GAME
CHANGERS

GAME CHANGERS

Twelve Elections That Transformed California

Steve Swatt WITH Susie Swatt,
Jeff Raimundo, AND Rebecca LaVally

FOREWORD BY Bruce E. Cain

HEYDAY

Berkeley, California
California Historical Society, San Francisco, California

Library of Congress Cataloging-in-Publication Data
Swatt, Steve.
Game changers : twelve elections that transformed California / Steve Swatt
with Susie Swatt, Jeff Raimundo, and Rebecca LaVally ; foreword by Bruce E.
Cain Heyday, Berkeley, California, California Historical Society, San Francisco,
California.
pages cm
Includes bibliographical references and index.
ISBN 978-1-59714-320-2 (pbk. : alk. paper) -- ISBN 978-1-59714-321-9 (amazon
kindle) -- ISBN 978-1-59714-322-6 (e-pub)
1. Elections--California--History. 2. California--Politics and government. I. Title.
JK8790.S93 2015
324.9794--dc23
2015018275

Cover and Interior Design: *the*BookDesigners
Printed in Saline, MI, by McNaughton and Gunn

Image Credits: All cartoons courtesy of Dennis Renault/*Sacramento Bee* except page
17, from *The Wasp;* page 49, from the *Los Angeles Times;* and page 71, courtesy of the
Sacramento Bee.

Game Changers was published by Heyday and the California Historical Society. Orders,
inquiries, and correspondence should be addressed to:

HEYDAY
P.O. Box 9145, Berkeley, CA 94709
(510) 549-3564, Fax (510) 549-1889
www.heydaybooks.com

10 9 8 7 6 5 4 3 2 1

CONTENTS

Reading California's Vivid Political History

LET'S BE HONEST. Most state political histories are tedious, inconsequential narratives written for no other reason than to provide instructional material for school civics requirements. By comparison, Californians are very lucky. Thanks to the colorful characters we elect to public office and the many political disruptions originating from our user-friendly direct-democracy system, California's political history is vibrant and, as this book attests, entertaining.

Californians like to walk on the political wild side. Cut property taxes drastically overnight? Why not? Adopt the harshest term-limit restrictions in the country? Let's do it! Make an Austrian-born Hollywood action hero governor? Sounds like oodles of fun. Now, whether these risky choices turn out to be good ones or not is another matter. Sometimes they work out well for us, and sometimes...not so much. But the more notorious cases only make the California story more interesting.

A rich history like this deserves an entertaining format, and this is what *Game Changers: Twelve Elections That Transformed California* provides. Written by a team of former Sacramento political reporters, legislative staffers, and campaign consultants, this book tells California's story through a critical elections framework. It focuses on a dozen contests that meaningfully shaped subsequent events, either through the election of notable figures such as Leland Stanford, Hiram Johnson, Pat and Jerry Brown, and Arnold Schwarzenegger, or by passing landmark ballot measures such as Propositions 13 (property tax cuts), 187 (denial of state and local services to undocumented immigrants), and 140 (drastic term limits).

The framework for each chapter begins with a narrative overview, then delves into each specific election, its backstory, and the consequences. In addition to drawing on relevant books, studies, and archival materials, the authors make effective use of interviews and oral histories, giving these historical events a more personal flavor. The authors themselves shy away from broad generalizations and abstractions, but some broad themes emerge from these various election stories. Let me point out just a few.

To begin with, it is sobering to realize how many scoundrels and sociopaths have played a significant role in California's political history. They include avaricious businessmen who used political power to advance their wealth (e.g., Leland Stanford, Charles Crocker, Mark Hopkins, and Collis Huntington), manipulative city and state officials (e.g., William Mulholland and Jesse Unruh), devious political consultants (Whitaker and Baxter, Michael Berman), and earnest political leaders who were guilty of what we now judge as horrible ethical lapses (e.g., Earl Warren and the internment of Japanese citizens and Japanese American residents). Ironically, many of these same flawed individuals did important things for the state, including facilitating the American West's expansion, building important infrastructure, and reforming political practices.

Political reforms now prevent many of the most questionable actions that public officials once undertook so casually. These days, blogs, social media, and opposition research magnify and instantly make public any personal shortcomings that political figures might have. Consider what contemporary politics has done recently to bold characters. The Hollywood action hero who ran for governor as a beloved celebrity in 2003 left as a tarnished and unpopular figure in 2010. The larger-than-life state legislators of the past—among them Jesse Unruh, Willie Brown, and John and Phil Burton—have been replaced by blander, consultant-coached, term-limited legislators. Time will reveal whether purer, cleaner politics leads to better outcomes, but the hitherto vivid California narrative will inevitably suffer.

Secondly, some of the most important elections in California's history attracted very low voter turnout at the time. Prime examples include creation of the "top-two primary" election system in 2010, when only a quarter of eligible adults went to the polls, and the 1905 Los Angeles municipal bond election that funded the Los Angeles Aqueduct and drained the Owens Valley of its water. Even Proposition 13, which lowered property taxes and fundamentally altered the state fiscal structure, was approved in an election in which less than half of eligible Californians participated. From one perspective, it seems undemocratic to allow major policy decisions to be made by such a small share of the electorate. But many years have passed since these measures were approved, and the public has not yet chosen to undo what the narrower electorates decided. So perhaps the problem is less dramatic than it seems. Proposition 13 is particularly instructive in this regard. While there have been minor changes over the years, the broad inequities of the law (e.g., huge disparities in the assessment of similar properties based on the time of purchase) remain, and the state still copes as best it can with a more volatile revenue stream than it had before the measure passed.

Another theme that runs through these stories is that elections often have ironic and unintended effects. Voters who enacted Proposition 13 certainly never intended for local governments to become more dependent on pro-cyclical state revenues. Big budget surpluses fueled the Proposition 13 vote, but several decades later the state had to mandate budget surpluses to hedge against the deficits produced by more volatile tax collections. Even ardent supporters of the term-limits law came to regret some of its unforeseen effects: weakened legislative capacity and enhanced lobbyist influence. The 1974 Political Reform Act ended the gifts and meals that legislators enjoyed on the lobbyists' expense accounts, but elected officials now depend on lobbyists to fund their campaigns and the two groups mingle regularly at fund-raising events. Jerry Brown, who initially rode to office touting the Political Reform Act, recently vetoed new ethics restrictions in his second stint as governor. A state heavily influenced by populist principles has enacted many super-majority rules. The list goes on.

Many of the chapters of this book also chronicle the path of the Republican Party to its current diminished position. To be sure, California's changing demography and national political dynamics have played significant roles, but one cannot help but notice the many mistakes the party has made along the way, among them the ill-advised swap of the US senate and governorship between Senator William Knowland and Goodwin Knight; the short-sightedness of Pete Wilson's reelection strategy targeting undocumented Mexican Americans even as they were becoming more politically relevant; Willie Brown outmaneuvering Republicans time and again in the California legislature during the 1980s and 1990s; Republicans overplaying their super-majority budget veto and eventually causing voters to remove that power; and repeatedly nominating inexperienced, self-financed candidates for important statewide offices. Democrats have of course made their fair share of political mistakes as well (e.g., the mishandling of the Gray Davis recall) and been involved in their own damaging political scandals, but the state's favorable demography gives Democratic office holders more room for error.

No doubt discerning readers will find other themes in these pages as well. But the search for meaning is not the main reason to read this book. Rather, the stories themselves are the draw. Californians should know their history and be familiar with events that brought us to where we are today. The *Game Changers* authors have made this enjoyable.

BRUCE E. CAIN, *professor of political science
at Stanford University and director of the
Bill Lane Center for the American West*

PREFACE

MORE CALIFORNIANS WATCHED the 1998 series finale of *Seinfeld* than voted in the 2014 general election, in which Governor Jerry Brown won a record-setting fourth term in the lowest-turnout election in state history. A student columnist for San Jose State University's *Spartan Daily* blamed the lackluster involvement of young Americans[1] on "ignorance, apathy and cynicism." "How can you convince people to vote when the truth is it may not actually make a difference?"[2] wrote the author. He could just as well have been talking about older voters.

Actually, we believe voting *does* make a difference, and this book illustrates how and why. California has been defined by its elections and by the new, often untested directions that voters have been willing to take. The book's title says it all: we look at twelve watershed elections that have transformed, and will continue to transform, California and its citizens for generations, past and future. We sought not to author a history or political textbook laden with mountains of facts and data. Instead, *Game Changers* is alive with stories, culled from archival and newspaper accounts, rarely read oral histories, and our own interviews, plus lively cartoons by Dennis Renault of the *Sacramento Bee*.

In pondering why so many people seem to find the electoral process less fascinating than we do, it occurred to us that perhaps they fail to realize the lasting impact that voters can have, even—or perhaps especially—in a place as populous as California. It is impossible to imagine, for good or ill, our state today without the constitutional revisions—including the initiative, referendum, and recall, not to mention women's suffrage—that male voters embraced in 1911.

Voters at critical junctures sent bigger-than-life leaders to the governor's office who proved capable of melding visionary notions of progress with the state's breakneck speed of growth. What if Pat

Brown, building on Earl Warren's legacy of postwar modernization, had not been around to push for a three-tiered system of higher education, a north-south water project, a modern network of highways? In contrast were the least successful leaders, who simply became bogged down in the enormity of it all. California's population has doubled many times over because it is a place like no other. While most Californians instinctively know this about the Golden State, they may not realize that voters—sometimes for better, occasionally for worse—have helped shape it that way. They also may not appreciate that events occurring in real time are consequences of what came before. Each chapter of this book puts game-changing elections into that historical context.

Together, the four contributors to this book have more than 150 years of experience in journalism, public policy analysis, and political consulting, most of it watching the sausage being made, as it were, at the state capitol. We're personally familiar with some of the stories used in this book to illustrate how interesting, even intriguing, politics and governance really are. Even so, determining which elections to emphasize, and researching what led to them and what followed, gave us a deeper understanding of our collective past—and in some cases an appreciation of our ability, as Californians, to overcome it.

Our research found many examples of people lamenting that politicians are more corrupt than ever before, that the influence of money is unprecedented, and that powerful special interests have put elected leaders in their hip pockets. We found complaints about high taxes, regulations that drive businesses out of state, and inequitable distribution of California's precious water. And all that was just leading up to the state's last constitutional convention in 1878–79. We also found that personal ambition and money played key roles in nearly every landmark election—from Leland Stanford, who used his position as governor to make himself and his business associates wildly wealthy, to Indian tribes that poured tens of millions of dollars into a campaign to gain voter approval of Las Vegas–style gambling on their tribal lands, to an action-hero actor's overthrow of an unpopular governor in California's most famous recall election.

The state's population has always been fueled by immigrants and newcomers—the fortune-seekers who rushed to the goldfields, pushing out or slaughtering native populations; the indentured Chinese imported as laborers; the Japanese who became farmers and shopkeepers; the Depression-era and postwar job-hunters pursuing a fresh start; the refugees from Asia and the Americas escaping poverty and conflict. The California experience is uniquely tumultuous, jumbling together the brilliant, the industrious, the adventurous, the hopeful, and the desperate. For much of its history, California's richly multi-layered culture has been tiered with the dominant and the subjugated, and those stories are told here, too. Ultimately, and perhaps inevitably, voter-approved intolerances were turned back by the courts, but often only after decades of injustice.

It should be mentioned that despite its diversity, California's political history following Spanish-Mexican rule is largely the result of the decision making of white males. To this day, no woman has been elected governor or lieutenant governor, and only two have served as US senators representing the state. So while these pages reflect the consequences of voters' decisions, they also mirror the historical whiteness and maleness of most of the candidates approved for California's top offices, including an almost universal exclusion of women from the halls of governance prior to the 1970s.

Just as any "Top Ten" list, whether of greatest rock guitarists or most memorable movie lines, is subjective, so too are our choices for the top dozen game-changing California elections. We have left out much more than we have included. We mention but do not emphasize the elections of Governors Ronald Reagan and Jerry Brown, for example. (The latter, while a historic figure, remains a work in progress.) We don't spotlight dozens of ballot propositions that have spent our tax money or filled our prisons or protected our environment—all important issues to be sure, but not the seminal watershed elections that we believe left the deepest imprints on the course of California's history. Those, we believe, are in the pages that follow.

STEVE SWATT, SUSIE SWATT,
JEFF RAIMUNDO, REBECCA LaVALLY
Sacramento, California

1

1861

The Railroad Begins Its Dominance with the Election of Leland Stanford as Governor

"[The railroad] owned governors, entire
legislatures and political parties. No one had
seen anything like it before, or have they since."
—Robert A. Jones, *Los Angeles Times*

TO THIS DAY, weather experts still talk about the Great Flood of 1862, the largest flood in California's recorded history. "This flood has been poured into the valley at a time when it is filled and covered with water on all sides, as far as the eye can reach," reported the *Sacramento Daily Union*, the state's dominant newspaper.[1] The January 10 inundation shared newspaper space with another major event that day: the inauguration of Leland Stanford as California's eighth governor. Floodwaters in Sacramento were about five feet deep, forcing Stanford to leave his recently purchased $8,000 house by rowboat to traverse the six blocks to the capitol, then located at I and Seventh Streets. One newspaper account said the new governor's inaugural address was "received with hearty applause, by clapping of hands, by stamping and shouting,"[2] despite Stanford's mediocre skills as an orator. He carefully adhered to a prepared text, and was described as someone who liked to think before he spoke.

Stanford had become president of the Central Pacific Railroad (CPRR) nearly seven months earlier and stressed the importance of building a transcontinental railroad, which fellow Republicans in Congress and the White House believed would help bind the West to the Union cause and help move Union troops and war matériel. Stanford called the railroad the "great work of the age" and noted that "the most difficult link" would have to blast through the imposing Sierra Nevada range.[3]

When Stanford returned home after the inauguration ceremonies, he found the lower story of his house flooded and the piano floating in a reception room.[4] He had to enter through a second-story window. Once the floodwaters subsided, Stanford set aside part of his home for his gubernatorial office, where he brazenly used his considerable public influence to advance his own private interests. Beginning with his two-year stint as governor, Stanford and his partners blasted through the great Sierra fortress and built a lasting monument to entrepreneurship and innovation, becoming multi-millionaires in the process.

At the same time, they created what muckraking journalist Charles Edward Russell called "incomparably the greatest political machine ever known,"[5] opening an era of unprecedented greed, corruption, and insidious railroad domination of California politics and public policy that endured for half a century.

THE BACKSTORY

Leland Stanford was an imposing figure with a neatly trimmed beard and mustache to go with his piercing eyes. He was always photographed in a three-piece suit looking resolute and determined. One of eight children, Stanford's ancestors were English, and the American branch of the family settled in Massachusetts in the mid-seventeenth century. A newspaper once described Stanford as "a man more noted for common sense and sound judgment than for brilliant qualities."[6] He was considered a calm and dispassionate businessman who carefully reasoned through issues, "arriving at decisions only after mature deliberations."[7] He came to California in 1852, on the heels of the Gold Rush.

Stanford's rise to political prominence paralleled the growth, both nationally and in California, of his new Republican Party, formed by antislavery activists in the pre–Civil War tumult of 1854. A lawyer, Stanford had a keen eye for commerce. He and his brother Josiah quickly realized that while a few gold miners might strike it rich, all of the thousands of fortune-seekers needed supplies. Josiah opened a general merchandise store in Sacramento, and Leland opened a store in El Dorado County. A year later, Leland moved to Michigan City in nearby Placer County and first tasted the allure of California politics, becoming justice of the peace. In 1856, he moved to Sacramento to manage the Stanford Brothers store on J Street, selling mining supplies, groceries, and liquor. An ad in the 1857 Sacramento City Directory promised, "Prices will be found as low as those of San Francisco."[8] While earning a good living running the store, Stanford stepped up his involvement in politics, helping to organize the fledgling Republican Party in Sacramento, which had few adherents in the early days. Stanford was choosing his friends carefully, quickly bonding with a cadre of leaders in the Sacramento Republican movement, including Collis P. Huntington, Mark Hopkins, and Charles Crocker, who would prove instrumental to both his business and political fortunes.

The Big Four, as they would become known, had taken similar paths to California, each attracted by the excitement of the Gold Rush. Huntington was a forty-niner from New York, described as a "frugal, energetic and no-nonsense man"[9] who tried mining for a while before teaming with another New York immigrant, Mark Hopkins, to sell hardware in fast-growing Sacramento. Hopkins was the oldest of the Big Four, thrifty and meticulous, "capable of making every dollar do the work of 105 cents."[10] Crocker, who would become an astute businessman, tried his hand at gold mining, peddling, and iron making before settling down as a dry goods merchant in 1852. Stanford also dabbled in mining, becoming president of the Bodie Bluff Consolidated Mining Company. Although it had a capital stock of $1.1 million, it proved to be a financial failure.[11]

California business and political leaders had been trying since the beginning of statehood to interest Washington politicians in an east-west railroad. In its initial session in 1850, the state legislature adopted the first of a series of nonbinding resolutions asking Congress to act on railroad construction. Congress turned a deaf ear, and numerous bills introduced to finance a railroad met with defeat. Democratic US senator William M. Gwin led the charge on behalf of railroad advocates. Gwin was a haughty, fervently pro-slavery Southern-born aristocrat who had once served as President Andrew Jackson's personal secretary. After a brief political career in Mississippi, Gwin moved to California in 1849 and immediately stated he wanted to be a US senator. He quickly became a leading architect of statehood at the 1849 state constitutional convention and saw his dream fulfilled when the state legislature sent him to Washington as one of California's first two US senators.[12] Described as an "opportunist who used political knowledge for financial gain,"[13] Gwin proposed his own rail route through the mountains. The *Marysville Daily Herald* noted in 1853, however, that the senator owned considerable property on his proposed mountain route: "The Senator, like a great many other modern patriots, has an eye to the filling of his own pockets in his labors of love for the public good."[14]

Gwin's efforts also met persistent opposition from his own Democratic Party, which before the Civil War was dominated by slave-state Southerners. They were wary of a railroad connecting northern free states, and of the federal subsidies and land grants that would finance it. Democrats by 1856 were giving lip service to the idea of a Pacific railroad, but the new Republican Party was aggressively urging its construction in its first party platform: "Resolved, That a railroad to the Pacific Ocean by the most central and practicable route is imperatively demanded by the interests of the whole country, and that the Federal Government ought to render immediate and efficient aid in its construction."[15]

Democrats still controlled Congress and the White House in 1858 when Senator Gwin made another of his dozen attempts over eight years to pass a railroad measure. When the Senate voted narrowly 25–22 to postpone action on the railroad bill, blame for continuous failures fell on the administrations of Franklin Pierce and James Buchanan and on "Southern states rights Democrats who are opposed to such works of internal improvement."[16]

Despite the setback, the *Los Angeles Star*, a newspaper that served what was then an arid pueblo of fewer than 10,000 residents, praised the senator as "indefatigable in his labors on this important subject." Why carry mail by sea and compel passengers to endure ocean hardships, including the "pestilent Isthmus," the newspaper asked, when "a speedy and safe mode of conveyance" could be built over American soil?[17] Still, western frustration boiled over. In some quarters, Gwin was accused of not trying hard enough. "He knows that the Democratic party, had it been united in favor of a bill, could have carried it through Congress at any time since 1853," one report said.[18] Some Californians thought about bypassing Congress and using the state's bountiful gold to finance a railroad. The *California Farmer and Journal of Useful Sciences* estimated that $50 million in gold could be dug from the state's soil each year. "California can build the railroad herself, if she will!...Here is the means; shall we use it? California has sent away from her shores, within the last ten years, gold enough to have built the railroad and entirely equipped it."[19]

As it turned out, the fate of a transcontinental railroad would hinge on the congressional and presidential elections of 1860. As expected, the Republican National Convention in Chicago adopted a pro-railroad plank in its platform, and it also nominated Abraham Lincoln for president on the third ballot.

The stars finally were aligning for Californians dreaming of an east-west railroad. Gwin, however, wouldn't be there to see it cross the finish line in the Senate. With Republicans ascendant, the Democratic Party in shambles, and his pro-slavery views anathema to sentiment in the state, Gwin served until March 1861 and declined to seek another term. It was a little-known surveyor and engineer, Theodore Judah, who became Capitol Hill's primary champion of a national railroad— not as a legislator but as a citizen advocate.

Judah was a visionary. As the chief engineer for the Sacramento Valley Railroad—the first railroad built in the West—he had earned the nickname "Crazy Judah" for urging a railroad through the fore-boding Sierra. He understood the potential of a transcontinental rail-road and had surveyed the mountains for a feasible crossing. After climbing to Donner Summit (named after the ill-fated Donner Party that was stranded there in the winter of 1846–47), Judah drew up plans for a route through the mile-high barrier. He "saw that the line could be built but only with government aid, since only the government had the resources to pay it."[20] To nudge Congress to act, Judah proposed that a company be created with private investments to ease the federal burden. At first, he sought capital from San Francisco businessmen but was turned down. Shortly before the 1860 presidential election, in a room over the Huntington and Hopkins hardware store, Judah pitched his idea to the four Sacramento business leaders who had become fast friends in Republican Party politics.[21] The Associates, as they liked to call themselves, were intrigued but noncommittal.

Lincoln narrowly captured California's four electoral votes on his way to a divisive sectional victory in a four-way contest in which he won 40 percent of the total vote and eighteen of thirty-three states— all of them in the North and far West. Republicans assumed control in the House for the first time. Lincoln and the Republicans were con-vinced that a Pacific railroad was necessary to hold the West's loyalty to the Union, particularly if the Southern states seceded. They envi-sioned more settlements in the West and development of the region's vast mineral and agricultural resources, leading to a huge boost of wealth and power for the entire country. A few days after Lincoln's election, South Carolina's two senators submitted their resignations. A month later, the South Carolina legislature voted unanimously to secede. Like wobbly dominoes, six other states had left the Union by February 1, 1861, even before Lincoln took office.

The young Republican Party had steadily increased its share of the vote in the previous four years, but once eleven Southern states seceded, Republicans dominated the House and assumed control of the Senate. The political prospects for a bill to fund a transconti-nental railroad looked better than ever, but with a Civil War appear-ing inevitable, there were concerns about such a project's toll on the national treasury. Senator John J. Crittenden of Kentucky argued that because the Union was "reeling about like a drunken man," it should be propped up before there was any talk about a railroad.[22] In his March 4 inaugural address, Lincoln made no mention of the railroad, concentrating instead on the questions of preserving the Union and dealing with slavery. But a railroad bill was the subject of growing debate in the new Congress. In a letter to the president, prominent Coloradan W. C. Jewett warned against "the Monster National Debt Pacific Railroad Bill."[23] The following day, rebels attacked Fort Sumter, South Carolina, and the war was on.

The Sacramento Associates saw the Civil War as a golden opportunity. They were convinced that Congress would approve and subsidize the railroad in an effort to bind the West and its resources to the North, a prospect that had the potential to make the railroad's owners rich beyond their dreams. On June 28, 1861, more than six months before Stanford's inauguration as governor, the Central Pacific Railroad was formally incorporated. Judah became one of its directors and was the railroad's chief engineer. Crocker ran the construction department. As treasurer, Hopkins was in charge of finance. Huntington became vice president and was tasked with getting loans and buying equipment and supplies. Stanford was elected president; his role was politics.[24] In a legal document filed a few months later, the Big Four reported combined personal assets of $100,000. Many skeptics believed the railroad owners were about to lose everything to push their railroad through the unforgiving Sierra. Ultimately, and thanks in large part to Stanford's political muscle, they parlayed the $100,000 into an estimated $200 million[25]—about $4 billion today.

THE ELECTION

Stanford had been nominated for governor a mere nine days before the railroad was incorporated. While his assumption of the Central Pacific's presidency and his simultaneous quest for the state's top office may have been suspect, he was characterized by the *Sacramento Daily Union* as an able merchant and a man of integrity. Stanford pledged to work on behalf of a Pacific railroad and suggested that electing a Republican as governor of California would sit well with the new Lincoln administration. By this time, Stanford already was a successful businessman, and the newspaper argued—naïvely, as it turned out—that his solid financial circumstances "place him above all temptations to make money by using a high public office for that purpose."[26]

Stanford had long been interested in politics, and it quickly became clear to his business partners that their enterprise would benefit greatly from his growing influence. He was one of the California Republican Party's founding fathers. His first election as a Placer County justice of the peace was nonpartisan, but he ran as a Republican in all his later races, including his failed campaign for state treasurer in 1857 and his distant third-place finish for governor two years later.

Throughout his political and professional careers, Stanford would have shifting views on one of the most volatile issues of the day: Chinese immigration. During his run for governor, Stanford embraced the popular nativist view that the Chinese must be kept out of California. In the years after gold was discovered along the American River, a flood of Chinese immigrants—mostly young men fleeing China's fifteen-year civil war—had streamed into California seeking riches they could take back home to their families. By 1852, they had become the largest of the state's foreign-born minorities, and they were often exploited and discriminated against. The immigrants brought with them different customs, languages, and cultures that agitated the white miners and settlers in California. An advertisement for the New William Tell House on J Street in Sacramento boasted that it had a bar stocked with choice liquors and cigars, along with this blunt notation: NO CHINESE EVER EMPLOYED IN THE HOUSE.[27] Stanford referred to the Chinese as "an inferior race." Asia, he said, "sends to our shores the dregs of her population....There can be no doubt but that the presence of numbers among us of a degraded and distinct people must exercise a deleterious influence upon the superior race."[28] Ironically, four years later, when Stanford's railroad required more laborers to work on roadbed construction, the Central Pacific's chief of construction reluctantly hired a few Chinese immigrants to bolster the workforce. Impressed with their work ethic and strength, the railroad hired thousands more, and the railroad even sent agents to China to recruit them.[29]

Stanford also campaigned on a platform of reform, accusing the incumbent administration of John G. Downey of corruption—another ironic and disingenuous stance in retrospect. But the overriding issue, particularly among the state's newspapers, was the newly ignited Civil War and California's allegiance. Stanford was a staunch Union supporter, certainly because of his Northern Republican roots, but there also was little doubt that a Union victory—especially combined with his election—would be good for his railroad enterprise. Stanford faced two opponents: John Conness, an antislavery Union Democrat, and Kentucky-born John R. McConnell, a Breckinridge Democrat with Southern sympathies. A distinct secessionist movement—complete with secret societies and militias supporting the Confederate cause— had grown primarily in sparsely populated Southern California, and some feared that McConnell's election would adversely affect California's loyalty and commitment to the Union.

In its best journalistic hyperbole, San Francisco's pro-Union *Daily Alta California* outlined the contest as one not about opposing parties but instead about "traitors" versus "true citizens." The newspaper endorsed Stanford as a "patriotic and able" man but was fairly kind to Conness as well. It left no doubt, however, that it considered McConnell to be one of the "traitors." It worried aloud about Conness and Stanford splitting the substantial Union vote, which could result in the "bare and remote possibility that their division may enable the enemy to triumph."[30]

The campaign was compressed into a frenetic five weeks. On July 30, Stanford began a grueling one-month tour of Northern California cities and towns, speaking in thirty-one different communities—starting in Yreka, near the Oregon state line; stopping at such tiny mining towns as Timbuctoo, Fort Jones, and Trinity Center; and ending in Petaluma, north of San Francisco.[31] At one point during the campaign, McConnell ventured to San Francisco and spoke at a Democratic gathering that the *Sacramento Daily Union* characterized as a "secession meeting." The article, originally carried in the pages of the *San Francisco Bulletin*, referred to McConnell as a "tall, swarthy man, with black eyes and black hair." It delighted to report that McConnell's speech was interrupted several times by hecklers.[32] On Election Day, the *Daily Alta California* breathlessly issued a stirring call to arms: "Arise fellow-citizens, arise; Gird on your armor for to-day's battle at the polls, which is to decide if Leland Stanford should be our Governor, and peace shall reign within our borders, or whether that Secessionist, McConnell, shall be permitted, by fraud and treachery, to gain that position."[33]

As it turned out, fears of a significant movement to withdraw California's support of the Union cause was overhyped. California's nearly 120,000 voters sent a clear pro-Union message. Stanford won comfortably with nearly half the votes, carrying twenty-six of forty-six counties. McConnell and Conness split the remainder almost evenly. Crowed the *Daily Union*: "Enough is known of the State election yesterday to justify the assertion that the enemies of the Government have met a Waterloo defeat."[34]

As candidate, and later as chief executive, the Central Pacific Railroad president never offered to separate his private business interests from his official responsibilities as governor. In fact, the railroad hierarchy embraced the potential of the public Stanford intersecting with the entrepreneurial Stanford. "I am trying to put my little road upon its legs, and it looks rather favorable, but like everything else, can do nothing with it until after the election," Judah said.[35] Public opinion approved of the arrangement as well, in the belief everyone would prosper if a transcontinental railroad were built.

THE IMPACT

Stanford's rise to the governor's office would prove fateful in the quest to shorten the time and distance between the two edges of a vast continent. A month after the election, the Big Four dispatched surveyor Judah to Washington to lobby lawmakers, as he had done since 1856, to sponsor the dreamed assault on the High Sierra. This time would be different, however. Now, Judah arrived as an official representative of an incorporated railroad enterprise, headed by none other than the Republican governor-elect of California, and he found a more receptive Congress to work with in the wake of the 1860 elections and widening Southern succession. Finally, Congress embraced the man with the vision. "Not leaving anything to chance, Theodore Judah got himself appointed clerk of the House Committee and as secretary to the Senate Pacific Railroad Committee—ideal positions for a lobbyist bent on pushing through funding for the project," wrote Edward Renehan, Jr.[36] It was a sensational coup, exploiting the lax ethics of the time concerning conflicts of interest. "We drafted the bill in our office, which, I think, became the foundation of the act of Congress,"[37] Stanford boasted.

Despite a more receptive Congress and the president's support, the railroad bill initially looked like it might be held up again in the spring of 1862. Debate over the rail plan focused on how much scarce national treasure—and how much federal lands—would go to Stanford and his friends. Others also wanted in on the action. Representative Thaddeus Stevens, for instance, owned a foundry in Pennsylvania and insisted that all rails and related ironwork be made in America.[38] That caveat accepted, the House passed the railroad bill 79–49 on May 6, 1862. Five weeks later, a depleted Senate sent the bill to Lincoln on a lopsided 35–5 vote that belied years of controversy.

On the night of July 3, the *Sacramento Daily Union* received word from Representative A. A. Sargent, author of the Pacific Railroad Act and himself a Californian, that the transcontinental link would become a reality. Its designated route was the thirty-second parallel; the line would head east from Sacramento, beginning only blocks from Stanford's home. The newspaper printed Sargent's comments the next morning: "The President has signed the Pacific Railroad Bill. Let Californians rejoice."[39] In celebration, Sacramento held a mile-long parade, "the most brilliant affair of its kind that has ever taken place in this city."[40] Sargent was lionized; the Central Pacific later would name a locomotive in his honor. Judah was feted as well. While on two payrolls—the government's and the railroad's—Judah had distributed $66,000 worth of CPRR stock to key members of Congress.[41] Sixty-one members of the

House and Senate gave Judah a written testimonial offering "our warmest thanks for your valuable assistance in aiding the passage of the Pacific Railroad bill through Congress....[Y]our indefatigable exertions and intelligent explanations of the practical features of the enterprise have gone very far to aid in its inauguration."[42]

The Pacific Railroad Act would provide the blueprint for the Big Four's first swindle, effectively spawning waves of government collusion with special interests into the next century. The new law specified that the Central Pacific Railroad eventually would meet the Union Pacific, which would build west from the Missouri River. The CPRR would receive huge land grants, including rights-of-way on both sides of the railroad over public lands, and ten square miles of public land for every mile of track laid. Two years later, a second Pacific Railroad Act would double the donation of public lands, a valuable asset. In November 1864, the railroad reported it had nearly 400,000 acres of land grants due from the government, all of which would "bring in far more than $1.25 an acre, because it was mainly superb agricultural land."[43] The federal government recognized the difficulty of laying track over steep and often snow-laden mountains that were 7,500 feet high and agreed to pay a significant premium for the effort. CPRR would receive $16,000 in government bonds per mile for level work, $32,000 per mile for construction in the foothills, and $48,000 per mile for track in the mountains, "said points to be fixed by the President of the United States."[44]

Pleading that the railroad needed higher initial subsidies, and thanks to some dubious surveying by California's state geologist, Josiah Whitney, the Big Four convinced Lincoln that the base of the Sierra started fifteen miles to the west of its actual location, thus securing hundreds of thousands of dollars in revenue it was not entitled to receive. Incredibly, Whitney at first suggested the base of the Sierra was the Sacramento River, which ran north–south through the city of Sacramento, itself at an elevation of twenty feet. He then pinpointed Arcade Creek, seven miles east of Sacramento, as the Sierra base, even though the terrain was nothing more than a gentle rise. In later testimony before the Pacific Railway Commission, Charles Crocker recalled that he had taken Whitney on "a little ride" and asked him—without prompting, Crocker insisted—to locate the western base of the Sierra. Crocker told the commissioners that Whitney's response was, "Well, the true base is the [Sacramento] river, but for the purpose of this bill, Arcade Creek is as fair a place as any."[45] Whitney's report was given to President Lincoln, who signed off on the lucrative deal. As noted historians James J. Rawls and Walton Bean put it, "The Big Four were now men who could move mountains."[46] Five and a half months after the president authorized construction of the railroad, Stanford told his mother, "My business prospects are very encouraging never more so." He noted that "newspapers find fault and slander and impugn my motives....I do what I think I ought and do not trouble myself about the consequences."[47]

On a cold, damp January day in 1863, a throng gathered at the foot of K Street in Sacramento to enjoy music, hear speeches, and watch Governor Stanford turn the first shovel of dirt for the railroad. "The *Sacramento Union* brass band played as 'proper' ladies gathered on the balcony of the What Cheer House across Front Street to watch the goings-on. The Legislature was in session, but it adjourned early for the day."[48] Stanford, speaking in a measured, deliberate tone, said work on the Central Pacific would proceed rapidly, without delays or uncertainty. "The blessings which are to follow the completion of the work which we this day inaugurate cannot be fully estimated," he told the crowd. "Agriculture, commerce, manufactures, wealth and population will feel its influence, and will commence with it a new era in progress."[49]

Despite Stanford's optimism, the Central Pacific faced an initial cash flow problem. The US government had a "build now, pay later" policy. Forty miles of railroad had to be constructed before the government would release the subsidy on it, and there were considerable up-front costs, including labor and equipment. Iron rails and locomotives had to be purchased in the East, at wartime prices, and transported to California by steamship. But money did come. Governor Stanford took full advantage of his political position to push the legislature to enact seven bills that directly and generously benefited his company, including a subsidy of $10,000 per mile of track put into operation. Stanford even included a lucrative contingency plan in case there was no money in the state treasury: the debt to the railroad would accrue 7 percent annual interest.[50] Sympathetic Stanford biographer George T. Clark, a one-time director of the Stanford University library, conceded, "This strikes one as an unethical proceeding, but we must remember that at the time, railroad communication with the Eastern states was California's most vital need, and that Stanford had been elected on a platform promising to accomplish all that was possible to meet that need."[51]

Stanford also induced the legislature to authorize votes in San Francisco, Sacramento, and Placer Counties for bonds to purchase large amounts of CPRR stock—totaling $1.15 million—and Sacramento gave the railroad thirty acres of public land.[52] In addition, the railroad began earning freight and passenger revenue even before the line was completed, charging for use of the initial tracks. And the Big Four's hiring of Crocker's construction company—a sham enterprise actually owned by the Associates—further boosted profits an estimated $10 million as the partners began paying themselves to build the railroad. Stanford even sought to insulate his railroad from negative court decisions by appointing Crocker's older brother, Edwin, to the California Supreme Court. Edwin Crocker happened to be the CPRR's chief legal counsel, and he served in both capacities until his court term expired in 1864.

To be sure, Stanford's behavior and the prospects of vast riches for the Big Four drew vitriolic criticism. Many Californians believed that the US government should have owned the railroad and that a gullible President Lincoln and Congress had been duped by Judah's persuasiveness to create a private monopoly at the public's expense. When Placer County voters were asked to contribute $250,000 to buy CPRR stock, a letter appeared in the *Sacramento Daily Union* calling the Pacific Railroad Act a colossal swindle and asked that the authorization vote be turned down. "Leland Stanford & Co. have, by logrolling and political juggling, bamboozled the Government and the people out of a stupendously magnificent franchise, worth hundreds of millions of dollars," the author wrote. "It is to them, and them alone, that all the benefits, and all the profits, inure." In reply, the newspaper's editor turned the argument on its head. "If it is worth so many millions, why should not the county of Placer become a subscriber, and thus obtain an interest in those millions?"[53] Voters authorized the stock purchase.

The Big Four also faced opposition from established transportation competitors, including Wells Fargo and Company, the California Stage Company, the Pacific Mail Steamship Company, and the Sacramento Valley Railroad. The companies and their financial backers worried their profits would shrink once the railroad was up and running. Before a San Francisco vote to pump $600,000 into the railroad, they circulated a 128-page pamphlet accusing the CPRR entrepreneurs of deceit and of putting profits ahead of the public good.[54] As in Placer and Sacramento Counties, citizens saw the opposition as "individual interest against the public interest."[55]

As shrewd businessmen, the Big Four obsessed over the bottom line and apparently weren't averse to cutting a few corners. As the transcontinental railroad neared completion, Huntington wrote to Crocker praising his decision to build a remarkable three hundred miles of railway roadbed in 1868. Huntington revealed that he was "glad to learn that you have made up your mind to go in for quantity of road instead of quality....I would build the road in the cheapest possible manner and then go back and improve it."[56]

From the beginning, Theodore Judah was a partner in the railroad enterprise, but he was never part of the inner circle of Associates. Judah, the inventive and farsighted engineer, was consumed with building a transcontinental colossus; his four colleagues were primarily interested in profits. Judah protested loudly when the Big Four put Crocker and his construction company in charge of building the railroad. He questioned their approach to financing the operation, was disillusioned by their ethics, and gradually lost influence with the four businessmen. In October 1863, Judah booked passage to New York in search of financial backers to buy out the Big Four. While crossing the Isthmus of Panama, he contracted yellow fever and eventually died in a New York hotel, seven days after the first rails of the great transcontinental railroad were laid at Sacramento's Front Street.

Criticism of Stanford would never really take hold. To most Californians, the transcontinental railroad was an economic necessity, and the daunting feat of its construction was an enormous source of pride in keeping with the nation's "can-do" spirit. The railroad put hundreds of men to work laying tracks, and sawmills in the Sierra flourished, providing lumber for the ties. Merchants turned impressive profits furnishing supplies. Chinese laborers, imported to blast tunnels into the Sierra's steep granite walls, did the most dangerous work, sometimes leading to severe injuries and deaths. Although Stanford's corrupt practices on behalf of his railroad were well documented in newspaper accounts, most citizens simply looked the other way.

Leland Stanford was the last California governor to serve a two-year term,[57] and he decided against seeking reelection. His brief stint in office, which began so ominously as the capital city lay under water, ended with his majestic overland enterprise well under way. Although he had used his public office to secure millions of dollars in government payments and land for his private venture, he was lauded a hero. He went on to serve in the US Senate from 1885 to 1893. His time in Washington would coincide with his $40 million endowment to found what would become a renowned university, named in memory of his son, on the rolling hills of his Palo Alto horse-breeding farm. Stanford and his wife, Jane Lathrop, had lost their teenager, Leland Stanford, Jr., to typhoid fever in 1884.

In December 1865, Stanford's successor as governor, Frederick Low, sent a message to the legislature commenting on recent correspondence he had received from the railroad president. Stanford had predicted—correctly, it turned out—that the railroad would reach Salt Lake City by early 1869. Low mentioned the sizeable government subsidies but called the transcontinental railroad a "great national work" whose completion "is demanded by the nation, on grounds of national policy."[58]

The Big Four would go on to buy out rival railroads, push for more public subsidies, and extend their rail network to San Francisco, the Central Valley, Southern California, and north into Oregon. They also continued to dole out favors. An influential senator who chaired the Pacific Railroad Committee was given 50,000 acres of land in the San Joaquin Valley.[59] Between 1875 and 1885, "graft cost the Central Pacific as much as $500,000 annually" (more than $10 million in today's dollars).[60] But for them it was worth every government bribe. Eventually, their railroad empire—by then known as the Southern Pacific—controlled 85 percent of railroad mileage in California.[61] It became the state's largest landholder, overseeing more than eleven and a half million acres of land through acquisitions and government gifts. The team of longtime friends also controlled state legislators, regulatory bodies, and local governments through intimidation and payoffs, becoming, in effect, California's shadow government. By setting arbitrary freight rates, they determined the success or failure of any California business that shipped products by rail.

Journalist Ambrose Bierce, who liked to refer to the former governor as Leland $tanford, was colorful and unrelenting in his criticism. In 1882, with Bierce as its editor, the San Francisco–based satire magazine *The Wasp* published a cartoon depicting the railroad monopoly as a giant octopus with tentacles ensnaring laborers, a stage coach line, an ocean vessel, and a farmer. One tentacle clutched bags full of money. This time the characterization stuck. Nine years later, turn-of-the-century muckraker Frank Norris fictionalized the Southern Pacific story with a vivid, lurid tale about "the galloping monster, the terror of steel and steam... symbol of a vast snatching power, huge, terrible, flinging the echo of its thunder over all reaches of the valley, leaving blood and destruction in its path...a soulless Force, the iron-hearted Power, the monster, the Colossus, the Octopus."[62]

THE CURSE OF CALIFORNIA

The Big Four never considered their behavior dishonorable. They felt they were transforming California and the nation with their daring and risky adventures. They saw no need to apologize. They believed that bribes and corruption were justified if the end product was worthy. As Stanford, Huntington, Crocker, and Hopkins saw it, they were unfairly attacked by scheming politicians and a hostile press that didn't have California's—or the nation's—best interests at heart. Years later, Crocker said the railroad tycoons had merely played defense. If the legislature had lacked the power or potential to interfere in their business dealings, he said, "we would have been glad to have kept entirely out of politics....We have always tried to prevent the passage of those laws that were going to ruin us just as any man would throw a bucket of water on a fire that had attacked his house."[63]

In the months after Leland Stanford took the levers of political power on that rain-soaked inauguration day in 1862, he seized opportunities that no other private business could reasonably expect to have. The outgrowth of his unique public-private leadership accelerated the building of the transcontinental railroad, helped accumulate vast riches for himself and his partners, and created an enduring culture of corruption. In later decades, there would be dozens of legislative attempts to rein in the railroad monopoly. Most were defeated by a determined Southern Pacific, which finagled governors' vetoes or managed to secure favorable court decisions. The railroad circumvented state regulations simply by making cash payments to members of the state's railroad commission. Critics won a few small victories along the way, but the railroad's vise-like grip on California would not be eased for decades, until voters enacted landmark reforms in 1911 aimed directly at a once-revered icon.

2

1879
Voters Ratify a Disputed Constitution for Tumultuous Times

"The movement which gave birth to the new
constitution...was crude in its aims and tainted
with demagogism in its methods. But it was evoked
by real evils and it sought however
ignorantly the public good."
—Lord James Bryce[1]

FOURTEEN-YEAR-OLD Michael Robins and his friends in the Temple Emanu-El Junior Youth Group were frustrated. They were having trouble finding a sidewalk location in downtown San Jose with enough foot traffic for gathering signatures on their petitions to President Gerald Ford. It was 1974 and they wanted the president to get the United Nations to rescind what they felt was an anti-Jewish resolution declaring that Zionism—support of Israel—was a form of racism. They decided to set up a card table on the parking lot near the entrance to the Pruneyard Shopping Center in nearby Campbell. The signatures came, but so did the center's security guards, who ran them off, saying the shopping center was private property.

In exasperation, the young petitioners turned to the temple board of directors for advice. Robins was the son of the temple's rabbi. The board discussed a lawsuit to force the center to let the teens set up their table. Board member Philip Hammer—the only attorney in the room, a family law specialist—was intrigued, and he agreed to take up their cause pro bono. Little did Robins or Hammer know at the time that six years later their case would become a landmark in American constitutional law—or that they would owe a debt of thanks for their victory to the men who created California's constitution more than a century earlier.

Some members of the synagogue board argued that the Pruneyard's owners had a right to expel those they felt interfered with their business. But Hammer had found a passionate dissent in an earlier case from California justice Stanley Mosk, who argued that the modern shopping center had become the equivalent of the town center. Building on Mosk's reasoning, Hammer contended the public no longer merely went to shopping malls to buy things. They gathered there as community.[2]

The California Supreme Court ultimately ruled four to three in favor of the youth group. Property owners appealed to the US Supreme Court, hanging their hopes on the court's 1976 finding that individuals do not have a First Amendment right to freely express themselves at privately owned shopping malls. On June 9, 1980, the high court agreed on that point but ultimately sided unanimously with Robins and Hammer on a separate pivotal point: under the principles of federalism, state constitutions may confer upon citizens broader rights than the federal Constitution provides. And the court found that the California constitution's free-speech protections do just that. Where the First Amendment of the US Constitution says "Congress shall make no law...abridging the freedom of speech," California's—coined in the second half of the nineteenth century— declares more affirmatively: "Every person may freely speak, write and publish his or her sentiments on all subjects, being responsible for the abuse of this right."[3]

Pruneyard v. Robins was a momentous acknowledgment that California's constitution "offers more protection to expression than does the federal counterpart"[4] and is "a document of independent force and effect particularly in the area of individual liberties."[5] The freedom of speech provisions "are not only as broad and as great as the First Amendment's, they are 'broader' and 'greater.'"[6]

There are numerous other examples of how courts have found California's constitution more progressive than the federal version. In 1890, six years before the US Supreme Court gave states permission in *Plessy v. Ferguson* to maintain "separate but equal" schools for black children, California's high court declared that "separate schools cannot be established for colored children."[7] It would be more than six decades before the US Supreme Court would catch up (*Brown v. Board of Education*), steered by Chief Justice Earl Warren, a former California governor. The 1879 charter also was the earliest in the nation to convey equal rights to women, stating they could not be "disqualified from entering or pursuing a business, profession, vocation, or employment."[8] And the California constitution also generated the first decision in America that found the death penalty unconstitutional;[9] while the Eighth Amendment of the US Constitution prohibits "cruel *and* unusual" punishment, California's charter bans "cruel *or* unusual" punishment—a much stricter test.

For all the acclaim given its progressive foundation and legal independence, however, the California constitution remains a confounding document. Although progressive in ways that benefited the civil liberties of Michael Robins and his friends, its evolution over more than a century has left it "a civic disaster."[10] Its harshest critics say it is too easily amended by voters—through the omnipresent election-year ritual of privately sponsored ballot propositions—but not easily reformed. It has become bloated by more than five hundred legislative amendments and citizens' initiatives, increasing its scope from 21,000 words in 1879 to more than 70,000 today. It is the third-longest constitution in the world. And perhaps the darkest lining to this silver cloud is its historic, officially sanctioned bias and discrimination against Indians, Chinese immigrants, foreigners of all stripes, homosexuals, and others.

"Elmo, we don't have jobs, don't speak the language, don't have any money and we didn't ask the Mexican government for permission — is this **legal**?"

THE BACKSTORY

The story of California's constitution is grounded in the unorthodoxy of the state's beginnings—formed by interlopers who claimed Alta California through war and bypassed established statehood protocols to make it part of the Union. They were explorers, military men, pioneers, settlers, visionaries, gold-seekers, fugitives, felons, eccentrics, and shameless land-grabbers. A determined if motley lot, they took California into statehood on their own terms. Although there was never a question it would be a free state, it entered the Union in a compromise over slavery.

Intent on expanding west, President James Polk formally declared war on Mexico on May 13, 1846. But word didn't filter to California for several weeks. Echoing the region's wild frontier personality, an emboldened band of American settlers, seeking an independent republic, launched a ragged insurrection against Mexico in June that became known as the Bear Flag Revolt. Their first revolutionary act was to seize a herd of horses intended for Mexico's military commander in Alta California. "Some further and more formal action was needed, lest the rebels remain merely horse thieves," recount historians James Rawls and Walton Bean.[11] So, thirty armed settlers surrounded the Sonoma home of Mariano Vallejo, a former Mexican commander sympathetic to the Americans, and announced he was a prisoner of war. Vallejo "invited the leaders in to explain what war he was a prisoner of, and when this proved a difficult question, he brought out bottles of *aguardiente*, or brandy, to aid in the discussion."[12] When the rebels and their prisoner sobered up, the Bear Flaggers threw Vallejo into a cell for a few days, though they never charged him with anything.

News of the war with Mexico still had not reached California, but hearing of the Bear Flag confrontation, Commodore John Drake Sloat landed with a small US naval force in Monterey, claiming Alta California for America. "The people were more astounded than indignant, and quite as intent over problems of preservation as measures of resistance," wrote Walter Colton, the expedition's naval chaplain, who soon would become Monterey's first alcalde (mayor).[13] When the American flag rose over the Custom House in Monterey on July 7, the nation had achieved its manifest destiny, stretching from sea to shining sea. The unchallenged American conquest short-circuited the Bear Flag Revolt less than a month after its stumbling beginning and launched a remarkable four-year wild ride in California. At war's end a year and a half later, Mexico officially relinquished California to the United States. As officials of both countries signed the Treaty of Guadalupe Hidalgo on February 2, 1848, they had no idea that gold had been discovered in the Sierra foothills east of Sacramento nine days earlier.

Already, pioneers had braved their way in a slow trickle across the Sierra Nevada. Some, like nearly half of the Donner Party in the winter of 1846–47, lost their lives in the effort. A few civic-minded early settlers who survived the pioneer trail schemed to separate California from Mexico, Oregon, and the United States to form a new nation. The discovery of gold at Coloma and the ensuing rush to riches quickly silenced that notion and just as quickly triggered growing concerns among many residents over raging lawlessness in the new territory—"a chaotic society on the edge of a wilderness."[14]

California's early population vaulted. Estimates vary widely, but it's generally accepted that there were about 2,000 adult white males in California in 1841, growing to 15,000 residents in 1848 and 165,000 in 1850—including approximately 10,000 "native Californians of Spanish-Mexican-Indian descent."[15] Sacramento's first real-estate salesman, Peter Burnett, who would become the state's first governor, lamented the rising tide: "We are, in fact, without government—a commercial, civilized and wealthy people without law, order or system."[16]

By late 1848 and early 1849, impatient assemblies were springing up in San Jose, San Francisco, and Sacramento, clamoring to form a territorial government. To head off that movement, General Bennett C. Riley, the last American military governor of California, convened an assembly of residents to establish a civilian government. On September 1, 1849, on the second floor of Monterey's Colton Hall, the first ten of forty-eight delegates elected from every region of the state launched a six-week convention that would set the stage for California to become the thirty-first state. Infuriated by Congress's dawdling, the participants attempted to force-feed the effort by creating a "state" constitution, bypassing the territory phase most pioneer states went through. Historian Joseph Ellison, in his series on the nineteenth-century struggle for civil government in California, wrote: "The people had an exalted conception of the importance of their state, whose gold, they claimed, had saved the impoverished east from bankruptcy." President Zachary Taylor complained of the "unprecedented" and "irregular" tactics employed by the unconventional Californians. "And they have, by and large, been prone to act in this manner ever since," historian Carey McWilliams wrote in 1949.[17]

It was a ragtag group of strangers who swiftly composed the 1849 constitution that McWilliams has called "an improvisation." Most delegates, new to the territory, had virtually no experience in government and little shared history. Only eight Mexican delegates were native Californians, the other participants a cross section of the still-young United States. The group included merchants, farmers, tradesmen, and one gentleman of "elegant leisure."[18] It was a leap of faith to think they could form a government so quickly, but they found surprising consensus.

Cobbling together parts of Alta California's Mexican law, the constitutions of Iowa (then the newest state) and other states, as well as the whim of individual participants in the exercise, they incorporated a two-house legislature and a diluted executive branch. They unanimously banned slavery and embraced a feature of Mexican law giving women the right to control their own separate property, acquired before or after marriage—a constitutional protection unprecedented anywhere in America. Henry Halleck of Monterey called on his fellow bachelors to support the proposal "because it would attract not only prospective wives, but *wealthy* prospective wives" to California.[19] Uneasy over rowdies with guns, the delegates rejected Pacificus Ord's proposal to guarantee that "every person has a right to bear arms for the defence of himself and the State," and they banned from voting or holding elective office anyone who would "fight a duel with deadly weapons, or send or accept a challenge to fight a duel with deadly weapons."[20] In the end, they produced in both English and Spanish what historian Robert Glass Cleland has called "a good, run-of-the-mill, workable constitution."[21]

Voters were asked to ratify the new constitution on November 13, 1849. "Rains of flood proportions and widespread political apathy reduced the voting to a minimum,"[22] but of the only 12,872 voters who went to the polls, a mere 811 voted No.

For most of the next year, "Congress practically neglected all other business on account of the heated debate over California and the slavery question in general."[23] South Carolina senator John C. Calhoun, the dying champion of the South, complained that admission of California as a free state "would destroy the equilibrium of the free and slave states in the Senate, and would finally lead to a civil war and the destruction of his beloved South."[24] But California was too valuable a prize to let get away; some worried it would become an independent republic. On September 9, 1850, eleven months after the state adopted its constitution, Congress finally welcomed California among the United States as part of a compromise that included abolition of slavery in the District of Columbia and use of federal officers to track down fugitive slaves.

Two days after voters approved that first charter, the *Alta California* had proclaimed: "From [the election's] results are to come the weal or woe of the new state, not only for a year but possibly for ten years."[25] Indeed, within less than a decade the 1849 Constitution proved inadequate to harness the burgeoning population, the rapidly changing social and economic conditions, and the real-life chaos faced by most residents.

One of the most tumultuous issues confronting the new settlers was where to settle. While the federal government encouraged colonization and homesteading in other pioneer territories with offers of 160 acres of "free land," the tide of California immigrants discovered, "with anger and amazement, that a large area of the best land had already passed into private ownership."[26] Eight hundred people held the title to fourteen million acres of claimed land in California, obtained from either the Spanish crown or the Mexican government.[27] Many of the land grants had been parceled out by Mexican governors to friends and family. Some were not clearly recorded anywhere, and still others were outright fraudulent. Yet, under the Treaty of Guadalupe Hidalgo, the United States agreed those land grants—even if questionable—should be "inviolably respected." Finding themselves unwelcome squatters, the new immigrants felt betrayed.

That first constitution failed to automatically grant the federal government title to public lands within California, as had been done in other territories, delaying the surveys of contested lands and the establishment of a system for settling disputes. That dysfunction led to "some of the worst social disorder and vigilantism in American history." With no public lands available, settlers "squatted, slaughtered the cattle they found on the land, and threatened violence if disturbed."[28] More than one hundred armed settlers marched through Sacramento streets on March 14, 1850, announcing they would resist with force any effort to evict them from the lands they had occupied. Landowners and city officials organized a posse that confronted the marchers in the streets. The ensuing "Squatters' Riot" left three people dead, including the city assessor, and many more injured. Order was restored only when five hundred members of the state militia came in to separate the two mobs.

Sometimes competing vigilance committees in San Francisco and elsewhere took over local governments, wreaking havoc in the name of justice. Over three months in 1856, the San Francisco Committee of Vigilance hung four accused murderers without a legitimate trial and sentenced thirty other men to deportation with orders to never return to San Francisco, on penalty of death. Even the newspapers got caught up in the lawlessness. A fatal rivalry played out tragically between James King, editor of the *San Francisco Bulletin*, and James P. Casey, publisher of the *Sunday Times*. Casey assassinated King only a couple of hours after King published a sarcastic editorial regarding a man named Bagley who had been charged with trying to kill Casey: "It does not matter how bad a man Casey had been, nor how much benefit it might be to the public to have him out of the way. We cannot accord to any one citizen the right to kill him, or even beat him, without justifiable personal provocation. The fact that Casey had been an inmate of Sing Sing prison in New York is no offense against the laws of this state; nor is the fact of his having stuffed himself through the ballot box as elected to the Board of Supervisors from a district where it is said he was not even a candidate any justification for Mr. Bagley to shoot Casey, however richly the latter may deserve to have his neck stretched for such fraud on the people."[29] On the day of King's funeral, about 250 armed associates of the Committee of Vigilance stormed the San Francisco jail and removed Casey and another accused murderer, hanging them "with great public ceremony." Alarmed, a competing "Law and Order" faction called on twenty-eight-year-old governor J. Neely Johnson to summon the state militia to suppress what it considered an insurrection. In the mayhem that followed, state supreme court justice David S. Terry stabbed one of the vigilantes. Although Terry was convicted of assault by the Committee of Vigilance, he was released with no punishment.[30]

Perhaps most glaringly, the 1849 constitution failed to provide sufficient tax support for the state's nascent government. Levies on land were the only form of taxation recognized in the constitution and were to be imposed "in proportion to its value" and "equal and uniform throughout the state." It failed to define "property" or a system for establishing uniformity. In any event, the vast majority of residents didn't have any property anyway. Joe Mathews and Mark Paul, in their examination of California's political evolution, called that first constitution "a recipe for disaster—and an early demonstration of the 'something for nothing' political culture that would be a constant burden to California" to this very day. Within five years, state government was broke.[31]

The three decades from 1849 to 1879 were the most tumultuous in the state's history. Economic depression, homelessness, foreclosure, drought and—worst of all—change had together conspired against an already rickety social structure. The population grew from just a few thousand before the discovery of gold to 261,000 four years later, and to 864,700 by 1880. California was dominated by immigrants—from eastern states, from virtually every European country, and from China—leading to factionalism that undermined community. The new residents considered native populations an insentient nuisance. By 1865, the cavalry, militia, and others had killed an estimated 15,000 indigenous California Indians.[32] Vaguely defined municipal structure invited corruption, malfeasance, and confusion. Where forty-niners had sought their own fortunes early in the Gold Rush, now mining was the province of salaried workers gathering gold and silver for wealthy capitalists.

Chaos over land ownership continued unabated. While the federal government had finally been given title to millions of acres of public lands, much of it intended for schools, swamp land reclamation, and public services had been "disposed of by speculators, often on the basis of insider tips and dummy buyers and without official survey or payment of agreed-upon prices."[33]

California's capricious weather cycles were devastating to agriculture in the 1860s and 1870s. Likewise, a shortage of workers left farmers frequently wondering if they could survive another season. Irrigation and water were especially expensive prior to the large water projects of the next century. When droughts extended over years, many landowners defaulted on their mortgages. According to Carl Brent Swisher in his exhaustive analysis of the 1879 constitutional convention, "As a result of these hardships, farmers throughout the state were deeply in debt, and it is not surprising that in the [1879] constitutional convention, we find them deeply exercised over the subject of the taxation of mortgages."[34] Farmers turned to the new Granger movement to gain political influence to deal with hardships. The Grange had grown rapidly across the country over the previous decade, becoming a farmers' cooperative to educate and supply struggling farmers and to fight such enemies as the monopolistic practices of the railroads and utilities. Grangers joined with the new Workingmen's Party, determined to break the transportation and freight monopoly of the Central Pacific Railroad, which had come to symbolize capitalist excess. By dominating shipping to market, the railroad's pricing monopoly bled the earnings of farmers and small businessmen.

Overhanging all of the turmoil was relentless antagonism toward Chinese immigrants, whom white Californians demonized for record rates of unemployment and countless other ills. By 1872, about 20 percent of the population of San Francisco—the state's largest city by a wide measure—were immigrants from the Far East, most of them Chinese. They held half the factory jobs in the city. Early on, many journalists, business owners, and politicians advocated the importation of Chinese labor under contract "as an alternative by which benefits of slavery might be enjoyed without some of the external appearance of the system."[35] But any hint of tolerance for those indentured workers was short-lived.

As he roamed the gold country to record details of the international phenomenon known as California, Scottish journalist John David Borthwick praised the Chinese camps as "wonderfully clean" and hospitable. Noting the servitude of many, he added, "It was well known that whole shiploads of Chinamen came…under species of bondage."[36] As Chinese workers took many low-wage or dangerous jobs in railroad construction, manufacturing, and agriculture, white labor resentments grew astride. The animosity saw its ugliest moment in 1871, when rioters lynched nineteen Chinese workers in Los Angeles. Racial hatred toward the Chinese would be another major motivation for the creation of a new California constitution in 1879, and the sentiment would continue unabated through the first half of the next century.

While California had attained mythic status abroad, economic conditions at home were horrible. White workers, many unemployed and others fearful for their own economic futures, began rallying during the spring and summer of 1877 on the "sand lots" near San Francisco City Hall, then under construction. Many of the participants were Irish—immigrants and Americans—who made up about 20 percent of San Francisco's population, the same proportion as Chinese residents. One of their own, Denis Kearney, a street-educated firebrand owner of a drayage business, quickly emerged as the leading and loudest sandlot voice castigating capitalists, monopolies, and government corruption. Kearney railed against the rich and called for redistribution of wealth, but he saved his most incendiary invective for those he claimed offered the greatest peril to white working men, barking in every speech, "The Chinese must go!" Laboring at lower wages and in greater numbers, Chinese immigrants provided a convenient butt for the pent-up anger of the white workingmen. During the summer of 1877, they vented that fury by "burning [Chinese] laundries, destroying their property wherever it could be found and driving them from their homes."[37]

At a sandlot meeting on Friday, October 5, the Workingmen's Party was formed, with Kearney among its officers. The Workingmen included a number of castaway members of the American constituency of the Marxist International Workingmen's Association, which had disbanded a year earlier; Kearney clearly was a socialist, which aroused fears among elites and newspaper owners throughout the state. Kearneyites favored not only deportation of Chinese but many progressive measures that eventually found their way into the 1879 constitution: the eight-hour work day, state regulation of railroads and other corporations, tax reform, compulsory education, and popular election of US senators.[38]

The party quickly gained adherents as pressures built to throw out the 1849 constitution and create a new one. Kearney continued his demagogic tirades, not only against the Chinese but against rich elites as well, pledging to "tax the millionaire." When a property owner on Nob Hill, one of San Francisco's most desirable vistas, refused to sell his choice parcel to Charles Crocker, one of the founders of the Central Pacific Railroad, Crocker built a high "spite fence" around the man's property. Kearney gave Crocker one month to tear down the fence or, he said, "I will lead the workingmen up there and tear it down and give Crocker the worst beating with sticks that a man ever got."[39] Linking both Chinese immigrants and corporate villains, another party leader, J. G. Day, proclaimed, "The young people will rise in this anti-Chinese movement, and deluge this city in blood, if not entirely destroy this city. We will show them the days of the capitalists are ended."[40]

THE ELECTION

Clearly, the turmoil stirred by the Workingmen's Party and encouraged by the Grangers wouldn't abate until California's most troublesome issues were dealt with. Three earlier calls for a second constitutional convention had been rejected by indifferent and lethargic voters in 1857, 1859, and again in 1873.[41] But in 1877, in the midst of growing disorder and a financial panic, voters finally said yes. They were an outraged populace demanding that delegates solve the myriad crises confronting the state. What they got were separate powerful factions plotting to protect their self-interests and emasculate their opponents.

Unlike the strangers who wrote the first constitution in 1849, those who gathered at the state capitol in September 1878 were political rivals, note Joe Mathews and Mark Paul in *California Crackup*. Workingmen—considered boors, demagogues, and communists by many elected officials and the conservative press—won fifty-one seats in a complex procedure to select delegates at local conventions and on a statewide ballot. Chagrined, the *Daily Alta California* took aim at one such delegate in particular, Dr. Charles O'Donnell, whom the paper called "a mere excrescence on the constitutional body," a man who "no sooner reaches the capital than, mountebank-like,…goes into the streets to split the ears of a crowd with ignorant harangues on Chinese 'leepers.'"[42] Seventy-eight delegates joined the convention as a coalition of "nonpartisans"—an uneasy alliance of Republicans, moderate Democrats, and a few independents assembled to combat the Workingmen. Traditional party supporters did not fare well, electing only eleven Republicans and ten Democrats. Grangers could be found among most of the groups.

Delegates assembled on Saturday, September 29, at the capitol and spent the first four days contriving to organize the gathering. It quickly became clear the Workingmen were not going to be able to dominate the convention. The nonpartisans promptly took control of presiding offices and procedures. But with two-thirds majorities required for adoption of any constitutional provisions, Workingmen found they could often control the outcome "by simply opposing the nonpartisans…on every single vote until the majority of delegates surrendered to their particular demands." It was a tyranny of the minority—"a difficult fact of California political life that endures today."[43]

The Workingmen allied with the Grangers on the three biggest issues of the convention: controlling the "corrupting power" of corporations, particularly the railroads, and making them more accountable; reforming and distributing the state's tax burdens more equitably; and suppressing the Chinese. They used their votes to leverage other progressive issues, among them restricting the legislature's power to benefit narrow interest groups, eliminating the requirement that only property owners could hold office, and expanding some women's rights, including granting them unconstrained access to universities, businesses, and professions, although failing to concede them the right to vote. Ultimately, they considered one of their most important achievements the creation of an elected railroad commission to stabilize and control shipping

rates and prevent the railroad from discriminating among its customers. The railroads would prove the reform irrelevant, emas-
culating the commission by stacking it with their own partisans
within two years.

Another key target of the Grange-Workingmen's coalition was
the inequitable tax structure. A finance system of that era forced
farmers to pay taxes on their mortgages, and the political system
levied them disproportionately on small farmers. Alas, "knotty
problems of finance were too much for most of [the proponents],"[44]
and although they succeeded in adopting provisions they thought
would curtail the money-lenders' abuses, they failed to enact any
usury provisions to prevent their creditors from merely raising
interest rates to cover the taxes. They did win approval of a state
board to equalize taxes, but they failed in their effort to block some
significant tax breaks to the railroads.

Most ignobly, the convention continued the assault against the
rights and freedoms of the state's Chinese residents. Article XIX of
the new constitution threw up economic and political barriers against
"aliens, who are, or may become...dangerous...to the peace or well-
being of the State," and it declared the "presence of foreigners ineli-
gible to become citizens...dangerous to the well-being of the State."
The new constitution legalized segregation, prohibited employment of
Chinese immigrants by corporations and government agencies, and
gave local government power to exclude Chinese people from many
areas. Although most of those provisions were eventually invalidated by
the courts, Article XIX itself was not repealed until 1952. California's
constitution became the template for enactment of the federal Chinese
Exclusion Act of 1882, and racist sentiments have continued to per-
meate the state's political culture right up to modern times.[45]

After five months and 127 days of meetings, delegates assembled for the last time on March 3, 1879. The secretary of the convention began to read the text of the now-behemoth document to
the delegates. Tired and no longer being paid for their time, the
members decided to suspend the reading and vote. Most likely not
read in its entirety by any of those present, the new constitution
was adopted by a vote of 120 to 15. Neither weary participants nor

critics were satisfied. "A majority of these men were utterly unfit for the duties they were called upon to perform," complained the *Sacramento Daily Union*. They embraced "new and untried propositions of the wildest character" and "have made scarcely a single change which is not a change for the worse."[46]

The statewide ratification election was set for May 7. Railroad interests immediately set up a $3 million fund to defeat ratification and were joined by banks, mining companies, water and gas companies, and three-quarters of the state's newspapers. Some Bay Area Workingmen also opposed ratification, feeling that the new constitution did not go far enough. But the people were not to be denied the reorganization of their government. After a two-month caustic campaign, voters approved the new charter—77,959 in favor to 67,134 against. Ninety percent of the state's potential electorate of 161,000 went to the polls.

In the end, the constitution of 1879 was constructed on pilings driven by "three diverse and incompatible groups, who were more concerned with the special interest of their constituents than the welfare of the State of California."[47] Despite the libertarian freedoms that managed to survive to the overall benefit of today's Californians, most historians generally agree with Mathews and Paul that the 1879 California constitution is "perhaps the greatest civic disaster in the history of a state with a talent for disaster."[48] The distrust the framers had in their elected officials was reflected in how they chose to allow amendments and revisions to the constitution. Unlike the more flexible processes followed in other states, the new constitution tied the hands of future legislatures by giving voters that ultimate authority—proceeding "on the principle that all legislatures are created incompetent and dishonest."[49]

THE IMPACT

Workingmen and Grangers succeeded in preventing the hated capitalists from enacting their version of constitutional reform. But while the Kearneyite-led minority was able to push through progressive reforms inside the convention, it couldn't sustain its influence outside of it. It was not until the state's second political revolution in 1911 that reformers were able to realize at least some of their goals through Hiram Johnson and the Progressive movement. By 1881, the Workingmen's Party had bled vast numbers of its members back to the Democratic Party and essentially was finished as a viable political force. Kearney had gone back to his package delivery business, and both the Republican and Democratic parties welcomed their members home from the nonpartisan alliance. When Democrats, Workingmen, and others split the Progressive vote in the 1880 election, Republicans took control of both the legislature and the executive branch, assuring that many of the most anticapitalist sections of the new constitution would not be enforced. The power and sophistication shown by the Central Pacific in seizing control of the very commission designed to control it demonstrated that the status quo would ultimately prevail into a new century.

But it wasn't just the anticorporate provisions that died on the vine. A number of significant discriminations written into the 1879 constitution—most notably those against the Chinese—were expunged by the courts within a few years, even though the language remained in the document for many decades. In 1886, the US Supreme Court sided with a Chinese laundry proprietor who challenged the constitutionality of a San Francisco ordinance that would have put him out of business. The case has been widely recognized as the foundation for modern equal-protection constitutional law.[50]

Most constitutions concentrate on loftier principles: organization of government and the judiciary, rights of individuals, manner of vote, and the like. From its inception in 1879, however, California's constitution has focused as much on baser matters traditionally left to statutory law. Thus, subjects as diverse as alcohol regulation, racial discrimination, gillnet fishing, tax levels, crime and punishment, the definition of marriage, and stem cell research have intruded to bloat the state constitution. That micromanagement approach to the constitution has plagued California ever since. Like an arm tattooed with the name of a former lover, California's constitution bears indelible scars that complicate the next beloved issue to come along.

California courts have generally given great leeway to the electorate on constitutional amendments. But not always. The courts have been particularly unfriendly to threats to the independent authority of the California constitution—the concept behind the ruling in *Pruneyard v. Robins*. Governor George Deukmejian led a string of law-and-order reforms in the late 1980s, culminating in Proposition 115 in 1990, an initiative to limit the force of the state constitution, asserting it "shall not be construed by the courts to offer greater rights to criminal defendants than those afforded by the Constitution of the United States." As approved by voters, Proposition 115 "could hardly be a plainer renunciation of the independence of the California Constitution," wrote former state supreme court justice Joseph R. Grodin. Only six months after the election, however, the California Supreme Court found Proposition 115 to be a change so dramatic that it amounted to a constitutional "revision"—something that can be initiated only by the legislature or a new constitutional convention.

That the 1879 constitution remains the foundation of California law is puzzling to many. Carey McWilliams observed in 1949 that California is a "giant adolescent [that] has been outgrowing its governmental clothes" for a long time.[51] While other states regularly revise and modernize their constitutions, "California still operates under an organic law enacted when its population numbered 860,000, long before vast economic and demographic changes made it, with thirty-eight million people, one of the most complex societies in the world today."[52]

Still, well-intentioned reformers continue every generation or so to advocate another convention—or at least a major legislative revision. It hasn't happened. The legislature has voted five times to refer the question of calling a constitutional convention to a vote of the people. In 1898, 1914, 1920, and 1930 two-thirds of voters said no. In 1934 they finally approved calling a convention, but the next session of the legislature failed to provide the enabling laws or necessary funds. "The state was in an economic depression and there was distrust as to what the convention might do in such troubled times," said historian Bernard Hyink.[53] Even today, some fear a runaway convention. Numerous proposals have withered because, once convened, delegates could take any action on any constitutional matter they choose.

Political commentators Mathews and Paul, who have called for a new "Great Unwinding of old rules," have identified five waves of constitutional change in California, sparked by "spasms of popular anger at the status quo," beginning with the 1849 attempt to bring order to a chaotic frontier. It was followed by a tumultuous three-decade struggle—culminating in the 1879 constitution—to "put meat on the bones" of the gaunt original. During the third phase, more than three hundred amendments were made over sixty years—including the Progressive reforms of 1911—"nearly all aimed at remedying the consequences, intended or not, of the 1879 disaster." Fourth came the post–World War II effort to purge the worst of those earlier amendments and "turn California's amateur government into a professional one." And since 1970, the fifth wave has been "a tsunami of ballot initiatives that, in the name of putting the fear of public anger in California's professional politicians, threatens the whole enterprise."[54]

It is in Mathews and Paul's fourth phase that some of the most sincere constitutional revision efforts were mounted. In 1947, the legislature created an interim committee, augmented by an advisory committee of 287 distinguished Californians, that developed a package of eight measures, seven of which were approved by voters in a special election in November 1949. The exercise eliminated some 14,500 unnecessary words from the constitution but made no substantive revisions. Amendments continued to pour into the document. By 1960, it stood at 80,000 words, leading state chief justice Phil S. Gibson to characterize it as "not only much too long, but...almost everything a constitution ought not to be." He said much of the fat in it "is so deeply imbedded in paragraphs containing sound and functioning provisions that the obsolete language cannot be excised without rewriting entire sections....Certainly, the people of California are entitled to something better than this."[55]

Whether better or not, the last significant revision came in the 1960s. Until then, voters could amend the constitution at the ballot box, but true "revisions" could only be achieved in a statewide convention—which hadn't happened since 1879. In 1962, voters approved Proposition 7, for the first time giving the legislature power to propose revisions, which would then be submitted to voters for ratification—a piecemeal approach to circumvent the need for a convention. Subsequently, voters agreed to delete thousands of words and accepted a handful of largely inconsequential revisions in 1966, 1970, and 1974. Only one of those revisions can truly be characterized as historic: the creation of a full-time legislature in 1966.

Will what has gone around ever come around again in California? Despite their sharp divisions in 1879, citizens came together in a public space to debate deeply partisan and polarizing issues. In the end, "delegates not only pursued a republican program, they exemplified a republican politics. Theirs was not a backroom caucus or a magnified focus group. It was a contentious and productive public assembly."[56] That it has been more than 135 years since the last convention legitimately raises the question whether any such exercise is possible today in such a large, complex state again held hostage by partisanship and polarization. "In these times of endless political rancor, that is a long shot," Mathews and Paul agree. "But that reality doesn't change another reality: the hostages must be surrendered before California can devise a system that works."[57]

3

1905

Los Angeles Votes to Spur Growth with a Giant Aqueduct

"[T]his water is more valuable to the people of
Los Angeles than to the Owens Valley."
—President Theodore Roosevelt

LATE ON A spring night in 1924 about forty men huddled on a
cow path north of Big Pine, California, to plot their attack. They
packed more than five hundred pounds of dynamite into a dozen
cars and caravanned southward more than thirty miles with their
license plates removed and headlights turned off. Twenty-seven
minutes after midnight on the morning of May 21, the remote
Owens Valley was rocked by an explosion that tore a hole in a
decade-old aqueduct carrying millions of gallons of snowmelt
from the Sierra Nevada to Los Angeles, 233 miles away.

According to the *Los Angeles Times*, "No one heard the
roar of the explosions," and word didn't reach Los Angeles
until 8:30 a.m. Upon hearing of the sabotage, the city's legendary water chief, William Mulholland, convinced the city council to offer a $10,000 reward for apprehension and conviction
of the dynamiters. A posse of Los Angeles detectives headed
north to the Owens Valley, and LA civic leaders denounced the

blast as a "dastardly" act committed by "cowardly criminals."[1] The city was forced to shut down the aqueduct for two days of repairs—costing an estimated $25,000—to a small tunnel at the base of a concrete spillway, where investigators said the dynamite had been placed. Jack Dymond, the lead inspector for the Los Angeles district attorney, traced the dynamite to a hardware store in the Owens Valley, where "a masked mob sawed through the shackle of a brass padlock" and stole several cases of explosives. No tracks were found at the scene, however, because such telltale signs had been "obliterated by grazing sheep."[2]

Dymond was certain the villains were prominent farmers and ranchers in the Owens Valley who for twenty years had watched Los Angeles scheme to divert their water south. He promised a sensation once their identities were revealed.[3] Los Angeles newspapers salivated at the prospects of a wild shootout once the suspects were named. "Plan to Nab 40 in Aqueduct Plot," screamed the *Evening Express* in a front-page banner headline. "Expect Battle Before Taking Bombing Gang."[4] Dymond's instincts were correct, and many valley residents knew who had dynamited the aqueduct. But despite the city prosecutor's best efforts, no witnesses came forward, no suspects were identified, and no charges were ever filed.

The aqueduct bombing, provoked by years of Los Angeles intransigence, was merely one stage in a long series of protests that included other explosions and water diversions. But they had little impact on the outcome of the state's water story. Los Angeles was rising. The city's population had more than quintupled since the turn of the century, overtaking San Francisco and cracking the nation's top ten. By the early 1920s, 100,000 men, women, and children were settling every year in Los Angeles, many of them dreaming of striking it rich in land speculation, oil, or motion pictures. It was the city of "salesmen, followers, and founders of cult religions and purveyors of strange health and rejuvenation fads and, of course, dreams."[5]

However, LA's future had been anything but certain as the twentieth century dawned. While the fertile valleys and streams flowing from the San Gabriel Mountains and other nearby ranges proved sufficient for modest population increases in the late 1800s, it was clear that the unrestrained growth at the turn of the century couldn't be sustained by the old sources alone. Local civic leaders were looking to create a major American metropolis. Agriculture and ranching were nice, but real wealth could be created only by residential and business development.

That meant Los Angeles would need water. Lots of it. And the city had a cadre of ingenious—some would say nefarious—conspirators who were up to the task. They were intent on seeking a stable water supply any way they could from the melting snows of the Sierra Nevada, making themselves rich and allowing the new metropolis to grow far beyond its natural limits. Agents for Los Angeles had surreptitiously purchased options on Owens Valley properties with water rights beginning in late 1904, and the powerful owners of the *Los Angeles Times* quietly bought up thousands of acres in the vast but dry San Fernando Valley, right where the Sierra water would be delivered. The *Times* had been among the most aggressive advocates for approval of municipal bond measures on the 1905 and 1907 ballots that financed the aqueduct. Beginning in 1913, Los Angeles would begin siphoning millions of gallons south to the thirsty city. To initially pay for land acquisitions in the valley, city officials—propelled by the unrestrained *Los Angeles Times* propaganda mill—had convinced local voters to approve a $1.5 million bond issue. The measure's success never was in doubt, but water historian Martha Davis has noted that to help ensure the desired outcome, the city's water utility created "an artificial water famine," even dumping water reserves into sewers at night. "In fact, LA's water supply became so scarce that, on the eve of the election, the city passed an ordinance forbidding people to water their lawns and gardens."[6] Mulholland denied any subterfuge.

Outraged and overmatched farmers, ranchers, and businessmen of the Owens Valley fought a simmering feud with the big city for several years until a withering drought hit California

in the early 1920s. Determined to quench the thirst of its growing population, Los Angeles pumped groundwater until shallow
wells ran dry. Many Owens Valley farmers and ranchers, beaten
down and desperate, sold out, took their money, and fled, devastating the local economy. Those who stayed behind grumbled
impotently about what LA had wrought. Adding insult to injury,
Los Angeles filed a suit on May 10, 1924, accusing some valley
farmers of illegally diverting city-bound water into irrigation
ditches. Two weeks later, the cold war turned explosive with the
bombing of the aqueduct. The story is the stuff of Hollywood
movies: double agents, powerful men, swindlers, greed, corruption, land speculators, beautiful scenery, and spectacular edi-
fices. It's a sordid tale of a water swindle that created the Los
Angeles of today and, with it, much of the California Dream that
has been celebrated since.

THE BACKSTORY

If Fred Eaton hadn't accompanied his father on a three-week camp-
ing expedition to the Owens Valley in 1880, who knows how long
it would have taken the tiny hamlet of Los Angeles to grow into the
sprawling behemoth it is today. Eaton, by then in his mid-twenties
and the superintendent of the Los Angeles City Water Company,
had been only the sixth American child born in the city—at a time
when its buildings were adobe and its few thousand inhabitants
relied on the unpredictable Los Angeles River and its crude system of dams and irrigation canals for sustenance. Eaton's father,
Benjamin, a cofounder of Pasadena, worried about the future of his
vineyards during a drought in the late 1870s and had heard about a
wealth of water in the Owens Valley. Father and son trekked north
more than two hundred miles and were awed by the majestic, per-
petually snow-covered Sierra Nevada and the abundant water supply in the Owens River that fed a large, teeming lake.[7] Fred Eaton
never forgot what he saw in that valley. He spent years warning
of water deficiencies spurred by a burgeoning LA population, and
advanced the idea of building a canal that let gravity carry water

from the eastern Sierra to Southern California. Eaton kept the idea alive when, in 1899, he became mayor of Los Angeles during one of the city's periodic dry spells.

When Eaton left office at the end of 1900, he set his sights on becoming a rancher but never abandoned his vision for the future of Los Angeles. He had an ally in William Mulholland, an Irish immigrant who had started his engineering career in 1878 as a ditch digger in Los Angeles and eventually rose to head its Department of Water and Power. The two men who would spearhead the city's water grab—one the scion of pioneering LA royalty and the other a pedestrian-born, self-taught overachiever—shared the same work ethic, fascination with water, and vision for their city. Despite their disparate backgrounds, both have been described as imperious. Eaton, as befitting his pedigree, was "an indefatigable go-getter...accompanied by a certain haughteur." He was active in numerous civic and social activities and, apparently, his alcohol, as he was "somewhat addicted to the cup that cheers." Mulholland had his own flaws. When he was approached

'It looks awfully dry here in California.
Is there enough water for 21 missions?'

in 1913 to run for mayor, he told a friend he had "temperamental unfitness" for the job, as well as "autocratic and unreasonably domineering" tendencies.[8]

Eaton and Mulholland understood that growth would be impossible if the city's water supply relied merely on artesian wells, the fickle Los Angeles River (which often dried up in the summer and overflowed in the winter), and the region's notorious long-term drought-and-flood weather cycles. At first, Mulholland looked at short-distance importation of water—from various creeks or rivers outside the city—but each alternative either promised insufficient supply or already was encumbered by legal claims. Eaton, now out of office and a private citizen, convinced Mulholland to look north to the Owens Valley. The only problem was that valley ranchers and farmers already had their own plans for the water, courtesy of the federal government.

In the spring of 1903, Theodore Roosevelt's new National Reclamation Service eyed the Owens Valley for a huge reclamation project to more efficiently use Owens River water. Landowners welcomed the project, "convinced that progressivism meant their salvation," while engineering reports indicated that a dam and reservoir would dramatically increase irrigated acreage and the value of agricultural production.[9] Joseph Lippincott, the chief of the southwestern region for the Reclamation Service, was sent to the Owens Valley to complete a water survey. Prior to joining Roosevelt's Reclamation Service, Lippincott had been a well-connected consulting engineer in Los Angeles. He had a solid reputation, but no one in the valley knew he had taken a substantial salary cut when he accepted the federal job, and no one suspected he might be moonlighting to make extra income. Lippincott turned out to be a double agent; employed by both the federal government and the city of Los Angeles. "Lippincott was a snake in the grass because he worked both sides of the fence for his own profit," notes John Walton, author of *Western Times and Water Wars*.[10]

Not surprising in retrospect, Lippincott cast his lot with the city, helping to scuttle the reclamation project by writing a report that favored an aqueduct to Los Angeles. He was paid the equivalent of half his annual federal salary under the table to write the pro-aqueduct report.[11] Meanwhile, Lippincott let Eaton inspect property records and water-rights documents up and down the valley. Telling locals he was scouting ranch land to retire on, Eaton quietly bought more than $1 million in property options and water rights on land where the Los Angeles Aqueduct would be built, which he later sold to the city. For the most part, Owens Valley residents isolated in rugged Inyo County didn't have a clue about the city's intentions, although occasional speculation surfaced. An article published on September 29, 1904, in the *Inyo Register* briefly noted the local presence of Eaton and Mulholland, with Lippincott as their guide. As far as anyone knew, it was merely an expedition to view federal reclamation plans. The trio "arrived a few days ago and went up to the site of the proposed government dam on the [Owens] River."[12] It was a classic tale of deception, insider dealing, outright lying, and conflict of interest; within two months the reclamation project had been suspended.

Once Eaton had obtained a key parcel of land and water rights from a valley rancher, the *Los Angeles Times* broke the secrecy with a journalistic roar that covered three pages and spared no hyperbole. Although the federal government had yet to sign off on the aqueduct project, the *Times* made it seem like the battle was over. "Titanic Project to Give City a River: Thirty Thousand Inches of Water to Be Brought to Los Angeles," bellowed the lead story. "The cable that has held the San Fernando Valley vassal for ten centuries to the arid demon is about to be severed by the magical scimitar of modern engineering skill."[13] Although the *Times* did refer to "unsuspecting ranchers," it asserted, "Everybody in the valley has money, and everyone is happy."

But everyone in the valley wasn't happy. Many of those who hadn't gotten a good price for their property were angry and scared. They had placed their faith in Lippincott and the National Reclamation Service and saw it shattered. "Los Angeles Plots Destruction: Would Take Owens River, Lay Lands Waste, Ruin People, Homes and Communities" headlined the *Inyo Register* in response to the *Times* article.[14] The newspaper outlined Lippincott's double-dealing and Eaton's secret scheme to make the Owens

Valley "the victim of the greatest water steal on record." In a separate article, the newspaper called for unity among those in the valley: "This is no time to mince words. The man who first gives the entering wedge its opportunity is a traitor to his community."[15]

Valley residents decided to take their case directly to the upper echelons of the Roosevelt administration. Nearly four hundred petition-signers demanded an investigation of Lippincott's betrayal and the Reclamation Service's complicity in the acquisition of "water rights in this valley for the City of Los Angeles instead of for the reclamation of arid lands."[16] Letters were written to the ultimate decider, President Roosevelt, urging him to protect the valley against "depopulation and devastation."[17] One "Dear Friend" letter was written by Lesta V. Parker, a farmer from the tiny community of Poleta. "Is there no way to stop this thievering?" she wrote. "As you have proven to be the president for the people and not the rich[,] I, an old resident who was raised here, appeal to you for help...I apeal [sic] to you in the name of the Flag, the Glorious Stars and Stripes."[18] Roosevelt's decision remained months away. Would he continue the valley reclamation project, or would he accede to the wishes of a growing economic and political power to the south? As the president weighed his decision, Los Angeles authorities moved quickly to schedule a public vote authorizing funds for acquisition of lands along the aqueduct's path between the Owens Valley and Los Angeles.

THE ELECTION

In mid-August 1905, the city set a $1.5 million bond election for September 7. It would be a frenzied three-week campaign to chart the future courses of both the City of Los Angeles and the rural communities in the eastern Sierra. The city's campaign for Sierra water almost foundered amid scandal. William Randolph Hearst, publisher of the *Los Angeles Examiner*, was not in the habit of getting scooped on big stories, and he felt snookered when the *Times* announced the water deal prematurely. For months, Los Angeles newspaper publishers had been aware of the city's plans for the

Owens Valley, but they were sworn to secrecy as operatives secured the valley's land and water rights. And they hadn't been told of the aqueduct's likely route ending in the San Fernando Valley.

When the *Times* jumped the gun and started crowing about its exclusive coverage, it ignited a good old-fashioned newspaper war. *Examiner* editor Henry Loewenthal smelled a rat. The story in the *Times* had referred to "regeneration of the San Fernando Valley." But why, he wondered, was it so interested in the valley? After all, it wasn't even a part of Los Angeles, and no one knew publicly that plans called for the aqueduct's southern terminus to be there. Loewenthal sent two reporters to poke around the valley, and on August 24, two weeks before the bond election, the *Examiner* stunned the city with its findings. An investigative story revealed that nine well-connected Los Angeles moguls stood to reap millions once the aqueduct was built. And who were their leaders? None other than *Los Angeles Times* publisher Harrison Gray Otis and his son-in-law, Harry Chandler. In fact, it was Otis who wrote a personal $50,000 check to secure the option to buy a key parcel in the San Fernando Valley: the huge Porter Ranch.

The *Examiner* disclosed that in late 1904 — well before the water scheme had become public and only six days after the Reclamation Service project had been suspended — the wealthy businessmen had formed a syndicate and bought options to purchase more than 16,000 acres in the San Fernando Valley for $35 an acre.[19] Many of the investors were personal friends of Eaton and Mulholland. The purchase was finalized on the same day that Eaton had secured a critical parcel in the Owens Valley and telegraphed Mulholland with the good news.[20] Otis steadfastly maintained that he quit the syndicate before the land purchase, but Chandler "proudly accepted the unofficial title of 'Father of the Los Angeles Aqueduct' until the day he died."[21] Once the San Fernando Valley was irrigated with Owens Valley water, and homes and orchards had appeared on its lands, the syndicate stood to see its investments multiply many times over. It became clear why the *Times* had pushed relentlessly for the Owens Valley project. In a follow-up editorial, the *Examiner* said the "company's officers [at the *Times*] seemed to have had advance knowledge" of the water scheme. "That these persons are moved by self-interest in the matter does not, of course, show that the project itself is bad, but it DOES weaken the force of what they serve, since the motive impelling them is purely mercenary."[22]

Revelations about the syndicate's insider knowledge threatened to torpedo the bond election, but the *Times* continued to tout the San Fernando Valley in both news coverage and advertisements. One full-page ad urged readers to buy lots for $75 to $250 in Pacoima, "The Garden Spot of Southern California." The San Fernando Valley Land Company, as the syndicate was called, promised "Pure cold mountain water piped to the rear of every lot."[23] To allay fears that voters might turn down the financing plan for the aqueduct, another full-page ad promised full refunds if the bond measure failed at the polls. However, "the moment it is announced that the bond issue has been voted, the price on every unsold lot will be advanced ten percent."[24]

Hearst, meanwhile, had been walking a tightrope. His *Examiner* had exposed graft and corruption involving the water deal, but he didn't want to appear to be opposed to an aqueduct plan that virtually the entire Los Angeles business establishment supported. Hearst was then serving in the US House of Representatives, but he had loftier ambitions, including the presidency. Shortly before the election, Hearst met with city leaders. Afterward, he personally wrote an editorial endorsing the Owens Valley project.

In the Owens Valley, the impending Los Angeles election was viewed with trepidation in some quarters, indifference in others. Many valley residents figured Los Angeles couldn't use all the water that the eastern Sierra provided. They fully expected the city would allow valley farms and ranches to use the surplus. But W. A. Chalfant, editor of the *Inyo Register*, attributed more sinister motives to the city's leaders. He wrote that the city was trying to obtain much more water than it needed, because "it is their ultimate intention to buy and divert from this county every inch of water in Owens Valley."[25] Also questioning the city's motives was Mary Austin, a noted Owens Valley resident who would enjoy a celebrated career as a novelist, poet, and playwright. She interviewed

Mulholland in Los Angeles and wrote a lengthy story for the *San Francisco Chronicle* recounting Lippincott's and Eaton's secret dealings and the confidence that the people of the Owens Valley had placed in the integrity of government. "Everyone who has ever read the reclamation act knows that it was instituted not to make rich cities but to provide homes for the people on otherwise unreclaimed land," she wrote. "It is the problem of how far it is well to destroy the agricultural interests of the commonwealth to the advantage of the vast aggregations of cities.... Is all this worthwhile in order that Los Angeles should be just so big?"[26] After Austin departed from her interview meeting with Mulholland, the Los Angeles water chief was quoted as saying, "By God, that woman is the only one who has brains enough to see where this is going!"[27]

Mulholland and the aqueduct promoters ran a panic campaign, abetted by the *Times*. The voters were told their water supply was in a precarious condition when, in fact, there was plenty of water to accommodate current demand. "Turn the entire volume of city water into one channel, and it would be but a little brook,"[28] argued *Los Angeles Times* reporter Allen Kelly. Actually, rainfall in Los Angeles had exceeded the average in most of the years leading up

THE TWO RIVERS.

One can be seen with a naked eye, the other hard to find with a spyglass.

to the election—and 1905 was a fairly wet year[29]—but in a stroke of good fortune for aqueduct backers, temperatures exceeded 100 degrees during the week before the election. City reservoirs receded. Mulholland was accused of attempting to manipulate the city's water supply to make conditions look more dire by releasing flows from reservoirs in the middle of the night. He responded that the city was merely flushing the reservoir system.[30]

Ultimately, the bond issue became a referendum on the city's future. Proponents argued future water supplies were necessary for Los Angeles to attain its manifest destiny. On Election Day, the *Los Angeles Herald* also pushed hard for passage, contending that water from the Owens River could be diverted to Los Angeles "without wronging the persons living in the valley."[31] It even quoted Los Angeles water commissioner J. M. Elliott as saying, "We intend to buy out the whole valley." The *Times* disingenuously editorialized that it carefully considered the issue and "is firmly convinced that it is for the highest possible good to all the people of the city."[32] It didn't mention, of course, that the measure's passage also would mean "the highest possible good" for the publisher's family, which had bought up more property than anyone else near the southern end of the proposed aqueduct.

A get-out-the-vote campaign formed by local business and political leaders shuttled voters to the polls by car and carriage. The measure passed by a fourteen-to-one margin—but out of a population of more than 200,000, a paltry 11,447 ballots were cast. Three months earlier, more than twice as many votes had been cast on a failed measure to close the city's saloons.[33] Before leaving for San Francisco to buy equipment for city surveyors, Mulholland said he felt "intoxicated, drunk with delight" at the election results.[34] The day after the election, the *Times* took particular enjoyment in ridiculing its chief adversary, Hearst's *Examiner*, which had unearthed the secret San Fernando Valley land scheme (and belatedly endorsed the Owens Valley water deal). A cartoon depicted three beautiful women—representing Los Angeles—in a three-horse chariot running over the dazed, prone body of *Examiner* editor Henry Loewenthal, who was scratching his head in disbelief with wheel tracks slicing through his legs. The caption: "He didn't stop her."[35] The San Fernando Land Company also stepped up its hawking of real estate, placing an ad in the *Times* offering round-trip excursions to Pacoima for fifty cents.[36]

THE IMPACT

Owens Valley residents, many of whom felt cheated and deceived, had one more card to play: Teddy Roosevelt. The president, after all, had a conservation ethic and frequently spoke of the benefits of the Reclamation Act, which opened "small irrigation farms to actual settlers, to actual home-makers."[37] Los Angeles, still needing approval to build its aqueduct across federal lands, also pressed its interests in Washington. California senator Frank Flint authored legislation to grant the necessary rights-of-way to Los Angeles, but Inyo County's representative in Congress, Sylvester Smith, offered an amendment—a compromise in which both the Owens Valley and the city would share the water. Because Los Angeles was acquiring the water for future uses and didn't need the water immediately, and since the Owens Valley had more than enough water for everyone, Smith suggested that local farmers and ranchers get first call on the Owens River bounty, with Los Angeles getting whatever was left over. Los Angeles forcefully rejected Smith's proposal.

On June 25, 1906, Roosevelt listened to arguments on both sides before dictating a letter to the Secretary of the Interior that dramatically ended the debate. "It is a hundred or a thousand fold more important to the State and more valuable to the people as a whole if [this water is] used by the city than if used by the people of the Owens Valley."[38] Roosevelt then successfully lobbied the House to reject Smith's amendment. In fast order, first the House, then the Senate passed the Flint legislation, giving Los Angeles unlimited access to Owens Valley water for irrigation and domestic uses. With the stroke of a pen, Teddy Roosevelt, the trust-busting, antimonopolist conservationist, had guaranteed untold riches for a handful of powerful and wealthy land speculators; he also secured the future for a growing metropolitan giant. A week later,

Joseph Lippincott quit his job with the federal government for a new position—with the City of Los Angeles as an assistant engineer on the aqueduct.[39]

A year after Roosevelt's momentous decision, Los Angeles had one more decision to make before it could realize its dream: where to find the money to finance construction of the aqueduct, now that voters had agreed to buy the rights-of-way. The project promised to be a monumental engineering challenge that would stretch the city's treasury to the limit. A $23 million bond measure was placed on the June 12, 1907, ballot. Proponents appealed to voters' civic pride, arguing it was their duty to approve the bonds. Alone among the city's newspapers, the *Los Angeles Evening News* fought against the aqueduct funding plan. It published a series of fourteen letters, signed "Veritas," that accused Mulholland of every imaginable misdeed, repeating the well-known charge he had deceived voters into believing that the city was in the throes of a water famine.[40] According to Mulholland's granddaughter and biographer, the water chief conducted his own personal get-out-the-vote effort on Election Day, first driving a ninety-seven-year-old man to the polls, then escorting Fred Eaton's father, who was in his mid-eighties, to his polling place.[41] The bonds passed in an eleven-to-one landslide. The *Times* exulted that "the opposition was cowed, overawed by the tramp, tramp, tramp by the early voters who marched to the polls to register in favor of the bonds."[42] The *Evening News*, its advertising pulled by a vengeful business establishment, folded soon after the election.

Construction of the huge water system took seven years. The city employed between 2,000 and 6,000 workers at any one time and built 120 miles of railroad track, 240 miles of phone lines, 500 miles of roads and trails, and 53 miles of tunnels. Forty-three workers died during construction, and families of eight of the dead received survivor benefits. (Of those, however, only three received cash settlements greater than $500. The city also paid each family $75 for burial expenses.[43]) On November 5, 1913, a crowd of about 40,000 gathered at the southern terminus of the aqueduct to watch the first water from the Owens Valley cascade into the San Fernando Basin after its journey "through the world's longest man-made conduit of steel, cement and solid granite."[44] Mulholland had prepared a formal presentation but apparently became tongue-tied when part of the celebratory crowd surged toward the falling water. He looked at the city's mayor, Henry Rose, and said simply, "There it is. Take it."[45]

Between 1905 and the end of 1913, the city's population had more than doubled to 500,000 — without the need for any Owens Valley water. Once the aqueduct started flowing, Los Angeles had more water than it could use, and San Fernando Valley farmers and land speculators wanted some of it. Under federal law, Los Angeles was prohibited from selling surplus water outside its city limits, so it embarked on an ambitious annexation strategy, beginning with the gigantic San Fernando Valley, a move that nearly tripled the size of the city overnight. The biggest financial beneficiaries included the owners of the *Times*.

In the north, meanwhile, predictions of dire consequences hadn't materialized, because the aqueduct's diversions of Owens Valley water were downstream from the most significant towns and agricultural areas. Then came several years of drought in the early 1920s, and LA responded by extracting more water from the valley. Public opinion began to turn on Los Angeles, and anger mounted. The *Bakersfield Californian* acknowledged LA's "selfish designs" but urged restraint and no violence.[46] Six months after the unsolved bombing on May 21, 1924, about seventy men commandeered the aqueduct's "Alabama Gates" spillway and diverted water into the dry bed of the Owens River. Inyo County authorities failed to heed demands from Los Angeles to arrest the trespassers. Protesters held vigils and picnics at the spillway for five days. Cowboy actor Tom Mix, filming a movie in the vicinity, brought his crew and a Mariachi band to the site.[47] Recapping two decades of what it called "injustice" and "broken faith," the *Inyo Register* asked, "For do you think that men who have been driven to the last ditch by schemers, who have openly said they would get the property for half price[,] would lay down?"[48]

Throughout the twenties and early thirties, there were eleven attacks at various aqueduct sites. Insurgents wanted to force Los Angeles to the bargaining table. Seething city officials responded to the rebellion by taking even more water, secure in the knowledge that neither federal nor state governments would intercede. "The city wanted rights to all the water that could be channeled its way, and no higher political authority wanted to restrain the impulse."[49] As the protests dragged on, Los Angeles lost additional ground in the public-relations war but didn't seem to care. In spring of 1927, editor Frederick Faulkner of the *Sacramento Union* trekked to the Owens Valley to create a devastating series of reports, one headlined "Water Sharks Wreck Valley." Los Angeles, Faulkner wrote, was "moving as an annihilating plague in the Owens Valley."[50] Valley property owners paid for a notice in Sacramento newspapers that clearly was aimed at state legislators: "We the farming community of Owens Valley, being about to die, salute you."[51]

Yet the legislature had passed the Reparations Act of 1925, which allowed cities and individuals in Owens Valley to seek damages caused by their loss of water. More than four hundred claimants—from grocery stores to barbers—sought nearly $3 million from Los Angeles. When the city council unanimously denied all claims, there was a new round of seven separate attacks on the aqueduct in the spring and summer of 1927 by the so-called Inyo Gang.[52] Los Angeles sent armed guards to patrol the aqueduct, and city investigators and private detectives were dispatched to catch the perpetrators. Pockets of the eastern Sierra resembled an armed occupation. Dynamite used in the latest round of blasts was traced to a rancher who blamed the city for drilling wells adjoining his fifty-eight acres and draining off all the water.[53] He and five others were arrested. In a preliminary hearing, defense attorney Rex Goodcell, the former head of the US Internal Revenue Service in Los Angeles, told the judge, "Is there any crime in men, ground down under the heel of a great and powerful city, seeking justice?"[54] The judge dismissed all charges.

By 1931, the rural-dominated legislature had grown to distrust Los Angeles, given its actions during the preceding twenty-five years in devastating agriculture and ranching in the Owens Valley. A special legislative investigation committee castigated the effects of the city's surface and underground water transfers. "The few remaining landowners find themselves confronted with a condition of isolation," its report said. "Their neighbors are gone. Their local markets are gone, and most of their ranches are being surrounded by complete desolation."[55] The legislature did approve a bill that protected areas where water supplies originated. It was too late to affect the Owens Valley, however; LA already had secured the rights to most of the water in the valley and the Mono Basin.

Aggrieved Owens Valley ranchers and farmers may have won a moral victory in the legislature, but they weren't making any headway with Los Angeles officials who continued to increase flows into the aqueduct. In an effort to move public opinion in the city, valley residents purchased radio airtime to argue that Los Angeles had no "moral or legal right to the underground waters of the Owens Valley." They insisted that "90,000 acres of fine farmland have gone back to the desert, former homes of residents have been burned, and orchard trees have been uprooted by tractors."[56] Los Angeles didn't budge; it bought as much valley property as it could get its hands on. Rather than fight the city, valley property owners haggled over price. In a letter to his congressman, the agent for thirty-one landowners in Bishop complained about LA's weak offers. He said he was being stonewalled by "the same tactics of broken promises they have been carrying on for twenty years."[57]

Los Angeles, with its insatiable appetite for water and the continuing assent of its voters, extended its reach another 105 miles north to the Mono Basin after voters in 1930 approved another water bond, this one for a whopping $38.8 million. Once again, the *Los Angeles Times* led the charge for its passage and—as in 1905 and 1907—voters were told the extension was critical to avert an impending water shortage. In the late 1960s, the city would build a second aqueduct to siphon even more water to Los Angeles. In the mid-1970s, the Department of Water and Power installed water meters on city-owned properties in the Owens Valley, prompting renewed vandalism. A bomb exploded at an aqueduct spillway, a DWP power boat blew up on Mono Lake, water meters were encased in concrete, and someone threw a Molotov cocktail at a DWP office in Independence.[58]

Not until the 1970s did the communities in the Owens Valley finally gain victories—in the courtroom. With both the federal government (National Environmental Protection Act) and California (California Environmental Quality Act) enacting sweeping environmental regulations, Owens Valley residents started winning legal battles. Los Angeles was forced to prepare an Environmental Impact Report to assess and acknowledge environmental damage caused by its second aqueduct, although it dragged its feet for several years until an appellate court judge took over management of the city's groundwater pumping. Other court decisions resulted in reparations and habitat and river restoration. In recent years, the city has spent more than a billion dollars to control dust in the dry Owens Lake. More than a century after Owens River water first flowed into Los Angeles, Mayor Eric Garcetti offered a measure of contrition. "The city has accepted its responsibility; we took the water," he said.[59] "Battles lost during the 1920s in the name of community were pursued and finally won in the 1970s under the auspices of environmentalism," wrote author John Walton.[60] "Remember Owens Valley" is a cry still heard today in the West when a community takes on a big, often remote city over water resources.

Notwithstanding the mayor's comment, the view from Los Angeles has been quite different. Samuel Nelson, who at one time was in charge of the aqueduct for the Department of Water and Power and later became the department's general manager, insisted the city was a benevolent owner. Los Angeles, he argued, prevented Owens Valley agricultural land from being sold for development, thus preserving the attractiveness of the region—which now depends on tourism for its economic well-being—and saving it from suburbanization. He contended that anti–Los Angeles sentiment came from valley newcomers. "The old-timers, the ones who have been there, they knew that when they sold their land to the department that they got more than a fair price for their property."[61] Walton, however, has another take: "The people wouldn't have been rebelling if they were happy."[62]

Lippincott left the employ of Los Angeles once the aqueduct was completed and returned to private consulting for another twenty-nine years, until his death at seventy-eight. But the endings

of Eaton and Mulholland resembled those in a Shakespearian tragedy. Eaton had retired to his vast land holdings in the Owens Valley,
and Mulholland negotiated to buy a small section of that land for
a city-storage reservoir dam. But when Eaton set the price at $1
million, Mulholland balked and built his dam in San Francisquito
Canyon, about forty miles northwest of Los Angeles. After the Inyo
County Bank failed in 1928, Eaton was ruined financially, and he
lived out his life as a pauper. That same year, shortly before midnight on March 12, Mulholland's St. Francis Dam collapsed, killing more than 450 people. In terms of loss of life, it remains the
second-greatest disaster in California history, next to the great San
Francisco earthquake of 1906. Investigators reported that the dam
was leaking shortly before the break, which sent more than eleven
billion tons of water to the Pacific Ocean. "Where once bloomed
flowering trees and other vegetation," reported the *Times*, "bodies
of those trapped in the rushing wall of water lay exposed on slimy
banks."[63] A coroner's jury blamed Mulholland and others for engineering failures. At the coroner's inquest, a despondent Mulholland
accepted responsibility and declared, "On an occasion like this,
I envy the dead."[64] He retired in disgrace. In response, the state
assumed regulatory oversight of all municipal dams.

Without the vision of Fred Eaton, the inventiveness of William
Mulholland, the double dealing of Joseph Lippincott, the scare tactics of the *Los Angeles Times,* and the complicity of the federal government, it is certain that Los Angeles would not have developed and
urbanized as quickly as it did, and the San Fernando Valley might not
be the suburban jumble of communities it is today. It has been clear
for years that the 1905 dream of civic growth as an engine of prosperity and wealth brought consequences—disappearing open space,
overdevelopment, congestion and sprawl—all of which have affected
quality of life for millions of people in the southland. In a final irony,
the vast underground aquifer in the San Fernando Basin—once filled
with fresh water cascading from the eastern Sierra—is now contam-
inated with hazardous chemicals. The basin continues to provide
drinking water for nearly a million Los Angeles residents, but half of
DWP's wells have been shut down. DWP blames improper storage,

handling, and disposal of chemicals used in aircraft manufacturing, automobile and equipment repair, dry cleaners, paint shops, chrome plating, and other commercial activities dating back to the 1940s.[65]

The influence of the *Times* owners on the history of the city and California's unique ethos cannot be overemphasized. The Los Angeles region and even California are what they are today, in many ways, because Harrison Gray Otis and Harry Chandler and their newspaper "envisioned it that way," said news media historian David Halberstam. "They did not so much foster the growth of Southern California as, more simply, invent it. There is water because they went and stole water."[66] Whether to promote their own financial interests, cement their political power, or expand their paper's circulation by fostering development of countless housing tracts, their vision became a metaphor for a new twist on the American Dream. If the nation's ethic insists that any American can pull himself or herself up by the bootstraps, then the California Dream suggests that its people can become who they want to be. And once the water flowed freely, Los Angeles became the destination for dreamers.

4

1910
Hiram Johnson's Election Brings Power to the People

"California's government no longer shall be an
asset of the Southern Pacific company."
—Governor Hiram Johnson

BUT FOR A would-be assassin's bullet, Hiram Johnson might not
have become one of California's greatest governors, and the state's
experiment with direct democracy might have taken a significantly
different course. The bullet wasn't intended for Johnson but rather
the chief prosecutor in San Francisco's sensational 1908 corruption
trial of Abe Ruef, a conniving political boss who controlled much
of San Francisco through bribery and intimidation.

To nab the powerful and arrogant Ruef and his political puppets, including Mayor Eugene Schmitz, local district attorney William H. Langdon chose Francis Heney to lead a dream team of
investigators and lawyers. The group included detective William
J. Burns, who later would direct the federal Bureau of Investigation (forerunner of the FBI) and found his own detective agency.
Also on the team was Hiram Johnson, a scrappy assistant district
attorney and emotional orator. "We shall protect no man," Langdon
said. "We shall persecute no man, but we shall prosecute every man

who is guilty, regardless of position or standing in the city."[1]

A week into the testimony, in a courtroom crammed with about two hundred spectators, an ex-con who had spent twenty years in San Quentin for embezzlement walked down the aisle toward the attorneys' table. Reaching into his coat pocket, he pulled out a pistol and fired point blank at Heney. The bullet passed between the prosecutor's jaws and lodged under his left ear.[2] Remarkably, Heney survived, although he was unable to continue the trial. Johnson took over as lead prosecutor, assisted by two other attorneys who "have responded to the call of civic patriotism and have given their time and talents, without thought of reward and at a pecuniary loss to themselves, to the cause of decency," declared the *San Francisco Call*.[3]

On December 10, 1908, the jury returned a guilty verdict against Ruef, who would be sentenced to fourteen years in San Quentin for bribery. Hiram Johnson quickly became a household name throughout California. The *San Francisco Call* published a huge photo of him addressing the jury with fists clenched, as if in a boxing pose. "With malice toward none and with equal justice toward all, the prosecution of crime in this community must go on," Johnson proclaimed.[4] He parlayed his new fame into a meteoric political career as a dauntless reformer. Two years after taking down "Boss" Ruef, Johnson was elected governor on an anti–Southern Pacific Railroad platform and carried with him a new Progressive majority in the legislature. Together, they won the support of California voters for sweeping reforms that ended the railroad's grip on state, city, and county governments—altering to this day the way public policy often is decided in California. Paradoxically, though, modern-day reformers argue the powers of direct self-governance that voters bestowed upon themselves at Johnson's behest have been hijacked by the very kinds of special interests they were intended to thwart.

THE BACKSTORY

By the election of 1910, Californians had been under the thumb of the barons of the Southern Pacific Railroad for decades. At first, the Central Pacific Railroad had been singularly focused on linking the continent with steel rail. Its heroic achievement of boring through the imposing Sierra Nevada and racing across vast deserts brought universal praise and commendation to the Big Four: Leland Stanford, Collis P. Huntington, Charles Crocker, and Mark Hopkins. From the start, they shrewdly realized the potential of their investment and quickly set their sights on huge riches through expansion and monopoly. They bought out the promoters of the California and Oregon Railroad and extended their influence up the Sacramento Valley, eventually to Portland. They acquired the Southern Pacific, owned by a number of San Francisco capitalists, and extended south, then east. They bought the California Steam Navigation Company and its river transportation network. And once they organized their own steamship line, they controlled ocean transport as well.

"In its dealing with cities and towns, the railroad was equally ruthless in putting its own interests ahead of the public's."[5] For instance, when the Big Four set their sights on the Los Angeles and San Pedro Railroad, which connected San Pedro to Santa Monica, Crocker resorted to extortion by threatening to leave Los Angeles off its main line unless it handed over the railroad and paid $600,000 to the Southern Pacific. As the Southern Pacific expanded east, the city of San Bernardino balked at the Big Four's asking price for rail service. To punish the city, the railroad built its division point a few miles away, bypassing San Bernardino entirely and creating the town of Colton, named for David Colton, one of the railroad's political operatives. The Southern Pacific became California's largest employer and landowner. It operated the longest rail system in the nation.[6] Politicians were paid under the table, and lawyer-legislators received secret fees for legal services. The railroad set exorbitantly high freight rates, simply because it could. Railroad accountants demanded to see shippers' books so they could set rates they thought the shippers could afford to pay.[7] "If merchants were found to be growing prosperous, rates were raised."[8]

In 1883, Californians received a rare peek into the Big Four's operating tactics when a series of letters from Huntington to Colton, the railroad's confidential manager of political interests in the mid-1870s, were revealed. Colton's widow had sued the Big Four, accusing them of swindling her late husband. She had the foresight to save Huntington's letters. They were released during the trial and caused a statewide stir. In an analysis many years later, the University of California's Bancroft Library said that the letters proved that the Big Four were guilty of "debauching Senators and Representatives, buying up Legislatures, publishing fraudulent reports, declaring dividends with money that should have been reserved to meet the railroad's liabilities, subsidizing newspapers and agents of the Associated Press, and misrepresenting the conditions and resources of the Southern Pacific Railroad." Excerpts from Huntington's correspondence to Colton concerning the railroad's interactions with Congress illustrate their money-for-political-favors mentality:

- "Friend Colton: I notice what you say of Conover, the Florida Senator. He is a clever fellow, but don't go any money on him." May 7, 1877

- "[I]t costs money to fix things....I believe with $200,000 I can pass our bill." January 17, 1877

- "Friend Colton: I don't think we can get any legislation this session for the extension of land grants...unless we pay more for it than it's worth." November 9, 1877[9]

In California, a newly ratified state constitution in 1879 created a commission to regulate the railroads, spurring more political manipulation by Southern Pacific. "By bribing two of the three original members of the commission, the company had made a mockery of state regulation," according to California chronicler Carey McWilliams.[10] In 1885, the Central Pacific and Southern Pacific reorganized under the single banner of the Southern Pacific Company, growing into a merciless transportation megacorporation, expert at playing power politics. Eventually this new "invisible third party," as McWilliams called it, controlled not only the regulators but the courts, the legislature, and city and county governments, including sheriffs and coroners. The railroad's strategy against opponents' lawsuits was to locate in every county a political manager who maintained a list of sympathetic prospective jurors. Its strategy in the legislature was to buy votes with cash and favors. When the legislature adjourned each week, Southern Pacific lobbyists scrambled to hand out passenger tickets to lawmakers, legislative aides, and news reporters. Even justices of the state supreme court got tickets that were good for free passage from Sacramento to San Francisco and back. One could take the San Francisco–bound train and scarcely find any passengers who had actually purchased a ticket. Perhaps it was little coincidence that the Southern Pacific won favorable rulings in fifty-seven of the seventy-nine rate cases to come before the California Supreme Court between 1885 and 1910.[11]

In his autobiography, legendary muckraking journalist Fremont Older, editor of the *San Francisco Bulletin*, said the Southern Pacific tried to control public opinion by getting as many newspapers as possible to do its bidding. Many smaller newspapers were satisfied simply to get annual free passes for the editors and their wives. Larger newspapers expected and received advertisements placed for lucrative fees. "There was hardly an editor who dared to criticize to any extent the railroad domination."[12]

Congress tried its hand at creating an investigative committee to look into railroad corruption but had similarly ineffective results. Accused of spending $3 million to kill anti-railroad legislation, Stanford suggested it wasn't money that defeated those bills but the effectiveness of his lobbyists in creating an "educated" Congress. He testified in 1887 that legislation the railroad had defeated had been proposed by lawmakers who "did not understand the subject, and whenever we could get such bills before a committee composed of fair-minded men, to whom we could explain the true nature and the necessary effect of such legislation, the bills helped to defeat themselves."[13] Apparently, Stanford had an insurance policy in case these "fair-minded men" were not disposed to see matters his way. When Senator William Stewart of Nevada became chairman of the Senate's Pacific Railroad Committee, the railroad secretly gave him 50,000 acres of land in the San Joaquin Valley.[14]

The Southern Pacific was untouchable. Creation of the railroad coincided with the nation's huge jump in industrialization and rapid economic growth. In the East, such industrialists and financiers as J. P. Morgan, Cornelius Vanderbilt, and John D. Rockefeller built huge empires and became fabulously wealthy. In California, the faces of plutocracy were Leland Stanford and his Southern Pacific colleagues. Beginning in the 1890s, however, cracks developed in the railroad's impenetrable fortress of political power. Many candidates no longer were cowed into being railroad lackeys. Democrat James Budd, a member of the original twelve-man graduating class of the University of California, campaigned for governor in 1894 on an anti-railroad platform. To protest the railroad, he refused to travel by train during the campaign, earning the nickname "Buckboard Jim." Budd won the election by a scant 1,200 votes in the first California gubernatorial election that used the new Australian—or secret—ballot.

During the 1890s, there were new outrages that prompted another round of reform attempts. Construction of the original railroad had relied on $28 million in federal loans, plus 6 percent interest, payable in thirty years. The Big Four paid themselves lavish dividends but made no effort to set aside funds to pay back the government loan. When the repayment finally came due, they offered Congress a shamelessly revised payback plan that would allow the railroad to delay payment for up to one hundred years and reduce the interest rate to one-half of 1 percent. Outraged legislators passed a resolution urging the federal government to foreclose on the railroad and take over its ownership and operation. Of Huntington's trip to Washington to push for passage of SP's proposed debt settlement, *San Francisco Examiner* columnist Ambrose Bierce's criticism was brutally descriptive. Bierce pointed to "the spectacle of this old man…his pockets loaded with dishonest gold" testifying before a US Senate committee. Huntington, he wrote, "took his hand out of all manner of pockets long enough to hold it up and be sworn."[15] The House defeated Huntington's measure, with Grove Johnson, Hiram's estranged father, the only member of the California congressional delegation to vote for passage.

After Huntington's setback, Governor Budd was so elated he declared the following Saturday a legal holiday. Even so, the Southern Pacific was at its zenith when Huntington, the last surviving founder, died on August 13, 1900. Historian Oscar Lewis said the SP was so powerful that "the major share of the profit of virtually every business and industry on the Coast was diverted from its normal channel into the hands of the railroad and its controlling group."[16] The Southern Pacific had its foot on the throat of the state's 1.4 million citizens. "California constituted for the railroad a private principality….Its control became absolute; its methods ruthless; its word law," noted J. Gregg Layne, president of the Historical Society of Southern California.[17]

But dark clouds loomed for the Southern Pacific as momentum gathered behind a nascent reform movement. It was propelled by a belief that if political power were given to the people, a cleaner and more responsive government would result. In 1898, San Francisco and Vallejo had become the first cities to adopt the initiative process, which allowed citizens to draft proposed laws and take them directly to the voters. Four years later, the Los Angeles City Council put the initiative, as well as referendum and recall, on the ballot. All three were approved, and in 1904 Los Angeles voters became the first to boot a council member out of office.

Although Progressives had won a few highly publicized skirmishes early in the twentieth century, they needed a comprehensive statewide strategy to win a war against corruption inside and outside of government. According to author and Los Angeles historian Thomas Sitton, the first spark that led to the statewide movement to rid California of the railroad's domination was a January 1907 dinner involving various reformers, including muckraking journalist

Lincoln Steffens and Dr. John Randolph Haynes, a force at the time although little remembered today.[18] Haynes, who had parlayed real-estate investments into significant wealth, had created both the Direct Legislation League of Los Angeles and a statewide counterpart. Steffens, who belonged to the formidable cadre of investigative journalists at *McClure's* magazine, had authored *The Struggle for Self Government*, a compilation of articles on political corruption. In the months that followed, organizational meetings were held to create an anti-SP political faction, while the arrogant railroad and the legislature seemed bent on plumbing new depths of malfeasance. San Francisco's "Boss" Ruef brazenly walked the floors of the assembly and senate—presumably off limits to non-members—and was seen whispering to legislators before crucial votes. "Certainly the Legislature of 1907 set new records for influence-peddling and outright bribery," noted Kevin Starr in his seminal history of the Golden State.[19]

On May 21, Haynes and several reform-minded reporters met at Levy's Café, one of Los Angeles's major banquet halls, to sift through a cornucopia of proposed reforms designed to drive a stake through the heart of the Southern Pacific's political machine. An outgrowth of their session was the creation two months later of the League of Lincoln-Roosevelt Republican Clubs,[20] dedicated to the election of a free and honest legislature via the nomination of party candidates through primary elections instead of state party conventions. "Leading Republicans Organize to Fight Boss Rule" screamed a banner headline in the *San Francisco Call*.[21]

By the 1909 legislative session, forces arrayed against the Southern Pacific likely made up a majority of both parties. The Democratic and Republican parties adopted platform planks supporting the initiative, referendum, and recall. With election reform high on the public agenda, laws were enacted to remove the option that allowed voters to cast a straight party choice on the ballot and to install the direct primary for all statewide offices, beginning in 1910.[22] Enter Hiram Johnson, the San Francisco hero who had successfully prosecuted "Boss" Abe Ruef for corruption. Although he had not held any elective office, Johnson was a longtime foe of railroad control and had been legal counsel to the San Francisco Teamsters Union for eight years. Chester Rowell, a cofounder of the Lincoln-Roosevelt Republican League and later a newspaper editor and university lecturer, called Johnson "the most effective orator in America."[23] Californians were clamoring for politics to be cleaned up, and Johnson seemed to be their eloquent, anointed champion.

THE ELECTION

Johnson was a self-made attorney, having dropped out of Berkeley in the middle of his junior year to marry his pregnant girlfriend. He studied law while working in his father's law office and even comanaged his father's successful congressional campaign in 1894. However, when Grove Johnson ran for reelection, son Hiram withdrew his support, suggesting that his father's advocacy for the Southern Pacific made his candidacy untenable. It caused a bitter family split: Hiram, the reform-minded lawyer who despised the Southern Pacific, and Grove, the railroad's water carrier. Grove Johnson lost his reelection bid but later would be elected to the state assembly, where his support for the railroad was unwavering.

Nervous, moody, insecure, but incorruptible, Johnson won the Progressive Republican nomination for governor in the state's first primary election. Physically, he was not an imposing figure—he was stocky, tended to be overweight, and wore spectacles—but he was a feisty, brilliant lawyer and had a flair for the dramatic. Twice he had been fined for striking opposing counsel in court. Johnson once confided to his son Archibald that he repressed demonstrations of affection yet had "a more intense temperament than usual."[24] He was a dynamic campaigner who knew how to connect with his audiences.[25] Aside from his hard-hitting campaign style, Johnson had several other things going for him: he was the Republican nominee in a state where Republicans controlled the levers of political power, and he was a San Franciscan. Northern California continued to dominate state politics just after the turn of the century, and San Francisco was by then the largest city in California and ranked eleventh in the United States.

Los Angeles, then the seventeenth largest city in the country, was just entering its growth spurt; in 1910, fledgling industries were taking shape that would change Southern California's landscape. D. W. Griffith directed *In Old California*—the first movie filmed in Hollywood. The same year, the city's Dominguez Field hosted the world's first air meet. Los Angeles's population would crack the nation's top ten by the 1920 census. General Harrison Gray Otis, the crusty, zealously opinionated publisher of the *Los Angeles Times,* carried on a lengthy public feud against Democrats, unions, and pro-labor William Randolph Hearst, publisher of the *Los Angeles Examiner*, which competed with the *Times* for readers. The Democratic Party was "a shameless old harlot," in Otis's view.[26] He equated organized labor with radicalism and the destruction of the American way of life, and he hated San Francisco because it was a union town. Hiram Johnson wasn't a Democrat, but he had two strikes against him in the general's book—he had worked for a union and he was a San Franciscan. To Otis, Johnson stood for everything that was evil: the politician believed in collective bargaining and wage earners' rights, including the right to sue employers. Otis called Johnson "a born mob leader—a whooper—a howler—a roarer."[27]

But Johnson gave as well as he got. In what became a landmark campaign speech in Los Angeles, Johnson shot back at the publisher:

> [W]e have nothing so vile, nothing so low, nothing so debased, nothing so infamous in San Francisco as Harrison Gray Otis. He sits there in senile dementia with gangrene heart and rotting brain, grimacing at every reform, chattering impotently at all things that are decent, frothing, fuming violently gibbering, going down to his grave in snarling infamy…disgraceful, depraved, corrupt, crooked and putrescent—that is Harrison Gray Otis.[28]

As the election year progressed, *Hampton's Magazine* ran a series of devastating anti-railroad articles authored by Charles Edward Russell, a socialist muckraking journalist who had helped found

the National Association for the Advancement of Colored People
the previous year. His articles traced the historical timeline of the
railroad, and its stranglehold on California's government, from the
early days of the Central Pacific to the dawn of the twentieth century, when it was "incomparably the greatest political machine ever
known." Russell argued that the railroad didn't simply control the
government, it *was* the government. "Discerning men that wished
to have a bill passed, a bill signed, an appointment made, a plan
adopted," Russell wrote, "wasted no time with the puppets who
nominally held office. They went directly to Mr. Stanford or Mr.
Huntington and asked for what they wanted."[29]

A month before the 1910 general election, Fremont Older,
clearly anticipating a Johnson victory, wrote a letter to the editor
of *Hampton's*: "Russell's articles in your magazine served a great
purpose and helped immensely to dethrone railroad domination of
California."[30] Socialist J. Stitt Wilson and Prohibition Party nominee Simeon Meads were afterthoughts with little chance of winning.
Democrat Theodore Bell, however, was a former Napa County district attorney and served in Congress. As Election Day approached,
the *New York Times* said the race was too close to call. "The contest is so fierce that not even good judges can predict who will win.
Many disgruntled regular Republicans who dislike Johnson will vote
for Bell."[31] As the campaign neared its conclusion, Johnson faced
a friendly, packed crowd of businessmen at San Francisco's Palace
Hotel. He conceded that some voters might consider his views on
remaking California's government too radical and anarchistic. But,
he said, honest merchants had nothing to fear from a Johnson administration. He did, however, have a pointed message for the railroad:
"You have got to keep your dirty hands off our politics and get out of
our government, or we will kick you out."[32]

Endorsed by Hearst's *Examiner*, Bell also denounced the
Southern Pacific during his campaign but nonetheless was attacked
as a tool of the railroad thanks to an untimely endorsement. William F. Herrin, the railroad's general counsel, considered Bell the
lesser of two evils and ordered Southern Pacific's managers to support him. The endorsement, once it became public, was the kiss of

death. A few days before the election, Johnson, speaking to a huge throng in San Francisco, dropped an eleventh-hour bombshell. He alleged he had "direct knowledge" that the Southern Pacific was pouring money into the Bell campaign and that Herrin had ordered railroad employees to vote and work for Bell. The frothing pro-Johnson *San Francisco Call* predicted the railroad would fire any employees who supported Johnson.[33]

The Southern Pacific's support, once so essential in California politics, likely cost Bell the election, along with a stronger-than-expected showing by third-place finisher Wilson. Johnson's Progressive Republican candidacy, promoted by the Lincoln-Roosevelt League, carried thirty-five of fifty-eight counties and captured the four-way contest with nearly 46 percent of the vote. He defeated Bell by slightly more than 22,000 votes statewide. Progressives also won big in the legislature. It had taken the Lincoln-Roosevelt League only three years to transform the political contours of California. In a post-election letter to one of his staunch allies, *Humboldt Times* owner Ralph Bull, Johnson said, "The cause for which we battle so valiantly has triumphed over special interests and disreputable politics, and has crushed the infamous alignment of allied villainies."[34]

THE IMPACT

Since the turn of the century, muckraking journalists had been assailing political and business corruption in vivid prose. Hiram Johnson and other governors of the Progressive Era—Robert La Follette of Wisconsin, James Cox of Ohio, and Theodore Roosevelt and Charles Hughes of New York—responded by seeking "to show how honesty and intelligence might provide the remedy," wrote historian Arthur Schlesinger, Jr. They stood for "the enforcement of middle-class standards of civic decency against greedy wealth and crooked politics."[35] A month after his election, Johnson took a victory tour, of sorts, to New York. He suggested California was the vanguard of revolt against special interests. For four decades, he told New Yorkers, "California has been a chattel of the Southern Pacific Railroad. Some of us decided that it was time to take the

state away from the railroad and give it back to the people."[36]

In his inaugural address, Johnson didn't let up on the Southern Pacific. The railroad was "the former political master" of California, "and instead of regulation of the railroads, as the framers of the new constitution fondly hoped, the railroad has regulated the State." Johnson reiterated his campaign promise of taking down the machine by way of political reform. He conceded that the initiative, the referendum, and the recall wouldn't take care of all of California's political malfeasance, but he argued the reforms would give people a mechanism to protect themselves."[37] Friendly newspapers heralded Johnson's call to arms. "As fast as it is possible to do so, Hiram W. Johnson, the new chief executive of California, is setting in motion those agencies which are calculated to return the government to the people," commented the *Sausalito News*.[38]

Acting with rare dispatch, the legislature placed twenty-three constitutional amendments on the October 10, 1911, special election ballot. The centerpiece of the reform package was a new system of direct democracy: the citizens' initiative, allowing voters to bypass the legislature and place their own proposals on the state-wide ballot; the referendum, to enable them to repeal laws enacted in Sacramento; and the recall, to permit voters to remove office-holders mid-term.[39] During legislative debate, the measure authorizing voters to recall officeholders, particularly judges, proved to be the most controversial. Still, it was sent to the ballot on a 70–10 vote in the assembly and a 36–4 vote in the senate. Other landmark propositions put before voters by the legislature on the crowded 1911 ballot proposed women's suffrage; comprehensive regulation of public utilities, including the railroads; creation of a board to supervise state finances; a package of labor laws that included a workers' compensation system, limits on child labor, and an eight-hour day for working women; greater autonomy for cities and counties; the nonpartisan election of judges and school officials; and new standards for school textbooks.

Despite the magnitude of the slate of constitutional amendments, voters didn't seem overly interested. "Many refused to go to the polls for the reason that they were unable to tell the merits or demerits of the propositions submitted," one newspaper commented.[40] Those who did vote swept all but one of the twenty-three measures into law. Fittingly, the only proposition to lose would have allowed public officials to receive free passes to ride on the railroads. Proposition 7, which gave California the initiative and referendum, was approved by more than 76 percent of the vote. Thus, California became the tenth state to allow citizens to circumvent their legislature by writing and approving their own laws. Proposition 8, the recall, was approved by nearly 77 percent of the electorate.

Woman's suffrage, however, was a cliffhanger. "Equal Suffrage in Doubt—Other Amendments Carried" headlined the *San Francisco Call* the day after the election.[41] Other newspapers jumped the gun with headlines reporting the measure's defeat. It was "the only proposition that imparted life to the occasion," said the *Amador Ledger*. "Suffragists and antis lined up on this question strongly. And it seems this is the only proposition out of the twenty three that went down to defeat."[42] When all the votes were counted, however, the measure barely passed with 50.7 percent of the vote. Since 1879 women had beseeched the legislature to give them voting rights. Finally, it was the electorate that made California the sixth state to give suffrage to women, nine years before passage of the Nineteenth Amendment to the US Constitution. As far away as Cincinnati, women's groups celebrated the California victory. "The winning of California seems too good to be true," said the president of Cincinnati's Twentieth Century Club.[43]

The complexity of the ballot and the sheer volume of homework that conscientious voters were required to perform set off a debate that still rages more than a century later. "It is hoped that we have seen the last of special elections on strictly law-making questions for many years to come," the *Ledger* argued.[44] Eight days after California voters charted a new course of direct democracy, the *New York Times* predicted citizens would become "muddled and puzzled and tired" of trying to understand and decide on a myriad of complicated issues presented to them in "small and nearly unreadable type." The *Times* argued that the best way to curb political machines wasn't a patchwork of reform proposals but the attentiveness of voters. Machines, the paper argued, prey on public indifference and have a knack for finding loopholes in reforms, simply maneuvering around them.[45] It was a farsighted analysis of the latent potential for special interests to take over the initiative process. In the second half of the century, Californians came to realize just how broadly initiatives could be used to try to control decision making in Sacramento. Well-heeled special interests and coalitions could—and did—pay signature-gatherers to circulate petitions, obtain the required number of voter names to put a self-interested or popular-sounding measure on the state ballot, and then bankroll campaigns to attempt to pass what the legislature might have rejected because of politics or policy. (In one example, Pacific Gas and Electric spent $46 million in 2010 to qualify and campaign for an unsuccessful measure that would have restricted the ability of municipal systems to compete against the giant utility.)

In 1912, California voters gave their brand-new electoral clout a test run. Death penalty foes failed to secure enough signatures to qualify a measure to abolish capital punishment, but three other initiatives did make the ballot, including one to prohibit bookmaking. All three failed. In later years, crime-related issues including the death penalty and prison-sentencing laws would be popular topics for ballot-box policymaking. In 1914, voters approved five of seventeen measures that qualified for the ballot, among them abolition of the poll tax and suspension of prohibition laws.[46] Meanwhile, the nationally popular Johnson had switched his party registration from Republican to Progressive. He had run for vice president on a third-party Bull Moose ticket in 1912 with former president Theodore Roosevelt and found many Californians receptive to the unorthodox move. The ticket narrowly won in California and finished ahead of incumbent Republican president William Howard Taft nationally, but Democratic challenger Woodrow Wilson ultimately won the presidency.

In seeking reelection as governor two years later, Johnson touted his California makeover. "Four years ago all over the state we gave one pledge—that the Southern Pacific Company should be kicked out of office," he told a Sausalito audience. "Whereas then the Southern Pacific Company regulated the state, now the state regulates the Southern Pacific Company. Graft and corruption have been eliminated from the State of California."[47] Johnson won in a landslide. In his second inauguration speech, he declared that "boss rule has been made permanently impossible by direct nominations, direct legislation and the recall."[48] Thanks to these and other changes, including a functional railroad oversight commission, California did, indeed, disentangle itself from the Southern Pacific's tentacles while transforming its political processes. Elections of city and county officials are nonpartisan to this day. Under cross-filing, another reform, candidates could seek nominations in multiple party primaries and, for a time, the system enabled the new Progressives to also retain the popular Republican label.

Cross-filing, however, contributed significantly to a Democratic hibernation that lasted until the dawn of the space age. In the 1920s, registered Republicans outnumbered Democrats by three to one. In the 1923 state assembly, Democrats could have caucused in a broom closet—they had only three members in the eighty-member lower house. And even when Democratic voter registration surged during the Depression, Republicans continued to dominate the state. Republican after Republican—including Governor Earl Warren in 1946—won elections in the primaries by capturing multiparty nominations and avoiding meaningful runoff elections. Not until 1958, when Democrats took control of the governorship and both houses of the legislature for the first time in generations, was cross-filing abolished.

Taken together, the reforms of the Progressives would emasculate political parties in California. Paradoxically, this created a political leadership vacuum at the capitol that was filled by alternative institutions—among them, special-interest lobbyists. It hadn't occurred to the reformers to regulate lobbying practices, because the only lobbyists who counted worked for the Southern Pacific, and the political influence of the railroad was eroding rapidly. Between 1880 and 1910 "there was, in effect, only one lobby, that of the Southern Pacific, and the function of the other lobbyists was to lobby this lobby," McWilliams explained of the era.[49] Machine politics, much as the *New York Times* had predicted, found ways to flourish after SP's influence was squelched. Gradually, the single most powerful and notorious lobbyist of them all, Artie Samish, took advantage of the capitol's permissive environment and thrived while representing a coalition of liquor, oil, trucking, banking, racetrack, and other interests.

While statewide referenda have been rare in recent decades and only one governor has ever been recalled,[50] the initiative has proven enduringly popular, both with special interests that sponsor them and with voters who support them. Since its inception, more than 1,600 initiative petitions have been circulated. More than a fifth of them have qualified for the ballot, and about 7 percent of the total have achieved voter approval. More than a century after Hiram Johnson's crowning reform achievements, Californians still debate the pros and cons of citizen lawmaking, its unintended consequences, and its effects on public policy.

Critics claim it has been perverted by special interests who pay professional signature-gatherers to qualify a measure, by sponsors who write special provisions into initiatives to benefit any interest willing to help pay the millions required to conduct a statewide

campaign, and by well-financed groups that quickly counter a dis-
agreeable initiative with their own measure on the same ballot as a
way to confuse voters. Still, the public clearly believes that voters
are better at policymaking than elected officials.[51] Citizens since
the 1970s have proffered and passed dozens of changes in law; they
have drastically cut their property taxes, made their coastline public and restricted beach development, earmarked a specific share
of the yearly state budget for schools, adopted and revised a "three
strikes" law sending repeat offenders to prison for life, designated
an elected state commissioner to regulate insurance rates, and
ended public affirmative action. Voter decisions that failed to survive court scrutiny include banning public education to undocumented immigrants and outlawing gay marriage.

Although twenty-four states grant their citizens the power of
initiative,[52] California's process is more narrowly tailored than most
others. Journalist Joe Mathews, coauthor of *California Crackup:
How Reform Broke the Golden State and How We Can Fix It*, believes
Hiram Johnson so distrusted politicians backed by powerful interest
groups—including his railroad-supported legislator-father—that he
deliberately removed lawmakers from having any meaningful role
in the initiative process. As a result, Mathews suggests, "We are governed by ghosts. The errors and decisions of voters long dead linger
in statutes unamended for decades, creating all sorts of unintended
consequences."[53] Voter-approved initiatives, for example can't be
fixed or amended by the legislature unless expressly permitted by
the wording of an initiative or ordered by the courts.

Even as Johnson basked in his remarkable achievements in setting
California on the path of direct democracy, he sensed that the reforms
could be used in ways contrary to their intent. "I am quite aware that
this year the referendum has been put to some base uses," he said in
1914. "I am aware too that the initiative may have been as you would
have preferred it should not be used." He predicted, however, that the
time might come again when reforms would be required. If it does,
"the most powerful weapons that you will have for your defense and
the perpetuity of what you hold most dear politically, will be the initiative, the referendum and the recall."[54]

5

1934
California's Dirtiest Election
Gives Birth to Modern Campaigns

"We're going to beat this son of a bitch
Sinclair any way we can."
—Kyle Palmer, *Los Angeles Times*

BY ALL ACCOUNTS, Frank Merriam was an unremarkable governor, barely a footnote between two other fairly nondescript leaders—predecessor James "Sunny Jim" Rolph and successor Culbert Olson. Rolph gave California its first sales tax, known as "Pennies for Jimmy," but was most remembered as the governor who endorsed the vigilante lynching of a confessed murderer. Olson, a pro-labor ultraliberal, broke a forty-year Republican stranglehold on the governorship in 1938, only to be swamped four years later by Earl Warren in his bid for reelection. Conservative Republican Merriam was once described as "a moon-faced Iowan who crept into Sacramento as lieutenant governor in 1930."[1] He does get a paragraph or two in especially thick history books for sending the California National Guard into San Francisco to quell a crippling longshoremen's strike, but what sets Merriam apart from all who preceded him was the unorthodox, grimy campaign that resulted in his election victory. Political campaigns, in California and nationwide, would never be the same.

In 1934, Democrats thought they were poised to win back the governorship after having wandered in the wilderness since the late 1890s. Two years into his presidency, Franklin Delano Roosevelt was extremely popular in California. Despite facing a huge deficit in voter registration, Roosevelt had swept the state as hundreds of thousands of California Republicans refused to vote for incumbent Herbert Hoover, who was widely blamed for the Great Depression. Hoover, a member of Stanford University's inaugural graduating class of 1895, was routed even in his adopted home county of Santa Clara. But in an election-year upheaval, Rolph died of heart failure, propelling bland and untested lieutenant governor Merriam into the governor's office. Merriam seemed hopelessly out of step with the majority of Californians, who had vigorously embraced Roosevelt's New Deal.

Thus, the table was set for a Democrat—just about any Democrat—to break the GOP's winning streak and occupy the capitol's corner office. Famed iconoclastic muckraker Upton Sinclair—a strident Socialist turned Democrat—nabbed his party's nomination and captured the imagination of hundreds of thousands of down-and-out Californians. As returns trickled in on August 28 and the breadth of Sinclair's primary victory became evident, shocked Democratic leaders panicked, convinced their party's nominee's anticapitalist ideas were toxic. Republicans also panicked, because they feared that Sinclair might actually win. To ensure Sinclair's defeat, Merriam supporters—or, more accurately, Sinclair opponents—lied and cheated on a scale never seen before or since in the Golden State. To carry out the mayhem, a former newspaper reporter and a chamber of commerce manager invented a new kind of political enterprise. Succeeding generations would bemoan mudslinging campaigns with their nasty, personal, and poll-tested ads and mailers fueled by heavily bankrolled special interests. But none would approach California's vile 1934 exercise in democracy, enflamed as it was by Campaigns, Inc., the nation's first full-service campaign management firm.

THE BACKSTORY

It took a devastating depression and record unemployment to breathe new political life into the California Democratic Party. Since 1898, Democrats had been an endangered species. Only a single Democrat had won statewide office: James D. Phelan, who benefited from a rift among Republicans by winning a three-way race for US Senate in 1914. Republicans had held a majority of state assembly and senate seats every year, and during one assembly session in the 1920s, Republicans boasted an unheard-of 77–3 edge against Democrats. However, with statewide unemployment surging as high as 28 percent by some estimates, Democratic politicians and voters awoke from their slumber. In the five elections before 1932, Democrats had won only seven of fifty-five California congressional contests. In 1932, Democrats won eleven of twenty races as party registration increased dramatically.[2]

In September 1933, writer Sinclair reregistered as a Democrat. He was twenty-seven years removed from his most highly acclaimed novel, *The Jungle*, a searing exposé of the meatpacking industry that led, in part, to enactment of the federal Pure Food and Drug Act and the Meat Inspection Act. Sinclair understood that his writings—which at that time numbered forty-seven books—had some effect on public opinion and government action, but "he wanted to push the implications of muckraking discoveries to their utmost practical conclusion."[3] He wrote a sixty-seven-page utopian platform that he hoped would catapult him to the governorship. His *I, Governor of California, and How I Ended Poverty: A True Story of the Future* sought to foretell his election and the subsequent redistribution of income he hoped to achieve. Invalids, widows with dependent children, and needy older Californians would receive monthly $50 pensions. Sinclair advocated heavy taxes on incomes, inheritances, public utilities, and banks. He wanted workers to produce goods for their own consumption, and he envisioned the state taking over foreclosed farms and idled factories. He blamed the profit system and concentration of wealth in a few hands for the workers' plight—a problem that would be remedied by government enterprises. In time, according to David M. Kennedy in his epic *Freedom from Fear*,

Sinclair hoped "these 'public industries' would drive private industry out of business."[4] His program was called EPIC—End Poverty in California—and more than two dozen candidates who supported it would win elections to the legislature.

When running as a Socialist Party nominee in California, Sinclair had struck out four times before—once for a House seat (1920), once for the US Senate (1922), and twice for governor (1926 and 1930). He was trounced in all of the contests and couldn't garner more than 4 percent of the vote in his gubernatorial races. He understood political realities enough to know he'd have to run as a Democrat to have any chance of success. In the early stages of his Democratic campaign, he was sanguine about the possibility of being elected, even if he captured the nomination. In late October of 1933, Sinclair sent a copy of his EPIC plan to Eleanor Roosevelt. "I will probably not be governor," he wrote, "but at least I hope to get some new ideas at work in this state."[5] Three months later, Sinclair wrote a second letter to Mrs. Roosevelt asking for her endorsement of EPIC. He thought he'd get it and hoped it would kick-start his campaign for governor. The First Lady's reply, marked "Private— not for publication," says she "heartily favors" some of his proposals. "I do not feel, however, that I am sufficiently in accord with your entire idea to make any public statement at present."[6]

Undeterred, Sinclair forged ahead by developing a grassroots organization. He formed EPIC clubs up and down the state in which members paid dues and sponsored radio broadcasts appealing for funds. He sold copies of his book to finance the campaign and published his own newspaper, *Upton Sinclair's End Poverty Paper*, which sold on streets for five cents. The newspaper's first issue (December 28–January 3, 1933–34) was headlined "Sinclair Book Stirs State as Crowds Jam Meetings." Sinclair wrote that "a little gray pamphlet is carrying a simple message of economic hope to sorely burdened taxpayers[,] and the despairing army of the unemployed is making history in California."[7] Mainstream media saw it differently. "EPIC received its full share of attention from Theosophists, spiritualists, vegetarians, Populists, Single Taxers, Rosicrucians, crackpots, faddists and cultists of every sort," sniffed Henry Luce's *Time* magazine.[8]

Democrats desperately tried to find someone to run against Sinclair. They wanted to reform the capitalist system, not destroy it. And they wanted to win. The early Democratic favorite was James Francis Thaddeus O'Connor, who led the FDR slate in Southern California and had been appointed US comptroller of the currency. O'Connor had connections and endorsements. The only problem was "he was having too good a time in Washington to run for governor in 1934."[9] A fractured Democratic Party couldn't agree on a single anti-Sinclair candidate, sending eight challengers against him.

While the Democratic establishment dithered, Sinclair gained traction, particularly with California's down-and-outers. By the end of March, there were nearly five hundred EPIC clubs; by late August there were a thousand. On the day of the primary election, the quirky ex-Socialist became the newly minted Democratic nominee for governor. He received more votes than the other eight candidates combined, polling the largest Democratic primary vote in state history. It was big news just about everywhere. "Votes for Upton Sinclair and his plan to 'end poverty in California' by state seizure of idle farm lands and factories piled up commandingly tonight as returns from today's primary election were received in volume,"[10] said the *New York Times*.

Despite the Democratic elite's fear that Sinclair was a pariah who would drive voters away, the party's registration increased significantly during his candidacy—spurred by the depth of the Depression, a popular new president and, to some extent, Sinclair's ability to articulate the concerns of California's working class. In August 1930, Republicans had outnumbered Democrats by more than three and a half to one. By primary day 1934, Democrats enjoyed a voter-registration edge of 75,000.[11]

Republicans, meanwhile, were embroiled in a much different drama. Frank Merriam had ascended to the governorship less than three months earlier from his quiet political backwater in the lieutenant governor's office. Immediately, he was confronted with a longshoremen's strike by 12,000 dockworkers who closed down the San Francisco waterfront, at that time the largest port on the West Coast. Teamsters, sailors, firemen, cooks, and stewards rallied behind the International Association of Longshoremen. Fights broke out when the port reopened with hired strikebreakers. A few hours after police fired into an angry crowd, killing a dockworker and a cook, Merriam ordered the National Guard to assume control of the waterfront. According to one account a year later, sending in the National Guard was a calculated political move by Merriam, who "black-jacked California's influential Republicans into nominating him against Sinclair by threatening to withhold State troops from the San Francisco strike."[12]

Merriam beat three other candidates in the GOP primary, setting up the showdown with Sinclair. One of the eight Democrats vanquished by Sinclair in August was prompted to suggest that voters would have "a choice between epilepsy and catalepsy. Sinclair has a fantastic, impossible plan, and Merriam is as modern as the dinosaur age."[13] As if the race didn't offer enough spice, a fairly strong third candidate, Raymond Haight, set out to capture the political center after winning nominations from the Commonwealth and Progressive Parties.

Lurking in the shadows were two young entrepreneurs who would forever change the nature of political campaigning: Clem Whitaker and Leone Baxter. They had just founded the pioneer consulting firm Campaigns, Inc. Whitaker was a lanky thirty-five-year-old former newspaper wunderkind and son of a Baptist minister. He was raised in tiny Willits in Mendocino County and cut his teeth as a teenaged crime reporter for the *Sacramento Union*. After a brief stint as the newspaper's city editor, he jumped to William Randolph Hearst's *San Francisco Examiner*. His son, Clem Whitaker, Jr., characterized him as "Hearst's leading crime reporter. Every murder that happened, every hanging that happened, whatever, that was my father's assignment."[14] Whitaker's transformation into politics was a financial decision. Like so many low-paid reporters of the day, he moonlighted on the side, including as a writer of speeches and press releases for politicians. While still in his early twenties, Whitaker created the Capitol News Bureau, a hugely successful service that supplied eighty California newspapers with news about state government and politics. After he sold the enterprise to United Press, he formed his own advertising company, headquartered on K Street in Sacramento. Leone Baxter, an elegant, immaculately dressed redhead, was a twenty-seven-year-old widow who had briefly worked for the *Portland Oregonian* and had managed the Redding Chamber of Commerce.

Whitaker's move into campaign management had begun a few years earlier, while he was getting a haircut. His barber complained that his trade association was having difficulty getting the legislature to approve a bill to create the State Board of Barber Examiners. Whitaker offered to help the barbers for a $4,000 fee. He tried a new approach to advocacy that has become a staple of campaign management to this day: grassroots organizing. Whitaker mobilized barbers to lobby their legislators, and the new strategy worked. In 1932, Whitaker successfully managed the state senate campaign of John B. McColl of Red Bluff. McColl authored a landmark water bill his rookie year in the legislature—the Central Valley Project Act—which was approved by voters to authorize the sale of $170 million in bonds to finance water storage facilities, hydroelectric power generation, and conveyance of Northern California water to towns and farms in the Central Valley.[15]

The Pacific Gas and Electric Company worried that it would lose its power monopoly under the new law. It sought to overturn it by referendum and was prepared to spend whatever it took to win. The statewide campaign in 1934 promised to be hard-fought, and backers of the Central Valley Project hired Whitaker to guide them through the electoral thicket. A lawyer working on the campaign introduced him to Baxter at the Redding Chamber and they hit it off immediately, getting married four years later. They formed a business partnership and together managed the campaign against PG&E. Forced to function on a relative shoestring, Whitaker and Baxter accepted contributions large and small to finance publicity and advertising. Shasta County, for example, sent separate checks for $3,500, $2,500, and $1,800, and the Madera Irrigation District chipped in $1,840. Their campaign files also noted a $2.50 contribution from Dolan Building Materials and $1 from a private citizen named A. C. Sikes.

Recognizing that the power of political parties had diminished since the dawn of direct democracy twenty years earlier, the pair used news media to communicate with voters. They placed advertisements in small newspapers, which—in gratitude—gave them news coverage. They created editorials, cartoons, and news releases for distribution to seven hundred daily and weekly newspapers, many with tiny staffs and huge holes to fill in their publications. They produced and distributed radio scripts. They bolstered the campaign's credibility by enlisting a Stanford professor of finance to write a paper on the project's importance to the industrial and commercial interests in Los Angeles.[16] Many of their tactics were inventive and cunning. And they worked. PG&E's referendum was defeated by more than 30,000 votes. Months following the election, on April 30, 1934, Whitaker and Baxter drafted a final statement of financial condition for the State Water Plan Association. It listed total deposits during the campaign of $40,037.01 and total withdrawals of $40,036.48, leaving a balance of fifty-three cents on deposit with the Bank of America.[17] Whitaker and Baxter had pointed future political consultants to another truism in campaign management: never leave money on the table.

THE ELECTION

Upton Sinclair's August 28 gubernatorial primary-election victory caught most political insiders off guard. With more than a touch of hyperbole, the *Washington Post* set the stage for a raucous campaign. "A new earthquake is rocking California, comparable in its intensity to the one that caused San Francisco's tall buildings to first shudder and then collapse on that fateful day in April, 1906."[18] Sinclair, of course, had predicted the outcome in his EPIC treatise written the prior year. On the day after his nomination, he set out to snag the biggest endorsement prize of all—Franklin D. Roosevelt—sending the president a telegram requesting a face-to-face meeting. Sinclair trekked to the source and spent two hours talking with the president in the library at his Hyde Park retreat. Roosevelt said he had read Sinclair's book on meatpacking and was aware of EPIC.

Sinclair quoted Roosevelt as saying, "My advisers tell me I have to talk to the people again over the radio and explain to them what I'm doing....I am coming out in favor of production for use." To that, Sinclair responded, "If you do that, Mr. President, it will elect me."[19] But it never happened. Roosevelt felt that an endorsement of Sinclair would cause irreparable harm to his New Deal, and he refused to answer any questions on the subject.

In California, prominent Republicans and disaffected Democrats began posturing against the Democratic nominee. A bitter Hamilton Cotton, who had managed a rival Democrat's losing primary campaign, was quoted by *Time* magazine as characterizing the August vote as "the rape of the Democratic Party in California by Upton Sinclair."[20] Republicans labeled Sinclair a communist bent on destroying the American way of life. As it turned out, the real campaign against Sinclair had yet to be unleashed. Before the campaign would conclude, two separate, lavishly funded independent advocacy groups—one headquartered in Los Angeles, the other in San Francisco—would hurl all manner of slime at Sinclair.

Three weeks after the primary, major Southern California businessmen, apoplectic at the thought of Sinclair as governor, pledged to raise hundreds of thousands of dollars in an all-out attack on the candidate. Billed as a nonpartisan organization, their United for California was funded by the wealthiest of Californians and fronted by a prominent judge. Two weeks later, the group publicly asked Californians to join its crusade against Sinclair's election, which would "strike at the roots of our most cherished institutions—the home, the church and the school."[21] In its initial salvo, tame compared to subsequent maneuvers, the organization accused pro-Sinclair forces of plotting to stuff ballot boxes. United for California sent Southern California employers a list of anti-Sinclair activities they could take to ensure his defeat, including sending their employees a not-so-subtle message to "soberly think of the danger to their jobs if Sinclair is elected."[22]

In the meantime, after the bold defeat of PG&E's referendum the year before, the fledging firm created by Whitaker and Baxter had caught the attention of the political establishment. Trying their hand at delivering votes for a statewide candidate, they signed on to manage every aspect of Republican George J. Hatfield's campaign for lieutenant governor, from strategy and media relations to advertisements, speechwriting, mail, and radio appearances. Republicans, however, found another use for the innovative team. Two months before the general election, Campaigns, Inc., was hired to manage publicity for a second, concurrent campaign—a bipartisan, supposedly independent drive targeting Sinclair and his radical ideas. Generously financed, the California League Against Sinclairism (CLAS) took advantage of Whitaker's specialty in manipulating California's small but influential weekly newspapers. This was the Depression, after all, and newspapers were hurting like other businesses. Whitaker's advertising company placed hard-hitting anti-Sinclair ads and reaped hefty commissions in the process. Operating sans latter-day notions of journalistic objectivity, newspapers responded by running Whitaker's publicity releases as news stories—usually unedited—as well as his "suggested editorials" and cartoons.[23] Whitaker would then reprint and distribute the articles, which now had the stamp of journalistic authenticity.

The news media proved to be a willing audience for the Whitaker-and-Baxter team's brand of persuasion. Vested in the establishment, most wanted to send Sinclair and his radical ideas packing. One radio station began broadcasting a report titled "The Unmasking of Upton Sinclair" twice a week. Harry Chandler's *Los Angeles Times,* which Sinclair ridiculed as "the fountain-head of so much unloveliness in California life,"[24] was particularly partisan. Sinclair, the *Times* said, was a "consorter with radicals" and a "threat to sovietize California." The newspaper insisted the Sinclair threat was not politics but war; "War knows no neutrality. If you are not against Sinclair and Sinclairism you are for them."[25] Every day for six weeks, the *Times* ran an unflattering Sinclair quote in a box on the front page. It ignored anything positive Sinclair had to say. According to author David Halberstam, when *New York Times* reporter Turner Catledge arrived in California to do a story on the governor's race, he picked up Chandler's *Times* to look for Sinclair's schedule but found only a negative story about how the candidate was anti-Christian. That night Catledge dined with Kyle Palmer, the *Los Angeles Times*'s chief political correspondent, and when he asked where Sinclair was speaking, Palmer replied, "Turner, forget it. We don't go in for that kind of crap that you have back in New York of being obliged to print both sides. We're going to beat this son of a bitch Sinclair any way we can. We're going to kill him."[26]

Sinclair, of course, didn't help himself with his natural naïveté that often played into the hands of the hostile press. In his record of the campaign, Sinclair recounted a conversation he had with reporters, jokingly telling them that if he were elected, half the nation's unemployed workers might come to California, "and we'll have to make plans to take care of them." A *Times* reporter told colleagues he wanted to lead the story with Sinclair's prediction of an invasion of unemployed. When reminded that Sinclair was obviously joking, he responded, "Maybe he didn't mean it, but he said it, and it's what my paper wants." The next day, a *Times* headline roared "Heavy Rush of Idle Seen by Sinclair," accompanied by a two-column editorial predicting California's ruin if five million jobless Americans flocked to the state. When Sinclair stated in a radio broadcast that his comment had been only in jest, the *San Francisco Chronicle* accused him of "jesting with human misery."[27]

Clem Whitaker and Leone Baxter were nothing if not thorough. They spent three days reading everything Sinclair had written and lifted quotes to suit their purposes; context was irrelevant. They hired a cartoonist who penned thirty separate drawings that appeared in print 3,000 times.[28] They had plenty of material. Sinclair's own words offered a treasure trove for his critics: attacks against Wall Street, the coal and oil industries, the church, the press, universities, the Boy Scouts, Hollywood, and others. Campaigns, Inc., churned out hit pieces in rapid succession. Some quoted Sinclair directly, others quoted fictional characters from his books and attributed the remarks to the candidate. Sinclair simply couldn't respond fast enough. One broadside quoted Sinclair as saying, "The sanctity of marriage...I have had such a belief...I have it no longer." Sinclair later explained that the quote was taken from a character in his novel *Love's Pilgrimage*, written more than two decades earlier.[29] In 1909, during a rough patch with his first wife, Sinclair did say he was "sorry he was married,"[30] but he had two subsequent marriages, one of which lasted forty-eight years. Whitaker and Baxter sent mail to voters linking Sinclair with Russia. They coaxed newspapers to run cartoons of Sinclair stamping out organized religion as well as to print articles about the unemployed flocking to California to take advantage of Sinclair's promised post-election giveaway. One editorial accused Sinclair of advocating free love. Newspapers received a statement from a leading Democrat suggesting the candidate was suffering from hallucinations.[31]

Whitaker and Baxter recognized the importance of repeating key messages on different platforms. They understood that if a message in a news story, for example, is repeated in editorials, mail, radio addresses, billboards, advertisements, and campaign speeches, it becomes a message that has a greater chance of being remembered. Twenty-five years later, in an extensive interview with *Harper's* magazine, Whitaker and Baxter seemed embarrassed to talk about their evisceration of Sinclair. "It was one we hated to handle," Whitaker said. "Sure those quotations were irrelevant," Baxter added. "He was a good man[;] we were sorry we had to do it that way. But we had one objective: to keep him from becoming Governor."[32]

Hollywood mogul Louis B. Mayer of Metro-Goldwyn-Mayer, who was chair of the Republican State Central Committee, had vowed to use all his influence to stop Sinclair. He even threatened to support the motion picture industry's move to Florida if the former Socialist were elected governor. MGM joined other movie studios in "donating" a day's pay from its employees—including the stars—to raise money for Merriam's campaign.[33] There were rumors of an actors' rebellion against the studios, but Californians learned little about this from the overwhelmingly anti-Sinclair daily newspapers. Late in the campaign, the issue gained traction, at least in the East. The *Boston Globe* reported that the Los Angeles County Grand Jury was being asked to investigate threats that stars would be fired if they voted for Sinclair. One threatened studio employee was said to be "Katharine Hepburn, film star."[34]

Nothing, however, affected the governor's race more than three widely viewed ersatz newsreels produced by Irving Thalberg, Louis B. Mayer's partner at MGM. They realized motion pictures had the power to transmit realistic and believable messages, whether they were true or not. "The movies have tasted blood—Upton Sinclair's blood," wrote *Harper's*.[35] Called *California Election News*, the "newsreels" were heavily scripted documentary-style shorts that featured so-called man-on-the-street interviews. Movie patrons saw supposed Sinclair supporters portrayed by menacing-looking actors with thick Eastern European accents praising Russia. Actors who depicted Merriam supporters, on the other hand, praised God and country. In one newsreel, an elderly woman said she was voting for Merriam "because I want to save my little home. It's all I have left in this world."[36] Another newsreel, released in theaters a few days before the general election, featured dozens of "hoboes" flocking into California by rail, expressly to get their hands on the taxpayer-funded largesse Sinclair would hand out after he won. "They were repulsive looking bums," noted *Harper's*, although "those with critical eyes wondered why the vagrants were wearing make-up."[37] A local judge, or what appeared to be a local judge, said, "I consider most of them to have radical ideas—some communist. If they stay in California, I don't know what will become of the working man."[38]

The visual images—forerunners of today's omnipresent television attack ads—had more impact than mere words in a newspaper or circular. Newspapers, among them the *Los Angeles Times,* the *Los Angeles Examiner*, and the *San Francisco News,* published what were purported to be graphic photographs and mocking cartoons of immigrants streaming into California. William Randolph Hearst's *Examiner* took a break from its daily anti-Sinclair rant on October 23 to feature the Ohio slaying of gangster Pretty Boy Floyd, but it still found room for a cartoon depicting two bums pining for California handouts once Sinclair was elected, as well as an editorial suggesting that a post-election "stampede of poverty" would make the Gold Rush look like an inconsequential migration. On October 24, an *Examiner* cartoon characterized Sinclair as a pied piper leading Californians with empty promises. The following day, the

Examiner ran a four-column photograph purportedly showing thirteen people disembarking from a Union Pacific boxcar, a "sample of influx of unemployed into California," according to the photo's caption.[39] Late in the campaign, EPIC headquarters received a phone call from a Sinclair supporter who worked in the publicity department of Warner Brothers. Some anti-Sinclair newspaper photos, EPIC was told, weren't news photos at all. They were still shots from the 1933 Hollywood movie *Wild Boys of the Road*.[40]

Sinclair was being hit from all sides—United for California in Los Angeles, the California League Against Sinclairism in San Francisco, nearly all of the state's newspapers, Governor Merriam, prominent candidate surrogates, and Whitaker and Baxter's other client, Lieutenant Governor Hatfield. The pair enlisted actor Wallace Beery, who was campaigning for Hatfield, to hit Sinclair hard. The text of one speech written for Beery declared, "Without the slightest exaggeration, this is probably the most import[ant] period in the history of Governments since the birth of Democracy."[41] In a radio address at Sacramento's KFBK, former assistant US attorney Albert Sheets urged his listeners, "Vote for reconstruction and recovery. Vote against radicalism and Communism." And in fliers distributed at the Republican State Convention in Sacramento, Hatfield said Sinclair's promise of "Utopia" cannot become a reality "unless we are willing to throw into the discard every principle of self-government and self-respect."[42] In an election-eve radio address, Hatfield insisted, "There must be a complete and overwhelming repudiation of radicalism."[43]

With full fury and bluster, the campaign finally lurched toward its inevitable conclusion. The Friday before the election, Scripps-Howard journalist Max Stern wrote from Los Angeles, "A reign of unreason bordering on hysteria has this sprawling city in its grip as the nation's ugliest campaign approaches zero hour." Stern characterized the anti-Sinclair movement as "a phobia, lacking humor, fairness and even a sense of reality." He reported on a fake "Young People's Communist League" leaflet endorsing Sinclair, and an appeal by a nonexistent "Citizens' Co-operative Relief Committee" for donations to help the millions of new citizens expected to arrive in Sinclair's new Utopia.[44]

Two days before Election Day, the *Times* ran a 1,200-word front-page editorial that dwarfed the day's other big story about a rumored reconciliation between silver-screen sweethearts Douglas Fairbanks and Mary Pickford. Under the booming headline "The Choice of California," Harry Chandler called the election the "most momentous decision" in California's history, one that would determine if the "apostle of hatred" would lead the state down the road to communism.[45] Sinclair limped to the finish line. "I'm anxious to get this campaign over," he said. "This campaign has shortened my life."[46]

Betrayed by fellow Democrats, attacked mercilessly by the press, cast adrift by Roosevelt, and targeted by a new breed of political consultants, Sinclair lost to Merriam by 259,000 votes under the onslaught of an unprecedented multimillion-dollar opposition campaign. Even so, Sinclair did well in the state's major urban centers of San Francisco and Los Angeles. Merriam claimed victory on election night during a radio broadcast that aired nationwide. The number of votes cast set a California record. Ten days after the election, and as required by California's Purity of Elections law, Merriam filed an official "Statement of Candidate's Receipts and Expenditures." When asked to name those who paid, loaned, or contributed funds to his election campaign, Merriam responded, "None. Certain moneys were paid to committees interested in my campaign and candidacy, the amounts, by whom paid, and to whom paid are unknown to me." When asked to name how he spent money on the campaign, Merriam listed a total of $464 for travel and other miscellaneous expenses.[47]

THE IMPACT

The 1934 midterm elections offered the first test of President Roosevelt's New Deal and, with few exceptions, it was a clean sweep. Democrats picked up an additional twelve seats in the House, giving them a better than three-to-one advantage over Republicans. In the Senate, they gained nine additional seats, reducing the GOP ranks to a mere twenty-five in the ninety-six-member body. "Never in the history of the Republican party had its percentage in either house been so low."[48] Democrats dominated the statehouse elections as well. Republicans retained only seven governorships. One of them, of course, was in California.

In the state assembly, twenty-four EPIC candidates were successful; in the state senate, three won, including Culbert Olson of Los Angeles, an attorney who specialized in investigating corporate fraud. Clearly, Sinclair's antipoverty ideas had caught fire with a sizeable sector of the electorate. In his concession speech, Sinclair acknowledged, "If we had had a better candidate, we might have won!"[49] He was right. In 1938, Democrats would put up a better candidate—Olson—who defeated Merriam's reelection bid to become the state's first Democratic governor in the twentieth century. EPIC clubs played a key role in Olson's victory and became a model for club systems in the future, among them the California Republican Assembly and the California Democratic Council.[50]

Three days after the election, Sinclair began work on his new writing project: *I, Candidate for Governor: And How I Got Licked,* a nonfiction sequel to his fictionalized original. "It is a revelation of what money can do in politics," he said with a prescience he understood best.[51] Sinclair traced his defeat to what he called the "Lie Factory" of relentless, well-funded attacks by his opponents that became too numerous—and too misleading—to adequately refute. "They had a staff of political chemists at work, preparing poisons to be let loose in the California atmosphere on every one of a hundred mornings." He recalled those daily front-page quote boxes in the *Los Angeles Times*. "Reading these boxes day after day, I made up my mind that the election was lost," he said.[52]

For a number of years, Campaigns, Inc., enjoyed a monopoly on campaign management. Between 1933 and 1955, it won seventy campaigns and lost only five.[53] Ironically, one of its rare losses came in 1938 when Whitaker and Baxter ran Lieutenant Governor Hatfield's challenge to Merriam in the Republican gubernatorial primary. In a speech written by Campaigns, Inc., for one of Hatfield's surrogate campaigners, Merriam was characterized as "the laughing stock of the country" because he had sold out the people's interest "for the sake of building up a political machine that will eventually place the governor in the White House."[54] In 1939, Campaigns, Inc., helped defeat Proposition 1, a so-called Ham and Eggs measure that would have levied a 3 percent income tax so seniors could receive $30 weekly pensions. In 1942, the firm managed Earl Warren's first gubernatorial campaign, advising the candidate on everything from issues to image. It flooded California with advertising and billboards but was terminated just before the election for issuing a press release without his approval. Three years later, Whitaker and Baxter got even. When Warren proposed compulsory health insurance for Californians, the California Medical Association hired Whitaker and Baxter to defeat it in the legislature. They vilified the plan as socialistic "political medicine," armed 9,000 doctors with campaign speeches, bought 40,000 inches of newspaper advertising, personally called more than 500 newspaper offices, and wrote postcards for constituents to send to their legislators. The Warren bill was defeated by one vote. When Warren tried a second time, Whitaker and Baxter again defeated it. "They stormed the Legislature with their invective," Warren later wrote.[55]

The political consulting giants had struck gold working with the medical establishment. When President Truman proposed comprehensive national health care in 1948 to "protect all our people equally against insecurity and ill health,"[56] the American Medical Association offered Whitaker and Baxter a $100,000-per-year retainer and gave the firm an annual budget of more than $1 million to defeat it.[57] The campaign spanned more than three years and successfully turned around public opinion. Every subsequent attempt to defeat national health insurance proposals borrowed from Whitaker and Baxter's campaign playbook: characterize the plan as "socialized medicine," demonize the proposal as taking away American freedom, and use a torrent of mail and advertising to mobilize the public and galvanize opinion.

The 1934 gubernatorial campaign, engineered by freelance campaign professionals for the first time, laid the foundation for today's multimillion-dollar campaigns by drowning voters in propaganda. In an interview twenty-five years later, Clem Whitaker and

Leone Baxter revealed the logistics of one of their typical statewide campaigns: 10,000,000 pamphlets and leaflets, 50,000 letters to key individuals and organizations, 70,000 inches of ads in 700 news-papers, 3,000 spot announcements on 109 radio stations, screen slides and trailers in 160 theaters, and up to 20,000 posters.[58]

Those political chemists Sinclair so despised ushered in a new era of electoral politics with what historian Arthur Schlesinger, Jr., characterized as the "first all-out public relations Blitzkrieg in American politics."[59] Words and images had become weapons, advertising markets were battlefields, and votes were the spoils that led to the trappings of office. Candidates became commodities, much like washing machines or toothpaste, and winning an election was all about manipulating public opinion and gaining market share— using slogans and chicanery, if necessary, to convince customers that one product was more worthy of their support than another. Political party bosses had been replaced by smart, ruthless outside consultants—spin doctors—who crafted aggressive, well-funded campaigns appealing to voters' fears through a variety of persuasion techniques. The use of streamlined themes, direct mail, concerted media outreach, polling, grassroots organizations, radio, and film— so new in 1934—have become de rigueur in modern campaigns. Many historians suggest the turning point in the Merriam-Sinclair contest was the use of the fake, highly charged movie newsreels, in much the same fashion many campaigns today turn on saturating the airwaves with misleading, emotional television ads.

Nearly twenty years after Merriam's victory, political ads made their debut on television. Republican Dwight Eisenhower made the greatest initial use of this new medium as he sought the presidency in 1952. His campaign aired a newsreel-style ad, "The Man from Abilene," and ran a series of twenty-second spots called "Eisenhower Answers America" in a dozen key states for three weeks in October. The ad buy cost $2 million. They were tame by today's standards, but they did attack the opposition. In one ad, a man says to Eisenhower, "The Democrats are telling me I never had it so good." Eisenhower, reading off cue cards, responds sternly, "Can that be true when America is billions in debt, and prices have doubled, and taxes break our backs, and we are still fighting in Korea? It's tragic and it's time for a change."[60] His Democratic opponent, Adlai Stevenson, also waged a television campaign, but it was old-fashioned and less effective. Many of his ads relied on uninspiring jingles and cartoons, and the candidate so distrusted the medium that he refused to appear in his own ads.

Stevenson speechwriter George Ball bitterly attacked the new campaign strategies: "I think the American people will be shocked by such contempt for their intelligence. This isn't Ivory Soap versus Palmolive."[61] Journalist Irwin Ross wasn't convinced that Whitaker and Baxter represented the future of political campaigns. The pair's methods were uniquely suited only to California, he suggested, because of the personal character of the campaigns and the lack of strong party identification in the Golden State. "To hire a PR firm to manage an entire major campaign would involve an unthinkable degree of abdication for a self-respecting political leader," said Ross.[62] Ball had a different take as America moved deeper into the postwar television era. "Presidential campaigns will eventually have professional actors as candidates," he predicted.[63] Only fourteen years later, a California actor named Ronald Reagan would hint at the disconnect between politics and fact in his race for governor. Not the first Hollywood figure to run for office in California, Reagan told his campaign manager, California PR executive Stuart Spencer: "Politics is just like show business. You have a hell of an opening, coast for a while, and then have a hell of a close."[64]

6

1942
Earl Warren Pilots California into a Postwar Boom

"It was…necessary for us to provide the governmental
services for a new city of ten thousand people
every Monday morning."
—Governor Earl Warren

SON OF A railroad man, Earl Warren had earned a far-flung reputation
as the fair-minded, corruption-fighting district attorney of Alameda
County, across the bay from San Francisco. When his own elderly
father was murdered by a home intruder in Bakersfield 250 miles
away, Warren vetoed the local police chief's suggested use of illegal eavesdropping to hunt down the suspect, who was never found.[1]
After a decade pursuing high-profile graft and crime at the helm of
the county prosecutor's office, however, Warren yearned to climb
higher. He saw enormous potential in the backburner post of state
attorney general—an elected job that, in effect, would make him
California's top lawyer. Warren went to work to reshape its mission. With the help of two of his office deputies, he cannily crafted
a successful initiative for the 1934 ballot to expand the powers of
the office and explicitly make its occupant—himself one day, he
hoped—California's chief law-enforcement officer.

Four years later, eleven Japanese residents of Alameda County, in an endorsement of Warren's candidacy for attorney general that would become poignantly ironic, commended his tenure as district attorney in an open letter to Japanese American voters. Their support for his election in 1938 was noteworthy given a history of state and federal legal restrictions, racist party slogans, and other overt prejudices against California residents of Asian descent that dated to the Gold Rush. The eleven vouched that members of the Japanese community had received fair treatment from Warren in Alameda County, "regardless of race, color or religion. Every resident has been treated equally. We cannot expect more from any public official," they wrote.

As it went on, the letter became even stronger: "He is too big a man to stir up racial prejudice against Japanese....[H]e is not the kind of man who would go out of his way to try to create trouble for the Japanese people of this state."[2] Warren's campaign bought ads that reprinted the letter in Japanese-language newspapers aimed at Nisei voters, the "second generation" Japanese people born of immigrant parents, who were themselves universally prohibited by federal law from becoming citizens.[3]

But within three years of Warren's inauguration as attorney general in 1939, the US naval fleet would lie in ruins in Pearl Harbor, massive wartime shipyards would begin rising from the bay marshes of Alameda and Marin Counties, and, as California's lead law-enforcer, Warren would lend his loud voice to the federal roundup and internment of more than 90,000 Californians of Japanese descent. Two-thirds of them were American-born citizens—the Nisei, who had been assured by their own that Warren would be fair and just. When the internment order came, properties belonging to Japanese immigrants and Japanese American residents—farms, shops, homes, and their contents—typically were sold at rock-bottom prices to exploitive bargain-hunters or were confiscated by the government, in some cases never to be returned. No war-related sabotage was ever traced to anyone of Japanese descent in the United States or Hawaii, but that did nothing to allay the public's fear.

Republican Warren sought the governor's office in the aftermath of Pearl Harbor, challenging Democratic incumbent Culbert

Olson. While it is impossible to know whether Warren deliberately exploited anti-Japanese sentiment for political gain, there is no question that he publicly promoted fears, suspicions, and the banishment of Japanese Americans at a time—the election year of 1942—when voters eagerly accepted those notions. It remains a lingering contradiction in this man of the law, who would become a champion of civil rights as chief justice of the US Supreme Court.

Whatever the electoral sentiments that initially propelled Warren into the corner office, he succeeded the lackluster Olson to become one of California's three biggest game-changing governors of the twentieth century. Riding the crest of a roaring wartime economy, his administration accrued more than enough capital to lead California into a postwar era of mindboggling population growth, guided by Warren's astute blend of prudence and vision. His nearly eleven-year legacy of public policy accomplishments built on the bold reforms of Hiram Johnson on one hand and laid the groundwork for Pat Brown's epic achievements on the other. It was Warren, shrewd and farsighted, who seemingly willed California into becoming the nation's most progressive state.

THE BACKSTORY

Japanese community leaders who had put their weight behind Warren for attorney general in 1938 knew they had ample reason to be wary of anti-Japanese sentiments in the Golden State. As far as many European-descended Californians were concerned, the state's riches were not for everyone. Notions of a "yellow peril" embodied by the "Chinese must go" slogan of the Workingmen's Party had persisted since the arrival of Chinese laborers during the Gold Rush. Targets of mob violence and discriminatory taxes in ensuing years, Chinese residents were relegated to low-paying jobs that included the dangerous work of blasting into the Sierra Nevada for the transcontinental railroad. Eventually they would be driven into urban Chinatowns.

Congress responded to the state's intense anti-Chinese sentiment by passing the Chinese Exclusion Act of 1882 to halt Chinese immigration nationally, and the follow-up Immigration Act of 1924 blocked those who were not white or of African descent from becoming natu-ralized citizens. Although an array of anti-Asian municipal ordinances, state statutes, and federal laws were initially aimed at Chinese laborers, within thirty years restrictions also targeted Japanese immigrants and their descendants, who had settled in enclaves as farmers and shop-keepers in the wake of Chinese exclusion. Governor Hiram Johnson, pressured by organized labor and the hardline farmer activists of the Grange, put his signature on the California Alien Land Law of 1913 to prohibit Asians who weren't entitled to become citizens under federal law from owning land in California. First-generation Japanese farm-ers, the Issei, were effectively forced to deed their property to their citizen children to get around the act.

Within a few years, California voters passed an initiative with the explicit intent of further tightening land restrictions against the Japanese. Arguments in the voter pamphlet supporting the Alien Land Law of 1920 candidly declared: "California seeks, as is her inherent right, to preserve her lands for Americans, precisely as Japan preserves her lands for the Japanese. Its primary purpose is to prohibit Orientals who cannot become American citizens from con-trolling our rich agricultural lands."[4] The arguments appeared over the name of V. S. McClatchy, who resigned his position as editor and publisher of the *Sacramento Bee* and its sister newspapers to lead the charge.[5] Opponents objected that the initiative, known as Proposition 1, violated the equal protection clause of the Fourteenth Amendment by favoring some residents over others. That line of reasoning was ignored for decades. Despite protestations from California's Japanese community that it represented less than 2 percent of the state's popu-lation and cultivated less than 2 percent of its farm lands, Proposition 1 passed with resounding 75 percent support. Not until 1952 would the Alien Land Law be overturned by the state supreme court, acting in the same year the federal government ended the practice of using race as a criteria for citizenship.

Although it never had the officially sanctioned framework of black slavery, California had since the Gold Rush developed its own legal and cultural patterns of bigotry against Native Americans, Mexicans, Asians, and African Americans—what historians James

J. Rawls and Walton Bean considered a "fixed belief in the innate superiority of whites over other races."[6] California's Indians probably endured the most "devastating experience," concludes historian Charles Wollenberg.[7] Involuntarily recruited as the state's first non-white workforce during Spanish-Mexican rule, they were felled by European diseases and deprived of their pastoral way of life, first under the Franciscan missions, then under the encroachment of American settlers who systematically hunted and slaughtered them, and finally under never-ratified federal treaties that forced them from their valley lands into the harsher mountains. Hardships nearly wiped out California's Indian population; by the late 1880s their numbers had plummeted from some 250,000 to just 20,000. Because the kidnapping of Indian children for servitude was so prevalent at the time of statehood, the first California legislature passed a law in 1850 declaring that custodians—called "masters"—of Indian children who failed to suitably feed and clothe them, or to treat them humanely, could be fined $10.[8]

Californians like to believe themselves free of the history of enforced racial segregation that marked the South and Border States. Warren himself, for instance, insisted that "no accepted policy of school segregation" existed in California when he was growing up at the turn of the twentieth century.[9] However, little more than two decades before his birth, the legislature had proclaimed that public schools should not accept children of African, Asian, or Indian descent, unless the last of these were living under the care of white people. In 1860, lawmakers granted the state superintendent of public instruction the authority to withhold funds from public schools that admitted non-whites, a move that prompted the establishment of the first Chinese school in San Francisco. It would not be until 1946, near the end of Warren's first term as governor, that state authorization of segregated schools was banished from the books.[10]

Warren grew up in dusty Bakersfield, then a railroad town dominated by the Southern Pacific. During his teen years, he worked as a callboy to summon train crews from bars, brothels, or wherever else they might be lounging as the trains were preparing to roll out. Bakersfield's environs gave him a lasting sensitivity to the ways powerful industries could oppress their own workers. "I saw minority groups brought into the country for cheap labor paid a dollar a day for ten hours of work only to be fleeced out of much of that at the company store where they were obliged to trade," he wrote in his *Memoirs*. He also witnessed even worse, and the awful memories would mold the district attorney, attorney general, governor, and chief justice he came to be: "I helped carry men to the little room called the emergency hospital for amputation of an arm or leg that had been crushed because there were no safety appliances in the shops and yards to prevent such injuries. I knew of men who were fired for even considering a suit against the railroad for the injuries they had sustained....The things I learned about monopolistic power, political dominance, corruption in government, and their effect on the people of a community were valuable lessons that would tend to shape my career throughout life."[11]

Aided by a father who had saved his railroad earnings so his son could attend college, Earl Warren headed for UC Berkeley. Self-described as a decent but hardly brilliant student, he relished fraternity life, thriving on the close-knit interaction as a natural networker. He was destined to blossom into a charismatic leader in social, professional, and political circles that ranged from UC's alumni organization to the statewide association of district attorneys to the Republican Party and beyond.

Graduating with a law degree, Warren landed a job as clerk of the Assembly Judiciary Committee, where he learned Sacramento's legislative ropes. It would be one reason why, decades later, he declared that his background for the job of governor had been as comprehensive as any candidate's in California history—despite the assertion of his *Memoirs* editors that he actually was a relatively modest man.[12] When he ran for election as district attorney in Alameda County in 1926, Warren later recounted, he and his wife, Nina, had agreed that to fund the campaign, he would devote a year's salary of $5,000— culled from their savings to buy a home—rather than take political donations. The approach epitomized his lifelong distaste for fundraising from anyone likely to want something in return; his *Memoirs* detail instances of losing friendships rather than granting expected political favors. At heart, Warren believed he was a nonpartisan. He declared himself independent of party influences in his campaigns and ran as a self-declared political independent even for governor.

Functioning on a spending shoestring in that first campaign, he made the rounds of poorly attended candidates' forums to argue his case. Because candidates typically spoke in alphabetical order, most voters had left by the time his name was called. One evening, he recounted, there was only one man remaining in the audience. "Nevertheless, I gave him my little speech, and in concluding thanked him for remaining to hear me. He replied, 'You are quite welcome, but I am entitled to no credit for remaining. My name is Young, and I am the next speaker.'"[13]

Warren won the DA's office by a landslide and was uncontested in future reelections. Strategically charting his political future, he developed relationships with district attorneys across the state in a self-made role as their Sacramento lobbyist. Although he was elected state Republican Party chair and would become a national committee member during the 1930s, he later conceded that he was a Republican simply because California was—at least until FDR's New Deal began raising struggling Californians out of the Great Depression. President Harry Truman, who would work with Governor Warren to complete the federal Central Valley Water Project years later, once playfully told a crowd gathered to hear the president speak from a train platform in Sacramento that Warren was a Democrat who didn't know it.[14]

Warren's avowed independence translated into winning Republican *and* Democratic nominations in primary elections for the same office, first for attorney general and then, in the postwar California of 1946, in his second bid for governor. Such resounding proof of his bipartisan appeal helped explain a legacy of left-leaning social reforms in working with a Republican-controlled legislature.

When Warren set his sights on the attorney general's office in 1934, it was a backwater whose officeholder, Ulysses Webb, made his real living by practicing law on the side. Warren's constitutional amendment on the 1934 ballot forbade future attorneys general from representing private clients, and in return, the annual salary rose from $5,000—hardly enough to support Warren's growing family—to a level equal to that of a state supreme court justice, then $11,000. Warren and his deputies also crafted a companion constitutional amendment to create a civil service system, removing most state jobs from political patronage.

Warren wrote ballot arguments for the successful measures, which were supported by organizations ranging from the League of Women Voters to the State Bar. As recounted by Ed Cray, Warren's biographer, the reforms helped cast Warren "as the embodiment of vigorous law enforcement and an opponent of corrupt political patronage." It made him the state's "most prominent 'good government' figure."[15] When Attorney General Webb in 1938 told Warren of his plan to retire at the end of his term, Warren was ready to run. Thanks to the 1934 overhaul he designed, the job had become the second-most-powerful position in state government.

Even before television screens could transform politicians into personal friends who shared living rooms with voters, Warren conveyed a larger-than-life presence. *Sacramento Bee* political reporter Herbert "Pete" Phillips, explaining Warren's appeal to Californians, made this observation to an oral history interviewer decades later: "In the first place, I suppose, his manner and appearance—a big man, above medium height, with a warm, pleasant smile which flashed on and off without appearing to be in the least contrived or synthetic, the kind of man Hollywood film makers would cast in the role of governor, the kind to whom the average voter is automatically attracted."[16] *Los Angeles Times* columnist Jack Smith, who covered Warren for United Press in Sacramento and in 1991 wrote that he considered Warren "the man of the century," described him as "a large, ruddy, fit man, full of confidence."[17] The *Los Angeles Times* editorialized after Warren's "spectacular victory" for reelection as governor in both primaries in 1946 that he was "an authentic leader. The people recognize him as such....He is a man possessed of a singleness of purpose which engages him to accomplish what he sets out to do."[18]

Warren was able to cross-file for the Republican and Democratic nominations beginning with his campaign for attorney general because of a voter-approved reform pushed by Hiram Johnson and other Progressives in 1913 to dilute the influence of political parties. The practice promoted the election of middle-of-the road candidates, but it was abolished in the late 1950s after Democrats won control of the governor's office *and* legislature for the first time in the twentieth century. Warren, a Hiram Johnson admirer all his life, even filed with the now-tiny Progressive Party when he ran for attorney general. He won all three nominations—Republican, Democratic, and Progressive—as Democrat Culbert Olson took the governorship, at least partly on the momentum of Franklin Delano Roosevelt's New Deal.

It didn't take Attorney General Warren long to begin forging a national reputation for tackling public corruption; in fact, it started on his first day in office. As it turned out, Warren learned, a spate of last-minute pardons for convicts had been sold through the private secretary of outgoing Republican governor Frank Merriam. The secretary, Mark Megladdery, would be indicted, convicted, and sent to jail.

Warren also sought long-delayed redress, at least in a token form, for California Indians, who, he believed, had suffered "perhaps the most shocking injustice that had ever come to my attention."[19] Indians, he wrote in his *Memoirs*, were naively talked into surrendering their lands for a pittance that was never paid. Although he sued and won more than $7 million in redress on the never-ratified treaties of 1851–52, it amounted to only about $350 for each of the 19,000 Indians remaining in California. The federal government, Warren groused, deducted every dollar that it had spent on Indian schools and health and social services in the intervening ninety years.

The attorney general was destined to take on duties that even he had not envisioned when crafting his reforms of 1934. As war widened on the European and Pacific fronts, many feared that California's coastline—stretching some 850 miles—would be vulnerable if the United States came under Japanese assault. After the Pearl Harbor attack, Warren assumed charge of the state's civil-defense plans. In this role, he publicized maps prepared for his office that depicted Japanese settlements scattered around military installations and other strategic facilities in California. In testimony to a congressional select committee meeting in San Francisco in early 1942, Warren declared these ownership patterns weren't accidental, and warned that organized sabotage posed "the greatest danger" to the country. Echoing sentiments of army general J. L. DeWitt, the regional commander with whom Warren kept in close contact, the attorney general said he took no comfort in a lack of any evidence that such sabotage actually existed.

Warren's testimony came just two days after Roosevelt had signed an executive order on February 19, 1942, authorizing military removal of people from areas deemed sensitive. Warren told the committee that it made little difference that two-thirds of California's Japanese residents were American citizens: "[O]pinion among law-enforcement officers of this state is that there is more potential danger among the group of Japanese who are born in this country than from the alien Japanese who were born in Japan." Sentiments against the Japanese were running high in California, he observed, and their continued presence "will unquestionably bring about race riots and prejudice and hysteria and excesses of all kinds." When Warren was asked by Representative Laurence Arnold of Illinois whether there were a way to determine if Japanese Americans were loyal, the attorney general replied: "Congressman, there is no way that we can establish that fact." He added that among members of "the Caucasian race" it might be possible to "arrive at some fairly sound conclusions....But when we deal with the Japanese we are in an entirely different field and we cannot form any opinion that we believe to be sound."[20]

Nine days later, DeWitt declared that by "military necessity" persons of Japanese ancestry would be relocated from the western halves of California, Oregon, and Washington. Japanese farmers, the *Los Angeles Times* reported, stood to lose $100 million in investments. Yet, a spokesman for the Japanese American Citizens League told the *Times*, no resistance would be offered. "We Americans of Japanese parentage are unified in our desires to aid national defense in any way possible," Mike Masoaka was quoted as saying. "We are unified in our belief in the inevitable victory of the forces of democracy. Now that the Army has ordered our evacuation from coastal zones we ask only for humane treatment consistent with America's belief in tolerance and fair play."[21]

Whatever its goals, the relocation lent authenticity to anti-Japanese notions even as most of the country's Italian and German immigrants and citizens were left largely alone during the years of Allied assaults on Axis powers.[22] A handful of sightings of Japanese submarines along the California coastline, accompanied by shellfire and blackout orders, gave credibility to perceptions of a frightening Pacific threat. While relatively little significant or lasting damage was done, Warren made clear in his oral history interviews that he believed California was essentially defenseless. No military response came to a submarine attack on two tankers off the coast of San Luis Obispo one morning, not long after Pearl Harbor, so the local district attorney phoned Warren. "I don't know who to call," the rattled official told him. "So I just called you." The attorney general in his own follow-up call to military brass learned there wasn't much they could do; all but two ships stationed along the entire West Coast were heading into the Pacific theater for what would become the pivotal Battle of Midway against the Japanese fleet.

The year 1942 proved a turning point for California voters, who would move their state onto a futuristic path after a series of caretaker chief executives. Warren professed to relish the attorney general's job, finding it a satisfying fit with his legal background and years-long interest in fighting crime syndicates and corruption. But he chafed under the shabby treatment he felt he was receiving from the governor's office. Olson left Warren out of defense briefings, "told me nothing about what he had done or intended to do, and would not have his subordinates consult with me."[23] The governor had even vetoed the attorney general's budget for civil defense in a dispute over who had ultimate charge of the matter. Warren lacked a significant campaign organization or financial base—and knew registered Democrats outnumbered Republicans by nearly one million in California. Even so, he told his wife one afternoon after an apparently seething drive across the Bay Bridge to their Oakland home from his San Francisco office, he couldn't handle the thought of another term as attorney general if Olson were in charge. If the only way to force Olson from office was to succeed him, Warren was determined to do it.

THE ELECTION

Announcing his candidacy for governor in the spring of 1942, Warren again filed for the Republican, Democratic, and Progressive nominations. In the wake of Pearl Harbor and with the country united against its foreign enemies, Warren insisted that partisanship was irrelevant. His campaign slogan would be "Leadership, Not Politics." He refused to endorse other Republican candidates, believing that would taint the image he sought to cultivate as an independent. Olson, meanwhile, filed for reelection as a Democrat only. Perhaps because Warren had persuaded the GOP to support Roosevelt's war effort in its platform, the hugely popular Roosevelt declined to actively campaign for Olson.

Although Warren favored running his own campaigns, he took the counsel of his friend Joe Knowland, publisher of the *Oakland Tribune*, to hire the no-holds-barred husband/wife team of Clem Whitaker and Leone Baxter to handle his press. As detailed in Chapter 5 of this book, Whitaker and Baxter had demonstrated ruthlessly effective skills in dominating mass-media messages in the elections of 1934, quickly establishing their hold over the emerging political-marketing business. They obtained an especially handsome photograph of the Warren family—six children assembled from tallest to shortest alongside their smiling parents—to help portray Warren as a man of people, not politics. Rival politicians wistfully labeled the Warrens an undefeatable family.

True to his politically unorthodox nature, Warren launched his campaign in the rolling foothills of the Sierra Nevada's mother lode not far from Sacramento—a world away from the urban coast where the votes lay. Before the year was out, Warren would be soliciting support at Democratic as well as Republican gatherings across the state. In a dinner speech to African Americans in Los Angeles, for instance, he argued for an end to discrimination and unfair treatment of racial minorities. "We of the United States will not have made good the principles of the Constitution until we have broken down the barriers of prejudice and ill will that separate any part of our people from their fellows,"[24] he declared. The remarks foreshadowed his landmark school-desegregation ruling in *Brown v. Board of*

Education as chief justice in 1954, yet they paradoxically overlooked what was happening at the moment to Japanese Americans and their immigrant parents in California.

Olson would take a somewhat softer stand on the Japanese evacuation in what Warren biographer Cray calls a political blunder. The governor suggested that, rather than idling in temporary venues such as racetrack stables while they awaited construction of military encampments, the evacuees could help harvest crops in the San Joaquin Valley that summer. Given the war's labor shortages, coupled with the demand to feed tens of thousands of GIs in training, farm labor was in dangerously low supply in the heart of California's agricultural valleys. As a practical matter, the disappearance of the Japanese from the agricultural scene during wartime was not ideal. Issei and Nisei by then were producing a huge share of California's "truck crops"—namely "half of the state's tomato crop, 75 percent of the celery, 80 percent of the peas, 95 percent of the strawberries and 60 percent of the processed spinach," the *Los Angeles Times* reported.[25]

Yet Olson's proposal was political dynamite, and Whitaker and Baxter were quick to ignite it. Attacks published in the press argued most farmers and citizens wanted no part of the governor's idea or the Japanese themselves. "Faced by the problem of saving the crops, the governor has no solution better than turning loose thousands of potential fifth-columnists, saboteurs and spies," declared Rex Hardy, an attorney and leading Democrat in Los Angeles who, the *Los Angeles Times* reported, was throwing his support to Warren.[26] Reinforcing that sentiment, a Gallup Poll found that nearly a third of those polled in West Coast states in 1942 didn't want Japanese Americans ever to return, even after the war was over.[27] The upshot, as Cray put it, was that "Warren appeared resolute, even patriotic, and Olson weak-willed. Warren stood with the great majority, Olson with a tiny minority."[28] Within a month, the federal government was importing Mexicans to the United States under a bracero program to harvest the crops.

Running against two political lightweights, Warren captured 635,230 votes to easily win the Republican nomination. More surprisingly, he also racked up a respectable 404,778 votes from Democrats, to Olson's 514,144. Although Olson had won his Democratic primary, Warren had secured more than twice as many votes from Californians, despite the Democrats' hefty registration edge.

The outcome of the November election loomed almost as an anticlimax. Whitaker and Baxter worked until the last weekend of the campaign, then abruptly parted ways with Warren after releasing an unauthorized statement that Warren and the Republican candidate for lieutenant governor, Frederick Houser, were on the same ticket. Honing his carefully cultivated image as a candidate independent of party influence, Warren had refused Houser's repeated requests to run as a GOP team, and upon learning of the press release, Warren ordered Whitaker by phone to shut down the campaign operation. Although this incident and its aftermath are recounted in Chapter 5, Warren's own account in his *Memoirs* illustrates his zest for a telling a good political story. "That was my last personal experience with Whitaker, and as far as I know it was his last important political [candidate] campaign during the years I was governor," Warren recalled. Yet, he observed, it would not be the last time Whitaker made trouble for him. California's powerful medical lobby would in future years hire Whitaker and Baxter at lucrative fees to crush, time and again, Warren's proposals for universal health insurance. Far from hurting Whitaker's business, Warren wryly conceded, "I was thereafter indirectly responsible for his making a fortune."[29]

Warren received 58 percent of the gubernatorial vote on November 3, 1942, winning every county but remote Plumas. The state's Democrat-dominated electorate gave him Republican majorities in both legislative houses despite FDR's continuing appeal.

Earl Warren would be sworn into office as the nation entered its second full year of war. But if the country were united behind its Democratic president, and Californians were ready for political independence in their chief executive, outgoing Democratic governor Olson apparently was less than enthused about wishing Warren well for the duration. Upon arriving for work in the capitol, Warren discovered, "Governor Olson had removed every document from the files....It took a long time for us to learn what the unfinished business of the previous administration was at the time I took over. In the meantime, we received many scorching letters for not responding to prior correspondence that we had no way of knowing about."[30]

In his first inaugural address, Warren laid out an ambitious blueprint of social and infrastructure reforms to remedy years of neglect—with aid from a hefty surplus linked to wartime job growth and an infusion of federal defense dollars. It was immediately obvious that Californians were not getting another partisan caretaker. "The address, clear, succinct and to the point, is the sort of utterance the public which elected him so overwhelmingly has expected from Earl Warren," the *Los Angeles Times* commented. "There was not a trace of exultation or a phrase of partisanship in his assumption of office; instead there was acceptance of the opportunity to serve."[31]

THE IMPACT

California had been well-suited to ramp up for war. Seemingly overnight it became home to military bases, shipyards, and aircraft plants that brought an instant end to the Depression. One of every eleven defense dollars would be spent in the Golden State. Prodded by civil rights activists, President Roosevelt had signed an executive order in 1941 that, as far as federal defense jobs were concerned, prohibited the common practice of discrimination against African Americans. Workers were in as much demand as building supplies, and hundreds of thousands arrived in a latter-day Gold Rush to California. Forty percent of the Los Angeles workforce in 1943 was female; child-care centers subsidized by federal contractors sprang up in defense plants.

As Warren noted in his *Memoirs*, California would become the biggest troop-training ground in the country; service members were shipped to war from ports in San Francisco, Oakland, Los Angeles, Long Beach, and San Diego. Many thousands, having tasted the sweet coastal climate and raw beauty of the Golden State, would come back when it was over, bringing their new wives and babies with them.

Jobs wrought by war would change the face of California once again. The number of African Americans, lured especially by ship-building jobs, nearly quadrupled during the decade between 1940 and 1950, growing to almost 4.5 percent of California's population.

Mexican immigrants and their offspring also filled thousands of defense jobs, comprising up to 15 percent of employees at aircraft giant Lockheed's Los Angeles plants in 1944.[32] Chinese immigrants and Chinese American residents, long confined to menial work and segregated Chinatown neighborhoods, finally moved into the wider job market. In 1943, Congress repealed the Chinese Exclusion Act, allowing immigrants to apply for citizenship. It would be more than two decades, however, before government-sanctioned race-based exclusions were ended with the 1965 Immigration Act.

California's wartime changes were swift and astonishing. Across the bay from San Francisco, a shipyard on Richmond's boggy marshes begun under Roosevelt's lend-lease program swelled into the behemoth Kaiser Shipyard to become the world's most productive of World War II. Although only 23,000 people had lived in prewar Richmond, the shipyard would employ more than 100,000 and launch an astounding 747 ships. Across the Golden Gate from San Francisco, on 25,000 pilings pounded into the tidal marshes of Sausalito, a second shipyard, Marinship, seemingly rose overnight. "Incredibly, in less than seven months after plans were drawn up, Marinship delivered its first vessel."[33]

Almost a year into his governorship, Warren continued to publicly voice suspicions about California's now-incarcerated citizens and immigrants of Japanese ancestry. He singled out detainees in the Tule Lake relocation center as particular threats to Americans, the Associated Press reported. "I have always felt that the concentration of these Japs—the reason for their concentration is based on military necessity and that the Army, which is charged with the external security in our country, is the only agency thoroughly familiar with the Jap and his machinations," Warren declared at a news conference.[34]

US representative Doris Matsui of Sacramento was born in the remote Poston internment camp in Arizona, where her Japanese American parents met and married after their forced relocation from California. Her father, who kept journals of the experience, described it as "the most horrible place," Matsui recalled in an interview shortly after her election to a sixth term in the House in 2014. The camp was a place of sandstorms, nonexistent privacy, and unappealing food. Her father, who had been a flower- and vegetable-seed farmer, managed to grow vegetables in the barren dessert. When he found a single flower that could thrive there, "everybody rejoiced over it," she recounted. "They had to survive and they made a life as much as they could."[35]

Governing a state that would swell by 1,500 new arrivals daily, Warren, of course, had plenty else on his agenda. "[N]one of these newcomers brought to our state any schools, hospitals, universities, highways, water, prisons, jobs, courts, or other necessities," he noted. "It was, therefore, necessary for us to provide the governmental services for a new city of ten thousand people every Monday morning, including a new public school for at least five hundred pupils every day of the week."[36] He charted a course that he liked to describe as neither liberal nor conservative in staying ahead of the onslaught during his tenure: "California was a new and fast-growing organism and our hope for the future depended on making progress day by day on as many fronts as possible."[37]

His hefty list of policy concerns would move California to the forefront of development in the fields of highway construction, water conservation, civilian defense, higher education, prison reform, public health, and many more. Warren's style tended to blend personal vision with a commonsense pragmatism and sheer determination. After he was kept awake at night by a disturbing tour of an insane asylum, for instance, Warren ordered nearly fifty buildings that had housed the mentally ill to be destroyed as unfit, with the stated goal of moving California from the age of asylums into the hospital era. He also believed an up-to-date general hospital should be within feasible driving distance of every Californian; local districts were created to finance community hospitals through revenue bonds.

The lax, disorganized penal system was so riddled with kickbacks to guards that two notorious criminals incarcerated at Folsom State Prison typically spent their weekends in San Francisco. Warren had the two nabbed and their arrests reported to the press; reforms proposed by his investigative committee on penal affairs were approved in short order by the legislature. On his watch, he reported in his *Memoirs*, management of California's prisons became a model for the nation. "I suppose I had a greater concern for our prisons than the preceding governor because, for twenty years before my election, I had been thrown incessantly in contact with their failure,"[38] he reflected.

Another Warren project made the state's average pension for senior citizens the highest in the nation by the end of 1943. Although Warren achieved the development of a forerunner of disability insurance, funded by employee contributions, he failed to secure unemployment benefits for working women before and after childbirth. The notion was, he decided, ahead of its time. The same apparently was true of his deep-seated desire to achieve universal health insurance financed largely by employer and employee contributions, a concept that has been staunchly opposed by the medical and business lobbies into modern times. Warren conceived his proposal for state-backed health insurance while laid up with a kidney infection in 1944 and pondering how ordinary Californians could possibly pay catastrophic health-care bills.

He was more successful, though, in waging a hard-fought legislative battle against oil company lobbyists. Despite intense opposition, Warren and proponents in the legislature succeeded in incrementally raising the state's gasoline tax by three cents per gallon, the profits to be used for constructing and upgrading networks of highways to keep pace with the state's exploding growth. The *Los Angeles Times* editorialized its support: "The state which lives by the automobile has a highway system 25 years out of date."[39] The resulting victory, Warren opined in his *Memoirs*, surely led to the best highway system in the world.

Meanwhile, as tens of thousands of veterans made good on their postwar benefits, the University of California opened campuses at Santa Barbara and Riverside, and UCLA expanded to become nearly as comprehensive as Berkeley. Three new state colleges opened in Long Beach, Los Angeles, and Sacramento, bringing the total to eleven, with combined enrollments of an eye-popping 380,000. The number of two-year colleges rose to seventy-seven.[40]

Although Warren agreed to lower taxes on personal income, sales, and corporate profits in view of the $60 million surplus, he also insisted on setting aside what he called a "rainy day" fund. Decades later, Republican governor George Deukmejian borrowed the term to justify prudently keeping hundreds of millions of dollars on hand as a hedge against emergencies and downturns, semantically preempting any inclination critics might have to label the practice "hoarding."

California's strides against racial discrimination would be unprecedented in the postwar years. Warren signed bills, for instance, to end racial segregation in the California National Guard and eliminate questions about race and religion from state employment applications. Even so, gains for the cause of civil rights could be elusive, especially when voters were involved. Although Warren proposed a relatively toothless fair-employment commission to seek ways to end discrimination against non-whites in the workplace, it died in two successive legislative sessions. Proponents responded by qualifying an initiative, Proposition 11, for the 1946 ballot to create a commission. Warren contended that version was too radical and refused to support it, engendering lingering bitterness among activists. In a serious setback for the cause, voters soundly rejected it, with less than 30 percent support. It would be another thirteen years before Governor Pat Brown put his signature on legislation to create a landmark Fair Employment Practices Commission with enforcement powers.

Ending arguably the most blatant denial of civil liberties in California's modern history, Japanese immigrants and citizens returned to a mixed reception after the US Supreme Court unanimously ruled in December 1944 that they couldn't be incarcerated indefinitely and thus should be released. Although their losses in possessions and freedom were enormous, and Warren openly supported their return to their communities, he could never bring himself to publicly apologize for his own role in promoting their evacuation. His son, Earl Junior, told biographer Ed Cray that Warren was infuriated by requests that he do so.[41]

Warren's record-setting election to three terms in the governor's office stood for sixty years until Governor Jerry Brown's third election victory in 2010 (and his fourth in 2014). The only election loss of Warren's career was a bid for vice president in 1948 with GOP presidential candidate Thomas E. Dewey. Incumbent president Truman gleefully upset them despite the opinion polls' unanimous prediction of a Dewey-Warren win.

A political and policy heavyweight by any measure, Warren would cut his final gubernatorial term short by more than a year to accept President Dwight Eisenhower's nomination to become chief justice of the United States. In that role, Warren proved a staunch defender of civil liberties, upsetting Eisenhower and others with the Warren Court's consistently progressive bent. Warren candidly observed in his *Memoirs* that Eisenhower "was widely quoted as having said that his appointment of me as Chief Justice 'was the biggest damn fool thing I ever did.'"[42] To Warren, though, the judicial branch differed from the political arena, where victory might amount to only a half a loaf, as he put it. The judiciary meant standing steady on principle. "If the principle is sound and constitutional, it is the birthright of every American, not to be accorded

begrudgingly or piecemeal or to special groups only, but to everyone in its entirety whenever it is brought into play,"[43] he explained. Only a few months into his tenure on the bench, Warren authored the unanimous decision in *Brown v. Board of Education* that found mandatory racial segregation of public schools inherently unequal and unconstitutional. The momentous ruling—which Warren said he deliberately wrote to be short, clear, and readily understood—would pave the way for civil rights gains by oppressed and vulnerable groups of Americans for decades to come.

If remorse over his role in the Japanese internment played any part in that landmark 1954 decision, or in subsequent rulings by the Warren Court on behalf of those who found themselves defenseless against overzealous institutional powers, Warren kept it to himself. He was not a man prone to admissions of wrongdoing, scholars have noted. During the remainder of his lifetime, including another fifteen years on the bench, he avoided expressing any public regret over his role in the mass evacuation of Japanese Americans. That would come, though. Warren, a father of six, uncharacteristically broke into tears when speaking to an oral-history interviewer about the impacts on children of their families' imprisonment in the guarded camps.[44] Then in his eighties, he wrote of his misgivings on a page in his unfinished *Memoirs*, which was not published until three years after a heart attack took his life in 1974. "I have since deeply regretted the removal order and my own testimony advocating it, because it was not in keeping with our American concept of freedom and the rights of citizens," Warren wrote. "Whenever I thought of the innocent little children who were torn from home, school friends, and congenial surroundings, I was conscience-stricken." It was wrong, he conceded, and had demonstrated "the cruelty of war when fear, get-tough military psychology, propaganda, and racial antagonism combine with one's responsibility for public security to produce such acts."[45]

In 1988, President Ronald Reagan signed legislation apologizing for the mass evacuation and providing $20,000 to each of the once-interned Japanese who were still living, forty-six years later. Those who pushed hard for its passage, after several previous unsuccessful efforts, included two Japanese American members of the House of Representatives who had been interned as children—Robert Matsui of Sacramento and Norman Mineta of San Jose. The redress had required a nationwide social movement, led by the Japanese American Citizens League, and a brand of retail politics in Washington that lobbied Congress "member by member," Matsui's widow, Doris Matsui, recently recalled. It was fitting, she believes, that the legislative branch enacted the redress with the signature of the nation's chief executive, acknowledging the wrong of a previous president. "There was a sense that this was important for the country. If it could happen once, it could happen again and there's a fundamental principle here,"[46] she said.

Writing about the redress ten years after its enactment, Robert Matsui—who was only a baby when taken with his American-born parents to Tule Lake—called it "a meaningful gesture toward healing decades-old wounds: it acknowledged the agony of the survivors who suffered the harsh conditions, the social stigma, and the traumatic aftermath of the camps."[47] His parents, he recounted, lost everything during the internment, including their Sacramento produce business and their dignity.

Warren left the statehouse in 1953 in the hands of Lieutenant Governor Goodwin Knight, a Republican who was less like him in political philosophy than successor Pat Brown, a Democrat who won the job in 1958. California's population had grown a remarkable 53 percent during Warren's nearly eleven years as governor, yet he professed to have relished the challenge of keeping pace—and, besides, acknowledging self-doubt was not in his political nature. "I believe we attacked all the issues that confronted us and made at least some progress on the vast majority of them," he reflected. "I would like to believe that it was a progressive administration."[48]

History would remember Governor Earl Warren kindly, as a leader who melded vision, administrative skill, and extraordinary opportunities with a desire to build on the legacy of Hiram Johnson—to continue casting California as a kind of grand experiment in progressive politics, farsighted policy, and intolerance for corrupt governance. The Golden State would emerge from his stewardship so strong it factored into the national well-being. "The state had developed a well-working sophisticated governmental apparatus, a highly productive, complex market economy, and viable social and cultural institutions," observed historian Edward Staniford.[49] Even hardened political reporters conceded Warren, untouched by personal or professional scandal, was an industrious leader whose loyalties lay in securing pragmatic achievements rather than furthering partisan or political interests.

7

1958
Pat Brown's Election
Ushers In Modern California

"We must dare to dream, to do, to build."
—Governor Edmund G. "Pat" Brown

PAT BROWN WAS struggling with a life-changing decision
that kept him awake at night. At a career crossroads in early 1957,
Brown vacillated between the pros and cons of each alternative.
He had been reelected California's attorney general three years
earlier and enjoyed widespread popularity as another election year
approached. Should he run for a third term as attorney general, the
safe alternative his wife, Bernice, favored? Should he bow to the
pressure of some Democratic Party leaders who believed Brown
had the best chance of taking the US Senate seat being vacated by
conservative Republican William F. Knowland? Or should he go
for the prize he personally coveted: the governorship of California.
Characteristically, he would change his mind several times.

According to Brown aide and confidant Fred Dutton, Bernice
was very practical, "always trying to look out for the family while
Pat was out fencing with windmills."[1] But she was almost alone
in urging Pat to seek reelection. Brown was the party's only statewide officeholder and its most popular figure. Democratic Party

leaders were putting pressure on him to set his sights higher. He had disappointed them when he declined to run for the US Senate in 1954 against incumbent Republican Thomas Kuchel. Now, suddenly, the state's other Senate seat had opened up with the shocking announcement from conservative Republican William F. Knowland that he would not seek reelection in 1958. It was widely assumed that Knowland had presidential ambitions and was eyeing California's governorship as a better springboard to the White House. Without an incumbent in the Senate race, Brown figured he'd be a solid favorite against whomever the Republicans might put up. "Knowland certainly is a strong man," Brown told reporters, "and his leaving will increase the chances of a California Democrat being elected to the United States Senate in 1958." Then, Brown told the reporters, he wanted to stop talking. "I've got to think this one out."[2]

The third option—a campaign for governor—was riskier, of course. He'd likely face in the general election either incumbent GOP governor Goodwin Knight, a moderate, or Knowland. Both were strong campaigners who easily had won their previous campaigns. Brown also singled out fellow Democrat and House member Clair Engle of Redding as a strong candidate for one of the posts.[3] In March 1957, Brown acknowledged only that he was considering all three possibilities and that a final decision wouldn't be made for several months. But privately during a spring visit with Engle in Washington, Brown confessed he was planning to run for governor, and he urged the congressman to seek the Senate seat. For Engle, the timing was perfect; he had served sixteen years in the House and had risen as high as he'd probably ever get in Congress. Engle agreed to make the Senate run, but Brown—typically cautious to a fault—immediately had second thoughts. The night after his meeting with Engle, Brown said he couldn't sleep, afraid he had made the wrong decision. The next day, he went to Engle's congressional office and told him, "Clair, I've changed my mind. I want you to run for governor and I'll run for Senate." Engle wanted nothing of Brown's change of heart. "Oh, no," Brown recalled Engle saying. "It's all set. You made a deal and I expect you to live up to it."[4] Brown stuck by the agreement but wouldn't make a formal announcement until the end of October. He continued to have doubts about whether he had made the right move, however, and he conceded in a letter to his son, Jerry, a seminary student at the time, "I can't help it. I just don't know what I am going to do. I may injure my chances by delaying, but would also injure them by too quick a decision."[5]

As late as August 1957, notwithstanding his pledge to Engle, Brown continued to dither. Knowland was sounding more and more like a candidate for governor, and Knight—the current chief executive—was sending reelection signals, too. Knight had met with top Republican financiers and said only apathy or "internal squabbling within our own party"[6] could derail GOP success. It was a clear broadside aimed at Knowland.

Meanwhile, a powerful conservative Democrat—multimillionaire oil magnate Edwin Pauley—was working to convince Brown to stay out of the governor's contest. Pauley counted both Brown and Knight among his friends. He didn't want the two of them running against each other and invited Brown and his family (except Jerry, who was away at school) to vacation at his private island in Hawaii so he could lobby the attorney general. Brown, he hoped, would run for reelection or for the open Senate seat. But Brown's young political adviser, Fred Dutton, wanted him to run for governor and recognized what Pauley was up to. While Brown was in Hawaii, Dutton devised a clever scheme to "neutralize" Pauley's entreaties. He sent letters to Democratic leaders, union officials, and donors, asking if they thought Brown should run for governor. As Dutton expected, he received fifty to sixty letters a day urging Brown to run. Dutton bundled them up and sent them to Hawaii. "Everybody likes to be asked. They're flattered," Dutton said. Apparently, the maneuver worked, for Brown cabled back to the mainland, "Tell all who signed not to have the slightest worry about next year."[7]

After waffling for several months, Brown had finally crossed his personal Rubicon and went on to become one of California's most accomplished governors. Viewed in hindsight, this "Architect of the Golden State" was the right man, in the right job, at the right time. If Brown had chosen an easier, more risk-averse political path, California would have lacked his extraordinary leadership in responding to the state's dramatic postwar growth explosion, and the state might have looked much different in the decades ahead.

THE BACKSTORY

California Democrats had been in political despair throughout the first half of the twentieth century. Although they had enjoyed a significant registration edge in California since the depths of the Depression in 1934, they were unable to translate that strength into sustained electoral success. They were due for a resurgence, but it wasn't going to be easy. The party needed a boost. It came in the form of a measure on the November 1952 ballot that altered the state's decades-old system of cross-filing, an innovation of Hiram Johnson and the Progressives designed to rid the state of political party bossism.

Cross-filing allowed candidates to run in any political party's primary election without listing a party affiliation. Many Democratic candidates couldn't even get into the general election under the cross-filing system because Republicans consistently secured nominations in both the Republican and Democratic primaries. Many political scientists at the time attributed this to the fact that confused voters may have assumed that candidates who appeared on their partisan ballots shared their party affiliation. Cross-filing also assisted incumbents—most of whom were Republicans—because of their advantage in name identification. Armed with nominations from both the Democratic and Republican parties, Republican William F. Knowland had been returned to the US Senate in November 1952 with a remarkable 88 percent of the vote. At that same election, however, voters approved a ballot proposition requiring future cross-filing candidates to list their party connections, thus removing "any uncertainty concerning the party affiliation of a candidate who cross-files in a primary election."[8]

The measure had the desired effect. In 1952, Republicans had won nearly half of the state's 131 races for the US Senate, House, and Legislature by cross-filing; two years later, Republicans won fewer than 14 percent of races by cross-filing, as partisan voter loyalties returned to the state's electoral system. Cracks began to appear in the Republican Party's longtime hold on state government. A year after voters modified the cross-filing system, leading Democrats formed the grassroots California Democratic Council, which selected and endorsed Democratic candidates and further enabled the majority party to regain the nominating process in its own primaries. After Democratic electoral successes in 1956, they celebrated their first president pro tem—the top post in the state senate—since 1891.[9]

By 1956, Democrats had a 900,000 voter-registration edge over Republicans, but as they looked forward to the statewide elections two years hence, they faced a considerable obstacle: incumbent GOP governor Goodwin Knight, whose political bloodline traced back to two of California's most popular governors, Hiram Johnson and Earl Warren. At the age of fourteen, Knight cut his teeth on politics handing out leaflets for Johnson.[10] In 1946, after a stint as a superior court judge, Knight was elected lieutenant governor during Warren's landslide reelection for a second term. Both easily won reelection in 1950. Three years later, when Warren left for the US Supreme Court, Knight became governor.

Knight was the epitome of the old-time backslapping, handshaking, baby-kissing pol. "Whenever two Californians get together," one Democrat said, "up pops Goodie Knight." He loved giving speeches, often sprinkled with corny jokes, and remembered the names of everyone he met. He had given up smoking in 1952 when he had half his stomach removed in an ulcer operation, and he kept in shape by tap dancing, shadow boxing, and eating healthy. (One of his favorite beverages was said to have been cabbage juice.)[11] Everyone called him "Goodie."

Although more conservative than Warren, Knight was smart enough to read the state's political tea leaves. Following Warren's example, Knight embraced the political center, expanded social programs in response to dramatic postwar growth, and gained significant support from labor unions. He preached the values of moderation and vowed, "I shall denounce the rigor mortis of all reactionary policies and shall welcome all workable programs for social betterment."[12]

Despite Knight's popularity and electability, conservative ideologues within the Republican Party wanted him removed as the party's standard-bearer. Warren's departure to Washington had left a leadership vacuum, and moderates were battling conservatives Knowland and Richard Nixon to fill it. For Nixon, part of his enmity was payback. Knight had actively urged that Nixon be dumped from the GOP ticket in 1956, and at the Republican National Convention in San Francisco, Knight delayed his endorsement of Nixon for renomination as vice president. The *Los Angeles Mirror-News* reported that California's angry pro-Nixon bloc wanted to draft a replacement for Knight at the top of the state ticket.[13] Knowland naturally fit that role. He was the state's conservative warhorse, appointed by Warren (a friend of Knowland's father) to fill the US Senate seat vacated when Hiram Johnson died in 1945. After his landslide reelection in 1952 and the death of Ohio senator Robert Taft, Knowland became the Senate majority leader and helped shape the nation's foreign policy. After Democrats regained control of the Senate, Knowland remained the minority leader.

The bull-shouldered Knowland, the son of the fiercely conservative owner of the *Oakland Tribune,* was not one to compromise. Once, in a fundraising letter on behalf of the Californian, President Eisenhower called him "stubborn, a bit of a lone wolf, and likely to follow his own conclusions and decisions, disregarding the opinions" of others. He was, Eisenhower said, "a bit of a bull in a china shop." Knowland was a mesmerizing public orator but had difficulty in one-on-one conversations. "I wish he wouldn't talk to me as though he were making a speech on the radio," one friend said.[14]

Knowland's problems with Knight were both political and personal. Not only did he think Knight was too liberal, he also considered him an obstacle to his own presidential ambitions. Knowland was setting the stage for a 1960 run for the White House after Eisenhower's eight years in office, and he believed that being a governor was a better stepping-stone to higher office than the Senate. If he had to steamroll Knight to become the state's chief executive, so be it. Knowland first broached the subject with his top staff in late 1956. Sitting in a lounge at the United Nations, he asked them, "What would you boys think if I ran for governor instead of senator in 1958?" Aide James Gleason didn't like the idea, believing that Knowland's Senate forum put him in a good position to run for president. But Knowland's mind was made up.[15] It would be a decision that would roil the Republican Party and dramatically change the political direction of California.

Shortly thereafter, on January 7, 1957, Knowland taped an interview with a CBS radio reporter. "We wonder if you are a candidate for the Republican [presidential] nomination in 1960," the reporter prompted. The senator demurred, suggesting the question was premature. At the end of the interview, with a few seconds of time remaining, Knowland was asked a throwaway question about his future plans. "I do not plan to be a candidate for reelection to the United States Senate in 1958," he responded, and then "Knowland instantly turned red," according to biographers Gayle Montgomery and James W. Johnson.[16] Knowland had stepped on his own scoop, announcing it matter-of-factly and well before he had intended. Knowland immediately went into damage control, informing his wife, Helen, his staff, leading Republicans, members of the Senate, and President Eisenhower of his premature announcement. He then held a late-afternoon news conference, stunning the Washington press corps.

As word reached Sacramento on the national news wires, an unsuspecting, unprepared Governor Knight was in the middle of his annual state of the state address. There had been rumors that Knowland might want to return to California, but his official announcement "stirred up a veritable hullabaloo among capitol politicos," noted the *Sacramento Bee*.[17] As soon as Knight concluded his remarks, reporters swarmed the rostrum and peppered him with questions about Knowland. Knight said he was surprised at the announcement, considering the fact that Knowland had mentioned nothing about his plans when they had chatted only three weeks earlier. Knight said it was hard to understand why Knowland would give up his position as Republican leader in the Senate. Knight also said he wasn't interested in seeking Knowland's senatorial seat.

There may have been another, more personal reason for Knowland's decision. Rumors suggested Helen Knowland demanded that her husband leave Washington and the clutches of Ruth Moody, with whom he was having an affair. In an interesting twist, Helen Knowland had carried on a secret affair with Moody's husband, Michigan senator Blair Moody, until his death in 1953.[18] Some suspected that if Knowland didn't return to California, Helen was prepared to cripple her husband's presidential ambitions by revealing his philandering to the public.

The race for governor, still more than a year away, had become a complicated mess for Republicans facing the potential of a bitter GOP primary. Kyle Palmer, the influential political editor of the conservative *Los Angeles Times*, sensed disaster. In his Sunday column after the Knowland announcement, he wrote that a contested primary would present "a truly shattering experience for the Republican Party in this State."[19] In subsequent months, Knight angrily announced he had no plans to step aside, and accused Knowland of using the California governorship as a launching pad to the White House. In August, Knight officially announced his reelection campaign; Knowland and Brown were playing it close to the vest.

Determined to quash a brewing donnybrook that was delighting Democrats, powerful forces behind the scene made Knight's position untenable. Richard Nixon and others threatened to cut off campaign funds and endorsements to Knight if he didn't change his mind. Norman Chandler, the powerful publisher of the *Los Angeles Times*, also urged Knight to reverse course, editorializing that the governor was losing the confidence of much of the party. "Kyle Palmer and Nixon and all the moneybags were going behind Knowland," Pat Brown remembered. "They didn't like Knight anyway because Knight had gotten way friendly with labor. So they just pulled the rug from under Knight."[20] Even Whitaker and Baxter, the governor's powerhouse political consulting firm, dropped him as a client.

Watching with glee as the Republican melodrama unfolded were California's Democrats, who were hungry to regain political power. Only once since January 1899 had a Democrat occupied the governor's office, and that was a brief one-term stint by Culbert Olson in the middle of the Great Depression. Other than Brown—the only Democrat elected to statewide office in 1954—the party had little bench strength. Amply jowled, stocky, and bespectacled, Brown often was described as "owlish." Like Knight, he seemed to relish campaigning and mixing with people, but a magazine profile in 1958 noted he was a worrier: "He worries about being liked, he worries about being disliked, and he worries constantly about being understood."[21]

Brown, himself, was a former Republican. He traced his family roots to the Gold Rush, and he had skipped college and studied law at night school while working in his father's cigar store. In 1928, at the tender age of twenty-three, Brown ran for the state assembly. A campaign flyer featured a photo of the young candidate and boasted "Twenty Three Years in the District." His opponent warned voters, "Don't send a boy on a man's job."[22] They didn't. Brown switched his affiliation to Democrat during the Great Depression, became San Francisco's district attorney and, after losing a bid for attorney general in 1946, won a second effort in 1950 to become California's top law-enforcement officer. By 1957, he was considered the Democrats' best hope for statewide success.

In the fall of 1957 clarity finally was brought to the approaching contest for governor. Brown always had qualms about facing Knight, a moderate who would be a formidable foe able to split the labor vote and tap into union coffers. As if to justify Brown's concerns, Joseph DeSilva, the influential secretary of the Los Angeles retail clerks union, urged Democrats to get behind Knight for governor and convince Brown to run for the Senate.[23] But party leaders, sensing the impending Republican train wreck, didn't budge. On October 3, two months after Knight announced he would run for reelection, Knowland concluded a month-long statewide speaking tour and made official what every political observer already knew: that he was prepared to take out a fellow Republican to win the governorship. The major issue? Controlling the power of unions. Knight, however, put it differently. The primary contest, he said, would be a battle between his progressive philosophy and Knowland's reactionary ideas. Either two high-profile Republicans would square off in a brutal, expensive primary or—as conventional wisdom predicted—Knight would be driven out of the race by conservatives who had taken control of the party.

Four weeks after Knowland formally entered the contest, Brown announced his candidacy and predicted that Knight would be forced to withdraw. Setting his sights firmly on Knowland, he characterized the senator as "a reactionary who views the state's highest offices as only a pawn in presidential power politics."[24] Brown proved to be prescient, and it was Vice President Nixon who negotiated Knight's surrender. A week after Brown's entrance into the governor's race, Knight went to Washington to consult with Eisenhower and Nixon, emerging from Nixon's office to say he was pulling out of the governor's contest and, instead, would run for the US Senate. As part of the deal, Nixon promptly endorsed Knowland for governor and Knight for the Senate. Republican power brokers finally had what they wanted: a prominent conservative without internal opposition to carry the party's standard in the gubernatorial campaign. The *Times* rejoiced and baldly dismissed suggestions that Knight "was under pressure from one source or another to drop out of the gubernatorial contest."[25] Democrats and their newspaper supporters portrayed Knight as a vanquished loser who was the victim of a cynical deal. "Never in the history of the state has there been anything like this," declared the *Sacramento Bee*.[26] Was the "big switch" a master stroke of political acumen, or was the ouster of a bipartisan and popular governor an act of hara-kiri?

THE ELECTION

Both Brown and Knowland decided to cross-file and seek dual Republican and Democratic nominations. Brown had token Democratic opposition and Knowland had no GOP challengers. Although the popularity contest would offer a sense of voter sentiment heading into the general election, there wasn't much of a campaign. Knowland, in fact, preferred to remain in Washington tending to Senate business and spent only fourteen days on the primary campaign trail. He left the campaigning to Mrs. Knowland and his two daughters, who drove an auto-trailer around the state handing out literature and playing the senator's recorded speeches.[27]

Early polling picked up an unmistakable trend: voters of all political persuasions were turning against Knowland in the wake of the "big switch." The unprecedented maneuver reinforced what Brown was saying as often as he could: that Knowland wanted to use the governorship as a catapult to the White House in 1960. Brown demanded that Knowland pledge to serve a full four-year term should he be elected. In Knowland's rare campaign announcements, he often seemed more focused on international affairs than the issues in California.

Knowland did campaign on one explosive state issue: he decried the rising influence of organized labor. While more than one million California workers were employed under union shop contracts, considerable backlash arose against what some saw as heavy-handed union tactics and stories of corruption. Antiunionists were pushing for a right-to-work law to limit collective bargaining and ban mandatory union dues. In late 1957, polling seemed to indicate that the issue would be a big winner for Knowland. One survey showed widespread opposition to mandatory unionism; nearly eight in ten respondents opposed the use of union dues for political campaigns.[28] The executive secretary of the Citizens' Committee for Voluntary Unionism said the poll was proof that "the people of this State are fed up with union corruption, power grabbing and political intimidation and are demanding that labor organizations be cleaned up."[29]

Union leaders fought back. Governor Knight had been a friend of labor who would have protected it from his perch in the governor's office and in upcoming redistricting battles, but he had been pushed out of the gubernatorial contest by the Nixon–*LA Times* cabal. In Knowland, labor faced its worst enemy. He had introduced legislation in the Senate to emasculate union clout and the power of labor officials, and was the leading voice in the right-to-work movement. Labor clearly recognized that it had to cast its lot with Pat Brown and the Democrats. Brown later recalled that the assault on organized labor was "the best thing that ever happened to me…because the money just poured in from the labor leaders. It was like manna from heaven. We didn't have to worry about fund-raising drives, or anything."[30]

As the spring progressed, polling indicated that labor's spending and grassroots strength was influencing voter sentiment on the right-to-work issue, which became Proposition 18 on the November ballot. But the unionists were just getting started, and Pat Brown was riding their coattails. In the warm-up for the fall election, Brown easily won the Democratic nomination by a six-to-one margin over Knowland, who won his own Republican primary over Brown by a three-and-a-half-to-one margin—with Brown capturing 662,000 more total votes in both primaries.[31] In vote-rich Los Angeles County, Brown and the Democrats "scored their greatest victory" in twenty years.[32] The stage was set for a bruising general election campaign that would be dominated by a single issue.

Knowland abandoned a tried-and-true GOP formula—precisely followed by Earl Warren and Goodwin Knight the previous sixteen years—to capture the middle ground in statewide contests. Instead, the Republican nominee campaigned as an aggressive and unapologetic archconservative who wanted to steer the state on a starboard course. Author Kurt Schuparra argues that the dual Knowland/Proposition 18 campaigns "gave many conservatives their initial sense of unity and mission" and thus kick-started the right-wing movement in California.[33]

Those campaigns also mobilized the labor movement in California like never before. Unions paid for campaign literature and precinct workers for Democratic candidates. They fought Proposition 18 with heavy media advertising buys and billboards, warning that the measure would "lower wages and reduce living standards for every employee in California."[34] Under the onslaught of labor's frantic campaign to defeat Proposition 18, public sentiment pivoted against the measure by the summer, and in a cunning move to cut into the measure's support, labor had qualified a so-called soak-the-rich initiative (Proposition 17) designed to reconfigure California's tax system by reducing sales taxes and hiking corporate and higher-bracket income taxes. The tactic forced state business interests to spend a half-million dollars battling the tax proposal, which diverted resources and energy that could have been used to fight the right-to-work measure.

Post-primary polls indicated that Brown was headed for a sizeable November victory. On the campaign trail, he played it safe, focusing on the relatively noncontroversial issues of schools, jobs, and highways—although he did campaign in favor of a controversial and expensive state water plan that had been bottled up in the legislature for years. He also continued to press the dual messages that Knowland was only interested in becoming president— what *New York Times* reporter Gladwin Hill called the senator's "Potomac myopia"—and that he wanted to "destroy the economy of the laboring class."[35]

The Republicans' internecine warfare, meanwhile, was quite a spectacle, aided and abetted by Helen Knowland's blunders on the campaign trail on behalf of her husband. In one stunning move that was emblematic of the friction within the party, Mrs. Knowland penned a seven-page letter to two hundred Republican leaders, writing that Governor Knight had a "macaroni spine" and was unable to stand up to the "labor-socialist monster which has latched on to the Democratic Party and to some Republicans as well, 'poor Goodie' being a perfect example."[36] Brown later confided that some Republicans were so angry at the vilification of Knight that they would "give me dope on things that were going on. I'd see Mrs. Knight at meetings and she'd say, 'I'm going to vote for you.'"[37]

With the situation steadily deteriorating and Election Day less than three weeks away, it was left to President Eisenhower to fly in and try to douse the GOP's self-immolation. In televised speeches in Los Angeles and San Francisco, the president urged an end to "family bickering." He also offered a harsh attack on California Democrats, who, he said, couldn't cope with labor bosses, "hoodlums[,] and racketeers." By then, however, California voter opinion had crystallized. Surveys taken four days before Eisenhower's speeches and four days afterward showed

the race virtually unchanged—Brown led Knowland by an astonishing twenty-one points.[38]

As the campaign approached its final, hectic days, Knowland
and his supporters hoped to gain traction with an assault on Brown's
record as attorney general. Full-page newspaper ads blamed Brown
for a dramatic rise in statewide narcotics addiction, particularly
among juveniles. "What has Brown done?...Brown has failed the
people. He has failed the parents. He has failed our children." The
ad, which featured a picture of a teenaged school girl and a hypo-
dermic needle, was placed by "Citizens for the Right to Know,"
describing itself as a nonpartisan committee designed "to reveal
Brown—the man behind the myth."[39]

For Knowland, however, nothing seemed to work. Even
elements of the reliably Republican press turned on him. The
vehemently antiunion *Los Angeles Times* stood by his side, as did
his father's newspaper, the *Oakland Tribune*, and many others.
But the conservative *San Francisco Chronicle*, which supported
Knowland in the primary, offered no endorsement and asserted
that "we have been unfavorably impressed with his subsequent
campaign."[40] Despite all the setbacks, Knowland put on a brave
face for the television cameras, enduring a twenty-hour telethon to close the campaign. Hollywood leading man Randolph
Scott headlined the telethon's guest stars. The Associated Press
reported that Knowland "was on camera nearly all the time and
showed no signs of fatigue."[41] Brown, meanwhile, predicted victory. "I think I'm going to win because I've talked sense to the
people of California and the opposition has talked nonsense."[42]

The election was a disaster for Republicans, bringing to an
end more than a half century of Republican domination of the
state's political institutions. Democrats swept every statewide
office except secretary of state, and for the first time since 1889
they controlled both houses of the legislature. Labor unions spent
$2.5 million to defeat Proposition 18 by nearly a million votes.
Thanks to labor's open wallet and the GOP's dysfunction and sharp
turn to the right, Brown defeated Knowland by more than a million
votes. Knowland carried only Alpine, Mono, Orange, and Santa

Barbara Counties. Both campaigns poured more than $1 million into the contest, with Knowland slightly outspending Brown. (He spent twenty-five cents per vote to Knowland's forty-three cents.)[43] Goodwin Knight, once the popular governor, was swamped by Clair Engle in the US Senate contest. In what many considered an apt observation, William A. Burkett, Governor Knight's superintendent of banks, joined the growing chorus and charged that Knowland's "mudslinging and ruthless tactics" had caused the "destruction" of the Republican Party in California.[44]

THE IMPACT

Clair Engle would serve four and a half years in the Senate before dying from a brain tumor. In perhaps a whimsical moment while reflecting on the election, he referred to Republican heavyweights Eisenhower and Nixon and noted, "Neither Ike nor Dick, nor all of Ike's men, could put the Republican Party back together again."[45] In subsequent elections, the party continued its rightward tilt, pausing only occasionally to embrace more moderate candidates. It enjoyed some success in gubernatorial elections, but only sporadically regained control of legislative levers.

As governor, Pat Brown was to put his imprimatur on the greatest extended period of growth in the state's history. He assumed office as California absorbed a large and steady influx of migrants—whites and minorities—attracted to good-paying jobs in aerospace, defense, electronics, and related industries. The state gained 75,000 new residents just between Brown's election and his inauguration. California's population was swelling—especially in Southern California—and during his tenure it increased by about 500,000 people per year. By 1963, California had surpassed New York as the nation's most populous state. The postwar baby boom fueled unprecedented demand for places to live, transportation facilities, and education.[46]

Brown and his brain trust knew that coping with that growth would be their paramount challenge. Warren Christopher, who later would become secretary of state under President Clinton, was charged with drafting the new governor's inaugural address. Five sentences into the speech, Brown established the framework for his administration. "Offered reaction by the radical right, the voters emphatically declined," Brown said. "Offered government by retreat, the people preferred progress." Brown called his version of progress "responsible liberalism," and he ambitiously outlined twelve priorities—including attacking air pollution and discrimination by employers and unions, reforming election practices, and boosting consumer protection and social services. Brown invoked the names of two legendary Republicans, Hiram Johnson and Earl Warren, and said, "No longer can we afford to stay on dead center, unresponsive and inert."[47] Three days later, the first of his dozen priorities was announced: legislation to prohibit employment discrimination based on race.

Brown once was told that he'd never be as popular as he was on inauguration day, and he understood from his study of political history that newly elected leaders have their best chance of success during their first year in office. Brown and his team moved quickly, negotiating deals and securing legislative commitments for his aggressive agenda. By the time the year was half over, Brown and the Democratic legislature racked up one remarkable accomplishment after another, including fighting air pollution, establishing a minimum wage, building freeways, boosting higher education, providing health care for the poor, and reorganizing state government. To close an inherited deficit approaching $100 million—and to replenish state coffers for additional spending on social services— the legislature approved Brown's proposals for tax increases on income, banks and corporations, capital gains, tobacco, and beer.

But it wasn't all public policy. Brown and his friendly legislature dealt Republicans a body blow by getting rid of cross-filing, that holdover electoral system from Hiram Johnson's days that Democrats believed had perpetuated GOP domination despite the Democrats' higher number of registered voters. "When we did away with cross-filing," Brown recalled, "that insured the defeat of the Republicans....Republicans always had better name recognition, always had more money, and they would always hide the fact that they were Republicans."[48] The *New York Times* noted that for the first time in nearly fifty years "it is impossible for California political aspirants to masquerade…as adherents of a rival political party."[49]

Part of Brown's early success can be traced to the personal relationships he developed with legislators. He loved being one of the guys, often inviting groups of lawmakers to dinner at the governor's mansion. Senator Walter Stiern remembered Brown asking his guests around the dinner table one evening, "Fellows, how do you think I'm doing? This is for you Republican fellows, too. Tell me what you think I'm doing that you don't like." Stiern said Brown always asked for advice. "Some people accused him of acting on the last advice he got. Whether that's true or not, I don't know. But he was searching for advice. And he was willing to wait before he made some decisions."[50]

Brown considered construction of the State Water Project to be his single most important achievement as governor. At the time, however, many believed it was unattainable. It was an age-old problem: Northern California had the water, and Central Valley farmers and fast-growing but dry Southern California needed more of it. Brown had dealt with water policy since his early days as attorney general, when he was a member of the California Water Project Authority. He recognized that Southern California was critical to the state's future prosperity, and that the region could thrive only with additional water supplies. "Every single year we create a city the size of San Francisco," he liked to say.[51]

When Earl Warren was governor, the legislature authorized studies for a statewide water project, but prospects fizzled under the weight of opposition from labor supporters and Northern Californians. Brown and his advisers agreed on a $1.75 billion bond measure to finance construction of a water project with a dam on the Feather River at Oroville as the centerpiece. The price tag was four-fifths the size of the governor's entire proposed budget ($2.19 billion) for 1959–60,[52] and the brain trust wasn't even sure how much the project eventually would cost. Was $1.75 billion enough? What if more money was needed and the legislature balked at providing extra funds? Brown had heard a story about how the Louisiana legislature wouldn't give Governor Huey Long money to build a road. In defiance, Long started the road, ran out of money, and left a big gap. The legislature was forced to finish the road. "Why don't you do that?" Brown told his advisers. "Build here and build here and then they'll have to complete it."[53]

Brown faced the daunting task of first getting the legislature to place the bond measure on the statewide ballot. In 1960—before implementation of the "one-man, one-vote" doctrine in district representation—the state senate was dominated by rural Northern California lawmakers, who provided a solid firewall against water raids from the south. Brown initially moved to secure the support of Fresno's Hugh Burns, a mortician by trade and the conservative Democratic leader of the senate. Burns, of course, wanted something in return, and got it: Brown's promise to reappoint a conservative Republican as the state insurance commissioner.[54]

Once Burns was in the fold, Brown coaxed and finessed votes from other recalcitrant senators. On the day of the critical vote, a Brown aide grabbed San Francisco's Eugene McAteer by the arm and pulled him to a phone off the senate floor that was connected to the governor's office. Minutes later, McAteer returned to his desk and voted for the measure. He had been promised that one of his friends would be appointed a judge. Although three-fourths of the senators represented areas north of the Tehachapis, Brown had horse-traded just enough to secure passage of the water plan by one vote. After the assembly agreed, however, the governor still faced the monumental task of convincing voters to incur a mountain of debt on a geographically divisive water transfer scheme.

The campaign to pass the water bonds—Proposition 1 on the November 1960 ballot—was not left to chance. The governor appointed a campaign committee full of people who could raise money. He campaigned up and down the state from Arcata to Imperial County, spending his reservoir of political capital and staking his reputation on the measure's success. "It's time to start moving dirt and stop throwing mud,"[55] Brown would say on the campaign trail. Ralph Brody, Brown's water adviser, recalled one visit to the *San Francisco Chronicle* editorial board. Halfway through the presentation, publisher Scott Newhall pushed away from the conference table and walked out of the meeting. "I don't care how good the program is," he said in a parting shot. "I don't want to see any water go south of San Francisco—period!"[56]

On election night, Brown and the Democrats gathered at the Beverly Hilton Hotel and nervously tracked election returns. By the time Brown went to bed at 3:00 a.m., the vote tally had the water plan narrowly losing. But not all the votes had been counted in Los Angeles, Orange, and San Diego Counties. Those tallies finally trickled in the following day and, combined with absentee votes, nudged Proposition 1 to victory. Reflecting the region's growing electoral clout, the measure carried only fourteen of the state's fifty-eight counties, most of them in populous Southern California.

In 1961, construction began on the 770-foot Oroville Dam on the Feather River in the upper Sacramento Valley. The California Water Project was a remarkable engineering feat—700 miles of an interconnected network of dams, aqueducts, pumping plants, power plants, pipelines, tunnels, and canals. Water had to be pumped 2,000 feet over the Tehachapis to Southern California. After a two-term governorship replete with accomplishments, Brown considered the north-to-south water transfer system his administration's greatest achievement, his legacy to the people of California. Brown always wanted the aqueduct to be a lasting monument to himself—the man who got it built against all odds. In the 1970s, Assemblyman Jack Knox of Richmond authored a measure to name the aqueduct after Brown. "It's a cinch to go through," Knox told the former governor. There was only one problem: then-governor Jerry Brown didn't like the idea. "Jerry called me up and said, 'Dad, I think it's a mistake to call the project after you at this time. When you're dead, then they'll name something after you.'" The elder Brown shot back at his son, "Hell, I won't know anything about it then!"[57] In December 1982, as Jerry Brown's tenure as governor was ending, the California Aqueduct was renamed the Edmund G. Brown California Aqueduct in his father's honor.[58] The elder Brown lived another fourteen years.

During Brown's tenure, there were other legacies and big-ticket achievements as well, many of which built on education, transportation, and civil rights initiatives begun by the progressive Earl Warren years earlier. With about 200,000 more children entering the first grade each year in California, Brown, thinking far ahead of his time, started planning for the day when those youngsters and their younger brothers and sisters would be ready for college. "We had to plan down the road for maybe 25 or 30 years, because you don't create a university overnight," he said.[59] On Brown's watch, the state created the Master Plan for Higher Education to coordinate massive growth and the development of the state's three branches of higher education—the University of California, the state college system, and the junior colleges—which often had feuded with each other. When he signed the master plan into law, Brown called it "the most significant step California has ever taken in planning for the education of our youth."[60] By the time Brown left office, three new university campuses had been built; in the next three decades, the state would add none.[61] In addition, four new state colleges were opened during Brown's tenure as governor, and California's system of higher education became the envy of the world.

Brown also set his highway engineers to work planning for a future that would see a dramatic surge in traffic to parallel the state's extraordinary population growth. Planners designed a massive system of freeways that would stretch for more than 12,000 miles, connect communities large and small, and dovetail with President Eisenhower's federal highway system. It was to be a Herculean $10.5 billion, twenty-year investment, financed in large part by California's gas tax, through which motorists would contribute to the highway treasury every time they filled their gas tanks. There were so many new motorists taking to the roads each year, Brown calculated the state wouldn't even have to increase the tax to pay the tab. The governor built 1,000 miles of freeways and highways during his tenure, but numerous factors put the clamps on the twenty-year plan—among them, higher construction costs from rampant inflation, and a burgeoning environmental movement in the 1970s. In addition, Ronald Reagan was elected to hold the

line on public spending, and Jerry Brown's "era of limits" virtually ground freeway construction to a halt.[62]

Beyond brick-and-mortar accomplishments, Brown put his reputation on the line when he fought hard to end racial discrimination in employment and housing, solidifying Democratic support from ethnic minorities in the process. He signed legislation creating the Fair Employment Practices Commission, finishing the job Warren had begun years earlier. The commission had legal enforcement powers and was years ahead of its federal counterpart established by the Civil Rights Act of 1964. Brown also signed the Rumford Fair Housing Act in 1963 to ban racial discrimination in housing sales and rentals, a particularly satisfying triumph for the governor. According to biographer Ethan Rarick, Brown had made fair housing the "linchpin" of his second term and considered the Rumford law one of his greatest accomplishments.[63] A year later, however, voters overwhelmingly approved Proposition 14, a constitutional amendment repealing the measure. The vote was a heartbreaking setback for Brown, but the California Supreme

Court would declare Proposition 14 unconstitutional two years later, leaving the antidiscrimination measure in place.

Politically, Brown's election as governor also provided the Democratic Party with a potent ally for generations to come. William Knowland's "right-to-work" obsession not only helped elect what then was only the second Democratic governor of the century, it unified labor behind the Democratic Party. The chasm between most unions and Republicans has been wide ever since.

Even as Brown was amassing one achievement after another, however, his public image was starting to erode. Much of it was self-inflicted—for instance, his vacillation over the death penalty in the case of rapist and kidnapper Caryl Chessman. Brown opposed capital punishment and briefly spared Chessman's life, then he later allowed Chessman and forty-one others to be executed in San Quentin's gas chamber. After a stunning reelection victory over Nixon in 1962, Brown simply wore out his welcome. He was blamed for mishandling student protests at the University of California, Berkeley, during the 1964 Free Speech Movement, and public opinion further turned against him the following year after violent riots in the Watts section of Los Angeles. In addition, Brown was still reeling from the stinging public defeat of fair-housing legislation. Voters decided eight years was enough. In 1966, he ran an uninspired campaign for a third term and was routed by up-and-coming political star Ronald Reagan, who gave voice to the widespread dissatisfaction with campus and urban turmoil. Brown later conceded that he rested on his early accomplishments and hadn't offered voters any new ideas.

In retrospect, Pat Brown was a perfect fit for the times. California was experiencing a postwar boom, with a robust birthrate and people flocking to the state from every corner of the nation. The treasury was flush with money—thanks, in part, to tax increases Brown engineered his first year in office. The people were in an expansive mood, aiming to make California a greater state. Many years later, in an oral history interview, Brown said he understood the mandate: "I had to build roads, and highways, and schools, and universities, and water projects, and beaches and parks, and everything else."[64]

8

1966
Voters Give Greater Power
to a Full-Time Legislature

"…perhaps the most important issue to face
[voters] in nearly a century."
—Gene Blake, *Los Angeles Times*

JESSE MARVIN UNRUH was ready to lay down the hammer. The imperial speaker of the California assembly—nicknamed "Big Daddy" for his sizeable girth—was used to getting his way, but recalcitrant senators disliked elements of his signature plan to create a full-time, professional legislature. In fact, the speaker's grand scheme was much more than that. Unruh had long believed that the state's gigantic, heavily amended constitution enabled executive branch dominance over the legislature, giving the governor the authority to set the legislative agenda and unduly influence legislation. To put the legislature on an equal footing with both the executive branch and the powerful Third House of lobbyists, Unruh had been on a campaign to create a more professional legislature to deal with problems facing a rapidly growing state. Lawmakers no longer would be temporary employees with little or no staff who spent a few months in Sacramento, then returned to their farms or businesses for the rest of the year. Instead, they'd be proficient, skilled professionals backed by competent, well-trained staff and research resources. Armed with information and expertise, the legislature—primarily Jesse Unruh's assembly—finally would become a true coequal branch of government.

In February 1966, a constitutional revision commission plopped a 212-page report into the legislature's lap, and Unruh ran with it. The report called for streamlining California's outdated, 80,000-word constitution and proposed a series of reforms that included annual legislative sessions and allowing the legislature to set its own salaries. It also recommended that qualifying an initiative for the ballot be made easier. Because the reforms required amending the constitution, they required a two-thirds vote in both the assembly and senate before being sent to the voters. Unruh's assembly moved decisively to force a public vote, quickly drafting a measure to place a comprehensive constitutional makeover on the November ballot.

Unruh recognized that outside the capitol the legislative pay raise provision had the potential to crush the entire plan. Initially, Unruh wanted legislators' salaries to increase from $6,000 a year to $25,000. Many newspaper publishers, still a potent political force in the mid-1960s, demanded not only that the proposed salary hike be scaled back but be accompanied by new conflict-of-interest rules. To make the package more palatable to the public and the newspapers, Unruh reduced the new salaries to $16,000 and tied separate ethics legislation to passage of the constitutional revision. That's when the senate balked, preferring weaker rules—or none at all. The capitol's most powerful lobbyists didn't like the plan either, because it would create a new staff barrier to their long-held easy access to lawmakers.

Unruh—always calculating and sometimes vindictive and over-bearing—seemed at his best when his back was against the wall. He usually could sense what a colleague needed and, as speaker, was in a position to make deals. Unruh's first target was conservative senate president pro tem Hugh Burns of Fresno, a fellow Democrat who wanted to be on good terms with the assembly leadership. Unruh's top aide acknowledged the speaker may have won him over by promising assembly support for the senator's legislation. With Burns on board, Unruh moved to neutralize lobbyist opposition. Two and a half months before the end of the session, Unruh summoned the most influential lobbyists to a meeting at the El Mirador Hotel, a favorite watering hole across the street from the capitol. They represented oil companies, truckers, liquor, racetracks, and other big commercial interests with a great deal to win or lose before legislative adjournment. Their opposition to the constitutional revision measure was gaining traction in the senate and threatened to prevent the plan from being placed on the November ballot.

Unruh sat next to Burns at the head table and, according to one lobbyist participant, started with a conciliatory gesture. "Gentlemen," Unruh said, "I want to know what you all want." The lobbyists took turns picking apart the constitutional revision package. Unruh responded that he'd be willing to accommodate many of their concerns without undermining the basic thrust of the constitutional amendment but insisted that professionalizing staff and upgrading resources were nonnegotiable. In case they weren't getting the message, he made it crystal clear: "We know that you're fully capable of marshaling the votes against us and could kill this proposition. But keep in mind," he sternly told the lobbyists, "everything you're interested in has to get through the two of us— the two houses. And we'll remember what you do."[1] Unruh chief of staff Larry Margolis recalled that the lobbyists filed out of the El Mirador meeting shaking their heads in resignation.

Once the assembly had overwhelmingly passed the constitutional revision and the pay and ethics measure, Unruh waited for the senate to act. The upper house dawdled and still hadn't passed the package by the last day of the session. With time running out, senators seemed to be stonewalling. One by one, they rose on the senate floor to offer long-winded testimonials to retiring or defeated colleagues. They wasted time passing inconsequential measures, such as a resolution praising Bobby Sox softball. As the deadline for action neared, it was clear that dislike for the ethics legislation threatened to doom Unruh's plan for a full-time legislature. That's when the powerful speaker reverted to the muscular politics he was famous for. Unruh and his lieutenants "black-jacked and cajoled" the senators by holding up their legislation in the lower house until the senators agreed to support the ethics bill.[2] They held for ransom one bill to expand the State Youth Authority by two members, which conveniently was designed to create jobs for two senators forced out of office by court-ordered redistricting. Under intense pressure, the senate cleared the conflict-of-interest bill for debate, with the fate of the huge constitutional revision hanging in the balance. As advertised, the measure would prevent legislators from profiting financially from any legislation they supported. Calaveras Democrat Stephen Teale complained the conflict-of-interest provisions were too stringent. "I'm afraid I wouldn't be able to get out of bed in the morning" for fear of violating the new ethics rules, he told his colleagues.[3] Another senator accused the state's newspaper publishers of demanding the ethics measure in return for their support of the pay raise. Finally, in the early evening, a reluctant senate approved the ethics bill with one vote to spare and handed Unruh his victory. In reality, the new law turned out to be considerably less effective than reformers had hoped. Nonetheless, it moved Jesse Unruh one step closer to building his empire and wielding power as no speaker before him. Next, he had to convince voters that a vastly bigger legislative branch was in their best interests.

THE BACKSTORY

Some people are groomed for success; Jesse Unruh fought for it. The youngest of five children who had grown up in poverty in Kansas and Texas, Unruh was a man in a hurry. After interrupting his studies at Wayland Baptist College in Texas to serve in the navy during World War II, Unruh settled in Southern California and became immersed in politics while finishing his studies at USC. Still in school in his mid-twenties, Unruh ran for the state assembly in 1948, finishing third in the Democratic primary. Undaunted, he unsuccessfully tried again four years later, then ran a third time in 1954. With a wife and a growing family to support, he couldn't take time off from his job to campaign and had no money in the bank. He scraped together $2,495 for a single district mailer while lobbyists poured money into the campaign of his incumbent Republican opponent.[4] Unruh won by six percentage points and launched his remarkable political career, representing Inglewood and other communities in southwestern Los Angeles.

In those days, well-heeled lobbyists had the run of the building. They had more staff and expertise on public policy issues than lawmakers and they spread money, booze, and women around to legislators all too willing to take their gifts and return the favors with votes. Legislators earned $500 a month plus a daily living allowance when the legislature was in session. Unruh spent the sessions living in a small $50-a-month room at the venerable Elks Club, two blocks from the capitol.

In 1960, *Reader's Digest* ran a blockbuster exposé about lobbyist influence in government. "This Is How Payola Works in Politics" was authored by an anonymous source known as Assemblyman X, as told to Lester Velie, the journalist who had made public the outsized influence of California mega-lobbyist Artie Samish more than two decades earlier. Through their lobbyists, Assemblyman X said, "pressure groups supply most of the [campaign] money—and later ask for their money's worth." The article detailed how Assemblyman X and a few other freshmen had arrived in the legislature as idealistic, somewhat naïve, do-gooders who pledged to turn their backs on lobbyists' gifts.

This new breed of legislator initially plotted strategies to elect like-minded politicians but finally concluded that only lobbyists had the resources to finance the campaigns of chosen candidates. Thus, Assemblyman X said, the band of lawmakers began "taking money from would-be corrupters—to elect men who would fight corruption."[5] Assemblyman X was, in fact, Jesse Unruh. Eventually, he became very good at taking lobbyist handouts and creating a political machine that funneled precious campaign dollars to confederates. In return, Unruh demanded loyalty from those he helped. Robert Finch, an up-and-coming Republican who years later would become lieutenant governor under Ronald Reagan, watched Unruh choreograph the flow of dollars. "He knew that a relatively small amount of money given to an incumbent or a new candidate at an early time was worth five times that much later on down the road."[6]

From the beginning, Unruh exhibited an astute knack for maneuvering through the legislature's complex processes. He forged relationships, built alliances, and picked winners. On his first day in office, January 3, 1955, Unruh had shrewdly provided a key vote that propelled Republican Luther "Abe" Lincoln of Alameda to the speakership in a GOP-dominated assembly. Unruh was rewarded with a Finance and Insurance subcommittee chairmanship, an important post, since the full committee decided the fate of business legislation that attracted large campaign contributions. In 1956, confident of reelection, Unruh spurned lobbyist contributions to himself but suggested that the cash be given, instead, to other candidates who needed help. And Unruh made sure he was given credit for the gifts. In 1957, with Republicans still controlling the lower house, Unruh again was rewarded for his loyalty. According to Unruh biographer Lou Cannon, "grateful" assembly members who had received funds directed by Unruh elected him chair of the full Finance and Insurance Committee.[7] Rarely had a legislator— particularly one whose party was in the minority—risen so quickly. In 1959, Democrats regained control of the assembly for the first time since the early 1940s and Unruh again made the right moves. He went to fellow legislators and secured votes to elect Modesto's mild-mannered assemblyman Ralph M. Brown as speaker. Once again, Unruh was rewarded with a plum assignment: the chairmanship of the prestigious Ways and Means Committee, which had power over both the budget and the amount of tax money that would be spent on each bill.

After six years in office, Unruh clearly was someone rocketing toward greatness; however, it was the 1961 reapportionment battle that cemented his stature in the legislature and vaulted him to the coveted assembly speakership. Pat Brown had defeated William Knowland for governor by a million votes in 1958 and, for the first time in eighty years, Democrats controlled both legislative houses and the governorship, putting them in charge of that decennial rite of political survival: the redrawing of political boundaries. Unruh maneuvered to get himself appointed to the Elections and Reapportionment Committee and soon mastered the intricacies of redistricting. Backed by expert outside help, he and committee chairman Robert Crown drew political boundaries that would keep Democrats in the majority for most of the next decade.

All along, Unruh set his sights on being speaker, at that time a post more ceremonial than powerful. He had two major obstacles before him: he needed to get a majority of the eighty-member assembly to support him, and the job wasn't vacant. Using his redistricting role as leverage, Unruh and a small group of confidants set out to grab the prize. First, Unruh secured the loyalty of a dozen Republican assembly members by creating safe districts for them. His greatest challenge, however, was figuring out a way to get Democratic speaker Ralph Brown out of the picture. Only in extraordinary circumstances will a politician willingly give up leadership, so Unruh brilliantly devised an offer Brown couldn't refuse. It was no secret that Brown really wanted to be a judge. He had told reporters in 1960 that he "would be honored to be an appellate judge, but I haven't been offered such a position."[8] And none was available. Yet Unruh concocted a way to maneuver Brown out of the speaker's chair and onto the bench by getting a bill passed to create a new appellate court in Fresno, near Brown's Modesto home. After getting Governor Brown's signature on the measure, Unruh then persuaded the governor to appoint Brown to the new court. It was an inspired move that would cement Unruh's reputation as a master strategist.

Shortly after Ralph Brown resigned from the assembly in September 1961, lawmakers met in a special Sunday session to elect a new speaker. It was Unruh's thirty-ninth birthday. One challenger emerged—Merced Democrat Gordon Winton—who simply couldn't stomach Unruh's heavy-handed tactics. A *Los Angeles Times* account of the speakership election described Unruh as "a disliked but respected man by some Democrats and many Republicans."[9] Winton received only one Democratic vote, his own, and lost the speakership contest 57–13. In his first official act as an appellate court judge, Ralph Brown swore Unruh into his new post. At the rostrum, Unruh thanked his supporters and was presented with a three-by-four-foot birthday cake that was topped with a large gavel. The son of sharecroppers so poor that he had gone without shoes even in the frigid Kansas winters, Jesse Unruh had used his cunning and intellect to become the leader of the assembly. In short order, he'd transform the speakership into a commanding power center with virtual life-or-death authority over every piece of legislation emerging from the capitol. He became the second-most-powerful politician in the nation's second-largest state.

Ironically, it was Pat Brown who had helped create the formidable rival who would tenaciously challenge the governor for many years. Brown was keenly aware of Unruh's rising-star power and hard-charging, can-do image, not only at the capitol but within the new Kennedy administration. (Unruh was the first major California Democrat to endorse John F. Kennedy's presidential bid in 1960.) Brown's persona, meanwhile, was suffering by comparison. *Time* magazine referred to the governor as "a political master of the hesitation waltz," who should be "no particular obstacle in the path of Unruh's drive for actual party power."[10] In subsequent years, the Brown-Unruh relationship would sour, particularly in 1966 when Unruh accused Brown of reneging on a pledge—denied by Brown—not to seek a third term as governor. Unruh thought it was *his* turn to run for governor. For his part, Brown regretted his "awful mistake" in creating the speakership vacancy. "If I could have done it all over again, I would never have made him speaker," he said.[11] In truth, Unruh had built up so much support in the assembly that eventually he likely would have become speaker anyway. The governor had merely made the task easier to accomplish sooner.

Never forgetting his working-class roots, Unruh now was in a position to put his stamp on an array of policy initiatives dealing with discrimination and consumer protection, and he was obsessed with restructuring the legislature to make it coequal with the executive branch. Unruh believed information was the currency of good legislating. He considered the legislature "deferentially inferior to the executive branch," primarily because it had no staff to independently analyze critical issues and legislation.[12] In fact, when he became chairman of the Ways and Means Committee, his staff consisted of a single secretary. That meant the legislature had to rely on the governor's Department of Finance or private lobbyists for vital information, which likely was biased to favor one position over another.

One of Unruh's first tasks as speaker was to begin developing competent, professional committee staffs to make the assembly less reliant on the executive branch, thus reducing the influence of the governor's office over legislation. Governor Brown took that move as a personal insult. Critics questioned the expense of hiring dozens of new staff members. Although Republicans benefited from the staffing surge, some raised a warning flag suggesting that many of the new hires were on the payroll to help Unruh and his cronies maintain their Democratic majority. They pointed to the Assembly Rules Committee's approval of an Unruh proposal to add ten specialists to the staff. The first hire, at $15,000 a year, was a longtime Unruh political associate, a detail that prompted Assemblyman Don Mulford of Alameda County to suggest the move was "a veiled effort to hire political hacks to support individual ambitions."[13]

Unruh understood that adding staff members merely worked around the edges of putting the assembly on an even footing with the governor's office. If he truly wanted to raise the stature of the legislature—and his speakership—he would have to tackle systemic barriers contained in the state constitution, which restricted the length of legislative sessions and limited lawmakers' ability to control their own agenda. On February 21, 1966, opportunity knocked, and Unruh made the most of it.

For three years, a special state commission had been studying ways to streamline California's gigantic, unmanageable, and outdated constitution. To improve it, dozens of prominent citizens toiled for thousands of hours—without pay—before handing their work product to the legislature. Overall, the commission's work covered about one-third of the existing constitution and proposed reducing that portion of the document from 22,000 to 6,000 words. The recommendation that received the most press attention would allow legislators to set their own salaries. It had been more than a decade since lawmakers had received a pay raise, which elevated their salaries to $500 a month and fixed the compensation figure in the constitution. Other recommendations included scrapping the part-time legislature in favor of annual sessions and reducing the percentage of voter signatures required to qualify an initiative for the statewide ballot. The commission's work product was just what Unruh wanted. In fact, he had collaborated with key members throughout the process.

Under the existing constitution, only the governor could place agenda items before the legislature in even-numbered years during its budget session. Thus, any legislative revision of the constitution in 1966 had to be sanctioned by the governor, approved by a two-thirds vote of both houses, and submitted to voters at the November general election. When the constitutional revision commission delivered its report at a ceremony in the governor's office, Brown noted there was resistance to the changes in the senate. In truth, Brown also had problems with the revision plan because it would have increased Unruh's political power at the expense of executive prerogatives. The *Sacramento Bee* reported that "at the very moment the ceremony was under way" the governor's office was announcing fourteen additional items for the legislative agenda. The additions did not include the constitutional revision. To effectively force the governor to add the issue to the legislature's agenda, Unruh turned to his tried-and-true playbook—horse-trading. Brown was about to ask voters to give him a third term as governor, and he desperately needed to get a budget-related bill through Unruh's assembly to avoid a pre-election tax increase that would hurt his chances. Unruh held up the bill until Brown agreed to put the constitutional revision on the legislative agenda.[14]

THE ELECTION

For Unruh, it had been a constant struggle maneuvering the constitutional changes through the legislature, and it wasn't until the evening of the last day of the session that the government overhaul squeezed through the senate and headed for the November statewide ballot as Proposition 1-A. Using his hold on the lower house to the fullest extent, Unruh had bullied reluctant lawmakers by threatening their pet projects in return for their support of the revision package. He applied the same tactic when he was forced to deal with Democratic attorney general Tom Lynch. The attorney general's office is charged with writing a title and brief summary for the ballot to describe the essence of each proposition at the top of the ballot. The wording is critical, because many voters read only the titles and summaries of measures before voting. According to Unruh biographer Bill Boyarsky, Lynch's office originally labeled the revision proposal a measure to raise legislative salaries. "That would have sunk the proposition all by itself," Unruh told an interviewer. In true "Big Daddy" fashion, Unruh called Lynch on the phone and gave him a choice—either change the title and summary to make it more neutral or never get another bill out of the legislature. Lynch rewrote the summary.[15]

Unruh understood that early in the campaign he had to secure the two endorsement prizes that mattered most: Governor Brown, with whom he had a deteriorating relationship, and Ronald Reagan, with whom he had no meaningful relationship at all. Brown had defeated Los Angeles mayor Sam Yorty in the Democratic gubernatorial primary but had received barely a majority of votes cast. Meanwhile, the fifty-five-year-old actor-turned-politician Reagan won a stunning victory over former San Francisco mayor George Christopher in the Republican primary.

Reagan had become a national political figure in 1964 after delivering a rousing defense of conservatism on behalf of GOP presidential candidate Barry Goldwater. Reagan had received between 4,000 and 5,000 adoring letters from Californians after that televised speech, many of which urged him to run for governor. Noteworthy was the fact that party officials had been lining up behind Christopher. "The farthest thing from my mind was running for political office," Reagan remembered. "It didn't look attractive to me at all. I liked my life."[16] Reagan, however, agreed to test the waters and travel the state making speeches to service clubs and chambers of commerce. He interviewed political consultants Stu Spencer and William Roberts, who initially had their doubts. "We wanted to know, is this a right-wing nut or what?" Roberts recalled.[17] The Spencer-Roberts team was hired to create and manage a grassroots "Friends of Ronald Reagan" organization, and the first thing they did was contact those thousands of Reagan fans and sign them up. Reagan, Christopher later said, had "no depth," but he acknowledged that Reagan had an "actor's ability to steal the scene."[18] He also had an ability to zero in on issues that voters cared about. One of those issues was bloated government and wasteful spending in Sacramento.

How could Unruh convince Reagan to endorse a significant and costly government buildup when the Republican candidate was campaigning to "cut, squeeze and trim" state government? And how could he persuade a skeptical governor to support a constitutional amendment that increased the independence of the legislative branch at the expense of the executive? Unruh was building a large support list among the state's newspapers. For years he had cultivated media backing for a constitutional rewrite. An early editorial in the *Napa Register*, for example, cited Unruh's arguments and concluded, "Without question a state as large as California requires more attention from the legislative branch of government."[19] Unruh also had bipartisan cover in the form of the star-studded Constitutional Revision Commission, led by an esteemed Republican former assemblyman. The commission included respected lawmakers from both major parties plus judges and community leaders; representatives of business, labor, and academia; and even the Hollywood president of the Artists Managers Guild.

Unruh decided to seek Reagan's help first, but he knew his fingerprints couldn't be on the request. After all, the day after the primary election, Unruh had participated in a Los Angeles news conference in which he, along with senate leader Hugh Burns and Governor Brown, had lobbed the first grenades in the fall campaign. Brown had warned against "turning California over to a government of negativism and retreat headed by an inexperienced actor and supported by the most immoderate and dangerous elements in our society."[20] Unruh turned to a number of Republican colleagues to reach Reagan and secure his endorsement through back channels.

Once Reagan was on board, Unruh secured Brown's endorsement of Proposition 1-A. Any reservations Brown might have had about a well-funded, professional legislature were outweighed by political considerations; the ballot measure enjoyed widespread support among the state's most important newspapers and policymakers, and further, Brown wouldn't have wanted to antagonize Speaker Unruh during his own reelection bid. To leverage the endorsements, Brown was named honorary chairman of "Californians for Yes on 1-A" and Reagan became honorary cochairman. Sherry Bebitch (Jeffe), a new staffer fresh out of college, watched Unruh at work. Nearly half a century later, she still marveled at Unruh's ability to aggregate real power. "It was astonishing to watch," she said. "He knew he wanted to make the legislature far stronger than it had been, and he chafed at the possibility of being under the thumb of the governor."[21]

In another brilliant stroke, Unruh hired the legendary political consulting firm of Whitaker and Baxter to manage the 1-A campaign. The firm had close ties to business organizations and Republicans, and Unruh knew that if there were going to be substantial opposition to the ballot measure it likely would come from groups Whitaker and Baxter had relationships with, among them the California Taxpayers Association, the California Chamber of Commerce, the California Manufacturers Association, oil companies, and utilities.

By 1966, the founder's son, Clem Whitaker, Jr., was running the company. "We went out and visited with all these groups very quickly," he said.[22] To demonstrate the bipartisan nature of the ballot measure during those "earthy discussions," Whitaker usually included Democrats Unruh and Burns as well as Republicans Robert Monagan from the assembly and Senator Jack McCarthy. Once an organization came on board, its endorsement was leveraged for more endorsements. The California Chamber of Commerce sent letters to seven hundred local chambers and one hundred other business organizations urging support of Proposition 1-A. It was an aggressive campaign, Whitaker said, and showed a united front.

Pat Brown and Ronald Reagan were always the centerpieces, and campaign press releases prominently mentioned their endorsements. Red-white-and-blue brochures featured sketches of the two candidates jointly declaring, "We support the revision of the State Constitution and urge all Californians to vote YES on Proposition 1-A."[23] The theme of the campaign materials was the modernization of California's out-of-date constitution, which hadn't been revised since Rutherford B. Hayes was president. The campaign slogan was "Update the State." Knowing that the basis for most opposition was the legislative salary provision, the campaign barely mentioned it in outreach materials. Money flowed into the campaign coffers. Unruh put the squeeze on special-interest lobbyists to raise funds, and legislators also did their part. The office of senate Republican leader John McCarthy of Marin County forwarded to Whitaker a $500 check from the Pacific Power and Light Company, along with a handwritten note from an aide that said, "Maybe we'll put [the good guys] back in style again in California politics."[24]

Brown and Reagan didn't spend much time on the campaign trail promoting 1-A; they were too busy fighting each other. GOP assemblyman Charles Conrad tutored Reagan on public-policy issues, and the candidate proved to be an effective campaigner. Reagan attacked California's welfare system, unemployment, high taxes, big government, crime, and student unrest. He was articulating a mid-decade malaise after eight years of Democratic control. Brown ran on his earlier record of accomplishments and reminded voters that it was an actor who killed President Lincoln. When Brown suggested Reagan merely was regurgitating rehearsed lines written for him by a campaign consultant, Reagan insisted that his standard stump speech be shortened and that speaking appearances include a question-and-answer session with the audience. "Someone may think that someone else wrote that short speech, but they'll have to know that nobody could write the answers to those questions," Reagan reflected years later.[25]

Under Whitaker's guidance, Brown and Reagan agreed to cut separate short television advertisements backing the proposition. Each spot featured the candidate walking toward the camera and delivering a couple of lines. Both stressed the fact that despite their differences and the rancor of the gubernatorial campaign, they were united on this one issue. "Besides wanting to be your next governor," Reagan said, "there is one thing Pat Brown and I agree on. That's Proposition 1-A, the long overdue constitutional reform measure." With Brown's spot, Whitaker wanted to keep a light touch. Thus, Brown says into the camera, "If there's one thing that Ronald Reagan and I agree on, besides motherhood, it's that Proposition 1-A—the constitutional reform measure—is good for California."[26] The simple but effective spots were played back-to-back. Brown and Reagan also signed a bland nineteen-word argument in the voters' guide urging support for the constitutional revision. Ultraconservative senator John Schmitz of Orange County, campaigning against the measure, insisted that the "passing of laws in a free country ought not to be a fulltime profession for anyone."[27]

Most of the underfunded, disorganized campaign against Proposition 1-A took aim at its Achilles' heel—the legislative pay raise. An early survey showed thirteen-to-one opposition to the provision in Los Angeles,[28] although later polls showed the measure as a whole was popular. Opponents scraped up enough money to run a few newspaper ads, but they were overwhelmed by the blast of media messages and editorial support for the measure. Despite a late September internal poll in Los Angeles County showing the proposition with a two-to-one lead, the campaign left nothing to chance. It blitzed the state with TV spots during the stretch drive: $38 for an ad straddling *Daniel Boone* and *Star Trek* in Eureka, $275 for an ad during the *Milton Berle Show* in Sacramento, and $1,450 for a spot during KNXT's newscast in Los Angeles. Leading up to the election, the campaign bought space on KTLA in Los Angeles in news, auto races, pro and college football, wrestling, soap operas, bowling, and *Divorce Court*. Meantime, media support kept pouring in. Given that Unruh had tied the possibility of higher salaries to new ethics requirements in the proposal, editorials were almost unanimously in favor of the ballot measure. Even the pay hike, with its 5 percent annual cap, received a great deal of favorable treatment. San Francisco's KPIX endorsed the ballot measure under the headline

"Let's Boost Their Pay." The *Los Angeles Times* called the proposed code of ethics "the toughest in the nation."[29]

The November 1966 election was seismic on many fronts. As a result of implementation of the 1965 court-ordered "one man, one vote" redistricting, masterminded by Speaker Unruh and his compatriots, the incoming California legislature would be dominated by urban interests—most notably those of Southern California—for the first time in the state's history. Los Angeles County, approaching seven million residents, went from being represented by only one senator to having fourteen upper-house representatives (plus another senator who represented both Los Angeles and Orange Counties). Based strictly on population, the fifty northernmost counties saw their representation in the forty-member senate shrink from thirty-one to eighteen. Unruh had created friendly districts for his friends and vaporized them for his enemies. After Gordon Winton lost the speakership contest in 1961, he refused to vote for Unruh in subsequent leadership elections. Unruh never forgot, and he reconfigured Winton's district, filling it with Republican voters and ending the Merced Democrat's career. Winton recalled Unruh once telling him, "In politics, you never get mad, you just get even." Unruh, Winton said, "did me out of office."[30]

The election also brought about a Republican resurgence in California. Despite a three-to-two registration edge for Democrats, Republicans nearly swept the state elections. They won five of six partisan statewide offices and picked up seven assembly seats, five senate seats, and three congressional seats. Reagan reversed the national Goldwater debacle of 1964 and easily won the election for governor. Voters were disenchanted with politicians—in both Washington and Sacramento. They resented the perceived welfare state, government waste, and student unrest—what Reagan called the "mess at Berkeley." They were fed up with crime and, particularly, the Watts riots that had occurred on Brown's watch. Many had voted two years earlier to strike down California's anti–housing discrimination law with which Brown was closely identified.

Benefiting from a white, middle-class revolt, Reagan took full advantage of a weak reelection campaign by Brown. Although

Reagan was quite conservative by California standards at the time, Brown failed to link the Republican to the ultraright John Birch Society as many had done with Goldwater, a move that had fueled suspicions the GOP presidential nominee was an extremist. Whereas Goldwater appeared to be an angry warmonger during his failed campaign for the White House against Lyndon Johnson, "along came this nice fellow" that everyone knew from the movies and television, said *New York Times* reporter Gladwin Hill.[31] Reagan had a pleasant demeanor and a golden smile. He ran an aggressive campaign against Brown, but unlike Goldwater, he was likeable and nonthreatening to a sizeable part of the electorate.

Voters gave Reagan a million-vote landslide victory. He carried all but three of California's fifty-eight counties, losing only in Alameda (barely), Plumas (barely), and San Francisco. Results were contradictory, however, because as voters sent a strong signal to reverse the direction of government and reduce the bureaucracy by electing Reagan, more than 73 percent of them also approved the first constitutional overhaul in nearly ninety years, to enlarge and modernize the legislative branch of government. Within a few years, independent critics would rank California's legislature as the best, most effective, and most accountable in the nation. It became a model for a nationwide movement to improve other legislatures. Jesse Unruh, with help from Pat Brown and Ronald Reagan, had conceived and built his monument. The cracks wouldn't show until he was gone.

THE IMPACT

The new full-time legislature that convened in Sacramento in January 1967 attracted young, smart public policy experts who staffed key committees and were eager to leave their marks on state policy. The legislature also was given an increasingly larger budget to hire personal staff. When Jesse Unruh began his capitol career in 1955, the legislature employed about 100 professional aides—fewer than one per member. By 1968, two years after the passage of Proposition 1-A, the legislature had an operating budget of $20 million and 500 staff aides. Nearly fifty years later, the legislative staff had grown to more than 2,100, with a budget of nearly $140 million.[32] But there were unintended consequences. In 1986, former Unruh staffer turned academic Sherry Bebitch Jeffe offered a blistering review of the legislature's staff buildup. "The policy experts have been replaced by political hired guns whose main job is to get their bosses elected," she wrote. "All of this has led to a dangerous shift in the function of legislative staff from being the professional arm of the Legislature to a taxpayer-funded political muscle."[33]

Over the years after voters passed Proposition 1-A, many capitol employees felt pressured to go off payroll in the run-up to elections, and to walk precincts in the districts of their bosses or vulnerable members. At the speaker's annual "End of Session Bash," a fundraising event instituted by assembly speaker Willie Brown in the 1980s, staffers were expected to sell tickets to lobbyists and other capitol habitués. The proceeds were used to fund Democratic campaigns. Staff members believed—even though it was never spoken publicly—that participation in these types of partisan efforts helped advance their careers. Unruh chief of staff Larry Margolis acknowledged that sending policy consultants to work on political campaigns diluted the assembly staff, even as far back as the late 1960s, but he insisted that was not Unruh's intention. "Whereas Unruh was devoted to building the capacity of the legislature to handle its own affairs and do its job effectively," Margolis said, "he had to fight off members—who were supporters of his—who wanted to use their staff positions for campaign aides."[34] Unruh even felt the need to lecture his committee chairmen about proper hiring practices. "If we want a legislature we can be proud of, then we have to restrain ourselves," Unruh told them. That meant preventing one of his committee chairmen from elevating his secretary to committee consultant "just because he's bedding her down."[35]

Since 1967, a two-tiered staff system has always seen some employees serving in political capacities for their bosses, and others serving the institution as policy consultants. Over time, the nonpartisan policy consultants found their roles morphing into service at the pleasure of the committee chairs who hired them. These are coveted, well-paid assignments in the capitol's hierarchy that may lead to elective offices. In 1960, for example, not one sitting member of the assembly had any previous experience as a political aide. By 1998, more than half had learned their craft at the legislative staff level. Staffing had become the "primary mechanism of politician candidate recruitment."[36] More recently, that number has diminished, but legislative staff service remains an important breeding ground for elective office. Legislators, even within the term limits enacted by voters in 1990, now make a full-time career out of lawmaking—what German sociologist Max Weber called "living *off* politics" rather than "living *for* politics."

Since Proposition 1-A was approved, the length of the legislative session has gone from fewer than one hundred days a year to nearly year-round, and salaries and benefits are no longer the token stipends they use to be. Legislative salaries have reached $100,000 a year, plus roughly $30,000 in tax-free per diem. In theory, the legislators' higher salaries obviate any necessity to seek special-interest handouts to supplement their incomes. Full-time legislators, however, still require barrels of cash to protect their careers and run reelection campaigns dependent on expensive ads and costly political strategists. By the 2013–14 election cycle, more than $132 million had been directly raised by senate and assembly candidates, which translated to $363,458 per day, or $15,144 per hour, twenty-four hours a day, seven days a week.[37] In addition, independent committees pumped more than $51 million into various legislative campaigns.[38] A March 2010 report by the state Fair Political Practices Commission identified labor unions, tribal gaming operations, and business interests as the largest donors to candidates. "The reality in politics is that money talks. Sometimes money shouts," the report concluded.[39]

One of Jesse Unruh's primary goals for Proposition 1-A was to boost the legislature's political clout, vis-à-vis the executive branch and the state's well-funded lobbying corps. But one of the least-discussed components of the proposition has had the opposite effect. By reducing the percentage of voter signatures required to qualify an initiative for the statewide ballot, Proposition 1-A made it considerably more attractive for well-funded special interests, as well as occasional citizen movements, to attempt to circumvent the legislature and enact new laws via initiative. In the forty-six years before the proposition's enactment, 206 measures were approved for signature circulation after receiving official titles from the attorney general; in the forty-six years since, the number cleared for circulation had increased more than seven-fold.[40]

Reagan's eight years as governor had its paradoxes as well. He demonized government, telling his inauguration audience, "We stand between the taxpayer and the tax spender."[41] Yet, he raised taxes by $1 billion on income, sales, corporations, liquor, and cigarettes in what was the largest tax levy in California history at the time. In the days before he took office, Reagan knew the state's finances were in a shambles, but he didn't know the scope, and the outgoing Brown administration wasn't very helpful. At a budget meeting between Brown's finance director Hale Champion and an incoming Reagan representative, a brusque Champion was quoted as saying, "We're spending $1 million a day more than we're taking in. I've got a golf game. Good luck."[42] As governor, Reagan's budgets increased faster than the inflation rate. He promised to cut government but created seventy-three separate boards, commissions, councils, and authorities his last year in office alone.[43] Most famously, Reagan angered conservatives by signing the nation's most liberal abortion law in 1967. He also signed an environmentalist-supported wild rivers bill and negotiated welfare reform with Democrats. Yet he brought with him a critical view of government's role, pulling the new conservative movement into the mainstream.

Despite Reagan's significant 1966 mandate, he was unable to put his stamp on a more permanent political realignment—at least in California. He did win reelection in 1970 by a half-million votes against a woefully underfunded Jesse Unruh, but Democrats regained control of both houses of the legislature, which they had lost two years earlier. Six years after Reagan left the governorship, Unruh had this assessment: "He was not as good a governor as his friends claimed, and he was not as bad a governor as many of his enemies had feared."[44]

By then, Unruh had resurrected a flagging political career by converting the backwater office of state treasurer into a powerful position that controlled the investment of billions of dollars in state funds. About six months before the 1986 primary election, as Unruh prepared to campaign for his fourth tour as treasurer, he sat down for his monthly lunch at Sacramento's Sutter Club with Steve Merksamer, Republican governor George Deukmejian's chief of staff. The two had become close friends and Unruh had given Merksamer valuable advice on dealing with Democrats in the legislature. Merksamer recalled: "He looks at me and says, 'Steve, have I been helpful to you?' I said, 'Yes, very much.'" Unruh continued, "Does George think I've been helpful to him? Have I done everything you've asked me to do the last four years?" Merksamer assured Unruh that he had. Unruh then told Merksamer he had prostate cancer and was refusing surgery because it would leave him impotent. "I'm going to die from it," Unruh said. "I'll be dead in a year or year and a half, and I have a favor to ask. I have this dream that I want to win reelection by the biggest landslide in California history." Unruh expected Republican US treasurer Bay Buchanan to run against him, and he asked Merksamer and Deukmejian to discourage her and any other prominent Republican from running. Merksamer took Unruh's request to Deukmejian, who decided, "Let's clear the field," and it was made known quietly to any potential GOP contender that Deukmejian would be supporting Unruh.[45] In November, facing no Republican and only token third-party opposition, Unruh received a record 5,589,633 votes and secured his fourth term as treasurer with 82.7 percent of the vote. Nine months after the election, Unruh died, allowing Deukmejian to appoint his successor.

In popular memory, Unruh's complex overhaul of the state constitution in 1966 is dwarfed by the dramatic ascension that year of Ronald Reagan to the California governorship—which put him on the path to the presidency and altered the course of the nation's history. Yet even as the fractured Republican Party has attracted a dwindling share of the state's registered voters, the impact of Proposition 1-A lives on in the full-time legislature. Reviews of

Unruh's grand experiment are mixed. In the decades that followed, disappointment with the partisan, gridlocked assembly and senate hit record highs. With public opinion polls occasionally putting the legislature's disapproval rate at 80 percent, critics tried and failed to qualify a series of ballot measures to return to a part-time legislature. Ronald Reagan's son Michael chaired one such effort in 2012. "I remember my father telling me there were only a few things he was disappointed with as governor. One was signing no-fault divorce, two was signing the abortion bill, and three was supporting Proposition 1-A."[46]

9

1974
Californians Pull Back the Curtain on Politics as Usual

"Money is the mother's milk of politics."
—Jesse M. Unruh, Assembly Speaker

IN 1949, following an embarrassing scandal, the California legislature banned notoriously powerful and arrogant lobbyist Artie Samish from entering the capitol and built new walls between lawmakers and special interests. Nearly a quarter-century later, another round of reforms seemed more necessary than ever. Money still flowed freely from lobbyists to legislators—in the form of free meals, liquor, and even cash stuffed in envelopes—and the public had little access to records showing who was paying for politicians' campaigns, or how much candidates were spending. Numerous electoral reform bills introduced early in the legislative session that year had languished without so much as a single committee hearing. Change was not an easy sell to a bloc of politicians who benefited daily from the largesse of special interests and who found little appeal in going beyond those inadequate 1949 reform laws.

As legislators scattered for their month-long summer recess in 1973, events unfolding 3,000 miles away gave new energy to reformers seeking to clean up government. In Washington, the

Nixon White House was unraveling under the relentless revelations of the mushrooming Watergate scandal that would shake the citizens' faith in their own government. By the time the legislature returned to Sacramento in August, senior Nixon administration officials had resigned (Nixon himself would hang on for another year) and the Senate Watergate Committee was capturing headlines with its nationally televised investigative hearings. State lawmakers quickly reacted to the scandal by approving a series of bills dealing with campaign contributions and spending, conflicts of interest, and open meetings. By September 15, the last day of the session, only one important reform measure remained.

At the request of Washington, DC–based Common Cause—an organization seeking greater transparency and honesty in government—Democratic assemblyman Ken Meade of Oakland had agreed to carry a measure to criminalize a number of widespread lobbying practices, including secret gifts and direct campaign contributions to legislators. Meade was a combative former reserve quarterback on the Cal football team in the late 1950s. He was elected to the legislature in 1970 and quickly forged an alliance with assembly speaker Bob Moretti, who supported the proposal. Meade's measure would require lobbyists to disclose whom they spent their money on and the legislation they were trying to influence.

Given the daily grind of Watergate news, Meade's bill appeared destined—at least publicly—for an overwhelming victory, particularly after it passed the assembly 74–0. Common Cause wasn't celebrating, though, and for good reason; success in the senate was far from assured. The upper house seemed to have a special relationship with lobbyists who liberally spread campaign cash and willingly picked up tabs at Sacramento restaurants and watering holes. It was in the senate that major lobbyists had unique access to power, representing such well-financed clients as liquor, racetracks, oil, Hollywood studios, insurance, unions, financial institutions, doctors, teachers, land developers, and private utilities.

Former state senator George Deukmejian, a Long Beach Republican who later would be elected attorney general and governor, recalled being summoned, shortly after his election in 1966, to the oversized office of senate president pro tem Hugh Burns, a burly Fresno mortician by trade, to talk about committee assignments. Deukmejian, who had previously served four years in the assembly, was seeking a seat on the Judiciary Committee and the chairmanship of the Elections and Reapportionment Committee. "I go in there to talk about my committee assignments and the room is filled with lobbyists," he said. "So Hugh asked me a couple of questions. There was a little discussion. It was sort of like, none of these lobbyists objected so I got the position. What really struck me, and it still does to this day—all those lobbyists were in there. They were all close to Hugh Burns."[1]

Big-time lobbyists wanted the Meade bill killed, and the old-boys network in the senate was happy to oblige. The first tactic was delay. The Senate Finance Committee had approved the measure several days before the end of session, but the bill had disappeared—literally. Other committee-passed measures had arrived on the senate floor, but not Meade's. He was convinced Democratic committee chairman Randolph Collier of Yreka had hidden the document in his car. Collier, he said, "had disappeared with the bill and literally wouldn't bring it back."[2] After newspaper coverage of the missing measure surfaced, the bill mysteriously made its way to the senate floor on the chaotic last day of the session. That night, as each house propelled toward adjournment, the voting was frenetic, rushing at a rate of one per minute in the assembly and about one every two and a half minutes in the senate. "I wandered to the back of the room to say hello to someone and when I came back I discovered I had voted on four bills," said Republican senator H. L. Richardson.[3]

Well after midnight, opponents—backed by their lobbyist allies—tried one last-ditch tactic, inserting a poison pill to either kill the measure or stall it until January. In a move that stunned weary observers, Jack Schrade, an old-guard senator first elected to the legislature from San Diego in 1954, proposed changing the definition of lobbyist. His amendment would require any citizen who communicated with lawmakers on legislation to register as a lobbyist. News reporters and editorial writers on legislative issues would have to register as well. With a straight face, Schrade said he merely was trying to make the bill stronger. The amendment passed narrowly after about an hour's debate and was sent to the assembly, which had already adjourned, thus preventing final action until January. "Few times in the session did members of the California Senate act together so smoothly," noted Robert Smith, the California Project Coordinator of Common Cause.[4]

Reformers did have a Plan B, however, based on the eventual likelihood that the legislature would balk. Common Cause had joined the Los Angeles–based People's Lobby and California secretary of state Jerry Brown to craft a parallel initiative—even stronger than the proposed legislation—to enact the toughest political reform law in the nation. They already had filed their 111-page reform document with state officials and would have to submit 325,504 valid signatures by December 24 if the measure were to appear on the June 1974 ballot. Sabotaged by the senate and facing a fast-approaching deadline for signature gathering, the small group of reform advocates went into overdrive. Thus was born Proposition 9, the state's landmark Political Reform Act, which still stands as an imperfect model for pulling back the curtain on once-hidden interactions among private money, public officials, and government decision-making. How were these reform advocates able to succeed against a well-entrenched establishment of powerful state legislators and savvy, formidable lobbyists who were used to getting their own way?

THE BACKSTORY

California's first electoral reform boomlet occurred in the 1890s as an increasing number of lawmakers dared to challenge the monopoly of the multi-tentacled Southern Pacific Railroad, which would continue its dominance of the state's politics and public policy for years to come. The reformers' first step was enactment of the Australian-style secret ballot for California voters in 1891, a move that brought structure, control, and privacy to elections. Two years later, Governor Henry Markham signed legislation creating the Purity of Elections law. Based on a ten-year-old English statute, it required candidates and their campaign committees to disclose contributions they received and how they spent the money. But the new law had a muted effect because disclosures were not available to voters until after an election was over. Further reform came slowly. Ballot measures would remain exempt from disclosure requirements for another twenty-eight years. Markham's successor, James Budd, failed to coax the legislature into imposing greater oversight over the railroad.

California voters, prodded by Governor Hiram Johnson and a likeminded legislature, finally drove a stake through the heart of the tenacious railroad's political supremacy in 1911. Legislators saw no need to clamp down on lobbyists, however, because the only ones with clout had been employed by the severely weakened Southern Pacific. Into that vacuum slipped a crafty, corpulent seventh-grade dropout who had learned the intricacies of passing and killing laws while serving as a legislative clerk. Artie Samish won his first legislative lobbying campaign in 1923 representing large chain stores that were battling small independent retailers at the capitol. By the 1930s, the massive six-foot-two, three-hundred-pound Samish had cornered the market on lobbying influence while representing such free-spending interests as racetracks, liquor, banks, chemical companies, and railroads.

Samish had offices at the Biltmore Hotel in Los Angeles and the Kohl Building in San Francisco. When the legislature was in session—on a schedule much more limited than those of modern times— he operated across the street from the capitol at the Senator Hotel, a Sacramento landmark with a pillared foyer and terrazzo marble floor modeled after the sixteenth-century Farnese Palace in Rome. The Brewers Institute paid his $3,000-a-month rent—a sum equivalent to more than $32,000 today. From the Senator Hotel, Samish directed his well-paid lobbying staff and more than two dozen informants— whom he called "my Gestapo"—taking astonishing advantage of an era when lax laws enabled lobbyists and their employers to spend unlimited cash to elect favored candidates or defeat those who dared to cross them. Samish never went to the capitol himself. Lawmakers came to *him*—to sample his well-stocked bar and sumptuous buffets.

He boasted that he kept a black book with information on every politician in the state and knew instantly if a legislator wanted "a baked potato, a girl, or money."[5]

Humility was a stranger to Samish. In his 1974 autobiography, he bragged that he elected legislators who were agreeable to his clients and unelected those who didn't toe the line. Once, in 1934, he engineered the election of a transient to the state assembly to replace three-term Republican Clair Woolwine, who represented skid row and other portions of downtown Los Angeles. Woolwine, who had upset one of Samish's clients, was considered unbeatable, regularly winning both the Democratic and Republican nominations in those days of cross-filing. But the client wanted to throw a scare into him. So Samish sent assistant Bill Jasper into the downtown Los Angeles headquarters of gubernatorial candidate Upton Sinclair. He found several dozen campaign workers—rounded up at soup kitchens and flophouses—tying bundles of literature and stuffing envelopes for fifty cents a day. "Any of you fellows from the Forty-fourth District?" Jasper called out. A tattered, unshaven fifty-year-old transient named John Pelletier raised his hand. Pelletier, a college graduate, was down on his luck, living on $12-a-month relief and what little he could make doing odd jobs. "How'd you like to run for the state legislature?" Jasper asked.

Pelletier, according to one account, "was skinny as a rail and his bad teeth made his jaw upswept like a ski jump." Samish cleaned up Pelletier, bought him two suits for $25 at a downtown tailor shop, and filed his papers for the Democratic primary, listing his occupation as "researcher." Samish had 100,000 cards printed with a twenty-five-year-old photo of Pelletier superimposed over a picture of the state capitol. Remarkably, Pelletier won the Democratic primary and went on to defeat Woolwine by 1,000 votes. Pelletier served six terms in the legislature before dying in office.[6]

Samish derived his influence from the huge bankrolls his clients provided him and his own strategic brilliance in devising ways to help those clients. His biggest employer, the Brewers Institute, raised $1 million by charging beer makers a nickel a barrel for six years. In typical fashion, Samish used the money to elect and entertain friendly legislators, and to defeat those who voted against the brewers.[7] Another client, whiskey manufacturer Schenley Industries, hired Samish to undermine its major competitor, Hiram Walker, whose Ten High bourbon was the best-selling whiskey in the state. When Samish learned Ten High was aged three years, he successfully pushed a bill requiring all whiskey sold in California to be aged four years or more. Governor Culbert Olson vetoed the Samish bill, but a pliant legislature overrode the veto and ran Ten High out of California.[8]

The Sacramento County Grand Jury investigated Samish in 1937 but returned no indictments. Twelve years later, Samish's inexhaustible hubris brought about his own downfall. The uber-lobbyist agreed to be featured in *Collier's* magazine. Samish posed for a photograph with a ventriloquist's dummy on his knee, referring to it as "Mr. Legislator." Writer Lester Velie quoted Governor Earl Warren, who first met Samish when Warren was a clerk for the Assembly Judiciary Committee in 1919, as saying, "On matters that affect his clients, Artie unquestionably has more power than the governor."[9] Samish later conceded that the *Collier's* exposé of 1949 was the beginning of the end of his political power. "You never saw such a whoop-de-do as followed those articles in *Collier's,*" Samish said. "I felt sorry for Earl Warren. He had taken a great deal of abuse."[10]

California's most famous and powerful lobbyist immediately had become a pariah. Embarrassed legislators who once did Samish's bidding launched an investigation of his activities and threatened to revoke his credentials as a lobbyist. Less than a week after the *Collier's* revelations hit the newsstands, lawmakers paused from flogging Samish and brazenly placed a measure on the special election ballot to triple their salaries, from $100 to $300. The official voter guide listed only one argument in opposition—from an assemblyman who insisted the salary increase wasn't high enough. Voters approved the pay hike.

Four months after the Samish scandal broke, a chastened Governor Warren—who the previous year had been the Republican nominee for vice president—convened a special session of the legislature to consider pension financing, school aid, and stringent regulations for the legislature's four hundred special-interest lobbyists (who outnumbered legislators more than three to one). Warren prepared a lobbyist control bill that "no honest man need fear"[11] and pressed for enactment by the end of the year. Opponents, like Senator Bradford Crittenden of San Joaquin County, complained the Warren-backed bill was "based upon the theory [that] members of the Legislature are a bunch of crooks or easily made crooks." The president of the Associated Farmers of California said a lobbyist wouldn't be able to give a legislator a cigar without accounting for it.[12] The legislature defeated Warren's bill but approved three weaker measures. Lawmakers also voted to ban Samish and his employees from ever lobbying the legislature again. Samish's boastings, the resolution said, "cast a slur and a shadow on the reputation and integrity of every member of the legislature."[13] Warren signed the legislation, calling it "half a loaf." The new law required lobbyists to register, disclose their employers, and list their receipts and expenditures with the legislature; however, in the ensuing quarter century, penalties for breaking the law were seldom if ever enforced.[14] After his conviction in 1953 for income-tax evasion, Samish spent twenty-six months in Washington's McNeil Island prison. He had to pay nearly a million dollars in back taxes on the slush funds he had built and managed.[15]

It didn't take long after Samish's exile for the lobbying corps, known as the Third House, to regain its swagger inside the capitol. Samish's former liquor clients were represented by a new breed of power brokers, including former assemblyman and superior court judge James Garibaldi, who lobbied for the liquor industry, horse racing, and other interests. The weak laws of 1949 were no match for Third House inventiveness. Lobbyists freely—and legally—plied legislators with cash, televisions, office refrigerators, free meals, and train trips to Nevada casinos. They filed reports that left more darkness than sunshine. "I had to report what I spent on a monthly basis...where I spent it, and how much," recalled Richard Ratcliff, who lobbied for Pacific Gas and Electric, Southern California Edison, and various irrigation districts in the early 1960s. "I didn't have to report on whom I spent it."[16]

Garibaldi soon became the senate's most influential lobbyist. Some legislators were free to sign Garibaldi's name to a bar tab even in his absence, and Garibaldi would automatically pay. Jerry Zanelli, then a top staffer for Hollywood senator David Roberti, recalled frequent trips in the early 1970s to a legendary watering hole a few blocks from the capitol. "You go to Frank Fat's and even a staff person would sign somebody's name. I would sign 'Judge Garibaldi.' He never knew."[17] Beer industry lobbyist Dan Creedon rented the entire top floor at the El Mirador Hotel, across the street from the capitol, which years later became a residential care facility. He left it open on Monday nights for a card game among select legislators, with an open bar. Wing Fat, owner-manager of Frank Fat's, would stop by at 11:00 p.m. with leftover food for the players. At times, the poker game would go all night even though many of the players had 8:00 a.m. committee meetings the next day. "We would wash, shower, order breakfast, sign the lobbyist's name, and go straight to the Ways and Means Committee on Tuesday mornings, without sleep,"[18] remembered William Bagley, who served in the assembly between 1961 and 1974. Assemblyman Willie Brown was one of the regular poker players. When he became chairman of the Ways and Means Committee and had to deal with exhausted, hungover committee members, he simply changed the hearings from Tuesdays to Wednesdays.

It was like a fraternity party. Assembly speaker Jesse Unruh once tried to sugarcoat the mayhem even as he acknowledged it: "If you can't eat their food, drink their booze, screw their women and then vote against them, you have no business being up here."[19] Lobbyists provided plenty of all three, although stories of the first two are more commonly circulated. On Thursdays, for instance, power and oil companies sponsored a bipartisan buffet called Moose Milk at the El Mirador; on Tuesdays, selected lawmakers enjoyed a free lunch at the Derby Club at Posey's restaurant. Bob Beverly, representing part of coastal Southern California in the assembly at that time, said he and other members of the Finance and Insurance Committee enjoyed a regular dinner hosted by banking, savings and loan, and insurance lobbyists the night before

'I don't want to read about any of you girls getting caught with a state legislator; this is a respectable house!'

committee meetings. They'd socialize at night and hash out legislation by day. Often, when legislators arranged their own lunches, they'd direct staff to round up a few lobbyists to pay the tab.

Since the reforms of Hiram Johnson and the Progressives, it had been illegal for the railroad to offer free passes to state elected officials. Lobbyists circumvented that law by purchasing round-trip tickets for them from Sacramento to Reno. Southern Pacific would hook up a private car on the back of a Chicago-bound train that left Sacramento at the end of the work day, and the railroad itself provided free steak dinners as the luxurious coach traversed the Sierra Nevada. Revelers would get off the train in mid-evening, gamble for about six hours in Reno, and take the westbound train back to Sacramento, often arriving around 9:00 a.m., just in time for the legislative session.[20]

During the 1950s and 1960s, some legislators, particularly those whose only official income was their $500 monthly salary, devised innovative ways to pad their incomes. Lobbyists often contributed hundreds of dollars to the campaigns of friendly incumbents—even if they were unopposed. Since it was not illegal for lawmakers to pocket excess campaign funds, some reelection years dramatically boosted a legislator's take-home pay. San Francisco Democrat John Burton, whose lengthy legislative career began with his election to the assembly in 1964, said the lobbyist-legislator relationship was an important informal custom. "You had cashier checks [from lobbyists] made out to 'bearer.' People could put it in their pocket or their campaign." Even key legislative staff members received lobbyist largesse. "I was stunned," Burton recalled. "Staff guys here had lobbyists buy their clothes."[21]

It was only a matter of time before an ambitious politician would seize on the freewheeling legislator-lobbyist culture as a potent campaign issue. In 1970, a year after being elected to the Los Angeles junior college school board, Edmund G. "Jerry" Brown, Jr., built a campaign for secretary of state around bringing special-interest politics and the cozy relationship between lobbyists and legislators under control. Since statehood, the office had been a sleepy backwater bureaucracy that rarely caused a ripple of public attention. Its early duties included maintaining state records and providing legislators with ink and stationery. In time, the office grew to oversee California elections, maintain state records and business filings, and commission notaries public. The post had become a family dynasty for Republicans Frank C. Jordan and his son, Frank M., who had served as secretaries of state for fifty-five of the previous fifty-nine years. Four weeks after Brown announced his candidacy, the younger Jordan died, leaving the post without an incumbent for the fall election.

Brown had two major advantages over possible challengers: his famous name and his father's rolodex. Jerry Brown was running for statewide election only four years after his father, Edmund G. "Pat" Brown, had lost his campaign for a third gubernatorial term to Ronald Reagan. In the LA junior college board campaign, the younger Brown had finished first among 133 candidates—receiving more votes citywide than the mayor. "I'm not fat-headed when I say he got them [votes] on my name," said Pat Brown years later.[22] In the Democratic primary for secretary of state, Brown faced Hugh Burns, the former senate president pro tem who had lost his twelve-year leadership post when Republicans took control of the senate in 1969. Burns had a mixed record of cooperation with Jerry's father when Pat Brown was governor, but he did coauthor and help muscle through the senior Brown's signature initiative, authorizing the California Water Project to transfer plentiful northern water to the arid south. In a letter to supporters and friends, Pat Brown referred to his son as "Ed" and asked for contributions to his statewide campaign: "Ed has an excellent chance to be elected, but he urgently needs your financial assistance." Former presidential peace candidate Eugene McCarthy, who benefited from Jerry Brown's service during the latter's tenure as McCarthy's Southern California vice chairman and treasurer in 1968, also sent out a fundraising letter on behalf of Brown.[23]

A full-page campaign piece, "Let's Take the Price Tag Off Public Office," announced Brown's agenda. Pictured in shirtsleeves, tie loosened, collar unbuttoned, the youthful Brown made the case for turning a quiet state bureaucracy into a headline-making office of election and lobbyist reform. Most candidates, Brown said, "are forced to accept money from paid lobbyists and special-interest groups. I believe this is inherently corrupting. This tragic situation must be changed. And the secretary of state—as California's chief elections officer—should play the central role in election reform."[24] Brown outspent Burns twenty-four to one and easily captured the Democratic nomination. In November, he became the only Democrat to win a partisan statewide election.

In the same November 1970 election, voters turned down a "Clean Air Amendment," placed on the ballot by the legislature as Proposition 18, to divert gas taxes from roads to anti-pollution programs, including local transit projects. Proponents had cobbled together $15,275 for the entire campaign and were outspent twenty-two to one by "Californians Against Street and Road Tax Trap," which was aided by four large, anonymous donations. "No one slips $95,000 under the door in a plain brown envelope," griped Proposition 18's author, San Diego senator James Mills. When it was revealed that Mobil Oil made one of those donations—a $30,000 contribution—Jerry Brown pounced. Although he had yet to be sworn into office, Brown accused the opponents of Proposition 18 of violating the state elections code. Contending it was "naïve to think tougher laws will make any difference,"[25] he simply called for tougher enforcement of those already on the books.

Shortly after taking office, Brown put his rhetoric into practice. He notified 134 candidates for state and local office in 1970 that they had failed to file detailed campaign disclosure reports and threatened not to certify the winners' elections unless the proper paperwork was filed. When eight candidates ignored the warning, he filed lawsuits. He sued oil companies for campaign violations and testified before a US House of Representatives subcommittee looking into the high cost of running for office. Later, he filed suit to strip the notary license of President Nixon's tax attorney. Along the way he became a media sensation, churning out press releases, generating attention, and capturing headlines with every lawsuit.

Brown had assembled a savvy cadre of young advisers. News pros Tom Quinn and Llewellyn Werner saw to it that Brown regularly remained in the headlines. Former Rand Corporation analyst Richard Maullin gauged public opinion and drafted strategy. Dan Lowenstein, a young staff attorney at California Rural Legal Assistance, joined Brown's team in 1971, specializing in election law and becoming chief deputy secretary of state. Midway through Brown's term, another lawyer, Robert Stern, joined the team after a brief stint staffing the assembly's committee overseeing elections. Together, they charted a new course of electoral and lobbying reform for California.

From the beginning, Brown was a young man in a hurry, seeing this post as a stepping-stone to higher office. Stern recalled his first meeting with Brown, ironically at Posey's Cottage, a lobbyist hangout one block from the capitol. "Jerry wanted to be governor," Stern said. "He told me, 'I need a platform.'"[26] As secretary of state, Brown had been helpful to the environmental coalition, sponsoring a landmark coastal protection initiative by publicizing special-interest donations to the opposition, but another issue—Watergate—with its tale of slush funds and cover-ups, was starting to attract national attention and public disgust. Brown had already sued major corporate campaign contributors and compelled candidates to comply with disclosure laws.

He told Stern to draft tough reform legislation, calculating that it never would pass a legislature that wanted few changes in the status quo. Brown wanted to make the legislature's obstinance the centerpiece of his campaign, but his plan almost backfired. Thanks in large part to the Watergate scandal, separate pieces of reform legislation were, in fact, being dislodged from the legislature and sent to Governor Reagan for his signature. Then, at 2:00 a.m. on the last night of the 1973 session, the senate killed Assemblyman Meade's strict lobbyist reform measure, handing Brown the issue he coveted.

Brown's political ambitions coincided perfectly with the fusing of the public-interest group Common Cause and People's Lobby, whose specialty was circulating petitions to qualify measures for the ballot. The pair had won a stunning victory in Washington state the year before with voter approval of a political reform initiative and decided to go after the big prize: California. They knew they couldn't rely on the legislature to pass a comprehensive reform package, so they wrote their own far-reaching initiative, which became Proposition 9 on the June 1974 ballot. Common Cause had more than 300,000 members nationwide and a $5 million annual budget. People's Lobby basically was a two-person operation—former used car salesman Ed Koupal and his wife, Joyce. In 1967 the pair had brashly tried to recall Governor Reagan. Their formula was simple: set up a table with a sign on the front that says, in big, bold letters "SIGN HERE." "Hell no, people don't ask to read the petition and we certainly don't offer," said Ed Koupal. "Why try to educate the world when you're trying to get signatures?"[27] If a table failed to get eighty signatures an hour, they'd move it to another location the following day.

The two groups had stylistic differences and a rocky relationship during the drafting of the initiative, both sides constantly arguing over provisions and fighting for control. At first they excluded Jerry Brown, because they were suspicious of his motives. Eventually, Brown and his staff played a key role in healing the rift between the two organizations, and they formed a triumvirate to move the proposal forward. Stern, who later became general counsel for the Fair Political Practices Commission, said Brown was thoroughly engaged in the Proposition 9 process that created the FPPC. Later, during his first stint as governor,

Brown would accrue a reputation as someone who flitted from issue to issue and was distracted by the plague of "Potomac fever," as he twice unsuccessfully sought the presidency; by contrast, Stern said, as secretary of state Brown read every one of the 18,000 or so words in the complex document, even offering input on punctuation.

The original draft of the proposition, finalized in June 1973, included campaign disclosure, lobbying reform, and conflict-of-interest requirements for state officials and top staff. A powerful new Fair Political Practices Commission would enforce the law and have authority to fine lawbreakers. Whether or not to include campaign spending limits became a major point of contention. People's Lobby pushed hard for them; Common Cause argued against them unless public financing of campaigns and contribution limits were included. Common Cause prevailed until Brown threw everyone a curve ball that threatened to unravel the deal only days before the coalition's final wrap-up meeting. Brown told Lowenstein and Stern he wanted spending limits written into the ballot measure to help his still-unannounced gubernatorial campaign. Brown said he had done some "hard thinking" about campaign budgets; lacking labor support and knowing he was likely to face a formidable array of opponents for the Democratic nomination, Brown worried about fundraising. He told Lowenstein that he thought he could raise enough money to "get me through the primary" but "what am I going to do for the general [election]? This experience has made me believe that we have got to limit spending. Because without the limit on spending, I have the pressure to raise more."[28] The coalition partners acceded. The final version of the initiative included spending limits for statewide candidates and ballot measures, and Brown had a golden set of Watergate-era campaign and lobbyist reforms to frame his run for governor.

THE ELECTION

Placing the reform initiative on the June 1974 primary ballot was not difficult. The legislature's attempts to undercut the measure had been blatantly disingenuous. Together, People's Lobby and Common Cause collected more than a half-million signatures, easily overshooting the 330,000 valid signatures required for qualification. Meanwhile, Watergate was in the headlines every day as the burgeoning scandal brought down the powerful in both Washington, DC, and California and propelled voter support for a citizens' measure that promised to clean up politics. By early March, Nixon's White House was coming apart at the seams. Vice President Spiro Agnew, the president's attack dog against liberals, the media, and antiwar demonstrators, had resigned after being accused of accepting bribes while serving as Baltimore County Executive, as governor of Maryland, and as vice president of the United States; President Nixon's personal counsel had pleaded guilty to charges of illegal campaign activities; the president had fired special prosecutor Archibald Cox; and seven of Nixon's top former aides and confidants, including former attorney general John Mitchell and chief of staff H. R. Haldeman, had been indicted.

Of particular consequence was the fact that there was a clear connection between Watergate and California, a link that ensured inordinate local news attention on the scandal, which itself further fed voter distrust in political institutions as a whole. Many of those involved in the scandal—from President Nixon himself to various administration officials—were Californians, and two months before the primary election, Republican lieutenant governor Ed Reinecke, vying to succeed Reagan as governor, was also indicted by the Watergate grand jury on three counts of lying to the Senate Judiciary Committee about financial arrangements for the 1972 Republican National Convention. Over a two-day period, the *New York Times* reported, "Reinecke was questioned for 10 hours," at times tied to a lie detector.[29]

Throughout the campaign, reform advocates had the wind of Watergate at their backs, the ire of a fed-up electorate on their side, and the support of the biggest name in the crowded Democratic state primary—who was staking his campaign on thwarting corruption at the California capitol. "We never learn which public officials are being wined and dined, which are taken on junkets, which are given expensive gifts," Jerry Brown exhorted.[30] In politics, there is no substitute for good timing. When reformers started drafting Proposition 9, they had no idea Watergate would mushroom into a national calamity, but they were lucky it did. Taking full advantage of the daily headlines, proponents insisted that wealthy special interests were dominating and corroding California politics and that a watchdog commission might prevent a future Watergate-type scandal from occurring in the state. A Common Cause memorandum argued that California law regulating lobbyists was vague and mostly ignored—not only by lobbyists but also those expected to enforce it. "The average citizen can only guess to whom his legislator is more responsive…to him, or to freewheeling lobbyists in Sacramento."[31]

Organized labor opposed the initiative, as did business groups and, of course, most politicians. Labor officials—concerned they would be disproportionately disadvantaged at the capitol and inhibited from supporting candidates of their choice—raised $115,000 in opposition. The California Taxpayers Association called Proposition 9 a "flagrant intrusion on the right of free speech and petition."[32] In ballot arguments that seemed tone-deaf to public sentiment, Republican state senator Clark Bradley said the reform measure was an unnecessary "over-kill attempt to legislate honesty. Powerful interests do not dominate California elected officials." Bradley suggested that of the 550 registered lobbyists prowling the halls of the capitol, "possibly five or six have to be watched."[33] That argument collided with the public's perception of reality and wasn't helped by newspaper reports indicating that business executives and corporations were dominating the financing of the state's leading candidates for governor.

In desperation, a handful of influential members of the legislature hammered home a new attack line—that Proposition 9 would create a commission of powerful, unelected czars with subpoena powers who would rule California political life. All but invoking George Orwell, senate majority leader George Moscone said the "commission's ability to collect and permanently maintain the names of each private citizen who contributes to each campaign is frightening," while assemblyman Jack Knox insisted this unelected commission would be given "fantastic power to do almost anything."[34] Five days after Knox made that statement, the state's largest newspaper argued in favor of Proposition 9, arguing that enforcement should not be left in the hands of elected officials.[35]

The Third House had to walk a fine line. Many lobbyists considered the measure an unnecessary and insulting intrusion into their business practices, but they feared reaction to a public display of opposition. Proposition 9 would tighten requirements on reporting the amounts they received and spent and the specific legislative decisions they were being paid to influence. It would ban lobbyists from making political contributions or guiding contributions from their clients, and they could only spend $10 a month on legislators for gifts, food, or drink. Throughout the campaign season, the capitol's top lobbyists continued to dole out campaign cash to incumbent legislators who had life-or-death authority over their bills.

Meanwhile, the primary race for governor had attracted eighteen Democrats, many of them politically prominent. The general consensus was that after eight years of Ronald Reagan, and following President Nixon's Watergate implosion, 1974 was shaping up to be a solid Democratic year. Aside from Jerry Brown, major challengers included former assembly speaker Bob Moretti, San Francisco mayor Joseph Alioto, congressman Jerome Waldie, and shipping magnate William Matson Roth. Each had something on his resumé that he hoped would attract votes. Moretti had taken a leadership role against Governor Reagan's unsuccessful property-tax-cut measure on the 1973 ballot, considered unduly drastic at the time; Alioto faced legal issues but had been easily reelected mayor of a major population center; Waldie had been a leading voice for the impeachment of President Nixon; and Roth was fabulously wealthy and would spend $800,000 of his own money in the contest. Skeptics expected Brown to fade once voters realized that it was Jerry, not Pat, who actually was on the ballot.

Brown's sponsorship of Proposition 9 cost him support from the important California Labor Federation, AFL-CIO, but he had a consistent lead in the polls, and Republicans considered him to be the toughest Democrat to beat in the fall. The political reform measure to which Brown was attached also had a lead in the polls.

The daily news reports brimming with the flotsam of Watergate had an interesting effect on the potential electorate. The scandal pulled many voters in different directions. Some became angry at the political process and wanted to make a statement at the ballot box, while others became so disenchanted with politics they didn't want to participate in the process anymore. Television, the public's primary source of news and information since the mid-1960s, contributed to this dichotomy. National news overflowed with Watergate coverage, while local television news departments gave short shrift to politics and politicians. With news ratings at the top of their agendas, many stations were perfectly happy to accept campaign cash for political advertisements even as they were concerned that viewers turned off by politics would be equally turned off by campaign coverage.

As it turned out, both apathy and anger were in play. Overall, turnout of registered voters was the lowest since 1946, but the anti-politician, pro-reform Proposition 9 captured seven of every ten votes. Only about $600,000 was spent by the initiative's supporters. The gubernatorial primary went according to form as well. Brown polled nearly 38 percent of the Democratic vote, double Alioto, his closest rival. Brown's general election campaign against Republican state controller Hugh Flournoy of Claremont, a former college professor, would prove much closer. Flournoy, a quiet, amiable moderate, had more than his share of good fortune during the GOP primary. Two potentially strong candidates — former lieutenant governor and Nixon cabinet member Robert Finch and attorney general Evelle Younger — decided not to run. The favored candidate, lieutenant governor Reinecke, had been badly wounded by his Watergate perjury indictment (later overturned), and although Reinecke remained in the race, Flournoy won by more than a two-to-one margin.

The fall campaign generally was listless. Brown's advisers determined that Californians wanted a noncontroversial governor, so he became a noncontroversial candidate who campaigned cautiously while protecting his big early lead in the polls. In the relatively new age of televised politics, Flournoy wasn't helped by his relaxed style of campaigning. "Sometimes I wish I had an electric prod," one of his aides told *Time* magazine. "Hugh is so good. But he comes on like Sominex."[36] Brown's lead against Flournoy reached its high-water mark during the summer, but it had the consistency of cotton candy. As the campaign progressed, Brown's lead steadily receded. California had elected only two Democratic governors since 1898. Would this scion of a Democratic icon let the governorship slip through his fingers?

As luck would have it, the long shadows of Watergate and Proposition 9 helped rescue the campaign from an embarrassing meltdown. President Nixon resigned in disgrace on August 8, and Flournoy—who opposed Proposition 9 along with much of the political establishment—was forced to spend time separating himself from the national Republican Party. A month later, in what many suspected was a sleazy backroom political deal, President Ford pardoned Nixon for his Watergate crimes, a move that crippled the Republican brand beyond repair. Brown won by fewer than 180,000 votes out of more than six million cast, the closest margin in a gubernatorial election since 1906. After the election, Flournoy said it was Nixon's pardon that had sealed his fate.

THE IMPACT

The new governor rejected the trappings of political opulence and turned his back on the perquisites of office. He scrapped Ronald Reagan's limousine in favor of a year-old light blue Plymouth that got better mileage and emitted fewer pollutants; more than any other symbolic gesture, showing up for events in a pedestrian used car made this son of a former governor look like a populist. Brown also ended the lease on Reagan's private jet and instead traveled by commercial air. He rejected the new $1.3 million suburban governor's mansion—a pet project of his predecessor—calling it a "Taj Mahal" and bunked down in a sparse $250-a-month state-owned apartment across the street from the capitol. Brown's criticism of the legislature and advocacy for Proposition 9 did not go unnoticed by lawmakers, prompting senate leader James Mills to comment, "When he became governor, the legislature had no use for him."[37]

Brown had taken his oath of office on January 6, 1975, as California faced rising unemployment and dwindling budget resources. He delivered an eight-minute inaugural address devoid of rhetorical flourishes or big plans. Noting that fewer than half of California's eligible voters cast ballots, Brown suggested this "vote of no confidence" could be addressed by following both the spirit and the letter of the new Political Reform Act. Under normal circumstances, the act would have taken effect on the day after voter approval. In a bit of sleight-of-hand, the initiative authors purposely set an implementation date of January 7—the day after Proposition 9 opponent Reagan left office. "We wrote it so Ronald Reagan couldn't make appointments to the FPPC," Stern said. "Even if Brown didn't win, we didn't want Reagan making the appointments."[38] On inauguration night, the bachelor governor eschewed the traditional gala ball, freeing some capitol habitués to enjoy one last supper at lobbyists' expense before the new reform law took effect. Senate staffer Jerry Zanelli went to one of Sacramento's fanciest restaurants with lobbyist Les Cohen. "I haven't had a $400 dinner since."[39]

California now had the toughest law in the nation for shedding light on the political process. For the first time, detailed records of campaign contributions and spending were available to the public. Ties between official votes and special-interest generosity—or, at least any appearances of a link—were there for all to see. A month after the new law took effect, the fledgling Fair Political Practices Commission held a school for lobbyists. Stern, the new commission's general counsel, walked them through the complexities. The $10-per-month gift ceiling particularly rankled. "I felt as though I had been reduced to second-class citizenship," mused Bank of America lobbyist Halden Broaders years later. "To believe that anybody's threshold of corruptibility could be as low as ten dollars...was quite an insult."[40] For Richard Ratcliff, the sting was more personal. "The characterization of lobbyists... was that we...would lie, cheat and steal. My mother had just gone into a home up in Redding and invited me to talk about lobbying, but she couldn't bring herself to call me a lobbyist. I was 'an attorney' with the legislature."[41]

Soon after the PRA passed, 136 lobbyists—nearly one-fifth of the lobbying corps—terminated their registrations.[42] Many were fearful of the hold the new enforcement commission had over their livelihoods. Lobbyist Ratcliff remembered working late with a top Brown administration official and then going to dinner afterward. They agreed to separate tabs, given the $10 monthly limit on gifts from lobbyists to legislators. "Well, he had too many drinks and went around socializing with his buddies and buying them drinks, putting them on my tab. Then he decided to leave and I was left with the tab. I didn't know what the hell to do."[43] Ratcliff paid the bill but sought guidance from the FPPC, which told him to send a bill to the government official for his share. Panicked calls to the commission for advice on the fly were not unusual.

The Political Reform Act endured numerous legal challenges. The Institute of Governmental Advocates, comprised of thirty-five lobbyists, challenged the new law—the centerpiece of Jerry Brown's campaign for governor—on the grounds it violated US constitutional guarantees of free speech and the right to petition government. Its selection of legal representation was not without irony, as it hired the high-powered Beverly Hills law firm of Ball, Hunt, Hart, Brown, and Baerwitz. The "Brown" of that team was former governor Pat Brown, a partner in the firm since shortly after his defeat for reelection in 1966. While the $10 limit on lobbyist spending was upheld, the elder Brown's law firm succeeded in getting struck down the ban on lobbyists making direct campaign contributions to candidates or arranging contributions from their clients. (Twenty-two years later, voters reinstated a direct ban on lobbyists' contributions with Proposition 208.) Given that the US Supreme Court had found federal campaign-spending limits unconstitutional unless accompanied by public financing, Proposition 9's spending limits also were struck down by California courts.[44]

Many veteran legislators disliked the new environment. They had thrived during the freewheeling pre–Proposition 9 days and resented the dismantling of many longstanding social institutions that had transcended politics and legislation. "Once I went to the senate Democratic caucus to brief them on the new law," Stern said. "[Senator] Dan Boatwright grabbed me by the neck, and he said, 'What are you doing to us?'"[45] Critics suggested that honest citizens, successful at business or other endeavors, would refuse to run for political office because they wouldn't want to comply with the law's strict conflict-of-interest provisions. In the ensuing four years, legislators would tweak regulations implementing the PRA more than one hundred times—establishing random auditing, reducing by half the number of audits of campaign committees and lobbyists, and raising the level of compulsory reporting of contributions and campaign expenditures.

Lobbyists and legislators soon realized they could take advantage of new disclosures on where—and how much—money was flowing at the capitol. Lobbyists could look up what their competitors were spending and get their employers and political action committees to up the ante, if necessary. Legislators were able to compare special-interest giving, too. Senator Paul Carpenter, it was said, often greeted visiting lobbyists by showing them a spreadsheet of campaign contributions on his desk computer. Turning the screen in the direction of a lobbyist, he'd note, "I don't see your clients on the screen."[46] The point was hard to miss. If lobbyists were reputed to have made a habit of stuffing envelopes of cash into the pockets of lawmakers, the reverse in many cases also was true; some legislators had their hands out to squeeze extra dollars from special interests that wanted something from the legislature.

Old habits died hard. One evening after the Political Reform Act took effect, a lobbyist hosted a lavish dinner for legislators and others at Sacramento's venerable Firehouse Restaurant—an elegant refurbished fire station originally built three years after California was granted statehood. It was Sacramento's fanciest restaurant, frequented by Pat Brown and having served as the site of Ronald Reagan's inauguration dinners. Outside the entrance to a separate room, the lobbyist had posted a sign proudly noting that he was hosting the dinner. Stern, the FPPC's chief counsel, happened to be dining at the restaurant that evening, and when he noticed the sign, he notified his staff and initiated proceedings against the lobbyist. Ross Johnson, who represented Orange County in the assembly and senate between 1979 and 2004, recalled how one of his Republican colleagues in the early 1980s would walk into Frank Fat's and brazenly admit, "I'm trolling for dinner." The lawmaker would stroll up and down the bar and restaurant booths until he found a willing lobbyist to pay for his meal.[47] Hedy Govenar, who for many years ran one of the capitol's largest and most successful lobbying firms, was a new and relatively unknown lobbyist in 1981. While at a downtown restaurant with a client, she noticed a large group of legislators seated at a long table. "One of them came over and said, 'Hedy, I would like you to pick up the dinner tab.' I didn't know what to do. I knew what the law was. I knew I couldn't do it. The client is frozen. I'm frozen. And right then another legislator from the table walked over, put his arm around me and said, 'Don't worry about it. I'm going to get it.'"[48]

The atmosphere for female legislators, lobbyists, and even journalists at the capitol was in transition in the early 1970s as societal changes and the national feminist movement drew considerable public focus on workplace inequality and salary inequity. Female lobbyists slowly increased their numbers and influence, morphing from trainees for big-time male lobbyists—or perhaps working as low-paid advocates on so-called female issues, such as education and health—to representing top, monied business clients and owning their own lobbying firms. Previously, members of the overwhelmingly male legislature and lobbying corps ate, drank, played, and developed public policy together, but many women saw Proposition 9 as a catalyst that—at least partly—helped create new opportunities for those once left out of the all-night poker parties or banned from the male-only private dining rooms. "Women wanted to get into politics because of the perception that now is the time to do it, because the old guy's network was falling apart," Govenar said.[49]

By the mid-1980s, the corps of female lobbyists had tripled. A few dozen of the most powerful, calling themselves "Women in Advocacy," met for monthly luncheons while the legislature was in session. Their meetings attracted female legislators, but no men were allowed—except for the waiters. Many of the participants earned six-figure incomes, had blue-chip client lists, and told stories of having to fend off the sexual advances of male legislators.[50] A few others openly pursued personal relationships with lawmakers. "I was friends with some who became quite successful in the business because of their involvements with powerful legislators," Govenar said. "When I came up here, a really smart man said to me, 'You are going to make a decision right away, because if you sleep with one, you will have to sleep with them all, because they talk.'"[51]

The new paradigm proved to be a boon to political law firms, which catered to big corporations, lobbyists, and politicians who needed help navigating the maze of new finance regulations. Guiding clients through the Political Reform Act maze was one part of their mission; finding loopholes to circumvent it was another. The PRA, for instance, banned direct payments from lobbyists to legislators but not payments from their clients. Before long, corporations, unions, and associations were shelling out lavish sums to gain "access" to key lawmakers. Now, lobbyist-supplied lunches and dinners were replaced by high-dollar client-sponsored events. "You can't buy someone a hamburger that costs over ten bucks, but you can take them on a junket to Asia," former senator John Burton complained.[52] In a not uncommon example of capitol activity, the Western States Petroleum Association in 2013 spent more than $4.6 million to influence legislation through lobbying and other activities. Two days before a high-stakes assembly floor vote on a bill to increase regulatory oversight on hydraulic fracturing—or fracking—the association spent thousands of dollars hosting a dinner for twelve legislators and two high-ranking legislative staff members at one of Sacramento's most expensive restaurants.[53] Lawmakers amended the bill to favor the oil industry, which caused many environmental groups to withdraw their support. If clients chose to pay enough to play, their lobbyists could enjoy privileged access to lawmakers at fundraisers just about any morning, noon, or evening the legislature was in session, as well as at luxury events, such as golf tournaments that could cost attendees $5,000 or more.

Critics—often former legislators who fondly recall the days before reform—contend today's partisan gridlock at the capitol is at least partly the result of Proposition 9. William Bagley, who served in the assembly before the PRA, suggested "free meals and a few goodies" fostered collegiality and a more workable legislative process because "we knew each other, learned to trust those who were worthy, and we governed through civility, camaraderie, and concern. There were no partisan aisles. Everybody knew the limited amount that was always forthcoming [from lobbyists]. Nobody had to call every lobbyist under the sun to raise a few bucks."[54] The Moose Milk lunches at the El Mirador faded away after Proposition 9. The California Derby Club, Sacramento's premier symbol of the lobbyist-legislator connection since the early Pat Brown era, continued until 1997 at Posey's, but to make the $10-a-month math work, the list of legislative attendees had to be trimmed at such gatherings so that lobbyists outnumbered lawmakers.

Whatever its promise or potential, the Political Reform Act alone could not end corruption at the capitol. Indeed, various federal and state investigations between the mid-1980s and 2014 led to indictments of nine sitting or former lawmakers. In addition, capitol staffers, a prominent lobbyist, a coastal commissioner, and others have gone to prison. A quarter century after its enactment, the legislature created a bipartisan commission to conduct a comprehensive review of the PRA. It solicited comments at fourteen public meetings, and the Institute of Governmental Studies at UC Berkeley conducted focus groups of the regulated community. Not surprisingly, those required to play by the new ground rules characterized the law as "overly complex and unduly burdensome." They made thirty-five recommendations to the legislature, many of which would have weakened disclosure requirements for political committees and public officials.[55] Only a small handful became law as legislators realized that any significant changes to the Political Reform Act would result in negative publicity and heightened public scrutiny.

Viewed through the prism of history more than four decades after its passage, there is no question that Proposition 9 was a watershed political event that—for the first time—gave Californians a detailed look at how state campaigns are funded. It wasn't the nation's first reform effort, but it was the most comprehensive. The Political Reform Act combined several ethics and disclosure elements into a single package covering election campaigns, lobby-ists, and the behavior of public officials. It opened a window, how-ever narrowly, to peek at the relationships between legislators and those who seek to influence them, and it enabled sanctions against those who refused to let in the government sunshine. California's experience shows that political reform is necessarily an ongoing, incremental process. Over the years, voters and occasionally the legislature itself have expanded Proposition 9's political reform legacy no fewer than nine times. Campaign reports, which used to be sporadic and of little use until *after* an election, are now more plentiful, and disclosures of large contributions and spending by independent campaign committees must be filed daily leading up to Election Day. These reports can be accessed online twenty-four hours a day. Journalists and voters can monitor how much money lobbyists are receiving from their clients and what legislation they are trying to influence.

Since 1974, hundreds of elected officials have been cited and fined by the FPPC for violating rules designed to keep the politi-cal process honest. This in turn provides grist to voters and oppo-nents at the next elections, and more than one politician has paid a high price for previous misdeeds. In 2008, state senator Carole Migden agreed to pay $350,000 in fines after the commission cited her for eighty-nine violations of reporting laws. She lost her next election. Insurance commissioner Chuck Quackenbush resigned in 2000 amid allegations of campaign-finance violations associated with insurance settlements after the 1994 Northridge earthquake. Such high-profile cases have likely served to keep other politicians in line.

Legislatures rarely reform themselves unless jolted by scan-dals and public pressure. The citizen-driven Political Reform Act was the most far-reaching of its kind in the nation, what journalist William Endicott called "a post-Watergate purging of the California political conscience" that became a model for others that followed.[56] Walter Zelman, a post–Proposition 9 director of California Common Cause, acknowledges the law did not inhibit "people's preparedness to give" to politicians, a point ratified by the extraordinary sums since spent on California campaigns. Instead, reformers Lowenstein, Stern, Zelman, and others believe the measure's greatest impact has been on the legislative process. "We have killed many pieces of bad legislation," Zelman says, "by being able to demonstrate who was behind that legislation, who was the sponsor of the legislation, and how much money they have given to key legislators."[57]

It remains indisputable that election reform advocacy and Proposition 9 helped launch Jerry Brown's record-setting career in public office. Ironically, as Brown prepared to embark on his quest for a historic fourth term as governor in 2014, FBI agents three floors above the governor's suite were raiding the capitol offices of a state senator running for California secretary of state who stood accused of attempting to trade political favors for campaign cash. Two other senators already were in trouble with the law, evidence that the cycle was continuing as usual. Brown, however, would stun the reform community six months later by vetoing several ethics bills dealing with gift giving, campaign spending, and public disclosure that a chastened legislature had approved in response to the scandal. The governor called the bills unnecessary regulation. Robert Stern, who more than forty years earlier had fulfilled Brown's mandate to craft tough reform legislation, felt "particularly disappointed." The once innovative and persistent reformer, he said, had "become the roadblock to meaningful reforms"[58] and was as unpredictable as ever.

10

1978
Proposition 13 Launches
a National Tax Revolt

"Death and taxes are inevitable. But being
taxed to death is not inevitable."
—Howard Jarvis, antitax activist

PETER BEHR GOT to know Howard Jarvis pretty well during the spring of 1978. The two political adversaries made for an odd couple as they traversed the state debating each other on the merits of Jarvis's proposed landmark property tax cut, Proposition 13. Behr, at sixty-three, was a refined and astute Yale-educated lawyer representing Marin County in the state senate. A liberal Republican, he had been engaged in public service for twenty-five years. Jarvis, a retired businessman who worked for the Los Angeles Apartment Owners Association, was a crusty, blunt-speaking, heavy-set seventy-four-year-old with slicked-back hair who was about to turn state government on its head.

The blustery Jarvis was the loudest voice in support of the contentious ballot proposition that not only would slash property taxes but also would make it more difficult for the legislature and local governments to increase taxes in the future. In describing Jarvis's shabby office at the association, one of his young campaign consultants observed, "He had one drawer that he would spit tobacco juice in and another drawer that he had a bottle of vodka in."[1] Behr, who had authored a legislative alternative to Proposition 13, remembered that Jarvis "wandered around in old shiny clothes. He was trying to sip vodka most of the time I was with him, but I never saw him vaguely drunk." Behr recalled one particularly testy exchange when he accused Jarvis of deliberately wanting to suck billions of dollars out of government. "I said to the audience, 'I don't think anyone who wants to destroy local government can be All-American.' And he rose up and he was as angry as I ever saw him before."[2] Sometimes, assembly speaker Leo McCarthy would join Behr on the campaign trail. McCarthy characterized Jarvis as "a curmudgeon who looked and often acted like a slob."[3] But for all their political and oratorical skills—not to mention their wardrobe advantage— Behr and Democrat McCarthy were no match for Jarvis. "If it was a live audience, they hooted us out of the hall," Behr recalled.[4]

Jarvis knew how to work a crowd. "I play on every emotion I can," he told an interviewer during the campaign's stretch drive. When taking on "dumb" politicians and belittling opponents, he'd often raise his right fist over his head in defiance. The audience would roar its approval. "I'm like a goddamn Baptist preacher. I tell them how government is clobbering them. I rev them up."[5] In a debate at the venerable Commonwealth Club in San Francisco, Behr recalled that Jarvis told jokes "which were pretty crude, and he was willing to say anything, whether it was true or not, that would further his cause."[6]

It was precisely Jarvis's bent on exaggeration that enabled his team to plot a devastating trap in forums along the campaign trail. Bill Butcher and Arnold Forde, two crafty Orange County political consultants, managed the campaign. Their simple strategy was to talk about how taxes—spurred by inflation-driven property reassessments—were forcing elderly Californians out of their homes and how the situation would only get worse if the initiative failed. Early in the campaign, Jarvis would tell audiences that property taxes would increase by 50 percent without Proposition 13. Then, as the campaign progressed, he stretched it to 100 percent. According to Joel Fox, who later would become president of the Howard Jarvis Taxpayers

Association, "Butcher wanted Howard to push the envelope a little bit and say, 'Your taxes are going to triple.' He was waiting for the other side to say, 'No, no, they're not going to triple, they're only going to double.' And then you've got 'em."[7]

Unencumbered by truth, blessed with hidebound opponents in government, and plugged into the electric outrage of millions of property-tax payers, Jarvis and Paul Gann (his Northern California sidekick) thus forged Proposition 13 into a campaign that to this day has defined the term "voter revolt."

THE BACKSTORY

An argument can be made that the greatest tax revolt in modern history owes as much to Russell Wolden as it does to Howard Jarvis and Paul Gann, the famed authors of California's storied Proposition 13. In the mid-1960s, Wolden unwittingly started a chain of events that imposed onerous property tax increases on homeowners—and became a key foundation of voter discontent. Wolden was part of a San Francisco dynasty, of sorts. Either he or his father had been the elected San Francisco County assessor continuously since 1916. In 1965, an accountant gave the *San Francisco Chronicle* file cabinets full of documents—including fee schedules and canceled checks—detailing how businesses had bribed Wolden to reduce their property tax bills by undervaluing their property.[8] The scandal rocked the state and prompted probes of assessors throughout California that exposed further abuses. Many assessors had not only accepted campaign cash from businesses but were found to have kept residential property values artificially low, likely as a way to curry favor with voters. State investigators estimated that California counties were losing hundreds of millions of dollars a year because of undervalued property assessments. In a San Francisco speech, Chief Deputy Attorney General Charles O'Brien declared: "Just try to find out what the assessor is doing. His records are more closely guarded than our atomic secrets. It would take an army of auditors to keep them honest. There just aren't enough cats to catch the mice."[9]

Wolden, described as a "bland and amiable public official,"[10] was the first assessor to stand trial. Known as the "Crooked Assessor," Wolden was convicted on nine counts of bribery and conspiracy after an exhausting sixty-day trial, during which the defendant spent nine days on the witness stand. The assessor in neighboring Alameda County then was convicted on eight bribery counts. A Los Angeles jury acquitted assessor Phillip Watson of bribery, while in San Diego, assessor John McQuilken had likely committed suicide by taking an overdose of barbiturates after an investigation into his office was opened.

Responding to what Attorney General Thomas Lynch hyperbolically called "the largest criminal conspiracy that has ever existed in California,"[11] the legislature stripped county assessors of much of their discretionary powers. Its reforms required all property to be uniformly assessed at 25 percent of market value, with subsequent, periodic reassessments. Wolden, for example, had been keeping homeowners content by requiring them to pay taxes on only 9 percent of their properties' market values, while commercial property—even after bribes—was assessed at 35 percent of market value.[12] Ridding the state of a property tax system ripe for corruption seemed like a prudent reaction to the scandal, but the new law had the effect of lowering taxes on commercial property and raising them for homeowners. Unhappy with the new assessment formula, some San Franciscans sported "Bring Back the Crooked Assessor" bumper stickers on their cars.

During the 1960s, home values had increased by only 2 or 3 percent a year. By the mid-seventies, they were escalating by 2 or 3 percent *each month*. As the economy boomed and inflation reached double digits, property soared in value and homeowners—although wealthier on paper—became frightened and indignant when their assessments kept pace. Compounding the jolt, most reassessments only occurred every three to five years. The cumulative effect of several years of inflation on home values resulted in sticker shock when homeowners opened their new tax bills.

Between 1970 and 1978, twenty separate initiative proposals dealing with property or income taxation failed to secure enough signatures to qualify for the statewide ballot, and those that did qualify were easily defeated. The measures were so complex that most voters had no difficulty finding some provision they didn't like. Phillip Watson, who successfully ran for Los Angeles assessor on the slogan "Stop Unfair Taxation,"[13] tried three times to enact a ceiling on property taxes that would shift most welfare and school spending to the state and increase other taxes to make up for the lost revenue. One proposed initiative failed to qualify, but two efforts, in 1968 and 1972, went before California voters and promptly attracted a Who's Who of opponents, from Governor Ronald Reagan and former governor Pat Brown to the California State Chamber of Commerce, organized labor, the NAACP, and the California Teachers Association. The teachers tried their own tax-shift proposal, but it also went down to defeat.

Sounding themes that would help propel him to the White House seven years later, Reagan advanced his own 5,700-word measure to comprehensively limit taxes in a 1973 special election. On a Bay Area television program less than two weeks before the election, Reagan was asked, "Do you think the average voter really understands the language of this proposition?" Quipped the governor in response, "No. He shouldn't try. I don't either." The Great Communicator, who should have known better, gave his foes a golden opening. In major newspapers throughout the state, opposition ads turned Reagan's comments against him. "When a proposition's chief sponsor doesn't understand it, it's time for the rest of us to vote no on Proposition No. 1."[14] The measure carried Orange County but lost in the urban centers of Los Angeles and San Francisco and was defeated statewide by eight percentage points.

While political insiders consistently failed to deliver meaningful property tax relief, a pair of veteran gadflies—cantankerous Howard Jarvis in Southern California and mild-mannered Paul Gann in Sacramento—joined forces in 1977 to take up the fight. Jarvis was one of those perennial political candidates who seemed to run for something every few years without success— US Senate, mayor of Los Angeles, state Board of Equalization.

After graduating from the University of Utah, Jarvis had borrowed $15,000 and bought a six-page weekly newspaper in his small hometown of Magna, Utah, and eventually owned a chain of eleven newspapers. He worked as a press aide in Herbert Hoover's 1932 presidential reelection campaign, joking that his job was to deflect rotten fruits and vegetables that angry voters hurled at the president. "I'll bet I saved him from getting hit with 500 tomatoes," Jarvis said.[15] Jarvis prospered in business after moving to California, then retired and turned his attention to his own political pursuits. He had failed to qualify property tax cuts four times, falling 400,000 signatures short the first time, 100,000 short the second, 10,000 short the next, and a mere 1,400 signatures short on the last try before Proposition 13.[16]

In Northern California, meanwhile, Gann had come to the tax fight later than Jarvis and was confronting similar disappointment. One of eleven children of an Arkansas minister, Gann learned Bible passages early on and often quoted them during his political campaigns. As a child, Gann's left leg had been crushed in a fall from a horse, and he subsequently contracted osteomyelitis—inflammation of the bone marrow—that caused severe swelling in his left knee and prevented him from walking. At first, his brothers and sisters wheeled him to school in a wagon. Eventually, his mother had to teach him at home.[17] He moved to a Sacramento suburb in 1935, and sold cars and worked in real estate for several years. He started a political advocacy organization in 1974. The following year, Gann tried to qualify a property-tax-cut initiative and found himself competing against Jarvis, who was working on one of his own. After both efforts fell short, Gann said he contacted a vice president with Jarvis's organization and arranged a meeting. The north-south pair teamed up and started collecting signatures for yet another tax-relief measure.

For all its impotence up to that point, the incipient tax revolt didn't go unnoticed at the state capitol. In his 1977 state of the state address, Governor Jerry Brown had declared that dealing with the property tax situation was "number one on the agenda," and politicians of every stripe called for tax reform. But they couldn't reach consensus to garner the necessary two-thirds vote in the legislature. As the legislature procrastinated, the state treasury was accruing an inflation-driven $5 billion surplus, mostly in income-tax revenues, which represented about one-third of the state's entire annual budget. Instead of perceiving the huge surplus as prudent fiscal stewardship, irate taxpayers viewed it as bureaucratic hoarding. Why, they asked, couldn't those billions be returned to the people in the form of tax relief? Many liberals in the legislature preferred to finance tax relief by raising income taxes on the wealthy.

As the months went by and an election year approached, some Republicans calculated that inaction in the Democrat-controlled legislature would work to their party's benefit. Thus, by the time the legislature adjourned on September 15, feuding factions ensured that nothing was accomplished, helping fuel an antigovernment sentiment that became a cornerstone of the Proposition 13 campaign. "And so," Senator Behr observed, "it was like the calico dog and the Cheshire cat who woke up one morning, and they were both dead. They'd eaten each other up."[18]

Two months after the legislature adjourned without addressing the plight of California's homeowners, Jarvis and Gann filed a record 1.2 million signatures with California's secretary of state to qualify an amendment to the California constitution. "It was amazing how rapidly it went," Gann recalled.[19] Their proposal, Proposition 13, would cut $7 billion a year in property taxes but offered no substitute funds for running government. Property assessments would be rolled back to 1975 market values, taxes set at 1 percent of assessments, and future assessment increases limited to 2 percent until the property was sold. And because the legislature would be unable to hike *any* taxes without a two-thirds vote, renters who didn't own property also had a stake in the measure's passage.

Stunned lawmakers returned to Sacramento in January 1978 with an incentive to head off the looming June ballot initiative; if it passed, they would face an immediate crisis in every city, county, and school district, all of which relied on property taxes. State politicians crafted a bipartisan compromise that promised homeowners about half the property tax relief of Proposition 13. It became

Proposition 8 on the same June ballot. "It's the only glimmer of hope left," declared Governor Brown, running for election to a second term that year.[20] With taxpayers fuming, Proposition 13 offered a drastic dose of self-interested relief. The June primary was only three months away, and the rest of the country slowly awoke to a historic showdown between California's political establishment and its angry voters.

THE ELECTION

In the early days of the campaign, the Proposition 13 political team perceived the alternative tax cut emanating from Sacramento as a threat. "We were fearful at first when the Legislature put it on the ballot," said strategist Bill Butcher. "But then we realized it wasn't working. Voters thought it was phony."[21] Early polls in mid-March indicated a tight race. Only about one-third of the electorate favored Proposition 13, but nearly four in ten voters were undecided. On the campaign trail, Howard Jarvis was in his element. He blustered and ranted. He led rallies like revival meetings. He skewered politicians. "It's either them or us, and we're for us," he'd shout.[22] One of the most effective television ads sought to debase the reputations of the politicians who were fighting the initiative. Over photos of resorts and world landmarks, ad copy read, "Each year, California politicians go on expensive junkets all over the world, stay at expensive hotels and hand taxpayers the bill. Your Yes vote on Proposition 13 will force an end to this kind of wasteful government spending."[23]

The opposition did not suffer for a lack of campaign funds. Organized-labor groups, particularly public employees, were strongly opposed to the measure and contributed generously to defeat it. Joining them was the business community, which feared a cut in property taxes would lead to higher offsetting business taxes. Opponents usually acknowledged the tax dilemma facing homeowners but primarily focused on the damage that Proposition 13's $7 billion tax cut would do to the finances of California's local government services. The Los Angeles Board of Education, anticipating substantial budget cuts if Proposition 13 were successful, sent a "Dear Vendor" letter that said the board was considering "adjustments" in purchasing policies and procedures. "It may be necessary," the letter said, "to curtail or even cancel certain existing contracts."[24]

The Proposition 13 team countered with Nobel Prize–winning economist Milton Friedman assuring voters that hyperbolic politicians were making false claims. While in Oakland for a speech, Gann received a phone call from a television reporter who told him there were signs at a local firehouse and library that said, "If you vote Yes on 13 this building will be closed." Gann met up with the reporter and Oakland's city attorney at the library. Turning to the city attorney, Gann said, "I'm gonna sue your tail off and this city's if you *don't* close this building after we've won."[25]

It was a storybook campaign pitting once untouchable institutions against a pair of insurgent iconoclasts supported by legions of fed-up taxpayers. The state's major newspapers acknowledged government was too inefficient but mostly agreed with the political elite that Proposition 13 was too draconian. The *San Diego Union* characterized Proposition 13 as "an unvarnished piece of demagoguery." It suggested the measure represented "the difference between putting a mechanic to work on an engine that's out of tune, and giving a chimpanzee a hammer to beat on it until it falls apart."[26] The *Los Angeles Times* stated its case against Proposition 13 on several occasions, arguing that its passage would close fire stations and libraries and cost 300,000 public jobs, including those of police officers, firefighters, and teachers. Under the headline "Getting the Message," the *Times* wrote that the "only message that Proposition 13 would send to Sacramento would be an SOS."[27]

Curiously, the contrarian *Los Angeles Herald Examiner*, under its liberal editor Jim Bellows, was the only major California newspaper to editorialize in favor of Proposition 13. Decades later, Bellows explained it was strictly business. The paper supported Jarvis "because the monster [*Los Angeles Times*] was against it. And you couldn't mimic the monster. The underdog paper must distinguish itself every way it can."[28] What Jarvis lacked in print support he made up on the broadcast circuit. KABC-TV in Los Angeles featured Jarvis debating an opponent every night for several weeks during the campaign. His bombastic style was good for ratings.

Proposition 13 opponents made critical mistakes, not the least of which was promoting an alternative (Proposition 8) that was overly complex and difficult to understand. Voters were confused by it, and confused voters tend to vote No. Further, the anti–Proposition 13 campaign team didn't talk about taxes, only the specter of devastating budget cuts. Hoping to persuade voters that such predictions were scare tactics, Jarvis released a copy of an apparently private letter that former governor Pat Brown had written suggesting that Communists wanted Proposition 13 to succeed. "If I were a Communist and wanted to destroy this country," Brown opined, "I would support the Jarvis amendment."[29] Still, in late April, a little more than a month before Election Day, public opinion surveys indicated that Proposition 13 might be awaiting the same fate as its failed predecessors. A *Los Angeles Times* poll reported that Proposition 8 held a nine-point advantage over Proposition 13. But change was coming; voters were listening to each other. A month later, the numbers were reversed as Proposition 13 began to surge.[30]

The dramatic about-face—in fact, the turning point in the entire election campaign—had nothing to do with Howard Jarvis, campaign consultants, or newspaper editorials. Ironically, the pivotal event that galvanized support for Proposition 13 was a surprise disclosure from a veteran Democratic activist who was on record opposing the tax-cutting ballot initiative. Alexander Pope had served as legislative secretary during Pat Brown's first term as governor. After stints with the California Highway Commission and the Los Angeles Board of Airport Commissioners, he had been appointed the Los Angeles County assessor by the board of supervisors and oversaw assessments of two million parcels within the county. On the last day of February, and after being on the job only a few weeks, Pope warned that upcoming property assessments—due to be released sometime after July—would increase substantially. Then, in mid-May, Pope surprisingly issued the detailed house-by-house assessment roll. Pope said he released the assessments early to blunt potential criticism that he was hiding them from the public before the primary election. Many homeowners found that their property values had doubled in the previous three years because of soaring inflation. They were considerably wealthier—on paper, at least—but liable for significantly higher taxes. Suddenly, Jarvis's claims didn't seem so outlandish, and the backlash was predictable. "Everything in life is timing, right?" said former Jarvis confidant Joel Fox.[31]

The Proposition 13 campaign team combed through property records and sent letters to homeowners notifying them of how much money they'd save if the ballot measure passed. Los Angeles County supervisor James Hayes, a supporter of Proposition 13, reported that a constituent in Palos Verdes saw her property tax bills increase ten-fold, from $600 to $6,000 in ten years. "She says it is now a question if she and her husband can pay the tax bill."[32] The opposition campaign, taking aim at prospective cuts in government services, simply could not compete against the cold reality of runaway taxes.

Public employees, in particular, faced a Hobson's choice when it came to Proposition 13. In the run-up to the election, opponents argued that $7 billion in tax cuts would force massive public-sector layoffs and cuts in services—to police, fire, parks, and libraries—that millions of Californians relied on. Should they hope the measure passed and risk losing their jobs in the budget-cutting aftermath, or should they hope for its defeat as they continued to struggle to meet their own escalating tax obligations as homeowners? At a campaign appearance in the San Fernando Valley, a middle-aged city surveyor acknowledged that his department would be cut by 30 percent if Proposition 13 passed, but he said he was going to vote for it anyway. "So I'll cut my throat," he said. "I'll get another job, go somewhere else." His home had just been reassessed from $32,000 to $63,000. "They're scaring the people by saying they'll cut back on the fire department and police," his wife said. "I don't believe it."[33]

Jarvis and Gann promised California's middle- and upper-middle classes relief from circumstances over which they seemingly had little control: double-digit inflation and bickering, inattentive lawmakers who lacked credibility and seemed incapable, or unwilling, to lend a hand. In the days leading up to the election, Jerry Brown could sense the direction of the political winds. He muted his criticism of the initiative and its backers. He even paid an unannounced visit to Howard Jarvis at his home in West Los Angeles one morning. Jarvis was home alone in his pajamas and suffering from the flu. Nonetheless, he threw on a robe, invited Brown in, and the two chatted for several hours about the state's budget surplus and property taxes. When Estelle Jarvis returned home, she made them lunch and scolded Jarvis for entertaining California's governor in his robe and bare feet.[34]

Shortly after Brown's visit, Proposition 13 swept to an overwhelming two-to-one victory. The measure carried fifty-five counties, and the legislature's less generous alternative was defeated. At the campaign's victory party at the Biltmore Hotel in Los Angeles, retired schoolteacher Fannie Cain declared: "My neighbors lost their land this year for taxes. We feed foreigners and welfare bums with our tax money and my neighbors, 100 percent Americans, lost their land. Does that make sense?"[35] As it turned out, voters had felt the status quo was more frightening than the consequences of change. "It was a case of anger versus fear[,] and anger prevailed," said Proposition 13 campaign consultant Bill Butcher.[36] Exit polls showed that nearly eight in ten seniors supported the measure, as did homeowners with no public employee in their household. Dazed political leaders had no choice but to start plotting ways to cope with the huge loss of tax revenue.

THE IMPACT

Overnight, Jarvis became a folk hero. He appeared on the cover of *Time* magazine with his right arm outstretched and his fist clenched. He would travel the country giving speeches and even scored a cameo role in the hit movie *Airplane*. Jerry Brown, meanwhile, had done some fancy footwork of his own. Despite his opposition to Proposition 13 during the campaign, Brown quickly embraced the voters' decision. Even as the votes were being counted, he was pledging to "seek a lid on state spending as well as on local spending

'If you liked my Howard Jarvis, you'll
LOVE my Ronald Reagan!'

in the spirit of what the people want. We will have serious and pain-
ful curtailments at every level of government."[37] Brown flipped so
quickly from critic to cheerleader that he earned the nickname "Jerry
Jarvis." It was a far cry from early in the campaign when Brown had
called Proposition 13 a "monster." *Time* magazine noted the change
of heart, observing that "Brown performed a pirouette that would
have dazzled" Russian ballet impresario Sergei Diaghilev.[38]

Republican attorney general Evelle Younger, who won the
GOP gubernatorial primary in June, had told reporters in late April
that after consulting more than one hundred sheriffs, police chiefs,
county counsels, and their deputies, he would vote for Proposition
13 but would not campaign for it. "The result will be traumatic, but
that's what proponents have in mind," Younger said.[39] During the
primary, a rival had characterized Younger as exciting as a "mashed
potato sandwich,"[40] but polls showed Younger with a narrow lead
over Brown five months before their November face-off. After a

bruising primary, the exhausted attorney general and his wife set out for some rest and relaxation in Hawaii while Brown stayed behind to begin implementing Proposition 13. Brown talked like a born-again tax cutter. In a ten-minute address before a packed joint session of the legislature two days after the election, the governor told solemn lawmakers, "Voters have told us they want a tax cut. They don't want a shell game." Standing in the rear of the chambers, Paul Gann basked in his victory. Referring to the governor, Gann said, "I'm happy he no longer thinks we're liars."[41]

By the time Younger returned from Hawaii, Brown had completely morphed into a Proposition 13 champion. His campaign ran radio ads touting the governor's work implementing the tax-cut measure and reminding voters that Younger had worked only on his tan 2,500 miles away. Younger also spent precious campaign time in the hospital for kidney stone surgery. "The next poll that came out had Jerry fifteen or sixteen points ahead of Evelle, and it was done. It was over," recalled Steve Merksamer, one of Younger's Department of Justice deputies at the time.[42] *San Francisco Chronicle* cartoonist Robert Graysmith called the governor "Browndini, the Incredible Escape Artist."[43] Even Howard Jarvis was impressed. During the fall campaign he appeared in television commercials for both gubernatorial candidates but later said he voted for Brown, who easily won reelection.

The governor's maneuvering had helped prove the point that the political optics of Proposition 13 could make or break political fortunes. Another beneficiary was a young conservative Republican, Dennis Brown, who experts thought was in over his head in an assembly race against veteran incumbent Democrat Fred Chel in the Long Beach–Lakewood area. Chel seemed so secure in his race that Republicans crossed the contest off their target list. Brown had little money, received no help from the party, and had twenty-three-year-old John Lewis running his campaign. Brown wrapped his candidacy around Proposition 13 during the primary before it was fashionable, and he then saw firsthand how it became the campaign's defining issue. Brown had enough money for a small survey. The first question was how people were voting in the head-to-head horserace, and Chel came out on top by sixteen points. "Then we asked a subsequent question," Lewis recalled. "'What if you knew that Fred Chel opposed Proposition 13 and Dennis Brown supports it?'" The numbers completely flipped to 45 percent to 27 percent in favor of Brown, an incredible thirty-four-point swing. Lewis shared the shocking poll results with other Republican campaign consultants, who started asking the same question in their contests.[44] Republicans added seven new members in the assembly—including Brown—who together became known at the capitol as the "Prop. 13 babies," pushing the GOP caucus to the right. Former assemblyman Bill Bagley, a moderate Republican, blamed Proposition 13 in part for "the deterioration of trust and collegiality" at the capitol as newly elected young Republicans "demanded less government but more partisanship."[45]

Governor Brown and the legislature faced a daunting task immediately following Proposition 13's passage: they had to completely rewrite the budget by the time the new fiscal year began in three weeks. That meant figuring out how local governments and schools could absorb billions of dollars in lost revenue and which programs and services would survive. From the beginning, most of the post–Proposition 13 debate focused on using the state's surplus—at least in the first year—to cushion the blow of local budget cuts. Some irritated lawmakers, however, wanted voters to see graphically the consequences of their actions. Democratic assemblyman Art Torres of Los Angeles was one of those suggesting that all $7 billion in cuts be taken out of local governments, as prescribed in Proposition 13, without any backfill from the state budget surplus. "You ought to just implement Proposition 13," he said, "and show the people what they really voted for."[46]

In the end, however, lawmakers siphoned $4.1 billion in grants and $900,000 in loans from the state to local government coffers to ease the pain. In addition, local governing boards created another cushion by enacting wide-ranging taxes and fees—for services such as hotel rooms, home inspections, local zoo tickets, and golf games—before the measure went into full effect in July. Brown pared the state budget considerably, halted state hiring, and angered state employees by eliminating pay hikes. Given the new reality that local government funds now flowed from Sacramento, Brown argued that keeping state salaries flat saved 18,000 local layoffs.

Thanks to the surplus and the state bailout, there were few visible signs that government services had been adversely affected during the first year of life after Jarvis. "How do we account for the fact that civilization as we know it has not come to a sudden halt?" asked Los Angeles city councilman Marvin Braude six months after Proposition 13's passage.[47] But budget dynamics had changed. Local governments—those closest to the people—previously had been sustained by local property taxes determined by local officials accountable to their neighbors. Now, cities, counties, and school districts were forced to come to Sacramento, hat in hand, and lobby for large chunks of general-fund dollars with strings attached. Property assessments and taxes may have been stabilized at local levels, but the health of the state budget relied heavily on volatile income and sales taxes.

As long as the economy was booming and generating a surplus, there was plenty of revenue to support state programs and a local bailout. But when the economy soured, as it inevitably did, a drained state treasury was insufficient to nourish this post–Proposition 13 coping strategy. A year after the election, Jarvis held a news conference outside the capitol. Jerry Brown watched with the tourists. A woman with a dozen small children in tow called out to Jarvis, "Do you care about the children? Your Proposition 13 is shutting down our preschools." As irascible as ever, Jarvis snapped, "That's your problem."[48]

Nearly four decades after Proposition 13's passage, the debate over its merits continues to rage. In reflecting on what he and Howard Jarvis had wrought, Paul Gann told an interviewer, "I think the thing we were trying to say was, number one, to make it possible for people to retain their homes. Number two was that we want less government, not more government."[49] By those criteria, Proposition 13 delivered. Although state and local governments have expanded over the years, growth certainly would have been significantly greater had Proposition 13 not been adopted. The

Cato Institute, a libertarian think tank, has credited Proposition 13 with ushering in an economic surge in the 1980s, and the Howard Jarvis Taxpayers Association estimates that California taxpayers have saved more than $500 billion since the measure's enactment in 1978. Joel Fox recalled flying around the state with Jarvis after the election: "Coming back to LA on the plane he'd look out the window at the houses and say, 'Look at all those homes I saved.'"[50]

Critics look at Proposition 13's machete approach to property taxes in a larger context. "It choked off a source of revenue, and the lack of that revenue has brought California to the edge," argued California historian Kevin Starr in 2011.[51] Communities, unable either to meet the two-thirds vote threshold to raise local taxes or to squeeze more dollars from Sacramento, faced tough decisions as to which services should be curtailed. Those decisions were even more difficult when the state's budget was in stress. Whether or not due in part to Proposition 13, California after Jarvis-Gann has seen layoffs of teachers, nurses, librarians, and counselors, and the elimination or curtailment of school enrichment instruction in art, drama, music, physical education, and what used to be called vocational education. In many communities, spending has been curtailed on recreation programs and park maintenance. Many libraries have reduced their days and hours of operation. Cities, prohibited from raising property taxes as they once did, have sought new sales-tax revenue by approving sprawling strip malls, auto malls, and big-box stores.

Forced to compete with local governments for state monies, traditional state-funded services have seen their share of the treasury crimped. The University of California, for example, received 5.09 percent of the state's general fund in 1980–81. By 2011, UC's budget share had dropped to 2.76 percent. To partially make up the difference, UC gradually pushed tuition and fees higher—from $710 in 1978 to more than $13,000 per year in 2014.[52]

Spurred by the success of Proposition 13 and the public's rebellion against the political establishment, Paul Gann returned the following year with another initiative, "The Spirit of 13," aimed at the back end of the capitol's tax-and-spend equation.

Fiscal conservatives had won the battle to restrict revenue collection, but they hadn't directly addressed spending. Fearing that lawmakers would increase other revenues to compensate for the loss of property taxes, Californians voted by a three-to-one margin to slap a spending limit on Sacramento, tying state spending to increases in inflation plus population growth. In addition, any revenue exceeding the Gann Limit had to be returned to taxpayers. In 1987, the legislature returned a surplus of $1.1 billion in eleven million checks—as low as $32 for lower-income earners and as high as $272 for the top income-tax brackets. Ironically, the rebates cost taxpayers $169 million in additional federal income taxes, and about 150,000 checks were returned as undeliverable.[53] In subsequent elections, voters severely weakened the limit by approving numerous exemptions.[54]

Besides altering government's budgeting structure, Proposition 13 ushered in an era of what veteran journalist Peter Schrag calls "plebiscitary rampage"—the surge of direct-democracy efforts to use the initiative to circumvent the legislature. In the thirty years before 1978, fifty-two initiatives had qualified for the state ballot; the number more than tripled in the thirty years afterward, as voters enacted laws on criminal justice, term limits, budget priorities, affirmative action, electoral reform, tribal gaming, wildlife protection, and many others.[55] Proposition 98, approved by voters in 1988, illustrates the vagaries of ballot-box budgeting. The measure not only guaranteed spending levels for K–14 education, it also required most surplus state funds be earmarked to repay schools for prior cuts. Lawmakers crafting the 2015–16 state budget had no choice but to spend billions of extra dollars on schools at the expense of other budget priorities.

The public's post–Proposition 13 penchant for direct democracy has dramatically increased the flood of money into campaigns and expanded new opportunities for a special breed of political operative. In the early days of California's experience with the initiative, sponsors were given unlimited time to gather signatures to qualify measures for the statewide ballot; they could do it with volunteers. In 1943, the signature-collection window was reduced to two years, and in 1973, it was cut to 150 days, forcing initiative sponsors to turn to professional signature-gatherers. Amassing signatures outside the neighborhood supermarket hasn't completely gone the way of the typewriter, but soliciting signatures—and contributions—by targeted, direct mail has turned into a thriving business for a few entrepreneurs. The median cost to qualify an initiative increased from less than $45,000 in the mid-1970s to nearly $3 million in 2006. In 2014, Silicon Valley entrepreneur Tim Draper spent $5.2 million in a losing effort to qualify a measure that would have split California into six states.[56]

Given the significant role money has come to play, well-heeled special interests arguably have co-opted the "citizens" initiative of Hiram Johnson. Far from curbing the trend, attempts to limit contributions to pass or defeat ballot measures have been thrown out in the courts. Since 2000, initiatives have attracted more than $2 billion in contributions from supporters and opponents. In 1911, voters had enacted direct democracy to rid the state of special-interest influence, primarily the Southern Pacific's grip on the legislature, courts, and press. "The irony became apparent when Southern Pacific itself took advantage of the initiative process [in 1990]," contributing significantly to qualify an initiative promoting rapid-rail transit.[57]

Despite criticism that the rash of initiatives has weakened representative government and contributed to the state's budget dysfunction, recent surveys indicate voters continue to distrust lawmakers and value the initiative system. Along with it, they prize their ability to weigh in on important issues, according to Mark Baldassare, president and CEO of the Public Policy Institute of California: "They believe there are times when the voters are better able to make public policy decisions than the governor and the legislature."[58] Yet some voter-approved measures have been poorly drafted, contradictory, confusing, and unconstitutional. As former California Supreme Court chief justice Ronald George has explained it, "sometimes dueling and conflicting initiatives" come before the court and "we're in charge of attempting to discern the intent of the electorate when they vote on these measures."[59]

In 2014, a coalition of government reformers, political activists, and business groups, frustrated by the unintended consequences
of California's sacred system of direct democracy, helped draft the
most significant change in the state's initiative process in modern
history. It promised to reduce drafting errors, promote compromise,
and curtail the avalanche of costly and divisive initiatives that began
after Proposition 13. The legislation, signed by Governor Jerry
Brown and hailed as "an important step to modernize and strengthen
direct democracy,"[60] offered initiative backers a chance to change
their measure during a public review period. It also allowed them to
voluntarily withdraw their measure later in the process, thus charting a potential course for proponents and legislators to find common
ground and avoid an election altogether. In addition, the initiative
signature-gathering period was extended from 150 days to 180 days,
and the public was given increased access to the identities of major
financial backers and opponents of individual initiatives.

Proposition 13's effect on California's initiative process is
merely one chapter in a thick volume dealing with the consequences
of the landmark tax revolt. After nearly four decades, Proposition
13 remains one of those seminal political events that jolted not only
California but the entire nation. Within five years of California taking the plunge, nearly half the states in the country imposed their
own tax-limitation measures.[61] Proposition 13 has withstood scrutiny
from both the California and the US Supreme Courts. Surveys have
shown that voters do agree, however, that one key provision should
be addressed. Because commercial property isn't resold as often as
homes, and a loophole allows some business properties to change
hands while avoiding reassessment, voters say they want commercial properties to be taxed at their current market values.[62] Over the
years, lawmakers and voters have tinkered with Proposition 13, but
the more fundamental the proposed change, the less successful the
effort. After nearly four decades on the books, and amid the continued din of strongly held opinions on the benefits and the adverse
consequences of the measure, Proposition 13 has held up well in
periodic voter surveys and likely would receive voter support today
comparable to its tally in 1978.

11

1980
Technology and Money Forever Change Political Campaigning

"California politicians think about campaign money
when they get up in the morning, they think about
it all day and they think about it at night."
—Art Agnos, California Assemblyman

HIS NAME IS almost lost to history, but Ed Skowron occupies a tiny niche in California's political timeline. Skowron was an entrepreneur of sorts. He sold insurance and owned the Valley Welcome Wagon, which packaged coupons, business brochures, and other goodies to hand out to new residents in the sprawling San Fernando Valley. He also owned a company called Addresses Unlimited that compiled and sold mailing lists. In 1973, he used his list-making talents to help an unknown thirty-year-old attorney get elected to the California senate.

Alan Robbins was running in a special election in the northeastern portion of the valley to fill the seat left vacant by the death of veteran Democratic senator Tom Carrell. Robbins was a self-made millionaire who had struck gold in real estate, and as a campaigner, he was indefatigable, mining for votes in supermarkets, coffee shops, and hair salons. "He swooped into four beauty parlors in less than ten minutes on a recent day of campaigning, pinning blue and white Robbins buttons on collars and introducing himself as the customers peered at him from under hair dryers," reported the *Glendale News-Press*.[1]

The unknown, untested Robbins was a decided underdog against assemblyman Jim Keysor in the Democratic primary. Robbins turned to Skowron to develop mailing lists of voters. Keysor, whose family manufactured vinyl records, ran a traditional election effort, sending out generic district-wide mailers and handing out recordings of presidential inaugural addresses.[2] He was endorsed by prominent Democrats and was confident of victory.

Political campaigning in the early 1970s, however, was beginning to undergo a technology-driven shift in direct-mail tactics, particularly with regards to data mining that enabled candidates to target voters with precisely tailored messages. Skowron didn't invent the strategy, but he knew how to use it. In those days, it was labor-intensive. "It relied on a lot of people," says Barry Brokaw, a longtime legislative aide and lobbyist who spent three months working for Skowron after graduating college. "Retirees would be taken down to the county registrar of voters to go through voter lists, scanning for any ethnic traits."[3] Jews would identify Jewish voters by their surnames, even down to their region of origin, such as Russia or eastern Europe. Italian Americans would identify fellow Italian Americans, Latinos would identify Latinos, and so on. Skowron noted which voters reliably went to the polls every election, culled voters' ages from Department of Motor Vehicles lists, and identified other demographic traits. In a valley warehouse that served as Skowron's base of operations, the names and individual characteristics would be categorized, coded, and fed into a tabletop automated mail sorter as the Robbins campaign staff tailored mailers to different age and ethnic groups. It was more costly than creating a single district-wide mail piece, but money wasn't a problem for the wealthy Robbins.

Robbins spent more than $300,000 in the special election, defeating the better-known Keysor in the primary and, in the general election, a well-financed Republican who had received campaign help from Governor Ronald Reagan. Robbins shattered spending records, mostly with personal loans to his own campaign. He paid Skowron's company more than $20,000 for the special lists.[4] Ross Johnson, then chief of staff to GOP assemblyman Jerry Lewis, remembers the impact: "Jim Keysor just didn't know what hit him." A few years later, as electronic technology continued to advance and Lewis was considering a run for the state senate, Johnson wrote his boss a memo about the value and expense of computer-targeted mail. "I was trying to lay out costs. I always remembered that [Robbins's election] as a model of what to do and how it had changed the culture of fundraising."[5]

At the same time Skowron was plying his trade, a young college dropout a few miles away also was experimenting with tactics to reach voters in more effective and compelling ways. Brainy and politically savvy, Michael Berman would advance and refine techniques of communicating with targeted voters, ultimately crafting campaigns that were more efficient yet also more costly, a factor that in turn challenged candidates to find the cash to pay for them. Political strategizing and fundraising would never be the same. By the end of the decade, Berman would be characterized as a tactical genius, and his skill at manipulating computers for political advantage would make him the Democratic professional whom Republicans feared most.

The election year of 1980 was a game-changer, not because of any one politician or ballot issue but because an array of forces—computerized voter targeting, stunning election upsets, an outlandish spiral in campaign costs, and a portentous upheaval in the assembly speakership—converged to permanently alter the way candidates win elections in California.

THE BACKSTORY

Michael Berman was something of a political prodigy. In 1965, he organized his high school class to walk precincts for a successful Los Angeles City Council candidate. A year later, in the days before computers, he learned data mining and rudimentary voter targeting as a strategist on David Roberti's 1966 campaign for assembly in Los Angeles. Roberti's young, unpaid campaign workers crafted differing messages for the district's various ethnic neighborhoods. Italian Americans had settled in Alhambra, for example, so the community received an Italian-themed campaign piece. Jerry Zanelli, who ran the Roberti campaign while a student at San Fernando Valley State College, said volunteers pored over precinct sheets to determine that Silver Lake residents tended to be reliable upper-middle-class voters, while Highland Park was working-class and conservative. "Each area was handled separately," and messages were suitably tailored.[6] Running a no-frills campaign, Roberti finished first in a Democratic primary field of eleven and won the runoff by 2,300 votes.[7] Two years later, twenty-year-old Michael Berman teamed with UCLA sociologist Howard Elinson to further refine his micro-targeting techniques. In a West Los Angeles assembly contest, the pair engineered the election of twenty-eight-year-old Henry Waxman by knocking off a fourteen-term Democrat in the primary and waltzing to a general election victory. "If there were twelve Armenians, they'd get a letter [tailored to them]," Elinson said.[8] Berman's emerging techniques and expertise were successful but still barely noticed by political insiders. Shortly, that would change.

During the nationwide Republican sweep of 1972, an unexpected assembly victory for a fairly obscure San Fernando Valley Democrat brought instant attention to this wunderkind. Michael Berman's older brother, thirty-one-year-old Howard Berman, a lawyer and former volunteer in the VISTA antipoverty program, won a landslide victory over veteran Republican Charlie Conrad. Republicans were stunned. How in the world could Conrad, a former actor who had won thirteen consecutive assembly contests, possibly lose so convincingly to such a newcomer in a district that overwhelmingly supported the presidential reelection of fellow Republican Richard Nixon?

Although Berman wasn't a complete neophyte—he had served a stint as president of the California Young Democrats in the late sixties—few gave him any chance of winning. As it turned out, he had a secret weapon in the campaign tutelage of his younger brother. "I walked precincts and coded every voter I talked to for purposes of future mail," Howard Berman recalled. "If you saw a peace sign on the door, you'd make a code. In those days we coded occupation (which was listed on voter registration forms), so you knew who the lawyers were, who the carpenters were. You knew who the doctors were." Berman and his brother's micro-targeting campaign successfully defeated the ten other Democrats in the primary, many of them backed by heavyweights in Sacramento. Howard knew whom to credit for his victory. "I slaughtered everyone else, not because of my natural great worth, but because our campaign was so much more sophisticated than everybody else's."[9] In the general election, if Berman found Republicans who might be persuaded to support his candidacy, he added them to the list and sent them a "Republicans for Nixon/Berman" mailer. Young voters received mail reminding them that Conrad had opposed allowing eighteen-year-olds to vote.

Within four years, Michael Berman had masterminded the elections of two men who later would serve decades together—first in the legislature, then in the House of Representatives—and create what became the powerful "Waxman-Berman" political machine that built alliances, cultivated wealthy Los Angeles liberals, doled out gobs of campaign cash to favored Democrats, and helped to elect friends with the skillful redrawing of election-district boundaries.

On the surface, Michael and Howard couldn't have been more different. Howard, hard-charging and ambitious, wore nice suits to work; Michael was disheveled. "In a good year, Michael must spend $200 to get his clothes pre-wrinkled," quipped his consulting partner, Carl D'Agostino, in a 1992 profile in the *Los Angeles Times*. Howard could be charming and engaging; Michael was a blunt and abrasive chain-smoking introvert. The décor of Michael's one-room condo above the Sunset Strip was described as "early library," with piles of books and magazines scattered everywhere. It was said that Michael's ability to count cards got him booted from Las Vegas blackjack tables. "The smartest person I know never graduated college," Howard once said. "My brother."[10]

In Sacramento, Howard promptly aligned himself with fast-rising secretary of state Jerry Brown and played a key role in the battle for assembly speaker to replace Bob Moretti, who had resigned the position after his defeat in the 1974 Democratic gubernatorial primary. The speakership is the assembly's Holy Grail. A decade earlier, Jesse Unruh had turned it into an autocratic post that by the late 1970s had near dictatorial control over the fate of all legislation. The speaker selected the members and chairs of assembly committees—and chairs exercised often decisive influence over bills that passed through their committees. Former assemblyman Vincent Thomas recalled that Unruh would cruise the assembly floor during roll-call votes. If the vote wasn't going his way, he'd walk up to a disobedient member, lean in closely, and snarl, "Change your goddam vote."[11]

A speaker could punish lawmakers who strayed by stripping them of chairmanships, key committee assignments, staff, and desirable offices. Most importantly, Unruh and subsequent speakers used their power over legislation to attract large campaign contributions from special interests with issues before the lower house, directing funds to friendly assembly candidates. It was a perfect circle of power: the speaker would help candidates win their elections and they, in turn, would owe their loyalty to the speaker and help keep their benefactor in power.

San Francisco liberal Willie Brown, bent on scaling heights unheard of for an African American politician, had been Moretti's handpicked chairman of the Ways and Means Committee and was considered Moretti's heir apparent for speaker. But another San Francisco liberal, Leo McCarthy, challenged Brown. Into the standoff stepped Berman, the leader of a half-dozen likeminded Democratic assembly members whose votes would determine the outcome. He and Brown were friends from their activist days with the Young Democrats, and Brown fully expected to get Berman's votes. It was a miscalculation. At the last minute, Berman delivered those votes and a narrow victory to McCarthy. Brown remembered Montebello Democrat Jack Fenton walking up to him after the vote and saying, "The black kid can't count."[12] McCarthy promptly rewarded Berman by anointing him the first freshman legislator ever to be named assembly majority leader.

Brown, meanwhile, suffered the consequences of running for speaker and losing. McCarthy stripped him of his chairmanship and moved him into an office "so tiny that the chairs for people waiting to see me were out in the hall."[13] Brown accepted his punishment as a risk of battle, but he never forgot the role Berman played in his demise. In subsequent years, did Brown harbor a grudge against Berman? "He should," Berman acknowledged. "I screwed him royally."[14]

In McCarthy's early years as speaker, Democrats not only had significant majorities in the legislature, Democrat Jerry Brown occupied the governor's office as well. Benefiting from the fallout of the Watergate scandal, they picked up six assembly seats in 1974 and two more in 1976 to assume a commanding 57–23 edge against a Republican party that was struggling to recover. Simmering below the surface, however, was a menacing volcano, and Democrats ignored the early warning sign: rising property taxes that ultimately led to the Proposition 13 voter revolt of 1978. Berman later lamented that majority Democrats could have approved "the greatest property tax relief bill any state had ever provided its constituents" to preempt Proposition 13; "We made a terrible mistake."[15] But frugal Jerry Brown hadn't wanted to spend a fast-growing state surplus on tax relief. McCarthy—who harbored ambitions to run for governor or the US Senate in 1982—was similarly convinced that a large property tax cut would wipe out the surplus and necessitate a remedial tax increase at a very critical time: just as he was asking Californians for their votes.

On McCarthy's watch, voters punished Democrats for their failure to respond adequately to the looming property tax crisis. Republicans picked up seven assembly seats in 1978, and many of the new Republicans—so-called Proposition 13 babies—were ideologues bent on securing a GOP majority. There is nothing more important to a legislator than reelection, and with redistricting on the horizon after the 1980 census, some Democrats were nervous that the election debacle of 1978 was the beginning of the end of the Democratic majority. Howard Berman was one of them. Further generating angst among Democrats was McCarthy's perceived inattention to his party colleagues.

After he had announced his ambitions for higher office, McCarthy became an instant short-timer who seemed to care more about his own personal future than the election fortunes of his panicked assembly flock. A Los Angeles fundraiser headlined by Massachusetts senator Ted Kennedy was the last straw. McCarthy committed a cardinal sin when he chose to set aside the $500,000 proceeds for his own future political war chest and not for his colleagues' reelections. Perhaps more egregious, McCarthy began his remarks at the Kennedy event by having the assembled Democrats stand as a group to be recognized instead of singling out each member. As trivial as that might seem to the public, lack of individual recognition—particularly in a ballroom full of wealthy donors— was an unforgivable insult.

Within twenty-four hours, there was talk of ousting McCarthy as speaker. Howard Berman had become a prodigious fundraiser for Democratic candidates by tapping wealthy West Los Angeles contributors, and many of his assembly colleagues owed him their careers. As McCarthy's right-hand man, he would have been first in line to assume the speakership when McCarthy moved on after the 1982 elections, but Berman couldn't wait. "I thought we were on a downward arc," he said.[16] Republicans were surging, Democrats felt insecure, and McCarthy was focused on himself. Berman's fundraising prowess—combined with brother Michael's exalted status as a campaign strategist—were strong attractions to Democrats worried about their political survival.

In mid-afternoon on December 10, 1979, Berman marched into the speaker's office, armed with a list of grievances, and told McCarthy to resign. He said he was putting together the votes to oust him if he refused. McCarthy had been tipped off to the coup attempt by one assembly member a few days earlier, but McCarthy hadn't believed it was true. "I said to him, 'It's impossible. It cannot happen,' because Howard was my right-hand man, and he and I had a close relationship, and I trusted him."[17] The December 10 showdown involved Berman, McCarthy, and their closest assembly confidants. It lasted eleven hours, into the next morning, with the two sides counting votes and airing their differences. Berman thought McCarthy would fold quickly, telling reporters he originally "thought this was going to be over in an hour."[18] He was clearly wrong. After his fruitless meeting with McCarthy, Berman resigned his job as majority leader and announced he was a candidate for speaker. It seemed madness to some, uncharacteristic of the shrewd Berman. Art Agnos, a McCarthy partisan, considered Berman "a talented, thoughtful, bright legislator....One week of politically demented actions do not wipe that out."[19] Little did any of the players know that the "one hour" insurgency would drag on for an entire year and pit Democrat versus Democrat in the upcoming elections. Republicans, watching from the sidelines, couldn't contain their glee.

THE ELECTION

California's 1980 legislative elections would shatter unwritten rules on campaigning and the accrual and flow of money in political contests. They were fueled by a bitter, seemingly unending internecine leadership battle in the assembly and by unexpectedly cutthroat partisan politics in the senate. By the time the dust settled on this most improbable and stunning election season, there would be leadership coups in both the assembly and senate, fratricide among assembly Democrats, a surge of Republican strength in both houses, and a record amount of money spent to win votes. In the morning-after hangover, it was clear that the approach to winning legislative campaigns had been changed forever.

The assembly was the first to undergo this transformation. Leadership battles are fought over politics and personal ambition, not policy, and the battle for the second-most-powerful political office in California offered a textbook study in how messy and uncompromising backroom politics can be. Years later, McCarthy insisted he lost two votes in the siege on his speakership because Berman coaxed his friend, Governor Brown, into promising judgeships to the two. McCarthy said he lost another vote when he refused to appoint a married assemblyman's girlfriend "to a nice, cushy job in the assembly staff."[20] For his part, Berman had made a critical tactical error by telling McCarthy of his coup attempt before actually lining up enough votes to replace him.

As the crucial 1980 election year dawned, the struggle between Berman and McCarthy had cleaved the Democratic caucus. There were constant procedural votes to remove McCarthy as speaker. All failed; no one budged. Players in the drama were killing each other's bills for spite. When it came time to choose sides, Willie Brown didn't struggle with his decision. "I had only two choices: vote for the speaker who defeated me or the majority leader who stabbed me in the back."[21] He went with the speaker.

Some assembly members joined with Berman, because with Howard they got both his rolodex of fundraisers and Michael, the consummate strategist. One magazine profile at the time characterized Michael Berman as "a restless, unsleeping political operator....He's ruthless."[22] The power struggle was taking its toll on friendships. "Guys we were close to, then all of a sudden we're not even talking to each other,"[23] recalled Assemblyman Frank Vicencia of Bellflower, a McCarthy loyalist. With the stalemate showing no signs of breaking, a frustrated Berman—reportedly at the urging of his brother—took the speakership fight to the voters.[24] Berman figured that the best way to demonstrate he was the right candidate for speaker was to raise large sums of money and elect more Democrats to the assembly, particularly those who would be loyal to him. "We then had a decision: do we have the resources to make this into a year-long fight? Based on funding commitments, oh yeah," he said.[25] Berman sought candidates to run in open seats and against a few vulnerable Republicans. He also startled his colleagues by breaking tradition and targeting a handful of incumbent McCarthy Democrats for defeat. Several assembly contests, therefore, had highly contested, well-funded Democratic primaries.

Jack Fenton was a first-generation American whose parents were Lithuanian immigrants. His father operated a delicatessen. Fenton practiced law in Montebello, east of downtown Los Angeles, and easily won the first of eight consecutive elections to the state assembly in 1964. He was universally liked by members of the Assembly Democratic Caucus and had championed worker

JUST MORE POLITICAL CAMPAIGN MATERIAL, MRS. FENWICK.

safety and consumer protection laws. He also was a McCarthy supporter in the bitter speakership fight. Fenton's district had changed
considerably over the years, and by 1980 it consisted of "a very
healthy list of registered voters with Spanish surnames."[26]

To pick up a vote in the caucus, the Bermans decided to take
out Fenton in the primary and replace him with Monterey Park city
councilman Marty Martinez. They held their fire until late in the
campaign, then bombarded the district with mail. Fenton was hit
for ignoring the district and being the "darling" of special interests.
The most effective mail pieces were targeted to the growing Latino
population. One hard-hitting letter, signed by Latino community
leaders, said Fenton "does not care about us." It urged a vote for
Martinez "por nosotros" ("for us"). Another piece urged support for
Martinez "out of concern for our Mexican-American community."[27]
The heated primary campaign may have focused on one enclave of
Los Angeles County, but word spread quickly in Sacramento that
Democrats were trying to oust their own incumbents. Republican

assemblyman Ross Johnson remembers walking through the capitol basement with GOP colleague Chuck Imbrecht when they ran into Democrat Rick Lehman, a Berman supporter. "Imbrecht asked him, 'Is it true you are going after Jack Fenton?' Lehman responded, 'How much mail can you fit in a Mexican's mail box in a week?'"[28]

The Berman assault worked. Steamrolled by the awesome efficiency of the Berman machine, Fenton was forced into retirement. Tom Bane, a Democratic assemblyman from Van Nuys who was allied with McCarthy, told an interviewer that Fenton's demise had shaken up many of his colleagues, "because they felt that if he [Berman] does that to member Jack Fenton, he'd do it to them."[29] Fenton's defeat also hardened feelings. Some Democrats said they never could support Berman after that.

With less fanfare, there were other battles within the Democratic family, including McCarthy's successful offensive against a Stockton incumbent. The amped-up primary contests set new records for campaign spending, nearly doubling 1976 outlays. Thirty-nine assembly candidates spent more than $100,000 each in the primary, representing "a four-fold increase in the number of Assembly candidates joining the 'Century Club,'" said election watchdog Tom Houston.[30] Much of the campaign cash was raised by McCarthy and Berman and transferred to their favored candidates.

In the fall, the electorate tilted to the right. Jimmy Carter conceded his landslide defeat to president-elect Ronald Reagan nearly three hours before the polls closed in California; with the presidential contest wrapped up early, it was estimated that hundreds of thousands of Californians skipped going to the polls. Post-election studies were inconclusive, but Democrats believed their candidates suffered the most. "Many in the Democratic establishment were furious with Carter,"[31] historian Douglas Brinkley noted, for hurting other Democratic candidates in the Pacific time zone. When the votes were counted, Republicans had gained three new members in the assembly, holding thirty-three of eighty seats. Democrats had lost ten seats in the two elections since Proposition 13's passage.

In the year-old quest for the speakership, there finally seemed to be some clarity. Berman had a better election night than McCarthy and assumed a narrow lead in the Democratic caucus. Two years earlier, in an interview with the *Los Angeles Times*, McCarthy had acknowledged the first rule of leadership: win or you're out. "If I lost a lot of seats," he said at the time, "then I think it would take on proportions of questioning my leadership."[32] McCarthy knew it was over for him; the day after the election he announced he would not be a candidate for speaker when the new assembly convened.

Berman assumed that the speaker's job was his for the taking. After a year-long gut-wrenching battle, he was the last man standing, but resentment and bad feelings prevented some fellow Democrats from joining the Berman team. Fenton's blindsided defeat "really angered us," said Vicencia. He said some members never would have supported Berman after that.[33]

A team of McCarthy supporters was established to negotiate terms of surrender to Berman. Meeting in Willie Brown's office, they asked Berman to retain committee chairmanships for a few of their members. But Berman refused; he had obligations to his loyalists, he explained. Brown reflected that had Berman not "slammed the door, the membership would have caved."[34] Instead, McCarthy's bloc of votes remained firm and sought another leader. Tradition dictated that the minority party rubber-stamp the majority's selection for speaker, but the Democrats still couldn't coalesce behind Berman. All along Republicans had been content to stand on the sidelines and watch the carnage. Once during an assembly floor session, they playfully showed up wearing hard hats. They also figured they would be able to dictate favorable terms to whomever emerged as a viable compromise candidate in return for delivering the bulk of their thirty-three votes. Few would have suspected that the white, ideologically conservative Republican caucus would cut a deal with black, liberal San Franciscan Willie Brown.

As it turned out, Republicans feared the political talents of the two Bermans and were ready for Brown's overtures. The Michael and Howard Berman operation "was a money raising machine, and coming from Southern California—with a whole lot higher population—we were scared to death" of Berman's fundraising ability, recalled Johnson, a key GOP player. "Plus Michael Berman was a map-drawing machine,"[35] and statewide redistricting was just around the corner. Republicans also analyzed Brown's campaign statements and determined that he didn't appear to be a particularly effective fundraiser. And they relished the prospect that the new face of the Democratic Party would be a pro-gay, pro-marijuana San Francisco liberal who had a closet full of expensive, perfectly tailored suits and drove fancy sports cars. "We really believed that Willie would self-destruct," assembly Republican leader Carol Hallett said. "We really felt that Willie's flamboyant approach would get him into so much trouble with his own caucus that he wouldn't last."[36]

In return for Republican support, Brown offered to consider Republicans for chairmanships, and he promised that committee chairs and vice chairs would not be members of the same party. He vowed to turn the assignment of bills over to the Rules Committee, which traditionally handled routine housekeeping matters, and he offered Republicans a redistricting budget so they could hire staff to analyze maps and demographics. Beyond that, terms of the deal remain in dispute. Republicans insist that Brown acceded to their demand that acerbic, bellicose Democratic assemblyman Lou Papan—a former FBI agent known as "the enforcer"—be removed as Rules Committee chairman. They considered him a heavy-handed, intimidating bully and they wanted him off the playground. "It took him [Brown] two hours to break that promise," Johnson recalled.[37] Brown remembers it differently, insisting he never made that deal.

With support from Republicans and fewer than half the Democratic members, Willie Brown ascended to the assembly's pinnacle of power. After the vote, and recalling his speakership setback six and a half years earlier, the victorious Brown remembered walking up to Berman and gloating, "The black kid *can* count."[38] Shortly after assuming the reins as speaker, Democrats in the New York legislature invited Brown for a visit. They wanted to know how he had put the leadership campaign together. Brown joked that Berman and McCarthy had spent $2.5 million to gain the speakership, while "I spent $40,000 on a wardrobe and won it."[39]

Although the speakership battle had roiled the assembly for a full year, it took only one day to shock the system in the less-partisan senate. The upper house was more decorous and genteel than the often raucous assembly, and incumbents rarely had to worry about reelection. Since 1975, ultraconservative senator H. L. Richardson, a blunt-speaking gun-rights champion, had established himself as the conservatives' answer to Michael Berman. His first foray into the new world of computer targeting came out of frustration with what he considered the National Rifle Association's old-fashioned methods of political activity. "The NRA's idea of maintaining political contact was to give $500 to an incumbent," he said.[40]

When a bill to ban handguns in California was introduced in the legislature, Richardson created Gun Owners of California and a direct-mail business to reach voters and pressure lawmakers. Eventually, Richardson would control several right-leaning political action committees. His pattern was to send mail advocating an issue and appeal for donations. He'd use the revenue to finance more mailings. In 1977, Richardson's Law and Order Campaign Committee sent out mailings to two million households and received hundreds of thousands of responses—as well as checks— as the legislature debated reinstatement of the death penalty in California. At one point, Richardson demonstrated the power of the computer letter by hauling twenty-seven bags of mail into the capitol in support of a pro–death penalty bill. When Governor Jerry Brown vetoed the measure, the intimidated Democratic legislature overrode the veto.

In 1980, Richardson was looking around for someone to run against Senator Albert Rodda of Sacramento, a white-haired, grandfatherly Republican-turned-Democrat who was the dean of the senate and one of its most respected members. Rodda had won a special election in 1958 and subsequently faced only token opposition in his solidly Democratic district. He was old-school. His idea of campaigning was to gather endorsements from civic leaders and place an ad in the *Sacramento Bee*. Richardson analyzed the district and Rodda's liberal voting record and figured he was vulnerable to a targeted computer mail campaign. "Everybody was telling me there was no way in the world you could touch him," Richardson said.[41] Gathering his key political staff as he did every Monday morning for a brainstorming session, Richardson was looking for a suitable opponent for Rodda. One of his employees, working for the Law and Order Campaign Committee, was twenty-nine-year-old John Doolittle. "So I just looked around the room and said, 'Any of you guys live in the district?' And John stuck up his hand."[42]

In the June primary, Rodda had received more than 79,000 Democratic votes, setting up what looked to be another easy general election bid. Doolittle, his unknown Republican opponent, had received barely 20,000 votes. But Rodda was blindsided in the fall. He ran his usual low-key campaign and didn't even spend all his money. Doolittle and Richardson, meanwhile, kept their powder dry until late in the campaign, then unleashed an aggressive mail barrage zeroing in on individual votes and using Doolittle's Mormon network to stagger the Democratic establishment. Democratic senate leader James Mills insisted Rodda had refused his offer of assistance. "Jim," Rodda said, "I'm not in any trouble. I know my district better than you do, and I wish you'd respect my judgment in that regard."[43] Doolittle won, and Mills—blamed for not doing enough to prevent Rodda's defeat—stepped down from his leadership post without a floor vote. Republicans had found their Michael Berman counterpart as once-complacent Democrats suddenly had to worry about the next sneak attack.

THE IMPACT

When the new legislature convened in Sacramento, pundits and even some legislators were sounding the death knell of the all-powerful speakership. Willie Brown had won "a speakership with relatively little power," wrote Ed Salzman in the *California Journal*. "Brown's acceptance of rules changes sought by the Republicans has further reduced the ability of a speaker to direct the flow of legislation in the Assembly."[44] In addition, there was continued speculation that since Brown won the post without a majority of his own caucus, his tenure would be short-lived. Both predictions were well off the mark. Brown served a record fifteen years as the self-described "Ayatollah" of the assembly, and he would have served much longer had it not been for voter-approved term limits—which many say he helped inspire with his righteous flamboyance. He ruled with an iron fist, dictated the success or failure of legislation, and made the Republicans regret they had ever conspired with him.

Brown's first move as speaker had been all about self-preservation. "When he got it [the speakership], he wanted to make sure he never lost it," Brown's San Francisco political pal John Burton said.[45] Now in command of the party's redistricting machinery and with help from his friends in Congress, Brown consolidated his power by ensuring the creation of comfortable 1982 congressional and state senate districts for potential adversaries. He didn't want to worry that Howard Berman might be lurking in the weeds preparing to stage a coup at the first opportunity. "One of the first things I did was get rid of all my enemies," Brown acknowledged. "Anybody with talent that might give me a problem, I got rid of them."[46] Brown didn't punish them; he promoted them—right out of the assembly and into Congress 3,000 miles away. Brown crafted extremely favorable congressional districts for Berman and two of his supporters, Rick Lehman and Mel Levine, assuring their elections to the House of Representatives. Favorable districts enabled Gary K. Hart and Bill Lockyer, two other Berman votes, to win election to the state senate. It was a brilliant stroke that helped ensure that Brown would occupy the speaker's throne for seven more terms.

Now safely ensconced in the speaker's chair, Brown set out to streamline and expand the flow of campaign dollars to Democrats by creating a "resource management" scheme that has endured at the capitol for decades. Recognizing that candidates often don't manage their money efficiently, Brown brought Democratic voter registration efforts, opposition research, and printing under his direction. Then, he centralized campaign funding. He compelled his caucus members, even those without significant electoral opposition, to constantly beg for campaign cash from special interests. Those who didn't need the money would help those who did through money transfers. In twenty-minute intervals at the Senator Hotel across the street from the capitol, Brown would sit down with agents for major special interests to persuade them to give to Democrats. He made sure that contributions went either to "needy" Democrats or to his own Democratic campaign account to distribute as he saw fit. At that time, there were no limits on contributions or transfers from one candidate to another. Large chunks of money—often in excess of $100,000—changed hands regularly.

In time, new senate leader David Roberti joined Brown in working the lobbyists and political action committees in tandem. Campaign fundraising that once relied primarily on district sources had pivoted to moneyed interests headquartered in the capital city with significant stakes in legislation—labor, doctors, lawyers, liquor, horse racing, tobacco. Republicans also were beginning to centralize their finances, although not on the same scale. The elections of 1980 taught everyone in the legislature a lesson: you better raise as much campaign money as you can, accept your leader's largesse when it's offered, and be wary of sneak attacks. "Everyone was scrambling," lobbyist Hedy Govenar said, "because they didn't want to get blindsided."[47] From that point on, "everybody desperately raised money," according to Ross Johnson, all of them aware that, "with last-minute [campaign fund] transfers, you could become the next Jack Fenton."[48] Legislators who wanted to move up the leadership ladder and attract loyal supporters had to be solid fundraisers as well, doling out cash to colleagues' political coffers.

Jesse Unruh deserves credit for creating the centralized system of campaign funding, but Willie Brown made it an art form and took it to a new level. In the late 1960s, Unruh had transferred about $300,000 to candidate campaigns during one election cycle. In 1981–82, Brown doled out nearly $4 million. In 1976, four years before the speakership fight, legislative candidates had spent $14.7 million on campaigns; by the 1996 legislative contests, spending had soared beyond $100 million, a dramatic increase, even allowing for inflation. Brown said the new arrangement of funneling money through him insulated his members from criticism by allowing them to accept campaign money they needed without "the political burden of having received it from, let's say, Phillip Morris." And Brown was in the best position to take the heat for accepting controversial contributions because it didn't matter to him. "My constituency was the membership, and my district didn't give a shit."[49]

Brown's cozy relationship with lobbyists and special-interest contributors—the new normal in Sacramento—spawned a spate of critical news articles that accused legislative leaders of tying the fate of legislation to political contributions. One lobbyist told reporter Dan Walters that the system had become an "abysmally corrupt shakedown," and San Francisco assemblyman Art Agnos conceded, "California politicians think about campaign money when they get up in the morning, they think about it all day and they think about it at night."[50] There was a growing perception "that Willie Brown had posted a 'For Sale' sign on the Capitol dome."[51] Brown has consistently denied that he ever linked legislation and contributions in discussions with potential contributors or rigged the legislative system to squeeze campaign cash from donors. "You can't sell the system and you cannot let anybody else sell the system," he said.[52] In the late 1980s, after assembly Republican leader Pat Nolan secretly suggested to the FBI that it look into Brown's fundraising activities, Brown escaped unscathed. Nolan, however, was snared in an FBI sting and later served more than two years in a federal prison after pleading guilty to racketeering.

The campaign-funding arms race has continued unabated since it was kick-started by the 1980 speakership melee and H. L. Richardson's takedown of a senator thought to be invulnerable. "Our kinds of campaigns require money, because a lot of mail goes out. And computer mail is more expensive than brochure mailings," Howard Berman said.[53] In 2014, 40 percent of senate campaigns cost more than $1 million each, with candidates and outside interests spending $11.5 million in one contest, and $8.5 million in another. In 2015, a special senate election attracted about $12 million in spending.[54]

In an effort to remove the domination of special interests in political campaigns, California reformers have tinkered with the system for decades, but without success. They could fill a library with their research studies. Fourteen other states offer public funds to candidates; the programs are voluntary, and candidates who accept the money must limit their campaign spending. But with the state legislature often saddled with low approval ratings, and corruption scandals making occasional headlines, would voters be willing to share public dollars with politicians in California? Previous efforts in the state have been unsuccessful. Yet would-be reformers are undaunted as they continue to seek significant changes in a system rooted in those fading 1980 battles for legislative supremacy.

12

1990
Californians Punish
Lawmakers with Term Limits

"Enough is enough."
—Pete Schabarum, Los Angeles County Supervisor

HEADS TURNED WHEN Pete Schabarum walked into the state assembly chamber in late August of 1990. Here was the man legislators feared most. The sixty-one-year-old rugged and rock-ribbed conservative was a member of the Los Angeles County Board of Supervisors and the face of a ballot initiative designed to run those eighty members of the assembly out of office in just a few years—and do the same to senators, the governor, and other constitutional officeholders. Square-jawed and resolute, Schabarum had been accustomed to rude welcomes on the gridiron as a star running back at Berkeley who later played for the San Francisco 49ers. Now, as the unbridled leader of the campaign for term limits and a nearly 40 percent cut in the legislature's budget, he was unceremoniously snubbed by assembly speaker Willie Brown.

Introduction of guests on the assembly floor was a common courtesy, particularly for former members like Schabarum, who had served from 1967 to 1972. But he wasn't a common guest on this occasion. When one conservative Republican tried to introduce him, Brown cut off his microphone. During debate on a bill concerning campaign spending, another assemblyman "tried to sneak in a reference to Schabarum," and he, too, was cut off. "You're not going to pull those kinds of stunts on me," Brown scolded from the rostrum.[1] A third attempt failed as well. Afterward, Brown, who would raise more than $2 million to try to defeat Schabarum's initiative, sparred with a reporter and insisted it had been an inappropriate time to introduce a guest. Schabarum had another take: "All you have to do is look at the way the legislature has and is conducting itself and you can suggest there is a dire need for change."[2]

If term-limit supporters wanted a fierce and aggressive pit bull for a leader, they had one in Schabarum. In a county-league softball game, he once scored a run by bowling over the catcher—a 135-pound grandmother. "That's baseball,"[3] he shrugged. Even though he spent twenty-four years as an assemblyman and supervisor, he seemed to have a genuine dislike for most politicians. In an interview with the *California Journal*, he referred to capitol lawmakers as "small-minded" and "arrogant." Legislative staff members were "turkeys" and "dumbos."[4] Fellow Republican Jerry Lewis of Redlands, who spent three years working with Schabarum in the assembly, remembered him as "an aggressive, persistent legislator with an abrasive style who didn't spend a lot of energy cultivating positive relations with his colleagues."[5]

Former GOP legislator William Bagley suggested Schabarum had sponsored term limits to get even with Sacramento colleagues who he felt "had mistreated him."[6] Fellow Republicans on the board of supervisors, Mike Antonovich and Dean Dana, also felt the occasional sting of Schabarum's ire. Schabarum was a lone dissenter on a three-to-one vote to require gas stations to obtain permits to sell alcohol. "Two alleged conservatives and a liberal just invoked another piece of government nonsense," he sneered. When Schabarum retired from the board, none of his colleagues showed up at his retirement party. Even one of his own press deputies called Schabarum an "ornery rascal."[7]

A month after Speaker Brown gave him the cold shoulder on the assembly floor, Schabarum again visited the capitol and his reception was a bit more cordial. He had been invited to testify before a legislative hearing looking into his term-limiting initiative. "The mood [among the electorate] is simple," Schabarum told the panel. "The folks are really ticked." He argued that the legislature needed to restore confidence by trading career politicians and staff for new blood. When asked how the legislature was supposed to operate efficiently with a reduced staff and slashed budget, Schabarum scoffed, "Forget staff. Why don't you do it yourself?" Democrat Tom Bane, at that time a twenty-two-year assembly veteran, concluded, "Our system of government is under attack."[8] So how was a prickly, underfunded Schabarum able to outmaneuver the state's political elite and persuade voters to slash state government and curtail the careers of its representatives?

THE BACKSTORY

The spark that ignited the push for California's state government term limits—an effort fueled by public disenchantment with the legislature—didn't come out of nowhere. In fact, it had been more than a decade in the making. Seventy-three percent of the state's voters had supported creation of a full-time, full-salaried, and fully staffed legislature in 1966, and with that vote of confidence had come elevated expectations. At first, there were few complaints. Despite political differences, members worked together respectfully and they were collectively recognized as a model legislature. Gradually, however, rising partisanship, gridlock, and perceived elitism engendered public dissatisfaction and the alienation of political leaders from the people who had put them into office in the first place. In one move, voters in 1982 overturned a curious Democratic-drawn redistricting plan that had jagged district boundaries zigzagging from one county to another in order to create districts that lumped enough Democrats together so as to ensure party dominance through the decade. Representative Phil Burton, who engineered the redistricting process, called it his "contribution to modern art."[9]

In tone and arguments, the term limits movement resembled the public uprising of 1978. In fact, it was bitter fallout from Proposition

13 that first stirred thought of an initiative to curtail politicians' terms. A new breed of Republicans, who had been elected as tax cutters campaigning against the "non-responsive" legislature, felt they had a mandate to shatter the status quo at the capitol. "We didn't come to Sacramento just to be part of a minority," said former legislator Ross Johnson of Orange County.[10] One of their first moves was to oust Paul Priolo—the moderate go-along, get-along assembly Republican leader—in favor of more conservative Carol Hallett, the first woman ever to lead her party in the legislature. Although Republicans had enabled Willie Brown to become speaker, they chafed under his stern rule. They made him the poster child of arrogance and abusiveness, and advocated for a ballot initiative to weaken Brown's power.

Paul Gann, who had gained fame and experience as a cosponsor of Proposition 13 and author of a subsequent voter-approved state spending limit, returned to take on the establishment in 1984 with another initiative aimed at reining in the power of assembly speakers. The ability speakers like Brown had to reward friends and punish enemies was a time-tested method by which they protected their leadership. Brown doled out plum assignments to his allies, and on occasion he used his authority to replace a recalcitrant committee member—at times, only for a single day—to help secure the passage of bills he supported. Gann's initiative would strip the speaker of that authority. Under his plan, the minority party would be given additional administrative clout, and the legislature's overall budget would be cut by nearly one-third, further removing the speaker's leverage over members.

In campaign arguments reminiscent of the antiestablishment Proposition 13 rhetoric, Proposition 24 supporters accused legislative leaders of being powerful bosses who "think they're above the law and accountable to no one, spending money on themselves like drunken sailors."[11] Voters approved the measure, but within twenty-four hours the majority Democrats sued on the grounds that the state constitution gives each house in the legislature authority to make its own rules. In striking down the statutory ballot measure five months later, Sacramento Superior Court judge James Ford said, "The will of the people must bow to the Constitution."[12]

In another stunning and unprecedented display of voter disenchantment with elements of the judicial elite, state supreme court
chief justice Rose Bird and two of her liberal colleagues, Joseph
Grodin and Cruz Reynoso, were thrown off the bench at their
reconfirmation elections in 1986. Republican governor George
Deukmejian, whose career was built largely on law-and-order
themes, was a major force in the drive by conservatives to ban-
ish the three justices appointed by his predecessor, the unorthodox Democrat Jerry Brown. A $7 million campaign, much of it for
television ads, pilloried the justices for being overly protective of
criminal defendants and for their dozens of votes against the death
penalty. After his defeat, Reynoso said the only thing that voters
knew about him was what they saw in hard-hitting thirty-second
television spots attacking his record and judicial philosophy. "If I
didn't know better," he said, "I would have voted against me, too."[13]

As the 1980s progressed, media accounts questioned the
value—and cost—of the capitol's staff buildup, considering that
many aides were purely political operatives. News stories also
revealed that the legislature had padded staff by creating seventy
joint, select, and other special committees that rarely met, did little work, and cost taxpayers millions of dollars. When reporters
pored through legislative spreadsheets for 1987, they found that
the legislature had spent more than $114 million in tax dollars on
itself—for salaries, per diem, staff pay, car leases, and other expenditures—triple what it had spent ten years earlier. (Interestingly, on
the day of the 1990 election, the legislature reported that its 1989
budget had increased to $141 million.)[14] The coverage led much of
the public to conclude that elected officials were receiving special
treatment at taxpayer expense.

Another news report asserted that lawmakers often occupied
themselves mulling over and then debating seemingly frivolous
legislation, such as making the banana slug the official state mol-
lusk and standardizing the content of goat milk products. One legislator contended that 85 percent of legislation was junk. "It's just
like fungus," said Senator H. L. Richardson. "It grows in the corner
of a damp bathroom. We've created the biggest damp bathroom in

the world, the state legislature."[15] An assembly member calculated he had voted for 46,000 bills in his thirteen years in the legislature and acknowledged there was no way he could have read many of them. One bill that made it through the legislature in 1988 offered a financial break to a sham West Sacramento shrimp processing company. The measure—planted by the FBI to nab corrupt legislators willing to swap votes for campaign cash—passed the legislature but was vetoed by a tipped-off Governor Deukmejian. Federal agents raided numerous capitol offices, and by the end of 1990, the first two of several legislators, staffers, lobbyists, and other officials had been convicted in what became known as "Shrimpscam."

With the legislature's public support continuing to slide, the likely coup de grâce was a series of reports by newspapers and broadcast news outlets revealing that eighty taxpayer-funded sergeants-at-arms were being used to chauffeur and run errands for legislators, prompting charges that the legislature "has virtually turned the sergeants into private servants." Records showed that one assembly member sent a sergeant to his home to turn off a crock-pot and put it in the refrigerator, while another had a sergeant take a blanket and snacks to her teenage son in Nevada City, sixty miles away. Sergeants chauffeured another lawmaker to lunch within walking distance of the capitol; others picked up laundry and stood in line at banks. One senator had a sergeant deliver cat food to his home.[16] The public, thus, was primed for a proposed constitutional amendment to punish lawmakers by limiting their terms of service and dramatically cutting their budgets.

Schabarum, the Los Angeles supervisor, and Lewis Uhler, founder of the National Tax Limitation Committee, had been friends for decades. In 1966, when Schabarum wanted to leave his land development business for the state assembly, Uhler signed on as a volunteer campaign cochair. More than twenty years later, Uhler joined with Schabarum and two other leaders in the state's antitax movement to form a core quartet that directed the term-limits campaign. Watching "wily Willie Brown" rule the assembly, Uhler said, "started us thinking that we've got to limit the length of service and the accumulation of power." The group settled on a maximum six years of service in the assembly and eight in the senate. "It was our experience that by the time legislators had served that many years, the fire in the belly was gone, they were relying more on staff, and were much more likely to be captives of lobbyists."[17] The group also included in the measure a 38 percent cut in the legislature's budget.

Schabarum's participation was critical. He was vulnerable to the charge of hypocrisy because he was a professional politician himself, having served two decades in public office enjoying a tax-paid salary and looking forward to a nice pension. But Schabarum was also a well-known, acerbic, and highly quotable front man who brought financial resources to a campaign in need of funds. A prolific fundraiser, Schabarum contributed $650,000 from his campaign treasury to hire a firm to gather signatures to qualify the ballot measure. Uhler, meanwhile, had written a book about profligate spending in Congress and was about to embark on "a very aggressive and vigorous" nationwide book tour. When it appeared that even Schabarum's money wasn't going to be sufficient to secure the required signatures, Uhler canceled his tour, oversaw a signature-gathering effort through mail and volunteer organizations, and barely qualified Proposition 140 for the November 1990 ballot. In midsummer, before the campaign had even started, Speaker Brown held a news conference at the capitol and in a "15-minute stream-of-consciousness diatribe" previewed the opposition campaign. "It's a mean-spirited effort," Brown said. "Would you prefer to be administered for your brain tumor by the surgeon who graduated this year or the surgeon who has been practicing for ten years and never lost a patient?"[18] In three months, Brown would get his answer.

THE ELECTION

The fall campaign was complicated by the fact that two different term-limit measures had been placed on the ballot: Proposition 140, with Pete Schabarum as primary sponsor, and a less stringent Proposition 131, which had been the brainchild of Democratic attorney general John Van de Kamp and was endorsed by consumer advocate Ralph Nader. Van de Kamp had hoped to ride the populist anti-legislature wave to the governor's office and had folded into his measure a provision for public financing of political campaigns. He hadn't counted on losing to former San Francisco mayor Dianne Feinstein in the June primary, and with his political career then in disarray, the campaign for Proposition 131 foundered, leaving Schabarum's antiestablishment term-limits proposal the only viable game in town.

On September 13, Speaker Willie Brown held a lavish fundraiser at the posh Beverly Wilshire to raise funds to defeat term limits. Inside the hotel's ballroom, hundreds of lobbyists and business interests in their finest formal attire had paid $1,000 each for a chance to rub elbows with legislators, eat dinner, and watch a show featuring the Temptations. Outside, supporters of term limits picketed the event. At the end of the evening, according to the *Los Angeles Times*, Brown addressed the crowd. "As you leave here tonight," he said, "drive carefully. But I don't give a damn if you hit the pickets."[19]

Brown was taking the campaign personally, and with good reason. As the legislature's most iconic member, he symbolized an institution that provoked strong public disapproval. He considered Proposition 140 to be an anti-democratic proposal clearly aimed at his leadership. Brown raised about $1 million for the "No on 140" campaign that evening and poured in more than another $1 million over the following weeks. His legislative colleagues transferred $1.3 million from their campaign treasuries for the cause, and more than 550 senate and assembly staffers ponied up between $100 and $1,000 each. Many capitol employees worried they'd be casualties of severe budget cuts if the initiative succeeded.

Schabarum's campaign committee had spent most of its money qualifying the initiative, but it had enough left to buy $500,000 worth of radio ads on forty-nine stations in the weeks leading up to the election. "Why would huge special interests like the oil companies oppose term limits?" one ad asked. "Maybe they believe California already has the best legislature that money can buy."[20] The campaign couldn't afford television spots in a state of thirty million people accustomed to learning about statewide issues via TV ads, but several television stations gave the campaign the equivalent of $105,000 in equal/free air time—ranging from a high of $20,250 at San Francisco's KRON to $86 at KHSL in Chico.[21] The campaign hit familiar themes, particularly that the advantages of incumbency rendered most elections futile exercises with foregone outcomes. Given this, the result was a legislature full of unresponsive, unrepresentative, and arrogant professional politicians who could rack up lengthy careers while staying insulated and shielded from voters they disregarded rather than served. As if on cue, and to prove the sponsors' point, two highly publicized federal court trials found state senator Joseph Montoya and former senator Paul Carpenter guilty of corruption just before the vote. Republican state senator Ken Maddy, an opponent of the term-limits measure, tried to focus the media on the larger picture. "Just because Montoya is convicted," he said, "doesn't mean you destroy the system."[22]

While published polls during the campaign showed Proposition 140 enjoying a comfortable lead, three additional developments boosted its momentum in the months preceding Election Day. When the legislature missed approving a new state budget by nearly a month, Republicans and Democrats blamed each other. Danville assemblyman William Baker, a Republican, asked Speaker Brown, "Do you think you won the press war last week? I don't think you won. I don't think we won. I think Schabarum won."[23]

On September 18, Oklahoma became the first state in the nation to enact term limits for its legislature. A few weeks later, Republican US senator Pete Wilson, who was locked in a tight race for California governor against Feinstein, joined the state's term-limits parade. During a debate televised by thirty-two California television stations, Wilson endorsed Proposition 140 and made the public's disenchantment with government a focal point of his stretch-drive strategy. "I share their outrage," Wilson said during the debate. Feinstein responded that Proposition 140 would not place term limits on bureaucrats or lobbyists.[24] Four days later, in a speech to the Sacramento Rotary Club, Wilson noted that exasperated voters in recent years had resorted to making their own public policy via ballot initiatives. "There should be a limit to public patience, and I think a limit to the term of legislative lifers who are not doing their job."[25]

Term-limit foes had raised considerably more money, but their more sophisticated paid-media campaign wasn't registering in the polls. With their careers on the line and public opinion running against them, legislative leaders called in the cavalry: popular actress Angela Lansbury. Californians had become accustomed to seeing Hollywood personalities pitch political issues—a practice that dated back to the 1930s—and the previous June, actors Charlton Heston and Jack Lemmon had squared off on opposite sides of a redistricting measure. Lansbury played an amateur detective on *Murder, She Wrote,* one of the most highly rated television shows in history and at the time in the middle of a remarkable twelve-year run on CBS. Speaking into the camera from a studio set, Lansbury said that with the passage of term limits, "special interest groups and developers will amass even more power," running roughshod over inexperienced legislators. "Don't be lured into the term-limit trap," she said. Proponents of Proposition 140 called for a boycott of Lansbury's hit TV show, but it didn't work. The following Sunday, the show continued to enjoy strong ratings. Democratic political consultant David Townsend said the actress brought considerable credibility to the campaign against term limits, but he questioned whether it would work at the polls. "Is it enough to calm down the anger and the fears of the voters of California? I don't think so," he said. "I think they'll need a little more than Angela Lansbury."[26]

Townsend was right. The Lansbury commercial, and another featuring actor Walter Matthau, helped close the gap in the final days of the campaign but fell short on Election Day. Proposition 131—term limits and taxpayer financing of campaigns—was easily defeated. Proposition 140 eked out a 52-to-48-percent victory and set the stage for extraordinary upheaval at the capitol and a national movement to restrict legislative service. Schabarum couldn't resist poking fun at the always impeccably dressed Speaker Brown—who boasted he wore $6,000 Brioni suits, $800 shirts, and neckties that would exhaust "a trust fund baby's monthly stipend."[27] "Election night," Schabarum said, "found [Willie] Brown shivering in his

Guccis."[28] Assemblyman Baker found a silver lining of sorts for himself and his colleagues. "Proposition 140 was punitive," he said. "It was designed to hurt us and it did. We're just lucky it didn't include hanging."[29] California voters also sent another message: despite the Democrats' 1.4 million advantage in voter registration, Republican Wilson narrowly defeated Feinstein—by a margin nearly identical to Proposition 140's victory edge.

THE IMPACT

Cathy Gardella, a staffer for assemblyman John Burton, walked into the capitol the morning after the election. "Everyone was stunned," she said. "People were walking around like zombies. It was like a punch in the gut."[30] For the legislature's 2,500 policy researchers, committee consultants, legislative aides, secretaries, political support staff, and other employees, the new term limits were the least of their worries; to them, immediate job security was far more important. The assembly and senate suddenly had been ordered by voters to slash nearly 40 percent of their budgets, a move that likely meant severe layoffs in every office. Legislators' base office allowances were reduced, and internal auditors looked at everything from travel and postage to phone expenses. Employees were offered four to five months of severance pay, or a boost in retirement benefits, if they resigned by the end of January 1991.

By February 1, 650 staffers had been coaxed to leave the legislature. On their last day as legislative employees, Willie Brown was presiding over the assembly. Briefly losing his composure, the tough, cagey twenty-five-year capitol veteran broke down, tears welling in his eyes. "It's a tragedy that we have to let these people go," he said.[31] The nonpartisan Legislative Analyst's office was decimated. The Senate Education Committee lost three of its four consultants, and departing colleagues presented the surviving consultant with a Lone Ranger mask.

In the assembly, the Ways and Means Committee lost some of its most respected consultants, including experts on taxation, local government, public schools, social services, and toxic substances.

The committee's demoralized and dejected chair, Democrat John Vasconcellos of San Jose, said he was debating whether to resign before his term was over. Vasconcellos had just been reelected to his twelfth assembly term with 63 percent of the vote. His district voters also approved Proposition 140. He told a reporter that he would reduce the time he devoted to the job from sixty to forty hours per week. "I'm not going to bust my ass for people who don't value what I'm doing. The only reason for me to stay," Vasconcellos said, "is to outlast that idiot Schabarum."[32] Vasconcellos, who was forced out of the assembly in 1996 by term limits, subsequently served two terms in the senate and retired in 2004 after thirty-eight years in the legislature. The parliamentarians from both houses also left, prompting one legislator to lament, "The players have gone; now even the referees are leaving." A job-placement office was set up in the capitol's basement.[33]

In response to the voter mandate, the legislature had begun to make cuts immediately and hacked more than $56 million from its $171 million 1990–91 budget.[34] Brown said the average salary of exiting assembly staffers was $33,000. Four months after the job cuts, eighty former senate staffers still hadn't found jobs, and the upper house had more cuts to make. Critics argued that the legislature's blanket use of severance incentivized many of the smartest public policy experts to leave. Republican Tom McClintock, in his fifth assembly term and one of a handful of legislative supporters of term limits, called the severance package "extravagant in the extreme." The exodus of top-flight policy experts, he said, left the legislature staffed by "political hacks who have no other employable skills."[35] As if to prove the point of that old saw about strange bedfellows, the moderate-to-liberal *Sacramento Bee* joined McClintock in suggesting the legislature was indeed in need of further housecleaning. It had "grown large and top-heavy with political hacks and hangers on. Salaries have been overly generous," the newspaper declared.[36]

Legislative leaders may have lost at the polls, but they refused to go down without a legal fight. But if they had expected any support from the state supreme court on term limits, those hopes were dashed quickly and with panache. In October 1991, a month after holding the first supreme court hearing ever to be broadcast live, Chief Justice Malcolm Lucas wrote a majority opinion that lawmakers considered demeaning, offensive, and insulting. Proposition 140, he wrote, "will free the entire process from the control of assertedly entrenched, apathetic, veteran incumbents, thereby allowing fresh creative energies to flourish free of vested, self-serving interests." Responded Oakland senator Nicholas Petris, first elected to the legislature in 1958, "Every guy that's been here more than six years resented his reference to apathetic incumbents." As Santa Clara University's law school dean Gerald Uelman observed, "He [Lucas] seemed to go out of his way to rub salt in their wounds."[37]

Lucas had picked a fight with a branch of government that not only had budget-making authority but was determined to get even. Four months after the court's decision, the assembly started its annual budget review, and in a move that no one considered coincidental, an assembly subcommittee voted to cut the supreme court's budget by 38 percent—the exact reduction that the court agreed should be imposed on the legislature. Lawmakers from both parties simply argued that California's budget, awash in red ink, needed trimming. "They've never taken any budget cuts and they seem to think we can," said Republican assemblywoman Cathie Wright. "We all have to take some pain." A senate subcommittee was only slightly less vengeful, cutting the court's budget by 30 percent. "We didn't set out to say, 'How can we sock it to the courts?'" said Democratic senator Dan McCorquodale. "We looked at an entity that hadn't been looked at for years."[38] Governor Wilson convinced legislators to make significantly smaller cuts in the court's budget. Wilson came to the aid of the justices a second time when he vetoed two bills that would have sliced judges' retirement pay. The episodes brought into sharp focus the question of judicial independence. Can justices truly rule objectively if they are worried that the legislature might punish the court in return? "It's like the alligator in the bathtub," said Richard Chernick, president of the Los Angeles County Bar Association. "You can claim that you're not looking at it when you're taking a bath, but it's hard to ignore."[39]

A subsequent federal court challenge of term limits took years to work its way through the system, but the results were the same. It also took several years for the full force of term limits to be felt. All assembly members who had been elected in 1990 or earlier had to be out the door by 1996. Many didn't wait. They jumped at the chance to seek other offices or take high-paying jobs in lobbying, business, or consulting.

Ultimately, Proposition 140 did not deliver the kind of fresh-blood improvement that many voters had expected from term limits. A spate of special elections and contests without incumbents helped send campaign spending—driven by special interests—to new heights. The cost of legislative races in 1996 increased by 22 percent over the previous election.[40] Turnover from legislative session to session was so high that some first-term legislators landed jobs as committee chairs with no particular knowledge or understanding of the policies they were administering. At the end of 1995, thirty-two-year-old freshman Republican Brian Setencich—whose prior lawmaking experience had been a few years on the Fresno City Council—was elected speaker of the assembly. He served four months and lost his reelection bid. During one two-year period, there was a spate of costly special elections precipitated by the premature departure of sitting legislators, the result of which was refreshing the legislature with rookies and prompting legislation requiring the state to reimburse local governments for millions of dollars in election costs.

On top of the departure of veteran legislative staff, many new members recruited staff from their corps of campaign workers—aides who often were more interested in helping their bosses win the next election than solving the state's problems. Critics say term limits led to increased partisanship and more stalemates in the capitol. Legislative officials have tried to teach new representatives and their staffs the deeper complexities of state government, finance, and policy, but with mixed results. "Who wants to stay up all night learning brain surgery when he can only practice for two years?" asked critic Peter Schrag.[41] Gregory Schmidt, a longtime senate chief executive, recalled an incident in which neither a committee chairman nor his staff apparently understood the basics of lawmaking, particularly the requirement that a bill must be approved in one house of the legislature before it is sent to the other. "A staff person showed up at the senate desk with a bill from the assembly," Schmidt remembered, "and he said, 'My chairman doesn't want to hear the bill so he told me to just send it to the senate.' I'm thinking, did this guy take eighth-grade civics?"[42]

Academic studies and interviews found that neophyte lawmakers and inexperienced staff increasingly turned to more seasoned political players to learn the ropes and get things accomplished — primarily the capitol's hundreds of savvy lobbyists, whose clients' agendas didn't always coincide with the greater public good. Relying on lobbyists always had been a capitol staple, but "a few new members confessed that in their first year, over ninety percent of their bills were drafted or given to them by lobbyists," and when staffers were unable to answer their questions, they turned to the lobbyists for explanations.[43] An investigation by the *San Jose Mercury News* in 2010 found a rise in the use of special interests not only to sponsor legislation but to shepherd it through the legislative process. As one-time term limit supporter Jim Brulte, chairman of the state Republican Party, explained, "When I was Republican leader in the assembly, special interests needed me. Today, the leadership in the legislature needs the special interests."[44]

New members — constrained by term limits — have quickly realized that they have to make their mark in a hurry so they can pad their resumes before their next electoral move. No longer patient with the pace of time-honored review and parliamentary procedures, lawmakers often accelerate bills along the legislative conveyor belt before they are fully developed, particularly in the assembly. Often, those bills — with serious legal or policy deficiencies — have been stopped in the senate. In addition, legislators focused on their own short-term futures have been less inspired to think about the state's long-term future. "It takes so much time to become proficient in water policy or transportation. You just can't do it," Schmidt observed. One assemblywoman told researchers Bruce E. Cain and Thad Kousser that the state's water policy affected her district but acknowledged she would "need ten years to learn enough to make a difference." Another conceded, "I felt like I was just beginning to become an effective member at the end of my third term in the Assembly." That disconnect between the learning curve for comprehending California governance and the reality of term limits also affected the annual ritual of enacting a state budget. As a body, the legislature has become "less likely to alter a governor's budget," and its own budget processes do not encourage fiscal discipline.[45]

The new-look legislature did, however, more closely resemble the demographic makeup of California. Legislators were younger, and women's representation increased dramatically. In the five post-term limit elections in the 1990s, sixty-one women were elected to the legislature, compared to eighteen in the previous five elections. Minority representation also grew substantially, coinciding with demographic changes in the state and a 1991 redistricting plan designed to boost minority representation by complying with the Voting Rights Act. In 1990, sixty-nine of the eighty members in the assembly were white. By 2000, that number had dropped to fifty-one, with minorities—primarily Latinos—climbing to twenty-nine. There was a similar trend in the senate.[46] In 2014, a third woman was elected speaker of the assembly—replacing a Latino man—and in the senate, Kevin de León became the state's first Latino president pro tem since the 1880s.

With consistent replenishment of new members and more competitive contests, advocates of term limits predicted a revitalized electorate and a boost in voter participation. "Why don't more people vote?" they asked in the official ballot arguments. "Because incumbents have rigged the system in their favor so much, elections are meaningless."[47] There was a dramatic boost in Latino voter turnout after term limits were fully implemented—possibly the result of forced retirements of incumbents and an increase in Latino candidates who were able to mobilize ethnic voters[48]—but overall, a CSU Sacramento study indicated that Proposition 140 actually may have helped depress voter turnout. New candidates have less name recognition among voters, and voters are less likely to vote for political unknowns.[49] Similarly, Proposition 140 failed to return California to an era of "citizen legislators." Political careerism has continued to flourish, but unlike the 1970s and '80s—when service as a legislative staffer frequently led to elective office—the post–Proposition 140 road to Sacramento often requires toiling on a city council, board of supervisors, or school board before serving in the legislature.

A quarter century after voters slapped the legislature with term limits, even some of Proposition 140's most ardent supporters had conceded that a number of unintended consequences have harmed the institution. Both Pete Schabarum and Lewis Uhler bemoaned the constant job-hopping among legislators with restricted shelf lives in the assembly or senate. "I don't recall that we concerned ourselves with that prospect," Uhler recalled. Voters modified the term limit measure in 2012, allowing lawmakers to develop seniority and specialized public-policy expertise by serving up to twelve years in either house. "As long as you have a date certain when somebody comes in and leaves, that is a vital dimension because it takes away the careerist attitude and mentality," he said.[50]

Uhler insisted that his landmark initiative was not aimed personally at Willie Brown or senate leader David Roberti but at reducing the power structure of the legislative leadership—something it accomplished. He and Schabarum had concluded that fundamental change in the legislature could be accomplished only with a complete housecleaning. Others, however, acknowledged partisan motives. John Caldwell, a Republican staffer at the time, said he voted for Proposition 140 "because I naively believed it would help Republicans by chasing out the professionals who are mostly Democrats."[51] Caldwell himself would become a casualty of the massive post-election budget cutting. In retrospect, he said, he concluded that many Democrats are working in government because they *care* about it and are willing to earn less by doing so; successful conservatives, however, tend to gravitate toward better-paying business careers, not politics.

Republican John Lewis, an early supporter of Proposition 140 while a state assemblyman from Orange County, also changed his mind. Like many other conservatives, Lewis wanted to rid the legislature of Willie Brown. "Looking back on it, I think the legislators with experience seemed to do a better job. For all of his [Brown's] faults, it's like Mussolini made the trains run on time."[52] And twenty years after standing with Schabarum, Uhler, and others, McClintock, still in public office as a member of Congress, would reverse course and acknowledge that term limits had "badly" harmed the legislature's effectiveness: "Of all the mistakes I've made in public life, the one I regret most is advocating for term limits for the legislature."[53]

After the shock of the initial cuts, the legislature's operating budget gradually increased and finally returned to pre–Proposition 140 levels—$170 million—nine years later. By 2014–15, total legislative spending approached $270 million. Elsewhere in the country, eighteen states have followed the initial lead of Oklahoma, California, and Colorado to enact term limits for their legislatures. Subsequently, two legislatures repealed their state's term-limit laws, and courts in four other states struck them down, although not on the merits of the laws but on technicalities.[54] As in California, proponents had seized on the failures and foibles of legislators and tapped into the public's alienation with its political institutions. "There's kind of a leitmotif in American history that you always hate the Legislature," said Schmidt, the senate's former chief executive. "That's a vein that you can always tap at any particular point."[55] Since 1990, there has been intense debate over the consequences of Proposition 140 and the one successful effort to modify it. Those who take the public's pulse say today, as then, the public wants a more effective legislature and generally continues to believe that one way to achieve it is to place limits on the power and political lifetimes of lawmakers.

Ironically, California voters have shown their willingness to make exceptions to term limits in a handful of cases. Most notable was the election in 2014 of Jerry Brown to his historic fourth term as governor of California. Brown surpassed the abbreviated three terms of Earl Warren, who had left the governor's office after ten years to become chief justice of the United States. Serving two stints three decades apart, Brown bridged the antigovernment tide that had begun at the end of his first two terms in 1983 and continues to this day. Because he first governed before Proposition 140, he was free to run again—for only two terms—in 2010 and 2014. But term limits finally caught up with him. Perhaps summarizing the view of many like him, facing their final campaigns for reelection to their last terms, he lamented, "I don't like to think about my last campaign. I find it a depressing thought."[56]

13

Still in the Game

JUDGING AN ELECTION'S enduring impact can take decades or longer. Who knew in 1861, for example, that a railroad line linking Sacramento to Omaha would lead to a single company dominating California's political institutions for nearly half a century? Who knew in 1934 that the election of a nondescript governor would revolutionize political campaign techniques? Beyond contests explored thus far in this book's chapters, several more-recent elections might be among the game changers, but their lasting effects have yet to be felt.

In 1994, California voters approved Proposition 187—heavily championed by Republicans—which would have allowed only legal immigrants and citizens of California to receive public education and health and welfare services. Although the initiative would later be invalidated by the courts and never take effect, the Republican brand has suffered ever since. Republican candidates have lost ground in subsequent decades, and they failed to win a single statewide election in both 2010 and 2014. Can the GOP recover in California?

Two contests in 1998 smashed national campaign spending records: the governor's race and a ballot measure to expand Indian gambling. Can Californians expect wealthy self-funded candidates to continue to dominate California's political landscape? And which special-interest groups will seek to have the most influence in future elections?

The 2003 recall of Davis found voters using 1911's tool of direct democracy against a California governor for the first time. Will this become a trend in California elections? Or was it merely a perfect storm of political fates that saw a chief executive as dull as his first name vanquished by a Hollywood action hero?

Finally, political polarization has dominated California politics for decades, preventing progress on numerous critical issues and angering an increasingly restless electorate. Recent voter-approved changes—particularly the "top-two primary"—seek to lessen partisanship. Will that result in charting a new centrist path for the state?

1994: Public Benefits Are Denied to Illegal Immigrants

A dozen miles southeast of downtown Los Angeles, in the heavily Latino city of Pico Rivera, a steady November rain fell as neighbors gathered outside St. Bartholomew's Church. Waiting with them in the dampness for the doors to open at 7:00 a.m. so they could vote, Ernesto Ricarte, Jr., told a *Los Angeles Times* reporter that he had brought his birth certificate with him. He explained that his boss once wanted to see proof of his immigration status and that he had to explain he was an American-born citizen. Since then, he said, "I carry it with me everywhere I go." Twenty-year-old Annabella Ramirez held her baby on her hip a short time later as she cast her first ballot. "I wanted to be part of the voting," she said. A poll worker, noting the surge in voter interest within a usually indifferent community, commented, "We have never seen anything like this."[1]

Ramirez and Ricarte were among the eight and a half million Californians who registered their sentiments on Proposition 187, the contentious "Save Our State" initiative of 1994 that roiled California with the goal of denying public benefits, including health care and education, to illegal immigrants. Under the initiative, state and local agencies would be required to report to authorities anyone they suspected of being in the country illegally. Schoolchildren would be expelled if their parents or guardians were unable to document their citizenship or residency status. Critics feared legal immigrants and citizens of color inevitably would be targeted too.

Just as Proposition 187 energized Latino voters in opposition, it also invigorated millions of angry and frightened Californians who were concerned that an estimated $2 billion a year for services for undocumented residents would drive the state into insolvency. "How many illegals can we educate, medicate, compensate and incarcerate before California goes bankrupt?" asked Harold Ezell, President Reagan's former western states chief of the Immigration and Naturalization Service.[2] The election also revealed California's less golden side, a streak that has run through much of the electorate since the Gold Rush. The leader of one anti-immigration group was defiant: "I have no intention of being the object of 'conquest,' peaceful or otherwise, by Latinos, Asians, blacks, Arabs or any other group of individuals who have claimed my country."[3] How did California find itself at the epicenter of such a tumultuous debate, and how would that shape a new generation of political and social institutions?

The first few years of the 1990s were difficult for California. The Cold War with the Soviet Union had ended, and Southern California's once-flourishing defense and aerospace industries were in retreat. Hundreds of thousands of laid-off engineers and other white-collar workers fled to states where jobs were more plentiful and taxes lower. It was the depression-era Dust Bowl migration in reverse. Housing prices had plummeted, the state's tax base had shrunk, poverty was on the rise, and Republican governor Pete Wilson had agreed to more than $7 billion in tax increases to help close the largest budget deficit the state had ever seen. In 1992, a prolonged budget deadlock in the legislature forced red-faced state officials to issue IOUs. As Californians were moving out, Mexico's own economic turbulence was propelling its citizens north across the border—legally or not—in search of low-paying jobs for unskilled workers.

In 1991, Governor Wilson's administration argued the state's budget was stretched too thin by public services for legal and illegal immigrants. Late in the year, Wilson met with White House officials, "pressing his argument that the cost of dealing with immigrants is overwhelming the state."[4] Wilson eventually filed three federal lawsuits seeking billions of dollars from the federal government to cover the cost of providing services to illegal aliens. They were combined into one suit and thrown out by a federal judge, who ruled there was no legal precedent for a state suing the US government for failing to enforce immigration laws.

Media coverage of Wilson's arguments began to register in the public consciousness, and prominent Democrats joined the debate as well. In an op-ed piece in the state's largest newspaper, Democratic US senator Dianne Feinstein noted there were 700,000 illegal residents just in Los Angeles County, with up to 5,000 Mexican citizens trying to cross the border each night. She called for increased border security and deportation of all illegal immigrants who committed felonies.[5] But it was Wilson—embroiled in a high-profile reelection campaign against state treasurer Kathleen Brown, the daughter and sister of two former governors—who set the agenda. Focusing on illegal immigrants in general and Proposition 187 in particular, Wilson drove media coverage that transformed an obscure issue into a headline-dominating crisis. By November 1994, "Wilson's internal tracking polls showed that more than 90 percent of voters knew Wilson's position on Proposition 187, more than the number of people who could identify Sacramento as the state capital."[6]

The "Save Our State" initiative, as it was billed by supporters, was born of failed legislative attempts by Southern California Republican assemblyman Richard Mountjoy to bar illegals from public schools and to restrict their medical care. He was "hooted down as a right-wing kook," *Los Angeles Times* columnist George Skelton wrote.[7] Once the legislative session ended in 1993, Mountjoy and a small band of frustrated immigration-restriction advocates met at a posh private club in Orange County to draft what would become Proposition 187. Two former high-ranking Reagan officials at the Immigration and Naturalization Service—

commissioner Alan Nelson and western chief Ezell—were selected to be the public faces of one of the most racially divisive ballot measures in California history. The initiative was California's first attempt to take aim at immigrants since 1920, when voters over-whelmingly prohibited those of Japanese descent from owning "our rich agricultural lands."[8] In May of 1994, sponsors submitted 600,000 signatures to qualify the measure for the November ballot.

Bogged down by a recession and inaction in Sacramento, Wilson's reelection campaign against Kathleen Brown had been foundering. At one point, he trailed the Democrat by twenty points in the polls. But Wilson found the boost he needed by tap-ping into growing antipathy toward undocumented aliens entering California. White anxieties "soon boiled over into racial resent-ment, driven in no small measure by Wilson's gritty, noir adver-tising that played to fears of lawless, dark-skinned immigrants overwhelming the state of California,"[9] noted Kathy Olmsted, a professor of history at UC Davis.

"They keep coming," an ominous voice declared as a pro-Wilson TV ad opened with footage of Mexicans running across the border into California, weaving in and out of traffic on Interstate 5. "Two million immigrants in California..." it continued before the ad broke to Wilson, who spoke directly into the camera: "For Californians who work hard, pay taxes, and obey the laws, I'm suing to force the federal government to control the border. And I'm working to deny state services to illegal immigrants. Enough is enough."[10] The ad sparked charges of racism and immigrant bashing. Dan Schnur, Wilson's campaign press secretary at the time, recalled the internal discussions about the ad. "We believed that because the footage came from the Border Patrol, voters would see it as a legiti-mate real-world argument. But we were so focused on the 60 percent of the voters who understood that argument that we didn't devote nearly the time and effort in talking to the 40 percent that didn't."[11] Believing Proposition 187 would boost the party's fortunes, the state GOP made the ballot measure the centerpiece of its voter mobiliza-tion efforts, featuring the immigration restriction measure in slate mailers, phone banks, and precinct-walking outreach.

Meanwhile, a "No on 187" coalition of Democrats and labor and civil rights groups was in a quandary, knowing the electorate then was 80 percent white. Their opposition campaign argued that "Proposition 187 does nothing to beef up border patrol" and would lead to more crime and graffiti by throwing as many as 400,000 children out of school. "Would they get deported back to their own countries? NO. Prop. 187 would deport them onto *our* streets."[12] Upset immigrants-rights organizations—a key component of the coalition—argued that this approach only reinforced the fears of white voters, but the campaign consulting team insisted it would resonate with those most likely to cast ballots.

Three weeks before the election, 70,000 demonstrators, many waving Mexican flags, marched through downtown Los Angeles in a grassroots protest against the immigration measure. Their march highlighted a new activism and engagement by Latinos who felt stigmatized regardless of their immigration status. It also, however, reinforced concerns many Californians had about a state that was shifting from white to brown. "This is the tragedy," said Jack McDowell, dean of the anti-187 consultants, who had been managing campaigns for twenty-three years. "They [the protestors] were trying to help [the campaign]. But the result was, I believe, they hurt [it]."[13]

Bolstered by the turnout of Proposition 187 supporters, Republicans enjoyed their best election since Ronald Reagan had been swept into office in 1966. With Wilson leading the way, they won five statewide offices and picked up an astonishing nine seats in the assembly. Although the GOP had a majority in the assembly for the first time in a quarter century, only slick maneuvering by Democratic speaker Willie Brown prevented Republicans from immediately assuming control.

The day after the election, Wilson announced he had signed an executive order directing nursing homes to halt new admissions of illegal immigrants and ordering health care workers to discontinue prenatal services for those who couldn't prove they were in the state legally. That same day, eight lawsuits were filed in various state and federal courts and, by mid-afternoon, a San Francisco

Superior Court judge had blocked schools from excluding illegal residents. Eventually, virtually every element of Proposition 187 was declared unconstitutional.

In 1994, the GOP reached its high-water mark in California. Energized Latinos, no longer diffident about civic engagement, parlayed their setback at the polls into a fresh political crusade. Those who were in California legally tried to become citizens, while those who already were citizens began capitalizing on the power of bloc votes at the ballot box. Two years after Proposition 187, nearly three-fourths of Latinos in California voted for Bill Clinton, who became the first Democratic presidential nominee since Lyndon Johnson to carry California. "This was the defining moment that influenced this community's political allegiances, much like African Americans became loyal Democrats after the party's civil rights commitment in 1964," said veteran Republican political consultant Richard Temple. In the years that followed, Republicans successfully pushed two other race- and ethnicity-related initiatives to outlaw affirmative action and bilingual education. "That's when the wheels started to fall off," Temple said. "You can't keep writing off blocs of voters and say, 'We don't need them.'" Republican primaries were being won by the candidate toughest on immigration. Minorities felt unwelcome in the party, and members of the middle class started to see the GOP as "wanting to have their white country club without letting anyone else in," Temple said.[14]

In the ensuing elections, Republicans face-planted as the state turned reliably blue. In 1998, minorities helped push Democrat Gray Davis into the governor's office with a twenty-point victory. Four years later, Republicans lost every statewide office. After a brief interlude with moderate mega-celebrity Arnold Schwarzenegger winning the governorship, Republicans returned to the wilderness, nominating a billionaire businesswoman in 2010 who spent $144 million of her own money but was nevertheless routed in seventy-two-year-old Jerry Brown's return to glory. By this time, the Latino vote, overwhelmingly Democratic, amounted to 22 percent of the electorate—two and a half times what it had been in 1994. The white vote had shrunk to 61 percent.[15] Four years later, Republican registration in the state would fall below 29 percent. "This is a party that, whether we like it or not, has been in decline for two decades in this state," California Republican Party chairman Jim Brulte told reporters in 2014.[16]

Can California Republicans rebound, particularly among the fast-growing Latino electorate? Ronald Reagan once said famously, "Hispanics are already Republican. They just don't know it."[17] Pollster Mark Baldassare agreed that "many Latinos have a conservative bent" and share certain values with Republicans. Immigration, Baldassare said, is not their top concern, but nonetheless it is an issue with a lot of close associations with human rights and civil rights, and the GOP remains negatively associated with that struggle.[18]

Complicating the GOP's comeback attempt were messages sent by Republican Party leaders during the national immigration reform debate beginning in 2013. "Make no mistake about it," Schnur said, "the immigration issue is a boulder in the road that is blocking the Republican Party's ability to compete seriously in large sections of the country."[19] That view, however, is not universal among conservatives, many of whom believe that Republicans would be more successful if they harden—rather than soften—their rhetoric on immigration issues. Writing in the *American Conservative*, Steve Sailer argued it was a myth that "cracking down on illegal immigration was political suicide for the GOP."[20] Pointing to Wilson's 1994 reelection victory, he suggested that racially charged campaigns may sacrifice the minority vote but more than make up for it by strengthening the white vote.

In 2014, the Republican consulting firm McNally Temple surveyed Californians on their attitudes toward Republicans and whether they believed there is a path toward resurrection. Richard Temple said the responses were encouraging. The survey showed that Latinos, Asians, millennials, and independents agree with Republicans that government should be efficient and prudent with tax dollars, that welfare should be temporary and basic, and that schools need to be more accountable. "Republicans have dug themselves a deep hole," Temple acknowledged. "We have to change our messaging but stay with our core values, and we have to change our messengers to be more diverse."[21]

Republican Party leaders took baby steps in that direction in 2014, fielding the most ethnically diverse slate of legislative candidates in memory and winning three contests with female Asian American immigrants. In 2015, at the party's state convention, delegates granted recognition to a gay Republican volunteer organization—a mostly symbolic move, but one that sent important signals about the party's rebranding efforts. As they try to keep up with changing demographics and revive the party's political fortunes in California, leaders understand the journey will take time. In surveying the political landscape, Temple conceded, "You can't reverse a stereotype overnight."

1998: Two Elections Shatter National Spending Records

In the business of politics it's called "carpet bombing"—saturating the television airwaves with advertisements, many of them negative and misleading. Long before the 1998 elections, expensive broadcast spots had supplanted in-person "retail" voter outreach as the dominant method of campaigning. As California's June 2 primary election approached, however, viewers in the state's major media markets were being subjected to an extraordinary onslaught of 527 TV spots a day just from the one Republican and three major Democratic candidates. There was no relief for viewers between *Good Morning America* and *The Price Is Right* in the morning, and *Seinfeld* and *Sabrina, the Teenage Witch* in the evening.[22]

The media persuasion blitz continued in the fall with a contentious ballot initiative sharing the spotlight with the general election for governor. With about 80 percent of a major, statewide campaign budget earmarked for production and placement of television ads, it took a combination of self-financing and furious fundraising to realize sufficient funds for the campaigns' media efforts. Indeed, California saw an unprecedented half-billion dollars spent on statewide and legislative races and ballot propositions in 1998.[23]

Once the books closed on the various campaigns—and the last political commercials had aggravated weary viewers—two national records had been smashed. Spending in the governor's contest reached nearly $125 million, making it the most expensive gubernatorial election in history at the time,[24] and more than $92 million was spent on Proposition 5 (impacting Indian gaming rights), which topped the charts among ballot propositions.[25] There had been so many ads on television for governor, US Senate, and major ballot measures that down-ticket hopefuls for lieutenant governor, attorney general, and treasurer complained they were frozen out of the TV market. "It's supply and demand," said a spokesman for Los Angeles powerhouse KABC-TV. "It's a matter of what's available." That was little solace to Curt Pringle, who had raised $1 million in his campaign for the Republican nomination for state treasurer but couldn't air his ads. "If you can't get the press to write stories, and you're frozen out of television, how do you communicate with voters?" he grumbled.[26]

JUNE 1998

The air war in the 1998 governor's race actually had begun ten days before Thanksgiving the previous year—an astonishing fifty weeks prior to the November 1998 general election. As people were getting ready to pick out their holiday turkeys, airline mogul Al Checchi introduced himself to California television audiences with an ad featuring a photo showing him celebrating his third birthday.[27] Known by journalists as "Al Checkbook," this upstart Democratic candidate for governor had publicly estimated his own net worth to be about $550 million. He had plunked $3 million into a campaign account on the last day of 1996 and immediately hired some of the biggest names in campaign management, voter polling, and ad development. He would continue to open his wallet to feed the campaign beast until he had dropped $39 million.

Potential rivals were near apoplectic. To them, it wasn't going to be a fair fight. While the courts had affirmed a limit of $1,000 on donor contributions, judges ruled that wealthy candidates could spend unlimited personal money on their own campaigns, reasoning that candidates can't corrupt themselves.

Gray Davis, one of those rivals, became obsessed with Checchi and what his wealth could buy in the governor's race. Checchi—untested and unknown, a social liberal and fiscal conservative—had never voted in a California primary or gubernatorial election, but now he wanted to be governor and had a boatload of money to finance a campaign. At forty-nine, he was handsome, looked good on television, and had a lengthy record of business success to tout. Davis had been Governor Jerry Brown's chief of staff for six years and, for all intents and purposes, ran the state when Brown was traipsing through New Hampshire, Wisconsin, and elsewhere campaigning for president in 1980. He had served two terms in the state assembly, then two terms as state controller and a single term as lieutenant governor. His political success, however, defied conventional wisdom in the television age. Gray Davis was unexciting, and his speeches tended to be sleep-inducing. He always seemed to be wearing the same dark suit, blue shirt, and red tie. A Stanford graduate and former army captain in Vietnam, he figured the Democratic nomination should have been his for the asking; he had earned it. But the state had just adopted a "blanket primary" system that allowed voters to cast ballots for any candidate, regardless of party, fueling Davis's fear that Republicans, enamored with Checchi's business acumen, would cross party lines to support the man who had turned around Northwest Airlines. Checchi, it seemed, had everything going for him.

Watching what he called the "Checchi phenomenon" was a skeptical George Skelton of the *Los Angeles Times*. "You can't go out and act like a rich guy and say, 'I'm smarter than anybody else,'" Skelton recalled years later. He wrote in a column that the mega-millionaire was "a baby boomer who still needs political training wheels."[28]

Five months before the primary election, the campaign entered a new phase. First, a federal district judge voided the contribution limits, enabling Davis to better compete for the nomination by accepting unlimited donations, particularly from his union friends.

A month later, three-term House representative Jane Harman of Torrance joined the contest, introducing a new dynamic. She was a fresh face but one with government experience, having served as a White House aide to Jimmy Carter and having won two tough congressional contests. As a member of the House Armed Services and Intelligence Committees, she had strong ties to Southern California's aerospace and defense industries. She was married to a wealthy electronics entrepreneur and wasn't afraid to spend millions of the family fortune on her campaign. Liberal on social issues and conservative on national security and economic matters, Harman characterized herself as "the best Republican in the Democratic Party." She also was the only woman in a Democratic primary in which significantly more women than men were expected to vote. "Hello, sisters," Harman greeted the women's caucus at the state Democratic convention. "May the best woman win."[29]

Her family-financed television ads had been running for only three weeks when a statewide poll vaulted her into the lead over Checchi and Davis. The night before the poll was released to the media, it befell Checchi strategist Darry Sragow to tell his client the bad news. "Al was stunned, absolutely stunned," Sragow recalled. "He had spent around $10 million, and all of a sudden, here's Jane, who had nothing as far as Al was concerned, and she was ahead of him in the poll. It was a major cataclysm in the campaign."[30] What followed was what the political cognoscente labeled, tongue in cheek, a "murder-suicide." Fueled by private fortunes, Checchi and Harman lobbed television grenades at each other, driving down the approval ratings of both, while Davis used other people's money to rise to the top using the line "Experience money can't buy." A *Washington Post* analysis a few days before the election found Checchi running 217 television spots a day throughout California, including 60 in the Los Angeles media market, where a single thirty-second ad in prime time cost as much as $25,000.[31] Davis strategist Garry South found that Checchi "wore out his welcome with viewers." When he showed a Checchi spot to participants in Davis focus groups, "people would go, 'Oh, God! Not him again.'"[32]

"Your honor, my client believes that campaign
spending limitations are a curb on free speech
because everybody knows money talks!"

By the time the last dollar was wrung out of the campaign,
Davis had defeated Checchi and Harman in the Democratic primary by comfortable margins. On top of Checchi's $39 million,
which translated to an astounding $52.45 per vote for him, Harman
spent more than $16 million and Davis just $9 million. Checchi's
total exceeded the combined spending of all one hundred assembly
and senate primary contests.

He and Harman weren't the first candidates to try to parlay personal wealth into high government office, but even in defeat, they
set a standard that others would follow. "That was the watershed
year where parties ceased to be a determinant factor," observed
Barbara O'Connor, former director of the Institute on the Study
of Politics and the Media at CSU Sacramento. "It really says to a
person who can't self-fund, you have to have a real tie to money in
order to run."[33] Having dispatched a pair of multimillionaires in the
primary, Davis cruised to an easy victory over Republican attorney
general Dan Lungren in the fall.

California lawmakers responded to the orgy of campaign spending by approving legislation that offered voters an opportunity in 2000 to impose strict contribution limits on candidate races. It didn't cover wealthy self-funded candidates, of course, who had court protection to spend as much of their own money as they wished. By this time, Davis was looking ahead to reelection in 2002 and, once again, worried about living under contribution limits while a wealthy opponent had no such constraints. Lawmakers delayed the effective date on statewide races until after the 2002 election cycle, and Davis signed the measure, sending it to the ballot for subsequent voter approval.

In the following years, fabulously wealthy candidates—many of whom had little or no record of prior public service—again stepped up to pour personal fortunes into runs for governor. Four years after Checchi and Harman were defeated, Republican businessman Bill Simon spent more than $10 million in a failed bid to block Davis's reelection. Republican Arnold Schwarzenegger, who earned $30 million acting in *Terminator 3: Rise of the Machines*,[34] would spend more than $15 million of his own money in the 2003 recall election and his 2006 reelection, although he forwent taking a state salary. Also in 2006, state controller Steve Westly, a venture capitalist, would fail to secure the Democratic gubernatorial nomination despite his infusion of $35 million into the campaign. In 2010, Republican businesswoman Meg Whitman shattered all records in reducing her net worth by $144 million to unsuccessfully run for governor against Jerry Brown. In the primary election, she had defeated former Silicon Valley entrepreneur Steve Poizner, who had poured $24 million into his campaign. Four years after Whitman's setback, Wall Street banker Neel Kashkari dropped three-fifths of his stated $5 million net worth into a challenge against Brown's reelection, losing by twenty points.

If there is a lesson to be learned from the 1998 governor's contest it's that an unlimited money supply—contrary to popular wisdom—does not ensure success in a major, high-profile contest. Although financial resources are often determinative in local, legislative, and "down-ticket" state races that attract little or no public attention, pouring additional money into a top-of-ticket campaign has diminishing returns beyond a certain point. Political consultants get rich, and media outlets pad their earnings, but candidates become intrusive and unwelcome guests who refuse to get off our TV sets. Between 1998 and 2014, wealthy candidates wrote personal checks in excess of $288 million for mostly quixotic campaigns for governor, time and again miscalculating that the size of their wallets could buy them the state's top political prize.

NOVEMBER 1998

His name was Mark Macarro, and by the time Californians went to the polls in November 1998, he had one of the most recognizable faces of the campaign season. The designated spokesman for the landmark Indian gaming initiative known as Proposition 5, Macarro had received more exposure through TV ads than leading gubernatorial nominees Gray Davis and Dan Lungren combined.[35] Even one of Macarro's political adversaries at the time, Stan McGarr of the Pala tribe, was impressed. "If I wanted someone out of Central Casting, I'd want him," McGarr said. For his part, the mild-mannered Macarro shrugged off his new celebrity status: "It's unsettling. I'd rather have remained a no-name nobody."[36]

Macarro traced his lineage through the Pechanga Band of Luiseño Indians in the Temecula Valley, where his ancestors had been pressed into servitude by Spanish missionaries and evicted from their traditional tribal land in the 1870s. Eight years after his graduation from UC Santa Barbara, Macarro stared into a commercial crew's TV camera and in a calm, understated manner told the California electorate that Proposition 5 "simply allows Indians to continue to have limited gaming on tribal lands." He urged Californians to "do the right thing."[37] Because of Indian gaming, he said in another ad, tribes have begun "the long march back from poverty and hopelessness to prosperity."[38]

The march from poverty had indeed been long for California's Indians, who would finally find their pot of gold in the losses of unlucky gamblers. As recently as 1989, according to the California

Research Bureau, the median family income on reservations was $13,489. Nearly half of families lived in poverty, the suicide rate was nearly twice the national average, and the alcoholism rate was 663 percent higher.[39] Many reservations were on dry, unfertile desert lands that offered little sustenance or opportunity for generating income. Desperate to raise their members' quality of life, a number of impoverished tribes had begun to pursue gaming to generate income. One of those, the Cabazon Band of Mission Indians near Palm Springs, had opened a card room in 1979 and then a bingo parlor, but it soon ran afoul of government officials who contended that high-stakes bingo violated state law. The state sued the Cabazons, but in 1987 the US Supreme Court handed California tribes a huge victory, ruling that they had a right to run gambling operations on their sovereign reservations.

As tribes rushed to build casinos, Congress moved hastily to regulate the industry. It required tribes to negotiate agreements, or compacts, with their states if they wanted to install lucrative video slot machines. Governor Pete Wilson balked, however. He contended the machines conflicted with state law, and refused to negotiate compacts permitting them. Despite threats of government raids, the gaming tribes defied Wilson and kept their casinos operating, piling up huge profits that were moving their members from poverty to wealth.

In the latter half of the 1990s, as their stalemate with Wilson dragged on, the gaming tribes found another use for their rapidly growing gambling profits: political advocacy. Realizing that the fate of their gaming operations ultimately would rest in the hands of state policymakers, the tribes hired consultants and lobbyists. In 1995, the gaming tribes had barely caused a ripple at the capitol, contributing a combined $78,117 to candidates for the legislature and statewide offices; by 1998, however, their contributions had increased nearly one-hundred-fold to $7.3 million, and they spent another $1.7 million on lobbying.[40] "They had garnered so much money, they were able to buy themselves into respectability," and they quickly joined the major players at the capitol, noted *Sacramento Bee* political columnist Dan Walters.[41] Money from

card rooms and racetracks—traditional powers at the capitol—
were being challenged by this new emerging force in politics.

After Wilson negotiated a compact with the Pala Band of
Mission Indians in San Diego County that placed strict limits on
the style and number of their video machines, many other gaming
tribes argued the new rules would be economic suicide for them.
By then, Indian gaming had become a $1.4 billion industry. The
sympathetic *San Diego Union-Tribune* editorialized that the deal
was "as big an assault on Indian rights as anything the cavalry did
last century."[42] The tribes decided to take their case to voters, setting up a classic battle among disparate gambling interests. It was,
at the time, the single most expensive ballot measure in US history
and an awesome display of political power.

In less than thirty days, the major gaming tribes collected a million signatures to put Proposition 5 on the November 1998 ballot. It
asked voters to allow them to continue to build their casinos around
video slot machines, and it played on the sympathies and guilt that
many Californians felt about past treatment of Indians. "We are not
asking for hand-outs," the ballot argument stressed. "We are asking
to take care of ourselves and get off welfare."[43]

In television ads that saturated the airwaves like never before,
the tribes argued that gaming limits would undermine their success
in reducing welfare by 68 percent and unemployment by 50 percent among Indians. Mark Macarro was everywhere, telling voters
that Nevada gambling interests were "funding the worst anti-Indian
scare campaign in modern history."[44] Led by $26 million in con-
tributions from the San Manuel Band of Mission Indians in San
Bernardino County, the tribes committed an unprecedented $66
million to the campaign.[45] "More people were aware of Prop. 5 than
were aware of who was running for governor," observed political consultant Allen Hoffenblum in the *California Journal*. Less
detached was Jack Gribbon of the Hotel Employees and Restaurant
Employees International Union, which fought the measure. "It was
a snowstorm from those guys and we were barely visible," he said.[46]

Gribbon and his union opposed Proposition 5 because it was
assumed that tribal sovereignty would insulate casinos from union

organizing efforts. The bulk of the nearly $26 million opposition, however, came from Nevada casinos, which studies indicated would lose up to $600 million a year from tribal competition.[47] The "Coalition Against Unregulated Gaming" flooded airways with overstated and low-key advertisements alike. One ad, warning of runaway gambling, depicted glitzy high-rise mega-casinos popping out of various locations on a map of California. Another featured a young mother sitting at her computer: "I want to help California Indians, but I'm voting no on Proposition 5."[48] A number of tribes also opposed the measure. Like the Palas, they had signed compacts with Wilson that limited gaming on their reservations; they worried that Proposition 5 would boost gambling statewide and increase their competition.

On Election Day, Californians chose sympathy over fear of the unknown and gave gaming tribes their blessing with 63 percent of the vote for Proposition 5. But the tribes had made a tactical blunder before the campaign had even begun. Months earlier, during five days of meetings at the Hyatt Hotel across the street from the capitol grounds, tribes had decided to seek a statutory initiative instead of a constitutional amendment, the latter of which would have required more signatures to qualify for the ballot; on a tight timeline, they were concerned they'd be unable to secure enough signatures by the deadline. What they did not predict then, but perhaps should have, was that the California Supreme Court would invalidate Proposition 5 because the state constitution—as amended by the voters when they approved a state lottery in 1984—expressly prohibited "casinos of the type currently operating in Nevada and New Jersey."[49] Video slot machines therefore remained illegal; the tribes would have to start over and get voters to change the constitution.

In March 2000, Californians again would express their sentiment that Indian tribes were entitled to gaming rights. This time, there was none of the rancor or profligate spending the state had seen with Proposition 5. Nevada casinos, singed by public opinion in 1998, decided not to throw their money away on what everyone knew would be a lost cause. As Governor Davis began ratifying fifty-seven separate compacts, Nevada interests unable to beat the tribes decided to join them, stepping in to operate their new, more lavish gambling resorts.

Only hours after the 2000 vote, Donald Trump's casino empire in New Jersey announced it had signed a letter of intent for a $60 million expansion of an Indian casino in California's Coachella Valley, and Harrah's Entertainment, Inc., said it would invest $110 million in a new gambling resort in San Diego.[50] In short order, the gaming tribes—fueled by billions of dollars in gambling profits—became the most influential special interest at the capitol, spending in excess of $400 million on candidates, ballot measures, and lobbyists between 1998 and 2014.[51] "If you don't have money, you don't have influence," said Chairman Robert Martin of the Morongo Band of Mission Indians. "That is the legislative process. If you don't have money, you don't have a seat at the table."[52]

And gaming tribes didn't merely get seats at the table, they reshaped it and nudged out previous occupants. Where liquor interests, racetracks, bankers, and insurance and oil companies had once dominated the flow of outside money into legislative campaign coffers, the tribes moved in as the new capitol kingpins, thanks to that 1987 supreme court decision and voter support. In 2010, the Fair Political Practices Commission reported that fifteen special interests collectively had spent a staggering $1 billion the previous ten years to influence voters and public officials. The Morongo, Pechanga, and Agua Caliente gaming tribes ranked in the top ten, with combined outlays exceeding $200 million.[53] Even so, the tribes were moving into another stage of maturation—playing defense instead of offense. "They just want to be left alone with their very lucrative monopoly," said political columnist Walters. "They don't want competition. It amounts to, 'We've got it, we want to keep it, and we don't want to share it.'"[54]

That attitude was on display in late 2014 when several gaming tribes helped finance a successful referendum that blocked a rival tribe—the North Fork Rancheria of Mono Indians—from building a large casino in the Central Valley city of Madera. The proposed casino would have been located thirty-eight miles outside the rancheria's original reservation land at a more desirable location off busy California Highway 99. Rival tribes worried about the precedent the Madera casino would set, as it could potentially lead to a rash of lucrative gambling palaces in urban communities that would siphon customers from casinos already built on more remote ancestral lands. Televised commercials for the opposition featured Mark Macarro, Pechanga's chairman, who sixteen years earlier had become a household name fighting for Indian gaming rights and Proposition 5. Once again, Macarro had become the public face of a once-destitute and politically impotent people who now commanded a maturing and powerful industry with enough wealth and savvy to influence public policy, rising to occupy an exalted spot in the top tier of California's political players.

Taken together, the primary election for governor in 1998 and the Indian gambling battle in the general election that year forever changed the game in California politics. While there always will be exceptions, the dominant presumption has become that candidates for the state's top offices and sponsors of ballot measures alike must raise extraordinary sums merely to participate in California politics. Self-financing by the rich, unlimited corporate funding now condoned by the courts, the willingness of labor unions to dig deep, and the wealth of individual special interests have raised new barriers to political involvement. Viability is no longer determined by good ideas or distinguished resumes; in most cases, only those who can muster millions are allowed on the playing field.

2003: Gray Davis Is Recalled from Office

On July 20, 1999, California governor Gray Davis walked into the *San Francisco Chronicle* editorial board meeting in a bad mood and loaded for bear. The night before, Davis—only six months on the job—had attended an event in the city with political donors, and he awoke in the morning to a scathing story on the *Chronicle*'s front page that gave voice to critics of his many "fundraisers with deep-pocketed special-interest groups whose economic fortunes are directly affected by his administration's decisions."[55] The report detailed how Davis had raised $125,000 from HMO executives a week and a half earlier, then asked key legislators to slow the progress of bills boosting regulatory oversight of the industry. As the editorial board meeting began, Davis pounced. He criticized the *Chronicle* for burying on page fifteen a story about him signing a tough assault weapons ban, and he addressed that morning's front-page *Chronicle* story, telling the editors, "That's just a chicken s— article." Davis also had plenty of words for legislative liberals who had been tangling with the more moderate governor over the direction of state policy. Noting that he had recently won a smashing twenty-point election victory, Davis bluntly said, "Their job is to implement my vision."[56]

The blowback was publicly restrained from Democratic legislative leaders who privately felt they weren't getting the respect they deserved from the dismissive governor. "We got elected too, you know, and we have to be accountable to our constituents," said assembly speaker Antonio Villaraigosa.[57] But the governor's remarks had strained his already tense relationship with leaders of his own party who had clashed over legislation and budget issues ever since his inauguration.

If the governor's outburst jolted the media and public, it didn't come as a shock to education secretary Gary K. Hart. Hart and Davis had shared a four-bunk room as fraternity brothers at Stanford, and both came to Sacramento in the mid-1970s — Davis as Jerry Brown's chief of staff and Hart as a member of the legislature. The governor made Hart his first cabinet appointee after the election. They were never close, Hart said, and "I could never quite figure out what made him tick." Hart said Davis was smart and focused, but he viewed him as "a loner who was very abrupt and always was in a sour mood." He recalled Sharon Davis coming into the office one day when her husband was grousing about something. "She came in and said, 'You've got to stop that. You're the one who wanted this job. This has always been your life's dream. And now that you've got it, you can't be complaining anymore.'"[58]

Seven months after his 1999 confrontation with the *Chronicle*, Davis picked another fight when he said his judicial appointees "should resign" if they didn't reflect his views. "They are not there to be independent agents," he said. "They are there to reflect the sentiments that I expressed during the campaign." Democratic senate leader John Burton bristled, "He doesn't support an independent Legislature, so why should he support an independent judiciary?"[59] Democrats in the legislature starting talking of sending a message to the "imperial governor" by organizing a veto override. "What's the difference between a Pope and a governor?" went one joke circulating the capitol. "The Pope only wants you to kiss his ring."[60] Despite solid approval ratings with the public, Davis was alienating traditional allies and testing their loyalty. Four years later, amid the turmoil of an unprecedented recall campaign, Davis would need all the friends he could get.

On November 5, 2002, in a crowded ballroom at the Century Plaza Hotel, Gray Davis made his way to the podium just before midnight to the cheers of "four more years!" He thanked Californians for giving him another term as governor and promised "to work as hard as I can" during his second stint. A reporter, however, thought he looked "more relieved than exultant." A *Los Angeles Times* exit poll earlier that day offered an explanation. Despite their apparent endorsement of him, 60 percent of voters said they disapproved of Davis's job performance over the previous four years.[61]

Davis had just defeated first-time Republican candidate businessman Bill Simon by a scant five percentage points and might not have won at all if moderate Los Angeles mayor Richard Riordan had been his general-election opponent. During the primary season, with Riordan seemingly headed for the Republican nomination and consistently attacking the governor, Davis aides conceived an unorthodox strategy: hit back at Riordan and soften him up for the general election. Davis initially opposed the idea, but at the urging of former president Clinton, he changed his mind. "You can't sit there and take it," Clinton told the governor.[62] The $10 million barrage of negative television ads damaged Riordan so much he lost the nomination to Simon.

Davis had handpicked his opponent and set up what appeared to be a cakewalk reelection, but his narrow victory was a harbinger of Davis's looming, unprecedented rejection by the California electorate. Three months later, a notice of recall was submitted to the secretary of state by Ted Costa, well known as a gadfly in Sacramento political circles. The petition accused Davis of "gross mismanagement" of California's problems—from its deficit-ridden budget to its skyrocketing energy costs.

Costa's bill of particulars drew a collective yawn from the political and media elite. After all, governors were always being threatened with recalls, and thirty-one previous attempts had failed to even qualify for the ballot. Besides, voters had seen fit to reelect Davis. But Costa thought he had a chance to make this recall succeed. He had worked on eighteen successful recalls—removing city council members, park commissioners, and other local officials from office—and was experienced in using radio for grassroots outreach. When he joined People's Advocate, Paul Gann's political advocacy organization, his first task was to repeal a pay raise for members of the local board of supervisors. "I went on a talk show and got six hundred calls," he related, and that led to thousands of signatures on petitions. "I thought we could do that with the recall."[63]

Californians might have just reelected their governor, but they weren't happy. The state budget was in a free fall, and fresh in the minds of its people were electricity blackouts that had shut down businesses and darkened homes in 2000 and 2001. The outages trapped people in elevators, crashed computers, triggered traffic accidents, and angered millions. California's power generation simply could not keep up with demand caused by the state's expansive job growth in the late 1990s, and the government had been slow to approve new power plants. Further, a drought in the Pacific Northwest decreased the amount of hydroelectric power for import, and the searing heat waves that sporadically hit parts of California put even more pressure on the power grid. Most importantly, Governor Wilson in 1996 had signed a bipartisan state deregulation plan—approved unanimously by the legislature—that was supposed to enable the free market to reduce electricity costs; instead, it led to higher wholesale energy costs and severe financial problems for a number of the state's utilities. Out-of-state wholesalers swooped in like famished wolves eyeing a flock of sheep. Houston-based wholesaler Enron reveled in California's woes. When a forest fire shut down a major transmission line, an Enron trader cackled, "Burn, baby, burn. That's a beautiful thing."[64] Later investigations revealed Enron conspired to artificially drive up prices by restricting energy deliveries.

Davis had opportunities to end the crisis by signing long-term contracts with energy wholesalers, but he was paralyzed by his risk-averse nature. "He was like a deer caught in the headlights. He just froze," observed columnist Dan Walters. "He just couldn't make a decision."[65] Eventually, Davis did sign those contracts, but the rates had escalated dramatically, and the governor was forced to propose sizeable rate hikes for consumers. To improve the political optics of the situation, Davis canceled a December 2000 fundraising dinner with energy producers. Even so, in the first eighteen months of his governorship, Davis had collected more than a half-million dollars from utilities, marketers, and producers.[66] Before the crisis, California was paying $7.4 billion for wholesale power. Those costs more than tripled to about $27 billion in both 2000 and 2001.[67]

Davis hadn't caused the energy crisis, but he had mishandled it. Similarly, Davis didn't cause the dot-com bubble to burst, but his actions unwittingly made the fallout worse. As California's economy boomed, Davis had signed a $99 billion 2000–01 budget that boosted spending by 18 percent and included substantial increases for schools, parks, health services, and transportation. He also set aside $1.4 billion to reduce vehicle-registration fees. He called the spending plan "fiscally responsible." Later that year, under a law signed by his Republican predecessor, Davis announced a billion-dollar sales tax cut because tax payments far exceeded forecasts.[68] Then the stock market bubble burst, and revenue from stock options and capital gains fell by half. By this time, the state was paying billions of extra dollars to keep the lights on. Even as the state budget was morphing from surplus to deficit, Davis gave prison guards—whose union was a top political contributor—a huge 35 percent pay hike over three years.[69] These events, taken together, laid the foundation for a credible attempt to recall a governor for only the second time in American history.

To qualify for the statewide ballot, the effort would need nearly 900,000 valid signatures. Working out of an office in a Sacramento strip mall, Costa had little money at first and his petition drive was off to a slow start, compounded by the fact that Davis allies had hired the top signature-gathering firms in the state and prevented them from working the recall. "They bought them all off," Costa said.[70] In desperation, Costa located the former owner of a California signature-gathering firm who was living in a St. Louis suburb. Tom Bader hadn't worked in California since 1986, but he agreed to accept what little money Costa had to work the recall. Without a steady bankroll, however, Bader couldn't keep his signature-gatherers in the field, and by the end of April 2003, Costa had secured a mere 65,000 signatures. There was no possibility of success unless a sugar daddy agreed to finance the drive. Enter Darrell Issa, a two-term Republican congressman and multimillionaire from San Diego County who had made his fortune manufacturing car alarms and fancied himself a future governor of California.

Issa agreed to launch a campaign—called "Rescue California"—with seed money of $100,000, hoping other donors would come forward. When they didn't, Issa added another $1.7 million and announced his own candidacy to replace Davis as governor. Issa's money flowed into the campaign in chunks of up to $200,000 every few days. Officially, these were listed as loans from Greene Properties, a company Issa co-owned with his wife. The goal was to collect the signatures rapidly—by mid-July—to place the recall on a fall 2003 special-election ballot, instead of waiting until the regularly scheduled March 2004 primary. Timing was critical. First, the

2004 primary, with a competitive race for the Democratic presidential nomination, would propel a torrent of Democrats to the polls. Second, if the recall were held in a special election in October or November, Issa could run for governor on the same ballot without having to give up his congressional seat.

Even after Issa's cash commitment, however, a number of party leaders considered the recall move misguided. Republican adviser Karl Rove told Sacramento consultant Dave Gilliard, who managed "Rescue California" for Issa, that Davis would never be recalled and that the mere attempt would hurt the party. State senate Republican leader Jim Brulte initially felt the same way, then abruptly changed his mind. "Brulte called me and said he had been at a Costco in Rancho Cucamonga where a table had been set up for recall signature gatherers," Gilliard remembered. "He said there was a line around the building."[71]

Publicly, Davis and his aides dismissed the recall attempt as sour grapes and just another crackpot idea. "We'll keep an eye on it. But the recall is collapsing under the weight of its own hype," said Davis spokesman Roger Salazar.[72] Even so, shortly after Issa's infusion of money into the campaign, Davis allies, led by the California Professional Firefighters, announced the formation of "Taxpayers Against the Recall" and donated funds and staff to try to block the effort. "Our message strategy was to go after Issa," said Carroll Wills, communications director for the firefighters union and on loan as the spokesman for Taxpayers Against the Recall. "Issa was the poster boy for right-wing ambition. And this was a right-wing power grab by an ambitious politician."[73] Journalist Joe Mathews, who chronicled the recall in *The People's Machine*, believes the focus on Issa may have damaged the congressman's credibility but was a tactical mistake: "Davis, by making the recall personal, missed an opportunity to look like a statesman rather than a partisan."[74]

Meanwhile, Davis faced a staggering $38 billion budget deficit and in June decided to triple the state vehicle license fee—the so-called car tax—at an average additional cost to motorists of $158 per year. Conservative talk-radio hosts had a field day, devoting countless hours to rants against Davis, often fueled by material fed by the recall campaign. Wills, the anti-recall spokesman, was a former radio reporter, but he wasn't prepared for this. Appearing on a popular show in Los Angeles, Wills had been told in advance by the producer that the hosts merely wanted to air both sides of the recall debate. Instead, Wills found himself under siege. "I was totally sandbagged and ambushed by these guys. My heart was pounding the whole time and I'm thinking, 'I'm screwed.'"[75]

Actor Arnold Schwarzenegger, a Republican, was flirting with a potential candidacy to replace Davis if the governor were recalled. On the Fourth of July holiday weekend, less than two weeks before recall petition signatures were due, Schwarzenegger's much-anticipated *Terminator 3* opened on more than 3,500 movie screens throughout the country. Tom Bader had the brilliant idea of sending his signature-gatherers to approach Schwarzenegger fans as they waited in long lines outside California theaters. By the end of the weekend, Schwarzenegger had another blockbuster hit, and "Rescue California" had 1.6 million petition signatures.[76]

The recall qualified easily, and the election was set for October 7. Voters had to deal with two questions: should Davis be removed from office and, if he were, who should take his place? Three days before the August 9 candidate filing deadline the dominoes began arranging themselves. First, Dianne Feinstein, the most popular political figure in the state, said she would stay out of the contest. That evening, Schwarzenegger announced his candidacy to a raucous, cheering crowd on *The Tonight Show with Jay Leno*. Also declaring their candidacies were Democrats lieutenant governor Cruz Bustamante and insurance commissioner John Garamendi, Republicans Bill Simon and state senator Tom McClintock, Green Party leader Peter Camejo, syndicated columnist and political independent Arianna Huffington, and scores of publicity seekers — from former *Hustler* magazine publisher Larry Flynt and one-time actor Gary Coleman to porn actress Mary Carey, who wanted to make lap dances a legitimate business expense. "The clown car had arrived, and people kept popping out of it," Wills said.[77] The day after Schwarzenegger threw his hat into the ring, Issa—the man who bankrolled the recall—realized he couldn't compete with the actor's money and star power and tearfully dropped out of the contest.

The recall ballot simply listed all 135 candidates, and whoever received the most votes (should Davis be recalled) would be California's next governor. As expected, Schwarzenegger's celebrity status dominated the contest. Davis no longer was running against a mere politician; he was running against one of the most recognizable brands on the planet, a former bikini-waxed Mr. Universe who captured headlines from Modesto to Moscow. Thanks to Schwarzenegger's celebrity appeal, a late September televised debate among the major candidates attracted a larger audience than had any of the televised debates between presidential contenders George W. Bush and Al Gore in 2000, with two-thirds of the viewers living in the greater Los Angeles area.[78] Davis wasn't included, sending a subliminal message to voters that the outcome of the recall was a foregone conclusion.

Bustamante claimed to be the Democratic alternative to Davis in case the recall succeeded, and throughout much of the campaign, the lieutenant governor enjoyed solid support as a replacement candidate. He held a narrow lead over Schwarzenegger until a judge ruled he had circumvented the state's contribution limits when he received millions of dollars from Indian gaming tribes. After that, it was clear sailing for Schwarzenegger.

Late in the campaign, a *New York Times* reporter sat in Gilliard's "Rescue California" office in Sacramento, watching him open envelopes stuffed with mostly small contributions supporting the recall. "We opened up an envelope and a $2,000 check fell out," Gilliard remembered. "We looked at it and the return address was Lake Wilhaggin Drive. I said, 'This person is Gray Davis's next-door neighbor.'"[79] Sniffing a story, the reporter trekked to the upper-middle-class suburban Sacramento neighborhood where Davis and his wife resided. Two previous governors had lived in the same house. Seventy-nine-year-old neighbor Charlotte Goland greeted the reporter in her bathrobe and said she had never been involved in politics before. Asked why she wanted Davis booted out of the neighborhood, she replied, "Because I don't like him." It had nothing to do with politics and everything to do with personality. "He's a cold cookie. Never changes his expression."[80]

More than 55 percent of the electorate voted to oust Davis, and Schwarzenegger received nearly half the votes in the crowded field to replace him. Pollster Mark Baldassare called the recall "an enhanced role for direct democracy in California governance."[81] In their malaise, Californians simply wanted a fresh start. Davis's personality undoubtedly contributed to his demise along with his budget performance and obsessive fundraising from special interests.

Davis's response to the state's energy crisis also illustrated what some saw as a broader flaw. "I think Gray's biggest problem was lack of courage and being too risk averse," said George Skelton of the *Los Angeles Times*. "The energy crisis was a great opportunity for him to show what he's made of. It was pretty obvious the power pirates were screwing us over. He should have ordered the National Guard to take over a power plant. He would have been a hero."[82] Hart, Davis's education secretary, said he could tell during the governor's first cabinet meeting in January 1999 that Davis worried unduly about the political implications of risk-taking. Instead of giving his new cabinet an encouraging pep talk as they embarked on fulfilling the administration's goals and aspirations, he issued a stern warning. "He said something like, 'Most of the stuff you people do is going to be wrong. You're going to screw up. I don't want anything bad happening on your watch.'" The new cabinet was "terrified," Hart said. "It was a clear message to be careful and very cautious, and 'Don't you do anything that's going to embarrass me.'"[83]

Schwarzenegger promised to shake up Sacramento and was so popular at first that the state's broadcast media—which had long since abandoned capitol coverage—returned to take advantage of of the public's fascination with the new governor. There was even talk of amending the US Constitution to allow Schwarzenegger, an Austrian-born naturalized citizen, to run for president. In time, of course, he was perceived as just another politician, and the television stations gradually closed their bureaus. Schwarzenegger ultimately had a mixed record as governor. On his first day on the job, he fulfilled a campaign promise by signing an executive order repealing Davis's tripling of vehicle license fees, and in so doing, he added $5 billion to the state's budget shortfall. He adopted a pro-business agenda and had some successes reducing regulations and reforming the state's workers' compensation system, but he failed to convince voters to cap state spending, ban the use of union dues for political purposes, and reform teacher tenure rules. Schwarzenegger's signature accomplishments were signing landmark legislation to combat global warming and pushing voters to revamp the state's electoral system in the hopes of reducing partisan rancor in state government.

After seven years in the capitol meat grinder, Schwarzenegger's approval rating plummeted to 23 percent. Republicans were no more supportive than Democrats, and only 12 percent of all respondents said California was moving in the right direction.[84] When he left office, the state faced a $25 billion budget deficit over eighteen months, the "pay-to-play" special interest culture was still ingrained in the capitol's ethos, and partisan acrimony showed no sign of subsiding.

To most Californians, it was politics as usual, and many of the principals in the recall were disappointed that it hadn't fundamentally altered state government. Ted Costa, the recall leader, who didn't get invited to Schwarzenegger's inauguration, conceded there was no fundamental change in how Californians are governed, even though that was a key goal of the recall effort. Still, he sees the recall as the "public's release valve," sending a potent message that the people are watching the powerful and that they value the little-used recall option that voters gave them in 1911.

The historic 2003 recall of Gray Davis likely was an isolated brush fire that resulted from circumstances at the moment. He was an unpopular governor with no residual goodwill who faced severe fiscal and energy crises and made them worse. To save his job, he had to square off in a popularity contest against a well-funded mega-celebrity who was idolized worldwide.

Paul Maslin, who polled for Davis during the recall, said, "The whole thing is democracy run amok, but it's still democracy. When the electorate gets unhinged, movements like this can happen."[85]

Ten years after his fall from grace, a philosophical Davis appeared at a Sacramento forum sponsored by the Public Policy Institute of California. He betrayed no hint of bitterness. "If you don't like the people's ability to make laws, to change laws, to kick you out of office," he said, "then you should find another line of work."[86]

2010: Californians Experiment with Electoral Reform

For Arnold Schwarzenegger and members of the California legislature, Valentine's Day 2009, a Saturday, was a disaster. They were sequestered all night at the capitol haggling over a budget crisis that defied resolution. Dinners were canceled, tempers were short, and progress on the budget was minimal. The marathon session would continue on Sunday. In the midst of a devastating national recession that forced state employee layoffs, furloughs, and the suspension of numerous services, the state's spending plan had an unfathomable $41 billion deficit that required a two-thirds legislative vote to plug. That meant at least three senate Republicans—most of whom had signed a "no tax" pledge—had to agree to any budget deal.

Schwarzenegger, who had sparred with Republicans over budget and environmental issues, had crafted an immediate fix-it plan with legislative leaders that called for a combination of borrowing, budget cuts, and more than $14 billion in temporary increases to income, sales, and gasoline taxes. After a weekend of horse-trading, Schwarzenegger had two Republican votes. He emerged from a closed-door meeting Sunday evening and said, "We're just searching for that one more vote."[87] A few days later, Schwarzenegger found his third Republican vote. It belonged to forty-one-year-old Abel Maldonado, an upwardly mobile senator from the central-coast agricultural community of Santa Maria.

Maldonado, a moderate Republican representing a swing district in the senate, had been climbing the political ladder since winning a seat on the Santa Maria City Council at the age of twenty-six, and he had visions of larger, statewide conquests. He often was at odds with hardline members of his own party, and he was frustrated with California's closed primary system, in which Republicans had to prove their conservative mettle in order to win nominations. In return for being the deciding vote for the budget and the tax increases that came with it, Maldonado named his price: he wanted to revamp the state's election rules that he believed stifled political moderates like himself. With Schwarzenegger's blessing, Maldonado linked his budget vote to a proposal that would dramatically alter the state's electoral system by allowing all voters to cross party lines in primary elections.

For more than a century, California legislators and voters had been tinkering with the state's electoral system to make candidate selection less partisan. In 1909, reformist legislators enacted a direct primary that gave control over nominating state party candidates to voters instead of machine politics. That same year, party labels were removed from judges and school officials. Two years later, county elections became nonpartisan. In 1915, the legislature enacted "the most extreme measure of its kind ever enacted in an American state" by making all legislative and statewide elections nonpartisan. It never took effect, however, because voters used their new direct democracy referendum tool to invalidate the law.[88] For nearly fifty years, the state experimented with "cross-filing," another Progressive reform, which weakened political parties by allowing candidates to seek multiple party nominations. In the mid-1990s, with partisan gridlock gripping the legislature and regularly delaying passage of the annual budget by a month or longer, the electorate overwhelmingly approved a "blanket" primary system, in which voters could cast ballots for any candidate regardless of that candidate's party affiliation. The law remained in effect for two state elections until the US Supreme Court struck it down, ruling that it violated a political party's freedom of association under the First Amendment.

Believing that the public felt disenfranchised and disillusioned by stridently partisan decision making in Sacramento, Steve Peace, a former state senator and finance director, founded the California

Independent Voter Project in the mid-2000s. He wanted to place election reforms on the ballot that would pass legal muster. At the capitol, Peace was known as a business-friendly Democrat. "Steve came to us and said, 'Can you draft something that will survive judicial scrutiny?'" recollected Steve Merksamer, former chief of staff for Republican governor George Deukmejian and a principal in one of the state's leading political law firms. "We wanted to create a situation where more centrist members of both parties could get elected." As luck would have it, that draft document became the bargaining chip for Abel Maldonado's budget vote, and it fit perfectly with Schwarzenegger's desire to establish a legacy as a political reformer. "It was personal to Abel and personal to Arnold," Merksamer said. "They came to us and took our draft without changing a comma."[89]

The Peace-Merksamer draft became a senate constitutional amendment that lawmakers approved as part of the deal to solve the budget stalemate, and it was sent to the voters as Proposition 14. The reform was called the "top-two primary" and was based on a system in use in Louisiana since 1975 and Washington state since 2008. It provided that all candidates for statewide, legislative, and congressional offices be listed together on the ballot in their respective contests. The top two finishers, regardless of party, would advance to the November runoff. By forcing candidates to run essentially a general election in the primary, proponents theorized that Democrats would move to the political middle as they competed for Republican and independent votes. Similarly, Republicans would moderate their views if they hoped to make the runoff.

As expected, California's major and minor political parties vehemently opposed Proposition 14. The major parties didn't like the idea of outsiders determining their nominees. "Just like baseball needs teams," said Republican Party chairman Ron Nehring, "democracy needs political parties in order to work. Otherwise you have chaos."[90] Minor parties knew their chances of getting a candidate in the runoff under the new system were infinitesimal. Beyond that, general-election write-in candidacies—on the books since 1850—were eliminated.

Despite their opposition, the parties decided not to invest their resources to defeat the measure. In contrast, Schwarzenegger's political committee and the state's business community spent nearly $5 million, convinced Proposition 14 would help voters send more pro-business Democrats to Sacramento. A radio ad claimed the measure would diminish "the influence of the major parties, which are now under the control of the special interests."[91] Maldonado called it "a huge game changer."[92]

By California standards, where hot-button ballot measures attract tens of millions of dollars in contributions that finance non-stop ad blitzes, the campaign for Proposition 14 was quiet. It didn't strike a raw, emotional chord with voters and was overshadowed by measures dealing with auto insurance and energy, as well as a Republican gubernatorial primary that saw former eBay executive Meg Whitman and wealthy insurance commissioner Steve Poizner combine to spend an astonishing $127 million to oversaturate the airways. Less than one-third of registered voters cast ballots in the primary—a record low for a non-presidential primary, although the record was broken again four years later. Thanks in large part to the public's dissatisfaction with the legislature's work ethic, voters narrowly agreed to experiment with a new system of electing lawmakers that promised to end the perennial brinksmanship and dysfunction at the capitol.

In the years following Proposition 14's passage, academic and anecdotal studies of the measure's impact have been contradictory and inconclusive, partly because the top-two primary was one of two significant reforms passed by voters with Schwarzenegger's encouragement. The other created an independent citizens' commission to remove partisan gerrymandering from the process of drawing legislative districts. An analysis of California's 2012 elections by UC Berkeley's Institute of Governmental Studies found that moderate candidates for Congress and the state senate fared no better under the top-two primary than they would have in closed-party primaries, mostly because voters "struggled to identify moderate candidates." However, writing for the *Monkey Cage*, a political science research blog, the study team did say the new primary system "may still moderate the behavior of elected officials."[93]

A subsequent study by the USC Schwarzenegger Institute, which compared legislative roll calls before and after the electoral reforms, found that lawmakers had, indeed, moderated their behavior. The reforms, it concluded, "are associated with an ideological shift in the State Legislature, toward the center."[94] Most of that movement came from Democrats supporting a more pro-business agenda, a stated goal of the drafters of the top-two measure. The most significant impact—at least early in the Proposition 14 historical timeline—appeared to be intra-party challenges in safe Democratic or Republican districts. Business interests that traditionally backed Republicans had stepped up their support of business-friendly Democrats in districts where Republicans were unlikely to succeed.

In a 2014 state senate contest in a heavily Democratic Sacramento-area district, Roger Dickinson comfortably finished first in the primary and faced fellow Democrat Richard Pan in the general election. Pan, a physician, benefited from more than $5 million in spending by independent committees (which are not subject to contribution limits) representing health care, insurance, and other interests. Mailers reached out to non-Democrats, who comprised 52 percent of the district. One geared toward Republicans touted Pan's support from local and statewide law-enforcement officials. Another stressed that he "worked with Republicans to protect tax incentives to help small businesses succeed and create new jobs."[95] Pan's cross-party appeal was considered a significant factor in helping him win the senate seat. Similarly, Democrat Steve Glazer appealed to Republicans and independents in defeating another Democrat in a 2015 special senate election.

Both contests also highlighted a number of unintended consequences—the hobgoblin of many ballot measures over the decades—in California's new electoral system. Without closed primaries, candidates have to run in the equivalent of two general elections, appealing to all voters in both the primary and general contests. That means earlier polling, more mail and, in some cases, earlier air time on television and radio. Campaign costs, therefore, have risen dramatically, particularly independent expenses financed by the same special interests whose influence the proponents of reform had hoped to diminish. Between 2008 and 2014 special interests' independent spending in legislative contests more than tripled in both the assembly and the senate. In addition, when two candidates of the same party face each other in the general election, they tend to have similar political philosophies and voting records and thus turn to personal attacks to sway voters.

Critics also point to "perverse and anti-majoritarian" results, because the system offers a "clear advantage to the party that runs fewer candidates for an office."[96] A prime example occurred in a 2012 congressional race in the Inland Empire of Riverside and San Bernardino Counties, where Democrats held an edge in voter registration. When four Democrats entered the primary and split the Democratic vote, it enabled two Republicans to advance to the general election. In addition, the system opens the door to mischief-making by allowing voters to cast ballots for any candidate regardless of party. During the 2014 governor's campaign, Democratic strategist Steve Maviglio acknowledged in an op-ed piece in the *Sacramento Bee* that he intended to vote for the weakest Republican on the gubernatorial ballot in the hopes his choice would advance to the general election and make Jerry Brown's reelection bid that much easier.

If candidates professing no party preference expected to thrive in the new electoral environment, they were disappointed. Dan Schnur, an independent candidate for secretary of state in 2014, sought to attract votes from both major parties with his antiestablishment message and background as chairman of the Fair Political Practices Commission. Schnur finished fourth behind a Republican and two Democrats—one of whom was a state senator indicted for corruption and gun trafficking. In reflecting on his electoral defeat, and the future of independent candidacies, Schnur conceded that political branding matters: "Even voters who are alienated from the parties still tend to take their cues from those party labels. If you don't have much information about a candidate, a D or an R after their name gives you some guidance on how to think about them."[97]

The jury is still out on whether California's new primary system—combined with more fairly drawn legislative and congressional districts—will reduce polarization in the legislature. The most visible example of legislative gridlock—the annual debate over enacting a state budget—was removed in November 2010, when voters discarded a seventy-seven-year-old requirement that the spending plan be approved by a two-thirds vote in each house of the legislature. The angry electorate changed the threshold to a simple majority, taking action a month after Governor Schwarzenegger had signed a budget that was one hundred days late. California lawmakers may have handed the state's business community a series of legislative victories, but a study by University of Chicago professor Boris Shor concludes California continues to have the most polarized legislature in the nation. The new electoral changes, he argues, are unlikely to reduce it.[98]

Only time will reveal whether the latest round of political reforms will bring more functional governance to the Golden State. Not every election, after all, is a game changer. Not every ballot measure has a noble purpose. Not every outcome is satisfying to every voter. Yet the elections described in this book—and many others right to the present—demonstrate that Californians do hold enormous power to shape their own destinies. Whether far-reaching or short-sighted, voters have molded a California that differs from the rest of the nation in ways that matter. If the past is any predictor, future rounds of civic experiments and perhaps another crop of visionary leaders await the judgment of tomorrow's voters. Competing with the state's storied history, however, sharply declining rates of voter participation pose troubling questions. Do Californians underestimate their own strength? Do they buy into the myth that their votes don't matter? Or will they show a continued willingness in the years ahead to flex their demonstrated power to influence their own lives, often as pioneers for a nation?

ACKNOWLEDGMENTS

WRITING A BOOK on California history relies, in large part, on the scholarship of historians who already have plowed the fields of the state's fertile past. Their contributions to *Game Changers* have been immeasurable. This glimpse at some of California's heroes and villains could not have been possible without the rich trove of research materials available to the authors—and in fact to all Californians with a thirst for history. California is blessed with some of the best research facilities in the country, where a sharp explorer can find nuggets of fascinating unpublished materials simply by looking in the right places.

We particularly want to recognize the reference librarians at the California History Room at the California State Library, who were extremely helpful during our research, and the helpful archivists at the California State Archives, particularly Melodi Andersen, co-leader of the Reference Program. The Archives has a wonderful collection of oral histories from many of the major players at the state capitol over the years.

At the University of California, Berkeley, the Bancroft Library is a gold mine for anyone interested in California history, and their librarians eagerly helped us locate obscure documents from California's past. Also at Berkeley, much of our initial encouragement and assistance came from Jack Citrin, Ethan Rarick, Marc Levin, and Paul King at the Institute of Governmental Studies. Throughout our project, they pointed us in the right direction and offered sage advice. Citrin, the institute's executive director, kept us focused throughout the process and provided valuable insight after reading our original draft manuscript. Rarick, author of an extraordinary biography of Pat Brown (*California Rising: The Life and Times of Pat Brown,* UC Press, 2005), also read portions of the manuscript and offered us guidance and the benefits of his rare talent as we worked on this project.

Besides Rarick and Citrin, we are indebted to many others who read all or portions of our draft manuscript and offered helpful suggestions, including Sherry Bebitch Jeffe, political analyst and public policy professor at the University of Southern California; Mark Paul, coauthor of *California Crackup* and senior scholar and deputy director of the California program at the New America Foundation; Dan Schnur, director of the Jesse M. Unruh Institute of Politics at the University of Southern California; *Los Angeles Times* political columnist George Skelton; and John Walton, author and research professor of sociology at UC Davis. We particularly want to thank Bruce E. Cain, professor of humanities and sciences and director of the Bill Lane Center for the American West at Stanford University, who wrote the book's foreword. We are also indebted to Dennis Renault, whose cartoons are sprinkled throughout *Game Changers*. Renault had a remarkable twenty-eight-year career as a cartoonist for the *Sacramento Bee,* lampooning politics, politicians, powerful vested interests, and voters alike.

This book was enriched by the cooperation of many political leaders and insiders who participated in and observed the important California public policy decisions of the last half-century and gave interviews to the authors. They included: Mark Baldassare, US Rep. Howard Berman, Barry Brokaw, Assembly Speaker Willie Brown, State Senator John Burton, John Caldwell, Ted Costa, Governor George Deukmejian, Joel Fox, Cathy Gardella, Dave Gilliard, Hedy Govenar, State Senator Gary K. Hart, Sherry Bebitch Jeffe, State Senator Ross Johnson, US Rep. Jerry Lewis, State Senator John Lewis, US Rep. Doris Matsui, Steve Merksamer, Barbara O'Connor, Sam Paredes, Ethan Rarick, Richard Ratcliff, State Senator H. L. Richardson, Gregory Schmidt, Dan Schnur, George Skelton, Robert Stern, Richard Temple, Lewis Uhler, Dan Walters, John Walton, Carroll Wills, and Jerry Zanelli.

From the beginning, we received encouragement and advice from Gary K. Hart, who ably served his Santa Barbara district in both houses of the legislature and spent a year as Secretary of Education in the Gray Davis administration. Hart provided a wise sounding board as we decided which game-changing elections to highlight. We also owe particular thanks to Heyday publisher Malcolm Margolin, acquisitions and editorial director Gayle Wattawa, and copy editor Lisa K. Marietta for their valuable insights and editing suggestions, and to the California Historical Society for honoring our work.

Finally, we'd like to acknowledge a number of friends and associates who also provided valuable assistance with the book: Lynda Cassidy and Trish Mayer at the California Fair Political Practices Commission; capitol staffers Bill Bailey and Joel Yang; political consultant Wayne Johnson; and Donna Lucas, one of Sacramento's foremost public affairs executives.

Without the help of these and other people too numerous to mention, this book could not have been written.

END NOTES

PREFACE

1. See "Survey of Young Americans' Attitudes toward Politics and Public Service," 26th ed. Harvard Institute of Politics, September 26–October 9, 2014. Among the specific survey findings on why young people don't vote, 12 percent answered "Don't know enough about the candidates," 11 percent said "Not interested," 10 percent said "No time/too busy," 7 percent said "My vote does not count/make a difference," 7 percent said "Don't like/trust the candidates/politicians in general," and 6 percent said "Don't like/follow politics/government." A variety of other reasons were cited in insignificant numbers.
2. Nicholas Ibarra, "Young People Don't Vote," *Spartan Daily* website, accessed November 16, 2014, spartandaily.com/126971/young-people-dont-vote-american-society.

CHAPTER 1
1861: The Railroad Begins Its Dominance with the Election of Leland Stanford as Governor

1. "Conditions and Prospects of Sacramento," *Sacramento Daily Union*, January 11, 1862.
2. "Inauguration Ceremonies," *Daily Alta California*, January 11, 1862.
3. California State Library Governors' Gallery, governors.library.ca.gov/08-Stanford.html.
4. George T. Clark, *Leland Stanford: War Governor of California, Railroad Builder and Founder of Stanford University* (Stanford, CA: Stanford University Press, 1931), 114.
5. Charles Edward Russell, "Scientific Corruption of Politics," *Hampton's Magazine*, June 10, 1910, 843.
6. "The Republican Nominees," *Sacramento Daily Union*, June 20, 1861.
7. Clark, 471.
8. Clark, 65.
9. Thor Severson, *Sacramento: An Illustrated History; 1839–1874, From Sutter's Fort to Capital City* (San Francisco: California Historical Society, 1973), 172.
10. Clark, 191.
11. Rodman Paul, *California Gold: The Beginning of Mining in the Far West* (Lincoln: University of Nebraska Press, 1947), 280.
12. US senators were elected by the legislature at the time and would not be directly elected by the people until passage of the Seventeenth Amendment in 1913.
13. Howard A. DeWitt, "Senator William Gwin and the Politics of Prejudice," Ohlone College, June 24, 2014, www.ohlone.edu/instr/english/elc/eng1163/williamgwin. html. In 1948, *San Francisco Chronicle* reporter Robert O'Brien wrote that Gwin and Congressman J. W. McCorkle once got into an argument at a racetrack and decided to settle the issue in a duel with rifles at thirty paces. Both men fired three shots and each missed his target, although a stray bullet killed a nearby donkey. The two men decided that if they continued, someone might get hurt, so they retired to a nearby bar for a round of bourbon. Source: Michael Colbruno, "Lives of the Dead: Mountain View Cemetery in Oakland," August 26, 2007, http://mountainviewpeople.blogspot.com/2007/08/senator-william-mckendree-gwin-october.html.
14. "Senator Gwin," *Marysville Daily Herald*, August 10, 1853.

15. Republican Party Platform of 1856, The American Presidency Project, UC Santa Barbara, www.presidency.ucsb.edu.
16. "Defeat of the Railroad and Telegraph Bills in Congress," *Sacramento Daily Union*, May 17, 1858.
17. "The Pacific Railroad Bill," *Los Angeles Star*, February 27, 1858.
18. "Speech of Gwin at Marysville," *Sacramento Daily Union*, August 15, 1859.
19. "Pacific Railroad," *California Farmer and Journal of Useful Sciences*, March 4, 1859.
20. Stephen E. Ambrose, *Nothing Like It in the World: The Men Who Built the Transcontinental Railroad* (New York: Simon and Schuster, 2000), 19.
21. James J. Rawls and Walton Bean, *California: An Interpretive History* (New York: McGraw-Hill, 2003), 171.
22. Carl Sandburg, *Abraham Lincoln: The Prairie Years and the War Years* (New York: Harcourt, Brace, 1954), 188.
23. Letter from W. C. Jewett to President Lincoln, April 11, 1861, quoted in David C. Mearns, *The Lincoln Papers* (Garden City, NY: Doubleday, 1948), 539.
24. Rawls and Bean, 172–173.
25. Ibid., 173.
26. Ibid.
27. Maryellen Burns and Keith Burns, *Lost Restaurants of Sacramento and Their Recipes* (Charleston, SC: American Palate, 2013), 35.
28. "Inaugural Address of Governor Stanford," *Daily Alta California*, January 11, 1862.
29. Severson, 179; Ambrose, 74.
30. "Which Is Stronger—Conness or Stanford?" *Daily Alta California*, September 1, 1861.
31. Clark, 106.
32. "The Secession Meeting," *Sacramento Daily Union*, August 3, 1861.
33. "The Necessity of Action," *Daily Alta California*, September 4, 1861.
34. "News of the Morning," *Sacramento Daily Union*, September 5, 1861.
35. J. R. Perkins, *Trails, Rails and War*, quoted in Ambrose, 74.
36. Edward J. Renehan, Jr., *The Transcontinental Railroad: The Gateway to the West* (New York: Chelsea House, 2007), 17.
37. Clark, 176.
38. Ambrose, 78.
39. "Pacific Railroad Bill Approved," *Sacramento Daily Union*, July 4, 1862.
40. Ibid.
41. Richard White, *Railroaded: The Transcontinentals and the Making of Modern America* (New York: W.W. Norton, 2011), 18.
42. Carl Wheat, *A Sketch of the Life of Theodore D. Judah*, quoted in Ambrose, 81.
43. Ambrose, 124.
44. Pacific Railroad Act, Sec. 5, Sec. 11, July 1, 1862, www.ourdocuments.gov/doc.php?doc=32&page=transcript.
45. Clark, 181.
46. Rawls and Bean, 175.
47. Correspondence of Leland Stanford, Leland Stanford Papers, Stanford University, http://stacks.stanford.edu.
48. *On Track*, California Railroad Museum, Sacramento, Spring 2013.
49. "Pacific Railroad Inauguration: Formal Opening of the Work," *Sacramento Daily Union*, January 9, 1863.
50. *University of California Publications in Economics*, Vol. 3 (November 13, 1913), 209; Spencer C. Olin, Jr., *California Politics, 1846–1920: The Emerging Corporate State* (San Francisco: Boyd and Fraser, 1981), 31.
51. Clark, 194.
52. Ambrose, 109.
53. "Railroad Question in Placer," *Sacramento Daily Union*, April 29, 1863.
54. Rawls and Bean, 175.

55. *Sacramento Daily Union*, April 29, 1863.
56. Huntington letter to Crocker, January 26, 1868, Huntington Library, in the Bancroft Library, UC Berkeley.
57. Subsequent governors were elected to four-year terms.
58. *The Journal of the Senate during the Sixteenth Session of the Legislature of the State of California*, December 4, 1865, 51.
59. White, 101.
60. Richard Hofstadter, *American Political Tradition* (New York: Vintage Books [Random House], 1948), 170.
61. Olin, 31.
62. Frank Norris, *The Octopus* (New York: Doubleday, Page, 1901), 51.
63. Clark, 278–279.

CHAPTER 2
1879: Voters Ratify a Disputed Constitution for Tumultuous Times

1. Lord James Bryce, *The American Commonwealth,* Vol. 2, 448. Lord Bryce was a British statesman and writer who chronicled the exploits of Denis Kearney and the Workingmen's Party of California, key players in the drafting of the state's 1879 constitution.
2. Philip L. Hammer, "The Temple Goes to Court," *California Lawyer* (June 2012): 104–105.
3. Constitution of the State of California, Article I, Sec. 2 (1879).
4. Joseph R. Grodin, Calvin R. Massey, and Richard B. Cunningham, *The California State Constitution: A Reference Guide* (Westport, CT: Greenwood Press, 1993), 26.
5. Gerawan Farming, Inc. v. Lyons, 24 Cal. 4th 468, 489–491 (2000).
6. Ibid., 491.
7. Wysinger v. Crookshank, 82 Cal. 588, 720 (1890).
8. Constitution of the State of California, Article I, Sec. 8 (1879).
9. California v. Anderson, 6 Cal. 3d 628 (1972).
10. Joe Mathews and Mark Paul, *California Crackup: How Reform Broke the Golden State and How We Can Fix It* (Berkeley: UC Press, 2010), 18.
11. James J. Rawls and Walton Bean, *California: An Interpretive History,* 9th ed. (New York: McGraw-Hill, 2008), 90.
12. Ibid., 90.
13. Walter Colton, *Three Years in California* (New York: S.A. Rollo, 1859), 13.
14. Robert Glass Cleland, Foreword to the Huntington Library's Centennial Edition of *The 1849 California State Constitution* (San Marino, CA: Friends of the Huntington Library, 1949), 9.
15. Carey McWilliams, *California: The Great Exception* (New York: A.A. Wyn, 1949), 42 and 66.
16. Ibid., 19.
17. Ibid., 5.
18. J. Ross Browne, *Report of the Debates in the Convention of California on the Formation of the State Constitution* (Washington, DC: John T. Towers, 1850), 479.
19. Rawls and Bean, 121.
20. Constitution of the State of California, Article XI, Sec. 2 (1879).
21. Cleland, 9.
22. Ibid., 9–10.
23. Joseph Ellison, "The Struggle for Civil Government in California, 1846–1850," *California Historical Society Quarterly,* September 1931, 221–222.
24. Ibid.
25. "The Election Results," *Alta California,* November 15, 1849.
26. McWilliams, 90.
27. Thor Severson, *Sacramento: An Illustrated History; 1839–1874, From Sutter's Fort to Capital City* (San Francisco: California Historical Society, 1973), 76.
28. Paul W. Gates, "Adjudication of Spanish-Mexican Land Claims in California," *Huntington Library Quarterly* 21, no. 3 (May 1, 1958), reproduced in *Readings in*

California History, edited by N. Ray Gilmore and Gladys Gilmore (New York: Thomas Y. Crowell, 1966), 171–172.

29. Winfield J. Davis, *History of Political Conventions in California, 1849 to 1892* (Sacramento: California State Library, 1893), 69.
30. Rawls and Bean, 138.
31. Mathews and Paul, 21.
32. Stephanie S. Pincetl, *Transforming California: A Political History of Land Use and Development* (Baltimore: Johns Hopkins University Press, 1999), 2.
33. Jeffrey Lustig, "Private Rights and Public Purposes: California's Second Constitutional Convention Reconsidered," *California History* 87, no. 3 (2010): 49.
34. Carl Brent Swisher, *Motivation and Political Technique in the California Constitutional Convention, 1878–79* (Claremont, CA: Pomona College, 1930), 8.
35. Paul Taylor, "Foundation of California Rural Society," *California Historical Society Quarterly,* September 1945, 194.
36. Philip P. Choy, "Golden Mountain of Lead: The Chinese Experience in California," in *Neither Separate Nor Equal: Race and Racism in California,* edited by Roger Olmsted and Charles Wollenberg (San Francisco: California Historical Society, 1971), 50.
37. Swisher, 10.
38. Russell M. Posner, "The Lord and the Drayman," in Olmsted and Wollenberg, 58.
39. In the end, Kearney never followed through on his threat. He was arrested and charged with inciting a riot two days after he led more than 2,000 Wokingmen to the top of Nob Hill, although he was soon released and the charges were dropped. More details can be found at http://foundsf.org/index.php?title=Crocker%27s_Spite_Fence.
40. Swisher, 12.
41. Ibid., 17. Swisher recounted that while a plurality of votes was cast in favor of a convention in 1857 and 1859, the propositions lost because they required support from a majority of those casting ballots. A significant number of voters did not vote on the measures. Swisher placed blame for the losses on "popular lethargy and indifference to the subject" as well as the active opposition by "great moneyed interests and corporations."
42. "Conventional Decency," *Daily Alta California,* September 30, 1878.
43. Mathews and Paul, 23.
44. Swisher, 73.
45. Lustig, 60.
46. "The Adjournment of the Constitutional Convention," *Sacramento Daily Union,* March 4, 1879.
47. Edgar F. Love, review of *Motivation and Political Technique in the Constitutional Convention, 1878–79,* by Carl Brent Swisher, *California Historical Society Quarterly,* March 1970, 87.
48. Mathews and Paul, 18.
49. Charles Aikin, review of *Motivation and Political Technique in the California Constitutional Convention, 1878–79,* by Carl Brent Swisher, *California Law Review,* November 1931, 109.
50. Yick Wo v. Hopkins, 118 U.S. 356 (1886).
51. McWilliams, 17.
52. Lustig, 46.
53. Bernard L. Hyink, "California Revises Its Constitution," *Western Political Science Quarterly,* September 1969, 639.
54. Mathews and Paul, 17–18.
55. From an address by the Honorable Phil S. Gibson, delivered November 16, 1955, at the fiftieth anniversary celebration of the University of Southern California Law School. *University of Southern California Law Review* (June 1956), 12.
56. Lustig, 64.
57. Mathews and Paul, 190.

CHAPTER 3
1905: Los Angeles Votes to Spur Growth with a Giant Aqueduct

1. "Two Trails Used in Hunt for Aqueduct Bomber," *Los Angeles Times,* May 22, 1924.
2. "US Probe on Plot to Blast Aqueduct, Hint," *Los Angeles Evening Express,* May 24, 1924.
3. Ibid.; *Los Angeles Times,* May 22, 1924.
4. "Plan to Nab 40 in Aqueduct Plot: Expect Battle Before Taking Bombing Gang," *Los Angeles Evening Express,* May 23, 1924.
5. Bill Boyarsky, *Inventing L.A.: The Chandlers and Their Times* (Santa Monica: Angel City Press, 2009), 82.
6. Martha Davis, "Stepping Outside the Box: Water in Southern California," speech at the UCLA Environment Symposium, March 3, 1998.
7. Catherine Mulholland, *William Mulholland and the Rise of Los Angeles* (Berkeley: UC Press, 2000), 30–31.
8. Ibid., 44, 74, and 230.
9. John Walton, *Western Times and Water Wars* (Berkeley: UC Press, 1992), 6 and 143.
10. John Walton interview, Sacramento, June 23, 2014.
11. Dennis McDougal, *Privileged Son: Otis Chandler and the Rise and Fall of the* L.A. Times *Dynasty* (Cambridge, MA: Perseus, 2001), 39.
12. *Inyo Register,* September 29, 1904.
13. "Titanic Project to Give City a River: Thirty Thousand Inches of Water to Be Brought to Los Angeles," *Los Angeles Times,* July 29, 1905.
14. "Los Angeles Plots Destruction: Would Take Owens River, Lay Lands Waste, Ruin People, Homes and Communities," *Inyo Register,* August 3, 1905.
15. "In Unity Is the Only Hope," *Inyo Register,* August 3, 1905.
16. National Archives, quoted in Walton, 146.
17. Ibid.
18. Ibid., 146–147.
19. "Will Make Millions by New Water Plan" and "L.A. Capitalists in San Fernando Had Company to Profit if Owens River Is Tapped," both *Los Angeles Examiner,* August 24, 1905.
20. William Kahrl, *Water and Power* (Berkeley: UC Press, 1982), 97; Marc Reisner, *Cadillac Desert: The American West and Its Disappearing Water* (New York: Penguin Books, 1993), 75.
21. McDougal, 468.
22. "The Owens River Water Scheme," *Los Angeles Examiner,* August 25, 1905.
23. "18 Miles—30 Minutes from Los Angeles," *Los Angeles Times,* September 3, 1905.
24. "San Fernando Valley: Sale of Pacoima Lots," *Los Angeles Times,* September 6, 1905.
25. "To All Property Owners," *Inyo Register,* September 7, 1905.
26. Mary Austin, "The Owens River Water Project," *San Francisco Chronicle,* September 3, 1905.
27. Helen MacKnight Doyle, *Mary Austin: Woman of Genius* (New York: Gotham Books, 1939), 218.
28. Allen Kelly, "Brook for the Village, Rivers for the City," *Los Angeles Times,* August 18, 1905.
29. Kahrl, 85; David Carle, *Water and the California Dream* (San Francisco: Sierra Club Books, 2000), 71.
30. Reisner, 78.
31. "Go to the Polls Today—Vote for Greater Los Angeles and an Adequate Water Supply," *Los Angeles Herald,* September 7, 1905.
32. "Progression or Retrogression?" *Los Angeles Times,* September 7, 1905.
33. "Anti-Saloon Ordinance Is Overwhelmingly Defeated," *Los Angeles Herald,* June 3, 1905.
34. Mulholland, 125.
35. "LA Progress," *Los Angeles Times,* September 8, 1905.
36. "It's a Go!! Pacoima," *Los Angeles Times,* September 8, 1905.
37. Roosevelt speech in Denver, Colorado, May 4, 1903, quoted in *The Bully Pulpit: Theodore Roosevelt, William Howard Taft, and the Golden Age of Journalism,* by Doris Kearns Goodwin (New York: Simon and Schuster, 2013), 352.

38. Elting E. Morison, ed., *The Letters of Theodore Roosevelt*, vol. 5, 315, quoted in *The Great Thirst: Californians and Water; A History*, by Norris Hundley, Jr. (Berkeley: UC Press, 2001), 155.

39. Los Angeles Department of Water and Power, "The Story of the Los Angeles Aqueduct: A Hundred or Thousand Fold More Important," 2013, http://wsoweb.ladwp.com/Aqueduct/historyoflaa/hundred.htm; Reisner, 82; Kahrl, 140; Hundley, 155.

40. Mulholland, 148–149.

41. Ibid., 152.

42. "Owens River Bonds Carried by Overwhelming Majority," *Los Angeles Times*, June 13, 1907.

43. Kahrl, 161; Reisner, 84.

44. "Silver Mountain River Now Flows to Los Angeles' Gates," *Los Angeles Times*, November 6, 1913.

45. Mulholland, 246.

46. "On the Defensive," *Bakersfield Californian*, August 3, 1921.

47. Walton, 164.

48. "How a City's Might Has Prevailed for a River of Farming Communities," *Inyo Register*, December 4, 1924.

49. Walton, 188.

50. Frederick Faulkner, *Sacramento Union*: "Water Sharks Wreck Valley," April 1, 1927; "Blooms Fade before Waste: Politicians Tear Up Verdant Orchards, Planted by Pioneer Matrons, to Make Way for Its Era of Desolation," April 2, 1927; "Water Greed Ruins Valley," April 3, 1927.

51. "A Message from Owens Valley, the Valley of Broken Hearts," *Sacramento Bee*, March 19, 1927.

52. Walton, 171–173 and 176.

53. Ibid., 177–178.

54. "Decision Today in Blast Trial," *Los Angeles Times*, March 19, 1928.

55. "Senate Special Investigating Committee on Water Situation in Inyo and Mono Counties," *Senate Journal*, May 7, 1931, in "Owens Valley Water Wars, from the Personal Files of Senator Joseph E. Riley," California State Library.

56. "Broadcast for the People of Owens Valley," in "Owens Valley Water Wars."

57. Joseph G. Riley letter to Rep. Harry Englebright, June 20, 1934, in "Owens Valley Water Wars."

58. Walton, 258–259.

59. Tom Knudson, "Outrage in Owens Valley a Century after L.A. Began Taking Its Water," *Sacramento Bee*, January 5, 2014; Adam Nagourney, "Century Later, the 'Chinatown' Water Feud Ebbs," *New York Times*, January 20, 2015.

60. Walton, 6.

61. Samuel B. Nelson oral history, conducted by Andrew D. Basiago, 1986, Center for Oral History Research, Young Research Library, UCLA, 30.

62. John Walton interview, Sacramento, June 23, 2014.

63. "100 Dead, 300 Missing, 47 Million Loss in St. Francis Dam Disaster," *Los Angeles Times*, March 14, 1928.

64. "Water Board to Demand Grand Jury Probe on Dams," *Los Angeles Times*, March 22, 1928.

65. "San Fernando Groundwater: LA's Most Threatened Resource," LADWP fact sheet in the author's collection, October 2013.

66. David Halberstam, *The Powers That Be* (New York: Alfred A. Knopf, 1979), 94.

CHAPTER 4
1910: Hiram Johnson's Election Brings Power to the People

1. "Heney Takes Up Cudgel against the Grafters," *San Francisco Call*, October 21, 1906.

2. Walton Bean, *Boss Ruef's San Francisco* (Berkeley: UC Press, 1967), 285.

3. "City's Ablest Lawyers to Take Up Ruef Trial Today," *San Francisco Call*, November 16, 1908.

4. "Hiram Johnson Declaring Ruef's Guilt to Trial Jury," *San Francisco Call*, December 11, 1908.

5. James J. Rawls and Walton Bean, *California: An Interpretive History* (New York: McGraw-Hill, 2003), 182.

6. Ibid., 231.

7. Ibid., 184.

8. Oscar Lewis, quoted in *Readings in California History,* by N. Ray Gilmore and Gladys Gilmore (New York: Thomas Y. Crowell, 1966), 250.

9. "How Congressmen Are Bribed: The Colton Letters," Bancroft Library, UC Berkeley, June 1939, archive.org/details/howcongressmenar00huntrich.

10. Carey McWilliams, *California: The Great Exception* (Santa Barbara: Peregrine Smith, 1976), 178–179.

11. Kevin Starr, *Inventing the Dream: California through the Progressive Era* (New York: Oxford University Press, 1985), 200.

12. Fremont Older, *My Own Story* (San Francisco: The Call Publishing Co., 1919), 21.

13. Testimony, United States Pacific Railway Commission 1887, quoted in Spencer C. Olin, Jr., *California Politics, 1846–1920: The Emerging Corporate State* (San Francisco: Boyd and Fraser, 1981), 33.

14. Richard White, *Railroaded: The Transcontinentals and the Making of Modern America* (New York: W.W. Norton, 2011), 101.

15. Ambrose Bierce, "His Deal with Pacific Mail: Huntington Forced to Tell the Truth by Senator Morgan," *San Francisco Examiner,* February 15, 1896.

16. Oscar Lewis, in Gilmore and Gilmore, 248.

17. J. Gregg Layne, "The Lincoln-Roosevelt League, Its Origins and Accomplishments," *Historical Society of Southern California Quarterly* 25 (September 1943), quoted in Gilmore and Gilmore, 257.

18. Tom Sitton, *John Randolph Haynes: California Progressive* (Stanford, CA: Stanford University Press, 1992), 89.

19. Starr, 205.

20. Ibid., 236.

21. "Leading Republicans Organize to Fight Boss Rule," *San Francisco Call,* August 2, 1907.

22. John M. Allswang, *The Initiative and Referendum in California, 1898–1998* (Stanford, CA: Stanford University Press, 2000), 14.

23. George E. Mowry, *The California Progressives*, quoted in Gilmore and Gilmore, 263.

24. Letter from Hiram Johnson to Archibald Johnson, July 17, 1917, *The Diary Letters of Hiram Johnson*, edited by Robert Burke (New York: Garland, 1983).

25. Starr, 265.

26. David Halberstam, *The Powers That Be* (New York: Alfred A. Knopf, 1979), 103.

27. Ibid.

28. Dennis McDougal, *Privileged Son: Otis Chandler and the Rise and Fall of the* L.A. Times *Dynasty* (Cambridge, MA: Perseus, 2001), 48.

29. Charles Edward Russell, "Scientific Corruption of Politics," *Hampton's Magazine*, June 1910.

30. Charles Edward Russell, "The Paying of the Bill," *Hampton's Magazine*, October 1910.

31. "Gives Democrats 23-Lead in House," *New York Times*, November 6, 1910.

32. "Merchants of City Welcome GOP Champion," *San Francisco Call*, October 15, 1910.

33. "Hiram Johnson Is Greeted by People as Conquering Hero," *San Francisco Call,* November 5, 1910; "Railwaymen Warned by Bosses: SP Political Bureau Uses Threats and Promises in Fight against Johnson," *San Francisco Call*, November 5, 1910.

34. "Letters from Hiram Johnson, August–December 1910," Hiram Johnson Papers, Bancroft Library, UC Berkeley.

35. Arthur Schlesinger, Jr., *The Age of Roosevelt: Crisis of the Old Order, 1919–1933* (New York: Houghton Mifflin, 1957), 18.

36. "Says the Interests Rule US: But the West Is in Revolt, Declares Governor-Elect Johnson," *New York Times*, December 15, 1910.

37. Hiram Johnson Inaugural Address, January 3, 1911, California State Library Governors' Gallery, governors.library.ca.gov.

38. "Hiram Johnson Now Governor of California," *Sausalito News*, January 11, 1911.

39. The legislature authorized votes on two separate initiative processes. The *direct* initiative required proponents of a statute or constitutional amendment to collect valid signatures of registered voters equal in number to 8 percent of the number of voters who participated in the previous gubernatorial election. In 1966, the threshold for statutory initiatives was lowered to 5 percent. An *indirect* initiative, which required a 5 percent signature threshold, allowed proponents to submit a measure to the legislature for enactment. Failing legislative approval, the measure then was placed on the ballot. The indirect initiative was rarely used and was eliminated by California voters in 1966. The signature threshold for a referendum was 5 percent. To place a recall on the ballot required signatures that equal a percentage of the total number of votes most recently cast for the targeted office: 12 percent for executive officials, such as the governor, and 20 percent for state legislators and judges.

40. "Constitutional Amendment Election," *Amador Ledger*, October 13, 1911.

41. "Equal Suffrage in Doubt—Other Amendments Carried," *San Francisco Call*, October 11, 1911.

42. "Special Election Farce," *Amador Ledger*, October 13, 1911.

43. "Suffrage Jubilee to Celebrate the California Victory," *San Francisco Call*, October 14, 1911.

44. "Special Election Farce," *Amador Ledger*, October 13, 1911.

45. "Anti-Democracy in California," *New York Times*, October 18, 1911.

46. "History of California Initiatives," California Secretary of State, 2013, www.sos.ca.gov/elections/ballot-measures/history-initiatives.

47. "Governor Johnson Speaks in Marin," *Sausalito News*, October 17, 1914.

48. Hiram Johnson Inaugural Address, January 5, 1915, California State Library Governors' Gallery, governors.library.ca.gov.

49. McWilliams, 199.

50. Gray Davis was recalled in 2003.

51. "The Initiative Process in California," Public Policy Institute of California, 2013.

52. National Conference of State Legislatures, "Initiative, Referendum and Recall," www.ncsl.org/research/elections-and-campaigns/initiative-referendum-and-recall-overview.aspx.

53. Joe Mathews, "The Bad Dad Who Cursed California," Zócalo Public Square website, June 13, 2013, www.zocalopublicsquare.org/2013/06/13/the-bad-dad-who-cursed-california/inquiries/connecting-california.

54. Hiram Johnson, October 16, 1914, quoted in *California Crackup: How Reform Broke the Golden State and How We Can Fix It,* by Joe Mathews and Mark Paul (Berkeley: UC Press, 2010), 27.

CHAPTER 5
1934: California's Dirtiest Election Gives Birth to Modern Campaigns

1. "California: After the EPIC," *Time*, May 20, 1935.

2. Royce D. Delmatier, Clarence F. McIntosh, and Earl G. Waters, *The Rumble of California Politics, 1848–1970* (New York: John Wiley and Sons, 1970), 252.

3. Richard Hofstadter, *The Age of Reform* (New York: Vintage Books, 1955), 198.

4. David M. Kennedy, *Freedom from Fear* (New York: Oxford University Press, 1999), 226.

5. Sinclair letter to Eleanor Roosevelt, in *Eleanor and Franklin,* by Joseph P. Lash (New York: W.W. Norton, 1971), 386.

6. Ibid., 386.

7. See Delmatier, et al., 275.

8. "Political Notes: California Climax," *Time*, November 22, 1934.

9. J. F. T. O'Connor, *Year Book Diaries*, in Delmatier, et al., 266.

10. "Sinclair Piles Up Commanding Lead in California Vote," *New York Times*, August 29, 1934.

11. "Historical Voter Registration and Participation in Statewide Primary Elections, 1914–1912," California Secretary of State, www.sos.ca.gov/elections/sov/2012-primary/pdf/04-historical-voter-reg-primary.pdf.

12. "California: After the EPIC," *Time,* May 20, 1935.
13. George Creel, in *California: An Interpretive History,* by James Rawls and Walton Bean (New York: McGraw-Hill, 2003), 334.
14. Clement S. Whitaker, Jr., oral history, conducted by Gabrielle Morris, 1988, 1989, State Government Oral History Program, California State Archives, Sacramento.
15. Greg Mitchell, *The Campaign of the Century* (New York: Random House, 1992), 129.
16. Whitaker and Baxter campaign files, Whitaker and Baxter Papers, California State Archives, Sacramento.
17. Ibid.
18. Robert Talley, "Earthquake Sinclair Causes Tremors in California's Golden Soil," *Washington Post*, October 7, 1934.
19. Upton Sinclair, *I, Candidate for Governor: And How I Got Licked* (Pasadena, CA: self-published, 1935), 82–84.
20. "Political Notes," *Time*, September 10, 1934.
21. Mitchell, 291.
22. Ibid., 328.
23. Ibid., 355.
24. Sinclair, 131.
25. "Merriam or Sinclair?" *Los Angeles Times*, August 29, 1934: "Stand Up and Be Counted," *Los Angeles Times,* October 5, 1934.
26. David Halberstam, *The Powers That Be* (New York: Alfred A. Knopf, 1979), 117.
27. Sinclair, 140.
28. Irwin Ross, "The Super Salesmen of California Politics," *Harper's*, July 1959.
29. Sinclair, 150.
30. "Ashamed of Wedlock," *Washington Post*, January 31, 1909.
31. Mitchell, 355.
32. Ross, "The Super Salesmen of California Politics."
33. Gilbert King, "Past Imperfect: The Traumatic Birth of the Modern (and Vicious) Political Campaign," Smithsonian Institution website, October 11, 2012, www.smithsonianmag.com/history/the-traumatic-birth-of-the-modern-and-vicious-political-campaign-70717968/?no-ist.
34. "Charges Threat to Movie Folk," *Boston Globe,* November 1, 1934.
35. Richard Sheridan Ames, "The Screen Enters Politics: Will Hollywood Produce More Propaganda?," *Harper's*, March 1935.
36. Sinclair, 169.
37. Ames, "The Screen Enters Politics."
38. Mitchell, 500.
39. *Los Angeles Examiner*, October 23–25, 1934.
40. Mitchell, 423.
41. George Hatfield campaign files, California State Archives, Sacramento.
42. "Hatfield States the Issues," September 20, 1934, George Hatfield campaign files, California State Archives, Sacramento.
43. Whitaker and Baxter campaign files, Whitaker and Baxter Papers, California State Archives, Sacramento.
44. Sinclair, 207–208.
45. "The Choice of California," *Los Angeles Times*, November 4, 1934.
46. "Political Notes: California Finale," *Time,* November 12, 1934.
47. Frank Merriam, 1934 Statement of Candidate's Receipts and Expenditures, California State Archives, Sacramento.
48. Jean Edward Smith, *FDR* (New York: Random House, 2007), 349.
49. Delmatier, et al., 281.
50. James N. Gregory, "Upton Sinclair," *California Journal*, November 1999.
51. Sinclair, 3.
52. Sinclair, 144.
53. Jill Lepore, "The Lie Factory," *New Yorker*, September 24, 2012.

54. Whitaker and Baxter campaign files, Whitaker and Baxter Papers, California State Archives, Sacramento.
55. Lepore, "The Lie Factory."
56. Harry Truman, "Annual Message to Congress on the State of the Union," January 7, 1948, American Presidency Project, UC Santa Barbara, www.presidency.ucsb.edu.
57. Lepore, "The Lie Factory."
58. Ross, "The Super Salesmen of California Politics."
59. Arthur Schlesinger, Jr., *The Age of Roosevelt: Politics of Upheaval, 1935–1936* (New York: Houghton Mifflin, 1960), 118.
60. "The Living Room Candidate," Museum of the Living Image, www.livingroomcandidate.org.
61. James T. Patterson, *Grand Expectations: The United States, 1945–1974* (New York: Oxford University Press, 1996), 258.
62. Ross, "The Super Salesmen of California Politics."
63. Joseph P. Natoli, *Memory's Orbit: Film and Culture, 1999–2000* (Albany: State University of New York Press, 2003), 258.
64. Mark Green and Gail MacColl, *There He Goes Again: Ronald Reagan's Reign of Error* (New York: Pantheon Books, 1983), 8.

CHAPTER 6
1942: Earl Warren Pilots California into a Postwar Boom

1. Ed Cray, *Chief Justice: A Biography of Earl Warren* (New York: Simon and Schuster, 1997), 95. Cray reports Warren did at other times resort to wiretaps in criminal investigations.
2. Earl Warren Papers, California State Archives, Sacramento, F3640: 269.
3. Cray, 92.
4. V. S. McClatchy, "Argument in Favor of Proposed Alien Land Law," California Ballot Pamphlet, November 2, 1920, 5.
5. Leo Katcher, *Earl Warren: A Political Biography* (New York: McGraw-Hill, 1967), 140.
6. James J. Rawls and Walton Bean, *California: An Interpretive History,* 9th ed (New York: McGraw-Hill, 2008), 140.
7. Charles Wollenberg, "Ethnic Experiences in California History: An Impressionistic Survey," in *Neither Separate Nor Equal: Race and Racism in California*, edited by Roger Olmsted and Charles Wollenberg (San Francisco: California Historical Society, 1971), 3.
8. Statutes of 1850, Chapter 133, California State Archives, Sacramento.
9. Earl Warren, *The Memoirs of Chief Justice Earl Warren* (New York: Doubleday, 1977), 4.
10. Wollenberg, 13.
11. Warren, 30–31.
12. Ibid., 176. His editors acknowledged that his accounts might have sounded pompous or prideful, a tone they attributed to Warren's inexperience at writing in the first person. They insisted that he "showed becoming modesty when in office," xii.
13. Ibid., 105.
14. Cray, 183.
15. Ibid., 72–73.
16. Herbert L. Phillips oral history, "Bee Perspectives on the Warren Era," conducted by Amelia R. Fry, 1972, Earl Warren Oral History Project, Regional Oral History Office, Bancroft Library, UC Berkeley, 4.
17. Jack Smith, "Let's Hear It for Earl Warren…Our Man of the Century," *Los Angeles Times*, March 13, 1991.
18. "Significance of California Primary," *Los Angeles Times,* June 6, 1946.
19. Warren, 153.
20. Cray, 120–122.
21. "Evacuation of Japanese Expected to Start Soon," *Los Angeles Times*, March 10, 1942.
22. A few thousand Italian and German immigrants and citizens were forced to relocate or were incarcerated for varying periods during the war, although never on a scale

approaching the Japanese internment. See Stephen Fox, *The Unknown Internment* (Boston: Twayne, 1990) for oral histories and background describing relocations of Italian Americans in California. Also see Gary R. Mormino and George E. Pozzetta, "Ethnics at War: Italian Americans in California during World War II," in *The Way We Really Were: The Golden State in the Second Great War*, edited by Roger W. Lotchin (Urbana: University of Illinois Press, 2000).

23. Warren, 145.
24. Cray, 131, citing Earl Warren Papers, California State Archives, Sacramento, 537A.
25. "Evacuation of Japanese Expected to Start Soon," *Los Angeles Times,* March 10, 1942.
26. "Olson Called War Failure," *Los Angeles Times,* July 15, 1942.
27. George Gallup, "Poll Shows How Coast Stands on Japs' Return," *Los Angeles Times*, December 30, 1942.
28. Cray, 130.
29. Warren, 165.
30. Ibid., 169.
31. "Gov. Warren Proves He Meant What He Said," *Los Angeles Times*, January 5, 1943.
32. Kevin Allen Leonard, "Brothers Under the Skin?: African-Americans, Mexican-Americans and World War II in California," in Lotchin, 192.
33. Arthur Verge, "Daily Life in Wartime California," in Lotchin, 19.
34. "Japs Constitute Peril to State, Warren Declares," Associated Press in the *Los Angeles Times,* November 6, 1943.
35. Doris Matsui interview, Sacramento, November 7, 2014.
36. Warren, 182.
37. Ibid., 170–171.
38. Ibid., 195.
39. "Let's Try a 5-Cent Gasoline Tax," *Los Angeles Times*, February 26, 1947, p. A4.
40. Warren, 223.
41. Cray, 520.
42. Warren, 5.
43. Ibid., 6.
44. James J. Rawls, "The Earl Warren Oral History Project: An Appraisal," *Pacific Historical Review* 56 (1987), 87.
45. Warren, 149.
46. Doris Matsui interview.
47. Robert T. Matsui, Foreword to *Achieving the Impossible Dream: How Japanese Americans Obtained Redress*, by Mitchell T. Maki, Harry H. L. Kitano, and S. Megan Berthold (Urbana: University of Illinois Press, 1999), x–xi.
48. Warren, 231–232.
49. Edward Staniford, *The Pattern of California History* (San Francisco: Canfield Press, 1975), 634.

CHAPTER 7
1958: Pat Brown's Election Ushers In Modern California

1. Fred Dutton oral history, "Democratic Campaigns and Controversies, 1954–1966," conducted by Amelia R. Fry, 1977, 1978, Regional Oral History Office, Bancroft Library, UC Berkeley, 110.
2. "Senator Knowland's Plan to Bow Out in '58 Has Explosive Effect in State Capitol," *Sacramento Bee*, January 8, 1957.
3. Edward H. Dickson, "Brown Says State Demo Slate Will Be Best in Years," *Sacramento Bee*, March 8, 1957.
4. Edmund G. Brown oral history, "Years of Growth, 1939–1966: Law Enforcement, Politics and the Governor's Office," conducted by Malca Chall, 1979, Regional Oral History Office, Bancroft Library, UC Berkeley, 234–235.

5. Letter from Edmund Brown to Jerry Brown, April 26, 1957, quoted in *California Rising: The Life and Times of Pat Brown,* by Ethan Rarick (Berkeley: UC Press, 2004), 91.

6. Robert J. Markson, "Knight Virtually Announces He Will Run Again," *Sacramento Bee*, May 10, 1957.

7. Rarick, 93–95; Dutton oral history, 111.

8. California Ballot Pamphlet, November 4, 1952, librarysource.uchastings.edu/ballot_pdf/1952g.pdf.

9. *California Blue Book* (Sacramento: California Secretary of State, 2000).

10. Greg Lucas, "Happy Birthday Governor Knight!" California's Capitol website, December 9, 2011, http://www.californiascapitol.com/2011/12/happy-birthday-governor-4/

11. "California: Don Juan in Heaven," *Time,* May 30, 1955.

12. Knight inaugural address, October 5, 1953, California State Library Governors' Gallery, http://governors.library.ca.gov/31-Knight.html.

13. "Nixonites to Gun for Knight in '58," *Los Angeles Mirror-News,* August 24, 1956.

14. Gale Montgomery and James W. Johnson, *One Step from the White House: The Rise and Fall of Senator William F. Knowland* (Berkeley: UC Press, 1998), 248.

15. Ibid., 228.

16. Ibid., 229.

17. "Knowland Plans to Bow Out in '58 Jolts Capitol: News Elates State Demos, Stuns GOPers," *Sacramento Bee,* January 8, 1957.

18. Montgomery and Johnson, 233.

19. Kyle Palmer, "Knowland Reshapes Battle Line," *Los Angeles Times*, January 13, 1957.

20. Brown, "Years of Growth" oral history, 238.

21. "Just Plain Pat," *Time*, September 15, 1958.

22. Sascha Rice, *California State of Mind: The Legacy of Pat Brown,* documentary, 2012.

23. "Labor Leaders Ask Demos to Draft Knight," Associated Press in the *Sacramento Bee*, October 30, 1957.

24. Herbert L. Phillips, "Demo Brown Will Seek Governorship," *Sacramento Bee*, October 30, 1957; Hal McClure, "Brown Also Expects Knight to Withdraw," Associated Press in the *Sacramento Bee*, October 30, 1957.

25. "Republican Prospects Improved," *Los Angeles Times*, November 6, 1957.

26. "Knight's Switch Proves Blow to Free Elections," "Unhappy Knight Leaves for Visit to New York; Knight Cabinet Is Unhappy Over Switch," all *Sacramento Bee*, November 6, 1957.

27. Totton J. Anderson, "The 1958 Election in California," *Western Political Quarterly* 12, no. 1, pt. 2 (March 1959), 284, www.jstor.org/stable/444055?seq=1#page_scan_tab_contents; Rarick, 103.

28. "State Right-to-Work Law Heavily Favored in Survey," *Los Angeles Times*, November 8, 1957.

29. Leonard Keeler, quoted in ibid.

30. Brown, "Years of Growth" oral history, 233.

31. Statement of Vote, June 3, 1958, California Secretary of State.

32. Dick Walton, "Big Demo Victory; OK on Chavez Leads," *Los Angeles Herald Express*, June 4, 1958.

33. Kurt Schuparra, *Triumph of the Right: The Rise of the California Conservative Movement, 1945–1966* (Armonk, NY: M.E. Sharpe, 1998), 28.

34. "Why Are the Promoters of Proposition 18 So Afraid to Tell the Truth?" *San Bernardino Sun*, November 2, 1958.

35. Gladwin Hill oral history, conducted by Carlos Vásquez, 1987, Regional Oral History Office, Bancroft Library, UC Berkeley, 76.

36. Clint Mosher, "Brown Lashes at Knowland for False Front," *San Francisco Examiner*, October 26, 1958; Anderson, 286.

37. Brown, "Years of Growth" oral history, 245.

38. Schuparra, 35; Anderson, 287–88; Kyle Palmer, "Party Feuds Must Go, Ike Warns," *Los Angeles Times*, October 21, 1958; "California Poll," *Los Angeles Mirror-News*, October 29, 1958.

39. "Brown's Black Record on Narcotics," *Los Angeles Times*, October 25, 1958.
40. "Governor," *San Francisco Chronicle*, October 30, 1958.
41. "Knowland Climaxes Drive with 20-Hour Telethon," Associated Press in the *San Bernardino Sun-Telegram*, November 2, 1958.
42. Rice documentary.
43. Statement of Vote, November 4, 1958, California Secretary of State; "Campaign Costs: How Much Have They Increased and Why?" California Fair Political Practices Committee, January 1980.
44. "Burkett Says Knowland Wrecks Party," Associated Press in the *Sacramento Bee*, October 30, 1958.
45. Anderson, 277.
46. *A Brief History of the California Economy*, California Department of Finance, www.dof. ca.gov/HTML/FS_DATA/HistoryCAEconomy/modern_economy.htm.
47. California State Library Governors' Gallery, governors.library.ca.gov.
48. Brown, "Years of Growth" oral history, 270.
49. Gladwin Hill, "California Shift Will Help Voters; With End of Cross-Filing, He Can Tell Aspirant's Party without a Scorecard," *New York Times*, April 28, 1959.
50. Walter Stiern oral history, conducted by Enid Hart Douglass, 1987, State Government Oral History Program, California State Archives, Sacramento, 157 and 160.
51. Rice documentary.
52. California State Budget: 1958 Budget Session, www.archive.org/details/californiastate5758uns.
53. Edmund G. Brown oral history, "California Water Issues, 1950–1966," conducted by Malca Chall, 1979, 1980, Regional Oral History Office, Bancroft Library, UC Berkeley, 16.
54. Dutton oral history, 102.
55. Rice documentary.
56. Ralph Brody oral history, "California Water Issues, 1950–1966," conducted by Malca Chall, 1980, Regional Oral History Office, Bancroft Library, UC Berkeley, 37.
57. Brown, "Water Issues" oral history, 24.
58. California Department of Water Resources, http://www.water.ca.gov/swp/milestones.cfm#1970.
59. Brown, "Years of Growth" oral history, 477.
60. United Press International, "Brown OKs Master Plan for Schools," April 27, 1960.
61. Rarick, 153.
62. Dave E. Dowall and Jan Whittington, "Making Room for the Future: Rebuilding California's Infrastructure," Public Policy Institute of California, March 2003, 14; Rarick, 129–130.
63. Rarick, 267.
64. Brown, "Water Issues" oral history, 34.

CHAPTER 8
1966: Voters Give Greater Power to a Full-Time Legislature

1. Larry Margolis oral history, conducted by Carole Hicke, 1989, State Government Oral History Program, California State Archives, Sacramento, 102–103.
2. Martin Smith, "Slow-Moving Legislators, in Spite of Plans to Contrary, Set Longest Session Record," *Sacramento Bee*, July 8, 1966.
3. Ibid.
4. Kenneth Reich, "Jesse Unruh, Key Political Figure in State, Dies at 64," *Los Angeles Times*, August 5, 1987; Assemblyman X, as told to Lester Velie, "This Is How Payola Works in Politics," *Reader's Digest*, August 1960.
5. Assemblyman X, "This Is How Payola Works in Politics."
6. Robert Finch, quoted in *Ronnie and Jesse: A Political Odyssey,* by Lou Cannon (Garden City, NY: Doubleday, 1969), 99.
7. Lou Cannon, *Governor Reagan: His Rise to Power* (New York: Public Affairs, 2003), 164.

8. "Stanislaus Legislator's Reelection Announcement Spies Rumors of Demo Fight Over Speakership," *Sacramento Bee*, March 4, 1960.
9. "Unruh Elected Speaker of State Assembly," *Los Angeles Times*, October 1, 1961.
10. "Big Daddy," *Time*, May 5, 1961.
11. Cannon, *Ronnie and Jesse*, 112.
12. Jackson K. Putnam, *Jess: The Political Career of Jesse Marvin Unruh* (Lanham, MA: University Press of America, 2005), 31.
13. Ed Salzman, "Mulford Warns Demos of 'Hacks' in Staff Plan," *Oakland Tribune*, August 20, 1964. Other criticism of Unruh's staff buildup is buried in the Unruh papers at the California State Archives in Sacramento. In an undated memo from top aide Jack Crose to Chief of Staff Larry Margolis about "kin on the payroll," the assembly's chief sergeant-at-arms, Tony Beard, Sr., was being inundated with requests to hire relatives of other assembly employees. One of them was the brother of an assembly member. Beard, going up the chain of command, wanted Unruh to create a policy statement against nepotism. In a handwritten response, Margolis wrote, "Jack—I told Jesse about this. He is not enthusiastic about taking all the heat, but OK."
14. Bill Boyarsky, *Big Daddy: Jesse Unruh and the Art of Power Politics* (Berkeley: UC Press, 2008), 167.
15. Sherry Bebitch Jeffe collection, in ibid.
16. Ronald Reagan oral history, "On Becoming Governor," conducted by Sarah Sharp, 1979, Regional Oral History Office, Bancroft Library, UC Berkeley, 3.
17. William E. Roberts oral history, "Professional Campaign Management and the Candidate," conducted by Sarah Sharp, 1979, Regional Oral History Office, Bancroft Library, UC Berkeley, 12.
18. George Christopher oral history, "San Francisco Republicans," conducted by Sarah Sharp and Miriam Stein, 1977, 1978, Regional Oral History Office, Bancroft Library, UC Berkeley, 45.
19. "Full-Time California Legislature?" *Napa Register,* February 24, 1964.
20. Richard Rodda, "Brown Fires First Salvo at Reagan," *Sacramento Bee*, June 9, 1966.
21. Sherry Bebitch Jeffe telephone interview, October 15, 2014.
22. Clement S. Whitaker, Jr., oral history, conducted by Gabrielle Morris, 1988–1989, State Government Oral History Program, California State Archives, Sacramento, 119.
23. Proposition 1-A campaign brochure, Whitaker and Baxter Papers, California State Archives, Sacramento.
24. Whitaker and Baxter Papers, California State Archives, Sacramento.
25. Reagan, "On Becoming Governor" oral history, 21.
26. Ibid.
27. "Proposed Amendments to Constitution," California Legislative Counsel/California Secretary of State.
28. Western Opinion Research Center, in the *Los Angeles Herald Examiner,* May 6, 1966.
29. "Let's Boost Their Pay," KPIX, March 22, 1966, Whitaker and Baxter Papers, California State Archives, Sacramento; "Constitution Reform Vital," *Los Angeles Times*, October 28, 1966.
30. Gordon Winton oral history, conducted by Enid Hart Douglass, 1987, State Government Oral History Program, California State Archives, Sacramento, 76–77.
31. Gladwin Hill oral history, conducted by Carlos Vásquez, 1987, State Government Oral History Program, California State Archives, Sacramento, 81.
32. J. P. Monroe, *The Political Party Matrix* (New York: State University of New York Press, 2001), 51; Sherry Bebitch Jeffe, "For Legislative Staff, Policy Takes a Back Seat to Politics," *California Journal*, January 1987; Jim Miller, "Assembly Hikes Pay for Many Employees, Including Highest Paid," *Sacramento Bee*, March 24, 2014.
33. Jeffe, "For Legislative Staff, Policy Takes a Back Seat to Politics."
34. Margolis oral history, 68.
35. Ibid., 68–69.
36. Monroe, 60.

37. California 2014 election review, Follow the Money, http://beta.followthemoney.org/election-overview?s=CA&y=2014.

38. "Late Independent Expenditures," California Secretary of State, http://dbsearch.ss.ca.gov/LateIndExpendSearch.aspx.

39. "Big Money Talks: California's Billion Dollar Club," California Fair Political Practices Commission, March 2010.

40. "Initiative Totals by Summary Year, 1912–2014," California Secretary of State, www.sos.ca.gov/elections/ballot-measures/pdf/initiative-totals-summary-year.pdf.

41. Steve Swatt, "Reagan: The Governor," KCRA-TV, January 1981; California State Library Governors' Gallery, http://governors.library.ca.gov/33-Reagan.html.

42. Reagan, "On Becoming Governor" oral history, 46.

43. Swatt, "Reagan: The Governor."

44. Ibid.

45. Steve Merksamer interview, Sacramento, November 5, 2014.

46. Paul Scicchitano and Kathleen Walter, "Michael Reagan Leads Effort to Make California Legislature Part-Time," Newsmax, April 17, 2012, www.newsmax.com/Newsfront/reagan-california-part-time-legislature/2012/04/17/id/436226/.

CHAPTER 9
1974: Californians Pull Back the Curtain on Politics as Usual

1. George Deukmejian interview, Long Beach, December 17, 2013.

2. Ken Meade oral history, conducted by Timothy Fong, 1987, 1988, State Government Oral History Program, California State Archives, Sacramento, 97.

3. James Dufur, "Legislative Session Closes in Bedlam," *Sacramento Bee*, September 16, 1973.

4. Bruce Keppel, "Open Government Initiative," *California Journal*, November 1973.

5. Arthur Samish and Bob Thomas, *The Secret Boss of California* (New York: Crown, 1971), 12.

6. Ibid., 57–58.

7. Richard Rodda, "Death of Artie Samish: Lobbyist's Legacy Lives," *California Journal*, March 1974.

8. Samish and Thomas, 97–98.

9. Lester Velie, "The Secret Boss of California," *Collier's*, August 13, 1949.

10. Samish and Thomas, 14.

11. "Solons Meet; Warren Urges Lobby Control," *Sacramento Bee*, December 12, 1949.

12. "Lobby Bill's Lawyer-Solon Curbs Are Hit," *Sacramento Bee*, December 15, 1949.

13. "Solons Vote Samish Ban, Near Recess," *Sacramento Bee*, December 21, 1949; "Solons Pass Three Lobby Bills, Adjourn," *Sacramento Bee*, December 22, 1949.

14. Rodda, "Death of Artie Samish."

15. Thayer Watkins, *Artie Samish: A Political Boss of California*, San Jose State University, http://www.sjsu.edu/faculty/watkins/samish.htm.

16. Richard Ratcliff interview, Sacramento, January 27, 2014.

17. Jerry Zanelli interview, Sacramento, March 11, 2014.

18. William T. Bagley, *California's Golden Years: When Government Worked and Why* (Berkeley: Berkeley Public Policy Press, Institute of Governmental Studies, 2009), 13.

19. Lou Cannon, *Ronnie and Jesse: A Political Odyssey* (Garden City, NY: Doubleday, 1969), 101.

20. Ibid., 96.

21. John Burton interview, Sacramento, January 7, 2014.

22. Steve Swatt, "Brown: The Governor," KCRA-TV, January 1983.

23. Roger Rapoport, *California Dreaming: The Political Odyssey of Pat and Jerry Brown* (Berkeley: Nolo Press, 1982), 129 and 132.

24. Ibid, 106.

25. "Proposition 18: Campaign Spending Controversy Continues," *California Journal*, December 1970.

26. Robert Stern interview, Los Angeles, December 15, 2013.

27. Carla Lazzareschi and Steve Duscha, "The Koupals' Petition Factory," *California Journal*, March 1975.
28. Daniel Lowenstein oral history, conducted by Carlos Vásquez, 1989, State Government Oral History Program, California State Archives, Sacramento, 96–97.
29. Wallace Turner, "Watergate Shadow Hangs over California G.O.P. Candidates for Governor," *New York Times*, March 21, 1974.
30. Swatt, "Brown: The Governor."
31. Jerry Gillam, "Prop. 9 Would Create Commission of Political Czars, Opponents Say," *Los Angeles Times*, May 20, 1974.
32. John M. Allswang, *The Initiative and Referendum in California, 1898–1998* (Stanford, CA: Stanford University Press, 2000), 121.
33. California Voter Pamphlet, California Secretary of State, June 4, 1974.
34. Gillam, "Prop. 9 Would Create Commission of Political Czars."
35. "Political Reform: Yes on Prop. 9," *Los Angeles Times*, May 24, 1974.
36. *Time,* "California: Brown v. Flournoy," November 4, 1974.
37. Swatt, "Brown: The Governor."
38. Stern interview.
39. Zanelli interview.
40. Halden Broaders oral history, conducted by Carole Hicke, 1990, State Government Oral History Program, California State Archives, Sacramento, 207.
41. Ratcliff interview.
42. Vigo G. Nielsen, Jr., "Is Proposition 9 Working?" *California Journal,* July 1975.
43. Ratcliff interview.
44. Herbert E. Alexander and Brian A. Haggerty, "Political Reform in California: How Has It Worked?" Citizens' Research Foundation, University of Southern California, February 1, 1980, 18; "Defining Acceptance of Contributions from a Lobbyist," FPPC memorandum, June 23, 2002.
45. Stern interview.
46. Ibid.
47. Ross Johnson interview, Sacramento, December 19, 2013.
48. Hedy Govenar interview, Sacramento, January 11, 2014.
49. Ibid.
50. Jerry Gillam, "Lobbyists in State Capitol: These Women Take Up Issues with All Things Being Equal," *Los Angeles Times,* November 8, 1987.
51. Govenar interview.
52. Burton interview.
53. Lobbying Activity/Western States Petroleum Association, "Report of Lobbyist Employer," July 1–September 30, 2013, California Secretary of State, cal-access.sos.ca.gov/PDFGen/pdfgen.prg?filingid=1799443&amendid=0.
54. Bagley, 8 and 69.
55. "Overly Complex and Unduly Burdensome," Bipartisan Commission on the Political Reform Act of 1974, July 2000.
56. William Endicott, quoted in Alexander and Haggerty, 63.
57. Walter A. Zelman oral history, conducted by Carlos Vásquez, 1989, State Government Oral History Project, California State Archives, Sacramento, 133.
58. Robert M. Stern, "What Happened to Jerry Brown, the Reformer We Once Knew?" *San Francisco Chronicle*, October 9, 2014.

CHAPTER 10
1978: Proposition 13 Launches a National Tax Revolt

1. John Marelius, quoting Stu Mollrich, "Prop. 13 Started Slowly, Turned into a Groundswell," *San Diego Union-Tribune*, October 4, 2005.
2. Peter Behr oral history, conducted by Ann Lage, 1988, 1989, State Government Oral History Program, California State Archives, Sacramento, 333–334.

3. Leo McCarthy oral history, conducted by Carole Hicke, 1995, 1996, State Government Oral History Program, California State Archives, Sacramento, 125.

4. Behr oral history, 344.

5. Ronald Soble, "Jarvis—Master of Crowd Psychology," *Los Angeles Times,* May 17, 1978.

6. Behr oral history, 333.

7. Joel Fox interview, Sherman Oaks, December 16, 2013.

8. Clarence Y. H. Lo, *Small Property Versus Big Government: Social Origins of the Property Tax Revolt* (Berkeley: UC Press, 1995), 11; Mark Paul, "Bring Back the Crooked Assessor," Zócalo Public Square website, June 10, 2012, www.zocalopub-licsquare.org/2012/06/10/bring-back-the-crooked-assessor/chronicles/who-we-were/.

9. "Tax Assessor Scandal Swells," Associated Press in the *Sarasota Journal*, June 21, 1966, news.google.com/newspapers?nid=1798&dat=19660621&id=VQwfAAAAIBAJ&sjid=-FowEAAAAIBAJ&pg=7097,2965084.

10. "Assessor's Marathon Trial—60 Days," *San Francisco Examiner*, May 29, 1966.

11. Jackson Doyle, "Final OK on Assessment Reform Bill," *San Francisco Chronicle*, July 1, 1966.

12. Paul, "Bring Back the Crooked Assessor."

13. Jack Jones, "Ex-Assessor Philip E. Watson Dies at 62," *Los Angeles Times*, December 9, 1986.

14. Bruce Keppel, "An Offer Californians Did Refuse," *California Journal*, December 1973.

15. Marelius, "Prop. 13 Started Slowly."

16. Joel Fox, *The Legend of Proposition 13* (Bloomington, IN: Xlibris, 2003), 50.

17. Burt A. Folkart, "Paul Gann Dies; Tax-Crusading Prop. 13 Author," *Los Angeles Times*, September 12, 1989.

18. Behr oral history, 330.

19. Paul Gann oral history, conducted by Gabrielle Morris, 1987, State Government Oral History Program, California State Archives, Sacramento, 20.

20. "Brown Throws Support to Behr Tax Bill," Associated Press in the *Santa Cruz Sentinel*, February 1, 1978 www.newspapers.com/newspage/62637735/.

21. Fox, *Legend of Proposition 13,* 84.

22. Bob Egelko, "Jarvis Is the Face of Property Tax Revolt," Associated Press in the *Santa Cruz Sentinel*, May 31, 1978, www.newspapers.com/newspage/63188098/.

23. Fox, *Legend of Proposition 13,* 86–87.

24. Howard Jarvis Collection, California State Archives, Sacramento.

25. Gann oral history, 22–23.

26. "The Wrench—Not the Hammer," *San Diego Union*, March 31, 1978.

27. *Los Angeles Times*, "Getting the Message," April 30, 1978.

28. Allan M. Jalon, "The 'Lion' in Winter," *Los Angeles Times*, April 14, 2002.

29. *Los Angeles Times*, "Letter His, Pat Brown Confirms," March 24, 1978.

30. George Skelton, "Dramatic Rise in Support for Proposition 13 Found," *Los Angeles Times*, May 28, 1978.

31. Fox interview.

32. Sid Bernstein and Barbara Baird, "County Reassessments to Be Mailed before Election," *Los Angeles Times*, May 17, 1978.

33. Egelko, "Jarvis Is the Face of Property Tax Revolt."

34. Fox, *Legend of Proposition 13,* 103.

35. Kenneth Reich and Penelope McMillan, "Jarvis Plans to Push His Fight Nationwide," *Los Angeles Times*, June 7, 1978.

36. John Marelius, "Campaign Manager Blamed for Failure to Win," *San Fernando Valley News*, June 11, 1978.

37. Reich and McMillan, "Jarvis Plans to Push His Fight Nationwide."

38. "Sound and Fury over Taxes," *Time*, June 19, 1978.

39. Richard Bergholz, "Younger Says He'll Vote for Jarvis Plan," *Los Angeles Times*, April 28, 1978.

40. John Balzar, "Ex-Atty. Gen. Evelle Younger Is Dead at 70," *Los Angeles Times*, May 5, 1989.

41. George Skelton, "Brown Asks Aid for Local Governments," *Los Angeles Times*, June 9, 1978.

42. Steve Merksamer interview, Sacramento, November 5, 2014.
43. Ed Salzman, "Life after Jarvis," *California Journal,* August 1980.
44. John Lewis telephone interview, September 2, 2014.
45. William T. Bagley, *California's Golden Years: When Government Worked and Why* (Berkeley: Berkeley Public Policy Press, Institute of Governmental Studies, 2009), 70.
46. Art Torres oral history, conducted by Steven D. Edgington, 2003, State Government Oral History Program, California State Archives, Sacramento, 87.
47. "Proposition 13 Revisited," California Taxpayers Association, June 6, 2013, www.caltax.org/Proposition13Revisited.pdf.
48. Carl Ingram, "The Heat Is On at Capital," *Los Angeles Times,* June 8, 1979.
49. Rebecca LaVally, "Proposition 13, Ten Years Later," *California Journal,* April 1988.
50. Fox interview.
51. Christopher Palmeri, "California Diminished by Tax Revolt of 1978 Shows How U.S. Invites Decline," *Bloomberg News,* October 16, 2011, www.bloomberg.com/news/2011-10-17/california-diminished-by-1978-tax-revolt-shows-u-s-in-decline.html.
52. University of California Budget News, www.admission.universityofcalifornia.edu/paying-for-uc/tuition-and-cost/; Terry Schwadron and Paul Richter, *California and the American Tax Revolt* (Berkeley: UC Press, 1984): *Proposition 13 Five Years Later* (Berkeley: UC Press,1984) 129.
53. Lisa Martin, "Exploring the Gann Limit: Then and Now," Cal-Tax Digest, Vol. 4, July 2000, 20.
54. Michael J. New, "The Gann Limit Turns 25," *Investor's Business Daily*, October 28, 2004, www.cato.org/publications/commentary/gann-limit-turns-25. Educators, who wanted to increase school spending with a portion of the surplus, won passage of their own constitutional amendment in 1988 to give schools minimum funding guarantees and a share of any revenue that exceeded the Gann Limit. Two years later, the transportation lobby pushed a measure that exempted gasoline taxes from the limit and reconfigured Gann's spending formula.
55. "Initiative Totals by Summary Year, 1912–2014," California Secretary of State, www.sos.ca.gov/elections/ballot-measures/pdf/initiative-totals-summary-year.pdf.
56. "Democracy by Initiative: Shaping California's Fourth Branch of Government," Center for Governmental Studies, May 2008, 11, policyarchive.org/collections/cgs/index?section=5&id=5800; Jim Miller, "Six Californias Initiative Fails to Make 2016 Ballot," *Sacramento Bee*, September 12, 2014, www.sacbee.com/news/politics-government/capitol-alert/article2609555.html.
57. "Democracy by Initiative," 3–4.
58. Mark Baldassare interview, Sacramento, September 5, 2014.
59. "Reforming California's Initiative Process," Public Policy Institute of California, October 24, 2013, www.ppic.org/main/event.asp?i=1392.
60. "Governor Brown Signs Ballot Reform Measure," Office of Governor Edmund G. Brown, Jr., September 27, 2014, gov.ca.gov/news.php?id=18735.
61. Stephen Moore, "Proposition 13 Then, Now and Forever," Cato Institute, July 30, 1998, www.cato.org/publications/commentary/proposition-13-then-now-forever.
62. "Californians and Their Government," Public Policy Institute of California, May 2013, ppic.org/content/pubs/survey/S_513MBS.pdf.

CHAPTER 11
1980: Technology and Money Forever Change Political Campaigning

1. "Robbins Wraps Up Senate Victory," *Glendale News-Press*, February 28, 1973.
2. Santa Clarita Valley Historical Society, http://scvhistory.com/scvhistory/lw2582a.htm.
3. Barry Brokaw interview, Sacramento, August 23, 2014.
4. Robbins Campaign Statement, 1973, California Secretary of State.
5. Ross Johnson interview, Sacramento, December 19, 2014.

6. Jerry Zanelli interview, Sacramento, March 11, 2014.

7. Statement of Vote, June 7, 1966, California Secretary of State; Statement of Vote, November 8, 1966, California Secretary of State; David Roberti Campaign Statement, 1966, California Secretary of State.

8. Harold Meyerson, "The Liberal Lion in Winter," *Los Angeles Times Magazine*, December 4, 1994.

9. Howard Berman interview, Berkeley, April 8, 2014; Berman/D'Agostino Campaign Files, Institute of Governmental Studies, UC Berkeley.

10. Alan Miller, "Mr. Inside and Mr. Outside: The Audacious Berman Brothers Built a Powerful Progressive Machine in California. But Can They Survive a New Political Order?" *Los Angeles Times*, March 29, 1992.

11. Vic Pollard, "Will the Imperial Speakership Survive the Assault on Government?" *California Journal*, May 1980.

12. Willie Brown interview, San Francisco, August 31, 2014.

13. Willie Brown, *Basic Brown* (New York: Simon and Schuster, 2008), 118.

14. Berman interview.

15. Ibid.

16. Ibid.

17. Leo McCarthy oral history, conducted by Carole Hicke, 1995, 1996, State Government Oral History Program, California State Archives, Sacramento, 169.

18. John Berthelson and Jeff Raimundo, "McCarthy Faces Sudden Challenge to Leadership," *Sacramento Bee*, December 11, 1979.

19. Claire Cooper, "McCarthy Lists Names of Supporters," *Sacramento Bee*, December 18, 1979.

20. McCarthy oral history, 169.

21. Brown interview.

22. Jeff Gillenkirk, "McCarthy vs. Berman: The Bitter Battle Rages On," *New West*, March 10, 1980.

23. Frank Vicencia oral history, conducted by Raphael Sonenshein, 1987, State Government Oral History Program, California State Archives, Sacramento, 149.

24. Miller, "Mr. Inside and Mr. Outside."

25. Berman interview.

26. Malcolm Schwartz, "Councilman Eyes Veteran Solon's Sacramento Seat," *Monterey Park Progress*, January 30, 1980.

27. Berman/D'Agostino Campaign Files.

28. Johnson interview.

29. Tom Bane oral history, conducted by Steven Isoardi, 1995, State Government Oral History Program, California State Archives, Sacramento, 224–225.

30. "Primary Election Campaign Costs Skyrocket," California Fair Political Practices Commission, September 16, 1980.

31. Douglas Brinkley, *The Unfinished Presidency: Jimmy Carter's Journey beyond the White House* (New York: Viking, 1998), 1.

32. W. B. Rood, "Speaker of the Assembly: From the Power Flow the Political Funds," *Los Angeles Times*, October 3, 1978.

33. Vicencia oral history, 150–151.

34. Brown interview.

35. Johnson interview.

36. James Richardson, *Willie Brown* (Berkeley: UC Press, 1996), 267.

37. Johnson interview.

38. Brown interview.

39. Ibid.

40. H. L. Richardson interview, Placerville, August 22, 2014.

41. Ibid.

42. Ibid.

43. James Mills letter to the *Los Angeles Times*, December 20, 1991.

44. Ed Salzman, "The Powder-Keg Speakership: How Long Can Brown Hold It," *California Journal*, January 1981.
45. John Burton interview, Sacramento, January 7, 2014.
46. Brown interview.
47. Hedy Govenar interview, Sacramento, January 12, 2014.
48. Johnson interview.
49. Brown interview.
50. Dan Walters, "Lobbyists Charge 'Shakedown,'" *Sacramento Union*, January 2, 1984.
51. James Richardson, *Willie Brown*, 321.
52. Brown interview.
53. Berman interview.
54. California Secretary of State, http://cal-acces.sos.ca.gov/Campaign/Candidates.

CHAPTER 12
1990: Californians Punish Lawmakers with Term Limits

1. Daniel Weintraub, "Schabarum Snubbed by Willie Brown," *Los Angeles Times*, August 30, 1990.
2. Steve Swatt, KCRA-TV, August 29, 1990.
3. Richard Simon, "Schabarum—End of an Era," *Los Angeles Times*, March 3, 1991.
4. Tom Waldman, "Pete Schabarum's parting shot," *California Journal*, December 1991.
5. Jerry Lewis telephone interview, September 29, 2014.
6. William T. Bagley, *California's Golden Years: When Government Worked and Why* (Berkeley: Berkeley Public Policy Press, Institute of Governmental Studies, 2009), 71.
7. Simon, "Schabarum—End of an Era."
8. Jon Matthews, "Lawmakers Battle Critic over Limits," *Sacramento Bee*, September 25, 1990; KCRA-TV, September 24, 1990.
9. John Jacobs, *A Rage for Justice: The Passion and Politics of Phillip Burton* (Berkeley: UC Press, 1995), 435.
10. Ross Johnson interview, Sacramento, December 19, 2014.
11. California Ballot Pamphlet, June 5, 1984, California Secretary of State.
12. William Endicott, "Judge Rejects Gann Curbs on Legislators," *Los Angeles Times*, November 30, 1984.
13. Philip Hager, "Justice Prevails: Cruz Reynoso Was Swept Off the Supreme Court with Rose Bird, but Now He's Found New Causes and a New Career," *Los Angeles Times*, August 13, 1989.
14. Herbert A. Sample and Ray Sotero, "Assembly Spending Soars 32 Percent in Two Years," *Sacramento Bee*, February 18, 1989; Herbert A. Sample, "Assembly, Senate '89 Costs Hit $141 Million," *Sacramento Bee*, November 25, 1990.
15. Swatt, KCRA-TV, February 19, 1990.
16. Teresa Simons, "Lawmakers' 'Bellboys' Cost Taxpayers $2.3 Million Yearly," *Los Angeles Times*, March 25, 1990.
17. Lewis Uhler interview, Roseville, October 1, 2014.
18. Greg Lucas, "Willie Brown Denounces Term-Limit Initiatives," *San Francisco Chronicle*, August 8, 1990.
19. Paul Jacobs, "Brown Bash Raises Cash to Fight Term-Limit Initiatives," *Los Angeles Times*, September 14, 1990; Paul Jacobs, "Schabarum Blasts Deukmejian for Lack of Effort," *Los Angeles Times*, September 15, 1990.
20. "California Committee to Limit Terms" radio ad, courtesy of Wayne Johnson.
21. Yes on Proposition 140 Committee Campaign Statement, October 1990, California State Archives.
22. Swatt, KCRA-TV, October 19, 1990.
23. Carl Ingram, "Fiscal Standoff May Aid Schabarum Initiative," *Los Angeles Times*, July 25, 1990.
24. Amy Chance and Rick Rodriguez, "Wilson Backs Prop. 140 Term Limits," *Sacramento Bee*, October 8, 1990.

25. Swatt, KCRA-TV, October 11, 1990.
26. Swatt, KCRA-TV, October 22, 1990, and November 2, 1990; Virginia Ellis, "Propositions 131 and 140: Brown, Roberti Draw Fire over Commercial," *Los Angeles Times*, October 24, 1990.
27. Willie Brown, *Basic Brown* (New York: Simon and Schuster, 2008), 9.
28. Peter F. Schabarum, *Enough Is Enough: Term Limits in California* (self-published, 1992), 24.
29. Greg Lucas, "Initiative Pushes Many to Leave Capitol," *San Francisco Chronicle*, January 31, 1991.
30. Cathy Gardella interview, Sacramento, September 20, 2014.
31. Dan Walters, "Politics of Pain Felt at Capitol," *Sacramento Bee*, February 1, 1991; "A Slap of Reality," *Time*, February 18, 1991; Robert G. Gunnison and Greg Lucas, "Peter Scissorhands," *San Francisco Chronicle*, February 2, 1991.
32. William Trombley, "Bitter Vasconcellos Threatens to Quit Politics," *Los Angeles Times*, January 31, 1991.
33. William Trombley, "Prop. 140 Forces Exodus of Experts from Legislature," *Los Angeles Times*, February 3, 1991.
34. "Legislative Expenditures and the Proposition 140 Limit: 1990–91 through 2014–15," California Senate, September 10, 2014.
35. Catherine Lewis, "The Proposition 140 Aftermath: Was the 'Golden Handshake' a Boon or a Bust?" *California Journal*, April 1991.
36. "Prop. 140's Hidden Blessing," *Sacramento Bee*, February 12, 1991.
37. Bill Ainsworth "Battle of the Branches: The Supreme Court vs. the Legislature," *California Journal*, January 1993.
38. Ibid.
39. Ibid.
40. "Candidates for the California State Legislature 1995–1996 Total Campaign Receipts and Expenditures," California Secretary of State, www.sos.ca.gov/prd/finance96/genlink2.htm.
41. Peter Schrag, "The Populist Road to Hell: Term Limits in California," *American Prospect*, December 19, 2001.
42. Gregory Schmidt interview, Sacramento, September 10, 2014.
43. Bruce E. Cain and Thad Kousser, "Adapting to Term Limits in California: Recent Experiences and New Directions," Joint Project on Term Limits, National Conference of State Legislatures, Washington, DC, 2004.
44. Mike Zapler, "Many Backers of Strict Term Limits Now Regret It, Saying They Only Made Things Worse," *San Jose Mercury News*, November 21, 2010, www.mercurynews.com/portal/politics-government/ci_15649835?nclick_check=1&_loopback=1.
45. Cain and Kousser, "Adopting Term Limits in California."
46. Ibid.
47. California Ballot Pamphlet, November 6, 1990, California Secretary of State.
48. Jack Citrin and Benjamin Highton, *How Race, Ethnicity, and Immigration Shape the California Electorate* (San Francisco: Public Policy Institute of California, 2002), 43.
49. Kimberly Nalder, "The Effect of Legislative Term Limits on Voter Turnout," *State Politics and Policy Quarterly*, CSU Sacramento, 2007, http://spa.sagepub.com/content/7/2/187.full.pdf+html.
50. Uhler interview.
51. John Caldwell interview, Sacramento, September 10, 2014.
52. John Lewis telephone interview, September 2, 2014.
53. Zapler, "Many Backers of Strict Term Limits Now Regret It."
54. National Conference of State Legislatures, www.ncsl.org/research/about-state-legislatures/legislative-term-limits-overview.aspx.
55. Schmidt interview.
56. Chris Megerian, "Jerry Brown Plans Final Touches on Legacy as California Governor," *Los Angeles Times*, November 5, 2014, www.latimes.com/search/dispatcher.front?Query=Jerry+Brown+Plans+final+touches+on+legacy&target=all.

CHAPTER 13
Still in the Game

1. Peter H. King, "They Kept Coming," *Los Angeles Times*, November 9, 1994.
2. Harold Ezell, "Enough Is More Than Enough," *Los Angeles Times*, October 23, 1994.
3. Gebe Martinez and Patrick J. McDonnell, "Prop. 187 Backers Counting on Message, Not Strategy," *Los Angeles Times*, October 30, 1994.
4. Vlae Kirschner, "Governor's Quest for Federal Help," *San Francisco Chronicle*, November 22, 1991.
5. Dianne Feinstein, "Perspective on Illegal Immigration," *Los Angeles Times*, June 16, 1993.
6. Ben Sherwood, "For Pete Wilson, His Political Ambition Is Never Blind," *Los Angeles Times*, July 23, 1995.
7. George Skelton, "Rational Talk on Immigration for a Change," *Los Angeles Times*, May 27, 1993.
8. California Ballot Pamphlet, November 2, 1920, California Secretary of State.
9. Kathy Olmsted, "California's Crisis and the Collapse of the Republican Party," Edge of the American West website, May 29, 2009, chronicle.com/blognetwork/edgeofthewest/?s=Proposition+187.
10. "They Keep Coming," Wilson campaign ad.
11. Dan Schnur telephone interview, October 18, 2014.
12. California Ballot Pamphlet, November 8, 1994, California Secretary of State; "What Kind of Message Would Proposition 187 Send?" Taxpayers Against 187, undated.
13. Marilyn Kalfus, "Opponents Hire a Proven Winner," *Orange County Register*, November 2, 1994.
14. Richard Temple interview, Sacramento, September 29, 2014.
15. CNN Exit Poll, cnn.com.Election/2010; "Voting in the 1994 Election," Field Institute, January 1995.
16. Josh Richman, "Will California Republican Party Resist Moderate Wave?" *San Jose Mercury News,* June 1, 2014.
17. Reuben Navarrette, "Remembering Reagan," *Latino Magazine,* Winter 2012.
18. Mark Baldassare interview, Sacramento, September 5, 2014.
19. Schnur interview.
20. Steve Sailer, "New Republican Majority?" *American Conservative*, May 8, 2006.
21. Temple interview.
22. William Booth, "In Calif. Governor's Race, It's Ads Infinitum," *Washington Post*, May 29, 1998.
23. In four separate reports, the California Secretary of State documented $512,600,509 in spending for statewide ballot measures and state candidates in 1998. See: www.sos.ca.gov/prd/bmprimary98-2/98primpropsmainpage.htm; www.sos.ca.gov/prd/bmprimary98-final/bmprimary98-final-mainpage.htm; www.sos.ca.gov/prd/finance-98/98primcandmainpage.htm; and www.sos.ca.gov/prd/finance98-general-final/98gencandmainpage.htm.
24. Donald August Gross and Robert K. Goidel, *The States of Campaign Finance Reform* (Columbus: Ohio State University Press, 2003), 34.
25. John M. Allswang, *The Initiative and Referendum in California, 1898–1998* (Stanford, CA: Stanford University Press, 2000), 234.
26. Dan Morain, "Many Political Ads Crowded Out of TV," *Los Angeles Times*, May 30, 1998.
27. Cathleen Decker, "Checchi Strikes First with TV Ads," *Los Angeles Times*, November 16, 1997.
28. George Skelton interview, Sacramento, October 28, 2014; George Skelton, "Checchi Not a Man for All Ages," *Los Angeles Times*, April 21, 1997.
29. George Skelton, "In the Ring, with Contenders for Governor," *Los Angeles Times*, March 23, 1998.
30. Gerald C. Lubenow, ed., *California Votes: The 1998 Governor's Race* (Berkeley: Institute of Governmental Studies Press, 1999), 119.
31. Booth, "In Calif. Governor's Race"; Mark Shields, "Golden State Gold," *Washington Post*, May 30, 1998.

32. Lubenow, 106.
33. Barbara O'Connor interview, Sacramento, October 21, 2014.
34. "Arnold Schwarzenegger Net Worth," the richest.com; "How Rich Is Arnold Schwarzenegger," thisismoney.co.uk, June 10, 2011.
35. Tom Gorman, "Prop. 5 Pitchman Has Starring Role," *Los Angeles Times*, October 25, 1998.
36. Ibid.
37. "Yes on 5" television ad, Californians for Indian Self-Reliance.
38. Michael Lombardi, "Long Road Traveled II," California Nations Indian Gaming Association (CNIGA), undated, www.cniga.com/facts/History_of_CA_Gaming_Part_2.pdf.
39. Roger Dunstan, "Gambling in California," California Research Bureau, January 1997, www.library.ca.gov/CRB/97/03/Chapt5.html.
40. "Stacking the Deck: Gambling Industry Emerges as Top Campaign Contributor in California," California Common Cause report, June 2000, updated July 2001, www.standupca.org/Local%20Government/fppc-and-fec/Stacking%20the%20Deck.pdf; Jay Michael and Dan Walters, *The Third House: Lobbyists, Money, and Power in Sacramento* (Berkeley: Berkeley Public Policy Press, 2002), 67.
41. Dan Walters interview, Sacramento, October 9, 2014.
42. "Indian Massacre: Wilson's Pact Is an Assault on Tribal Rights," *San Diego Union-Tribune,* April 9, 1998.
43. California Ballot Pamphlet, November 9, 1998, California Secretary of State.
44. "Yes on 5" television ad, Californians for Indian Self-Reliance.
45. " Yes on 5" Campaign Reports, California Secretary of State.
46. Claudia Buck, "A Gamble that Paid Off," *California Journal*, December 1998.
47. "No on 5" Campaign Reports, California Secretary of State; KCBS-TV, July 29, 1998.
48. Coalition Against Unregulated Gambling, "Internet Mom."
49. California Constitution, Article IV, Sec. 19 (e).
50. Kevin Fagan, "Big Casinos Move Fast to Cash In: Trump Signs $60 Million Deal after Prop. 1A Wins," *San Francisco Chronicle*, March 9, 2000.
51. 1998–2014 Campaign Reports, California Secretary of State.
52. Keith Matheny, "Once-Poor Tribes Parlay Casino Revenues into Political Power," *Palm Springs Desert Sun,* January 27, 2013, archive.desertsun.com/article/20130126/NEWS06/301260014/Once-poor-tribes-parlay-casino-revenues-into-political-power.
53. "Big Money Talks," California Fair Political Practices Commission, March 2010.
54. Walters interview.
55. Robert B. Gunnison and Greg Lucas, "Critics Say Davis Kowtows to Donors; Access Being Sold, They Charge," *San Francisco Chronicle,* July 20, 1999.
56. Gunnison, "Davis Says He Calls All the Shots; Legislature's Job Is 'to Implement My Vision,'" *San Francisco Chronicle*, July 21, 1999; "The Angry Governor," *San Francisco Chronicle*, July 21, 1999.
57. Dave Lesher, "Tensions Flare Between Davis and His Democrats," *Los Angeles Times*, July 22, 1999.
58. Gary K. Hart interview, Sacramento, November 9, 2014.
59. "Davis Comments Draw Fire: Judicial Appointees 'Should Reflect My Views,'" Associated Press in the *San Jose Mercury News,* March 1, 2000.
60. Hallye Jordan, "Davis' Attitude Brews Challenges: Perceptions of Arrogance by Governor Irritate Traditional Political Supporters," *San Jose Mercury News*, March 20, 2000.
61. Mark Z. Barabak, "Davis Narrowly Defeats Simon," *Los Angeles Times*, November 6, 2002.
62. Mark Z. Barabak, "Clinton Was Key to Davis Strategy," *Los Angeles Times*, November 8, 2002.
63. Ted Costa interview, Sacramento, October 15, 2014.
64. Joel Roberts, "Enron Traders Caught on Tape," CBS News, June 1, 2004, www.cbsnews.com/news/enron-traders-caught-on-tape.
65. Walters interview.
66. Dan Morain, "Davis Faces Growing Criticism on Power Crisis," *Los Angeles Times,* December 31, 2000.

67. Christopher Weare, "The California Electricity Crisis: Causes and Policy Options," Public Policy Institute of California, 2003.

68. Dan Morain, "With Pomp, Davis Signs $99-Billion State Budget," *Los Angeles Times*, July 1, 2000; Dan Morain, "Booming Economy Triggers 1/4-Cent Cut in Sales Tax," *Los Angeles Times*, October 26, 2000.

69. Larry N. Gerston and Terry Christensen, *Recall!: California's Political Earthquake* (Armonk, NY: M.E. Sharpe, 2004), 22.

70. Costa interview.

71. Dave Gilliard telephone interview, October 10, 2014.

72. Dan Morain and Gregg Jones, "Rep. Issa Launches New Davis Recall," *Los Angeles Times*, May 6, 2003.

73. Carroll Wills interview, Sacramento, October 15, 2014.

74. Joe Mathews, *The People's Machine: Arnold Schwarzenegger and the Rise of Blockbuster Democracy* (New York: PublicAffairs, 2006), 123.

75. Wills interview.

76. Mathews, 128–129.

77. Wills interview.

78. "The Recall Campaign: Debate Viewed in 2.4 Million Homes," *Los Angeles Times*, September 26, 2003.

79. Gilliard interview.

80. Michael Lewis, "All Politics Are Loco!!!" *New York Times*, September 28, 2003, www.nytimes.com/2003/09/28/magazine/28CALIFOT.html.

81. Mark Baldassare and Cheryl Katz, *The Coming Age of Direct Democracy: California's Recall and Beyond* (Lanham, MD: Rowman and Littlefield Publishers, 2008), 2.

82. George Skelton interview, Sacramento, October 28, 2014.

83. Hart interview.

84. Field Poll, September 28, 2010, www.field.com/fieldpollonline/subscribers/Rls2357.pdf.

85. David Lesher, "The Rise of Voters," *California Journal*, September 2003.

86. "Reforming the Initiative Process," Public Policy Institute of California, October 24, 2013, www.ppic.org/main/event.asp?i=1392.

87. Jordan Rau and Eric Bailey, "One Vote Shy, State Budget Remains Stuck," *Los Angeles Times*, February 16, 2009.

88. Rebecca LaVally, *California's Laws of the Century* (Sacramento: Senate Office of Research, December 1999).

89. Steve Merksamer interview, Sacramento, November 5, 2014.

90. Alex Pepper, "Proposition 14 Puts Primaries Shakeup on California Ballot," June 4, 2010, ABC News, abcnews.go.com/Politics/Media/proposition-14-puts-primaries-shakeup-california-ballot/story?id=10809262.

91. Jack Dolan, "Party Chiefs Wary of Prop. 14," *Los Angeles Times,* May 24, 2010.

92. Ibid.

93. Jack Citrin, Gabriel Lenz, and Doug Ahler, "Can California's New Primary Reduce Polarization? Maybe Not," The Monkey Cage, March 27, 2013, www.themonkeycage.org/2013/03/27/can-californias-new-primary-reduce-polarization-maybe-not/.

94. Christian Grose, "The Adoption of Electoral Reforms and Ideological Changes in the California State Legislature," USC Schwarzenegger Institute, February 25, 2014, www.schwarzenegger.usc.edu/institute-in-action.

95. Pan campaign mailer, November 2014.

96. Harold Meyerson, "California's Jungle Primary: Tried It. Dump It," *Los Angeles Times*, June 21, 2014.

97. Schnur interview.

98. Boris Shor, "Measuring American Legislatures," *Washington Post*, January 14, 2014, http://americanlegislatures.com/2014/01/14/new-preliminary-2013-data-on-polarization/.

SOURCES AND
SELECTED BIBLIOGRAPHY

CHAPTER 1
1861: The Railroad Begins Its Dominance with the Election of Leland Stanford as Governor

This chapter draws extensively from nineteenth-century newspapers that colorfully reported on Leland Stanford's campaign for governor, his activities in office, and the development of the transcontinental railroad. Among them are the *California Farmer and Journal of Useful Sciences,* the *Daily Alta California,* the *Los Angeles Star,* the *Marysville Daily Herald,* the *New York Times,* the *Sacramento Daily Bee,* and the *Sacramento Daily Union.* The California State Library houses a large collection of California newspapers, and the California Digital Newspaper Collection (cdnc.ucr.edu) makes many historical newspapers available online. The State Library's Governors' Gallery (governors.library.ca.gov) has an online collection of California governors' inaugural addresses. Other key sources include:

Ambrose, Stephen E. *Nothing Like It in the World: The Men Who Built the Transcontinental Railroad.* New York: Simon and Schuster, 2000.

Bryant, William Cullen, and Sidney Howard Gay. *Bryant's Popular History of the United States.* New York: Charles Scribner's Sons, 1881.

Burns, Maryellen, and Keith Burns. *Lost Restaurants of Sacramento and Their Recipes.* Charleston, SC: American Palate, 2013.

Clark, George T. *Leland Stanford: War Governor of California, Railroad Builder and Founder of Stanford University.* Stanford, CA: Stanford University Press, 1931.

Delmatier, Royce D., Clarence F. McIntosh, and Earl G. Waters. *The Rumble of California Politics, 1848–1970.* New York: John Wiley and Sons, 1970.

Gilmore, N. Ray, and Gladys Gilmore. *Readings in California History.* New York: Thomas Y. Crowell, 1966.

Hofstadter, Richard. *American Political Tradition.* New York: Vintage Books (Random House), 1948.

Kazin, Michael. "How the Robber Barons Railroaded America." *New York Times,* July 15, 2011.

Lewis, Oscar. *The Big Four.* New York: Alfred A. Knopf, 1938.

McAfee, Ward. *California's Railroad Era, 1850–1911.* San Marino, CA: Golden West Books, 1973.

Mearns, David C. *The Lincoln Papers.* Garden City, NY: Doubleday, 1948.

Norris, Frank. *The Octopus.* New York: Doubleday, Page, 1901.

Olin, Spencer C., Jr. *California Politics, 1846–1920: The Emerging Corporate State.* San Francisco: Boyd and Fraser, 1981.

Rawls, James J., and Walton Bean. *California: An Interpretive History.* New York: McGraw-Hill, 2003.

Renehan, Edward J., Jr. *Transcontinental Railroad: The Gateway to the West.* New York: Chelsea House, 2007.

Sandburg, Carl. *Abraham Lincoln: The Prairie Years and the War Years.* New York: Harcourt, Brace, 1954.

Severson, Thor. *Sacramento: An Illustrated History; 1839–1874, From Sutter's Fort to Capital City.* San Francisco: California Historical Society, 1973.

White, Richard. *Railroaded: The Transcontinentals and the Making of Modern America.* New York: W.W. Norton, 2011.

Williams, R. Hal. *The Democratic Party and California Politics, 1880–1896.* Stanford, CA: Stanford University Press, 1973.

CHAPTER 2
1879: Voters Ratify a Disputed Constitution for Tumultuous Times

Information for Chapter 2 was drawn chiefly from works by leading California historians, from official judicial opinions, from legal journals, and from contemporary newspaper accounts (1879 and earlier). Particularly important to understanding the foundations of the California constitution were Carl Brent Swisher's *Motivation and Political Technique in the California Constitutional Convention, 1878–79* (Claremont, CA: Pomona College, 1930) and former state supreme court justice Joe Grodin's seminal treatise, *The California State Constitution: A Reference Guide*, co-written by Calvin R. Massey and Richard B. Cunningham (Westport, CT: Greenwood Press, 1993). Other key sources include:

Cleland, Robert Glass. Foreword to the Centennial Edition of *The 1849 California State Constitution.* San Marino, CA: Friends of the Huntington Library, 1949.

Ellison, Joseph. "The Struggle for Civil Government in California, 1846–1850," *California Historical Society Quarterly,* September 1931.

Gates, Paul W. "Adjudication of Spanish-Mexican Land Claims in California." *Huntington Library Quarterly,* May 1, 1958.

Gerawan Farming, Inc. v. Lyons, 24 Cal. 4th 468, 489–491 (2000).

Hunt, Rockwell Dennis. "The Genesis of California's First Constitution (1846–49)." *Johns Hopkins University Studies in Historical and Political Science,* August 1895.

Lustig, Jeffrey. "Private Rights and Public Purposes: California's Second Constitutional Convention Reconsidered." *California History* 87, no. 3 (2010).

Mathews, Joe, and Mark Paul. *California Crackup: How Reform Broke the Golden State and How We Can Fix It.* Berkeley: UC Press, 2010.

McWilliams, Carey. *California: The Great Exception.* New York: A.A. Wyn, 1949.

Olmsted, Roger, and Charles Wollenberg, eds. *Neither Separate Nor Equal: Race and Racism in California.* San Francisco: California Historical Society, 1971.

Pincetl, Stephanie S. *Transforming California: A Political History of Land Use and Development.* Baltimore: Johns Hopkins University Press, 1999.

Posner, Russell M. "The Lord and the Drayman." In *Neither Separate Nor Equal: Race and Racism in California,* edited by Roger Olmsted and Charles Wollenberg. San Francisco: California Historical Society, 1971.

Rawls, James J., and Walton Bean. *California: An Interpretive History.* 9th ed. New York: McGraw-Hill, 2008.

Sandmeyer, Elmer Clarence. *The Anti-Chinese Movement in California.* Urbana: University of Illinois Press, 1991.

Sargent, Noel. "The California Constitutional Convention of 1878–79." *California Law Review,* November 1917.

Severson, Thor. *Sacramento: An Illustrated History; 1839–1874, From Sutter's Fort to Capital City.* San Francisco: California Historical Society, 1973.

Taylor, Paul. "Foundation of California Rural Society." *California Historical Society Quarterly,* September 1945.

Working Papers of the Constitutional Convention of 1878–1879, California State Archives, Sacramento.

Wysinger v. Crookshank, 82 Cal. 588, 720 (1890).

Yick Wo v. Hopkins, 118 U.S. 356 (1886).

CHAPTER 3
1905: Los Angeles Votes to Spur Growth with a Giant Aqueduct

Among the numerous newspapers consulted on Los Angeles's early twentieth-century acquisition of Owens Valley water, and the valley protest movement that followed, are: the *Bakersfield Californian*, the *Inyo Register*, the *Los Angeles Evening Express*, the *Los Angeles Examiner*, the *Los Angeles Herald*, the *Los Angeles Times*, the *New York Times*, the *Sacramento Bee*, the *Sacramento Union*, and the *San Francisco Chronicle*. Valuable material was drawn from "Owens Valley Water Wars, from the Personal File of Senator Joseph E. Riley," a collection housed in the California History Room at the California State Library in Sacramento. The collection includes radio broadcast scripts, correspondence, and government documents. An account of key events in the history of the Los Angeles Department of Water and Power can be found at ladwp.com and in the oral history of the department's former general manager and chief engineer, Samuel B. Nelson (interview conducted by Andrew D. Basiago, 1986, Center for Oral History Research, Young Research Library, UCLA). Other key sources include:

Boyarsky, Bill. *Inventing L.A.: The Chandlers and Their Times*. Santa Monica: Angel City Press, 2009.

Carle, David. *Water and the California Dream*. San Francisco: Sierra Club Books, 2000.

Caughrey, John, and LaRee Caughrey, eds. *Los Angeles: Biography of a City*. Berkeley: UC Press, 1977.

Doyle, Helen MacKnight. *Mary Austin: Woman of Genius*. New York: Gotham Books, 1939.

Faulkner, Frederick. "Water Sharks Wreck Valley," *Sacramento Union*, April 1, 1927.

———. "Blooms Fade before Waste: Politicians Tear Up Verdant Orchards, Planted by Pioneer Matrons, to Make Way for Its Era of Desolation." *Sacramento Union*, April 2, 1927.

———. "Water Greed Ruins Valley." *Sacramento Union*, April 3, 1927.

Goodwin, Doris Kearns. *The Bully Pulpit: Theodore Roosevelt, William Howard Taft, and the Golden Age of Journalism*. New York: Simon and Schuster, 2013.

Guinn, James Miller. *Historical and Biographical Record of Southern California*. Chicago: Chapman, 1902.

Halberstam, David. *The Powers That Be*. New York: Alfred A. Knopf, 1979.

Hundley, Norris, Jr. *The Great Thirst: Californians and Water; A History*. Berkeley: UC Press, 2001.

Inyo Register. "Los Angeles Plots Destruction: Would Take Owens River, Lay Lands Waste, Ruin People, Homes and Communities." August 3, 1905.

Kahrl, William L. *Water and Power*. Berkeley: UC Press, 1982.

Los Angeles Times. "Titanic Project to Give City a River: Thirty Thousand Inches of Water to Be Brought to Los Angeles," July 29, 1905.

McDougal, Dennis. *Privileged Son: Otis Chandler and the Rise and Fall of the L.A. Times Dynasty*. Cambridge, MA: Perseus, 2001.

Mayo, Morrow. *Los Angeles*. New York: Alfred A. Knopf, 1933.

McWilliams, Carey. *California: The Great Exception*. Santa Barbara: Peregrine Smith, 1976.

Mulholland, Catherine. *William Mulholland and the Rise of Los Angeles*. Berkeley: UC Press, 2000.

Reisner, Marc. *Cadillac Desert: The American West and Its Disappearing Water*. New York: Penguin Books, 1993.

"Senate Special Investigating Committee on Water Situation in Inyo and Mono Counties." *Senate Journal*, May 7, 1931.

Walton, John. *Western Times and Water Wars*. Berkeley: UC Press, 1992.

Walton, John, interview, Sacramento, June 23, 2014.

CHAPTER 4
1910: Hiram Johnson's Election Brings Power to the People

This chapter relies on colorful newspaper and periodical coverage of the Southern Pacific Railroad's dominance in California during the late nineteenth and early twentieth centuries, and the rise of the progressives. Sources include: the *Amador Ledger, Hampton's Magazine* (which published a comprehensive series of articles by Charles Edward Russell critical of the railroad in the months before the 1910 gubernatorial election), the *Los Angeles Herald,* the *New York Times,* the *Sacramento Daily Record-Union,* the *San Francisco Call,* the *San Francisco Examiner,* the *Sausalito News,* and the Zócalo Public Square website (www. zocalopublicsquare.org). The state library's California Research Bureau and the California Secretary of State both document the state's use of the initiative process, and the Hiram Johnson Papers at the University of California's Bancroft Library offer a treasure trove of information on California's twenty-third governor. Other key sources include:

Allswang, John M. *The Initiative and Referendum in California, 1898–1998*. Stanford, CA: Stanford University Press, 2000.

Bancroft Library. "How Congressmen Are Bribed: The Colton Letters." Berkeley: University of California, June 1939. archive.org/details/howcongressmenar00huntrich.

Bean, Walton. *Boss Ruef's San Francisco*. Berkeley: UC Press, 1967.

Burke, Robert, ed. *The Diary Letters of Hiram Johnson*. New York: Garland, 1983.

Gilmore, N. Ray, and Gladys Gilmore. *Readings in California History*. New York: Thomas Y. Crowell, 1966.

Halberstam, David. *The Powers That Be*. New York: Alfred A. Knopf, 1979.

Hiram Johnson Papers. "Letters from Hiram Johnson, August–December 1910." Bancroft Library, UC Berkeley.

Layne, J. Gregg. "The Lincoln–Roosevelt League, Its Origins and Accomplishments." *Historical Society of Southern California Quarterly* 25 (September 1943).

Mathews, Joe, and Mark Paul. *California Crackup: How Reform Broke the Golden State and How We Can Fix It*. Berkeley: UC Press, 2010.

McDougal, Dennis. *Privileged Son: Otis Chandler and the Rise and Fall of the L.A. Times Dynasty*. Cambridge, MA: Perseus, 2001.

McWilliams, Carey. *California: The Great Exception*. Santa Barbara: Peregrine Smith, 1976. First published in 1949 by Current Books.

Older, Fremont. *My Own Story*. San Francisco: The Call Publishing Co., 1919.

Olin, Spencer C., Jr. *California Politics, 1846–1920: The Emerging Corporate State*. San Francisco: Boyd and Fraser, 1981.

Rawls, James J., and Walton Bean. *California: An Interpretive History*. New York: McGraw-Hill, 2003.

Samish, Arthur, and Bob Thomas. *The Secret Boss of California*. New York: Crown, 1971.

Schlesinger, Arthur, Jr. *The Age of Roosevelt: Crisis of the Old Order, 1919–1933*. New York: Houghton Mifflin, 1957.

Sitton, Tom. *John Randolph Haynes: California Progressive*. Stanford, CA: Stanford University Press, 1992.

Starr, Kevin. *Inventing the Dream: California through the Progressive Era*. New York: Oxford University Press, 1985.

White, Richard. *Railroaded: The Transcontinentals and the Making of Modern America*. New York: W.W. Norton, 2011.

Williams, R. Hal. *The Democratic Party and California Politics, 1880–1896*. Stanford, CA: Stanford University Press, 1973.

CHAPTER 5
1934: California's Dirtiest Election Gives Birth to Modern Campaigns

Upton Sinclair's candidacy for governor attracted considerable national attention at a time when the popular press made little effort to hide its own partisan leanings. This chapter draws on news coverage and commentary from the *Boston Globe*, the *Los Angeles Examiner*, the *Los Angeles Times*, the *New York Times*, the *San Francisco Chronicle*, *Time*, and the *Washington Post*. The campaign against Sinclair was the first to employ video persuasion techniques (newsreels), the forerunners of today's omnipresent television advertisements, and "The Living Room Candidate" (livingroomcandidate.org) has a fascinating collection of presidential campaign commercials that aired between 1952 and 2012. Recollections of Clem Whitaker's career as a journalist and groundbreaking campaign consultant come from his son, Clem Jr., in an oral history conducted by Gabrielle Morris in 1988–89 for the State Government Oral History Program, California State Archives, Sacramento. Other key sources include:

Ames, Richard Sheridan. "The Screen Enters Politics: Will Hollywood Produce More Propaganda." *Harper's*, March 1935.

Delmatier, Royce D., Clarence F. McIntosh, and Earl G. Waters. *The Rumble of California Politics, 1848–1970*. New York: John Wiley and Sons, 1970.

Halberstam, David. *The Powers That Be*. New York: Alfred A. Knopf, 1979.

Hofstadter, Richard. *The Age of Reform*. New York: Vintage Books, 1955.

Kennedy, David M. *Freedom from Fear*. New York: Oxford University Press, 1999.

King, Gilbert. "The Traumatic Birth of the Modern (and Vicious) Political Campaign." Smithsonian Institution website. October 11, 2012. www.smithsonianmag.com/history/the-traumatic-birth-of-the-modern-and-vicious-political-campaign-70717968/?no-ist.

Lash, Joseph P. *Eleanor and Franklin*. New York: W.W. Norton, 1971.

Lepore, Jill. "The Lie Factory." *New Yorker*, September 24, 2012.

McWilliams, Carey. *California: The Great Exception*. Santa Barbara: Peregrine Smith, 1976. First published in 1949 by Current Books.

Mitchell, Greg. *The Campaign of the Century*. New York: Random House, 1992.

Natoli, Joseph P. *Memory's Orbit: Film and Culture, 1999–2000*. Albany: State University of New York Press, 2003.

Patterson, James T. *Grand Expectations: The United States, 1945–1974*. New York: Oxford University Press, 1996.

Rawls, James J., and Walton Bean. *California: An Interpretive History*. New York: McGraw-Hill, 2003.

Reinhardt, Richard. *Treasure Island: San Francisco's Exposition Year*. San Francisco: Scrimshaw Press, 1973.

Rolle, Andrew F. *California: A History*. New York: Thomas Y. Crowell, 1963.

Ross, Irwin. "The Super Salesmen of California Politics." *Harper's*, July 1959.

Schlesinger, Arthur, Jr. *The Age of Roosevelt: The Politics of Upheaval, 1935–1936*. New York: Houghton Mifflin, 1960.

Sinclair, Upton. *I, Candidate for Governor: And How I Got Licked*. Pasadena, CA: self-published, 1935.

Smith, Jean Edward. *FDR*. New York: Random House, 2007.

Time. "Political Notes: California Climax." November 22, 1934.

Whitaker and Baxter Papers, California State Archives, Sacramento.

Whitaker, Clement S., Jr. Oral history conducted by Gabrielle Morris, 1988, 1989, State Government Oral History Program, California State Archives, Sacramento.

CHAPTER 6
1942: Earl Warren Pilots California into a Postwar Boom

Research on Earl Warren and his era was aided by the Bancroft Library's Earl Warren Oral History Project, a massive enterprise of more than fifty volumes of transcripts from interviews with Warren, his colleagues, journalists, and others spanning his years of public service in California. Stories from the *Los Angeles Times* recounted Warren's successful campaign against incumbent governor Culbert Olson in 1942; the tenor of sentiment in California against people of Japanese ancestry in the aftermath of Pearl Harbor; and the ongoing news conferences, proposals, and actions by Warren as governor. In an interview with the authors (Sacramento, November 7, 2014), US Representative Doris Matsui of Sacramento recalled efforts by her late husband, US Representative Robert Matsui, and others to successfully steer reparations legislation through Congress for survivors of the Japanese internment. Other key sources include:

Cray, Ed. *Chief Justice: A Biography of Earl Warren*. New York: Simon and Schuster, 1997.
HoSang, Daniel Martinez. *Racial Propositions: Ballot Initiatives and the Making of Postwar California*. Berkeley: UC Press, 2010.
Katcher, Leo. *Earl Warren: A Political Biography*. New York: McGraw-Hill, 1967.
Leonard, Kevin Allen. "Brothers Under the Skin? African-Americans, Mexican-Americans and World War II in California." In *The Way We Really Were: The Golden State in the Second Great War*, edited by Roger W. Lotchin. Urbana: University of Illinois Press, 2000.
Lotchin, Roger W., ed. *The Way We Really Were: The Golden State in the Second Great War*. Urbana: University of Illinois Press, 2000.
Maki, Mitchell T., Harry H. L. Kitano, and S. Megan Berthold, eds. *Achieving the Impossible Dream: How Japanese Americans Obtained Redress*. Urbana: University of Illinois Press, 1999.
McWilliams, Carey. "Liberty in Limbo: Japanese Relocation." In *Readings in California History*, edited by N. Ray Gilmore and Gladys Gilmore. New York: Thomas Y. Crowell, 1966.
Rawls, James J., and Walton Bean. *California: An Interpretive History*. 9th ed. New York: McGraw-Hill, 2008.
Verge, Arthur. "Daily Life in Wartime California." In *The Way We Really Were: The Golden State in the Second Great War*, edited by Roger W. Lotchin. Urbana: University of Illinois Press, 2000.
Warren, Earl. *The Memoirs of Chief Justice Earl Warren*. New York: Doubleday, 1977.
Weaver, John D. *Warren: The Man, the Court, the Era*. Boston: Little, Brown & Co., 1967.
Wollenberg, Charles. "Ethnic Experiences in California History: An Impressionistic Survey." In *Neither Separate Nor Equal: Race and Racism in California*, edited by Roger Olmsted and Charles Wollenberg. San Francisco: California Historical Society, 1971.

CHAPTER 7
1958: Pat Brown's Election Ushers In Modern California

A number of oral histories proved to be essential primary sources for this chapter, especially those that detailed personal recollections from decision-makers during Pat Brown's campaigns for governor, his two terms in office and, particularly, Brown's signature accomplishment—the California Water Project.

From the Regional Oral History Office at the University of California's Bancroft Library:
Brody, Ralph. "California Water Issues, 1950–1966." Conducted by Malca Chall, 1980.
Brown, Edmund G. "Years of Growth, 1939–1966: Law Enforcement, Politics and the Governor's Office." Conducted by Malca Chall, 1979.
Brown, Edmund G. "California Water Issues, 1950–1966." Conducted by Malca Chall, 1979, 1980.
Christopher, Warren. "The Governor's Office Under Edmund G. Brown, Sr." Conducted by Amelia R. Fry, 1978.
Dutton, Fred. "Democratic Campaigns and Controversies, 1954–1966." Conducted by Amelia R. Fry, 1977, 1978.

Hill, Gladwin. Conducted by Carlos Vásquez, 1987.

Kline, Richard. "The Governor's Office Under Edmund G. Brown, Sr." Conducted by Eleanor Glaser, 1977.

And from the State Government Oral History Program, California State Archives, Sacramento:

Burby, John F. Conducted by Carlos Vásquez, 1987.

Margolis, Larry. Conducted by Carole Hicke, 1989.

Stiern, Walter. Conducted by Enid Hart Douglass, 1987.

Also particularly helpful in researching the Pat Brown era were articles by the Associated Press, the *California Journal*, the California's Capitol website (www.californiascapitol.com), the *Capitol Weekly*, the *Los Angeles Herald Express*, the *Los Angeles Mirror-News*, the *Los Angeles Times*, the *New York Times*, the *Sacramento Bee*, *San Diego Magazine*, the *San Francisco Examiner*, and United Press International. Other key sources include:

Allen, Don A., Sr. *Legislative Sourcebook, 1849–1965*. Sacramento: Assembly of the State of California, 1965.

Anderson, Totton J. "The 1958 Election in California." *Western Political Quarterly* 12, no. 2, pt. 2 (March 1959). www.jstor.org/table/444055?seq=1#page_scan_tab_contents.

Clark, Ray Leon. "The 1958 California Gubernatorial Election: How Republican Party Infighting Affected the Outcome." Master's thesis, CSU Long Beach, 1999.

Delmatier, Royce D., Clarence F. McIntosh, and Earl G. Waters, *The Rumble of California Politics, 1848–1970*. New York: John Wiley and Sons, 1970.

Findley, James C. "Cross-Filing and the Progressive Movement in California Politics." *Western Political Quarterly* 12, no. 3 (September 1959). www.jstor.org/stable/443867?seq=1#page_scan_tab_contents.

Hundley, Norris, Jr. *The Great Thirst: Californians and Water; A History*. Berkeley: UC Press, 2001.

Jacobs, John. *A Rage for Justice: The Passion and Politics of Phillip Burton*. Berkeley: UC Press, 1995.

Mills, James R. *A Disorderly House: The Brown-Unruh Years in Sacramento*. Berkeley: Heyday Books, 1987.

Montgomery, Gale, and James W. Johnson. *One Step from the White House: The Rise and Fall of Senator William F. Knowland*. Berkeley: UC Press, 1998.

Pitchell, Robert J. "The Electoral System and Voting Behavior: The Case of California's Cross-Filing." *Western Political Quarterly* 12, no. 2 (June 1959). www.jstor.org/stable/443983?seq=1#page_scan_tab_contents.

Putnam, Jackson K. *Modern California Politics*. San Francisco: Boyd and Fraser, 1984.

——. "The Pattern of Modern California Politics." *Pacific Historical Review* 61, no. 1 (February 1992).

Rarick, Ethan. *California Rising: The Life and Times of Pat Brown*. Berkeley: UC Press, 2005.

Rawls, James J., and Walton Bean. *California: An Interpretive History*. New York: McGraw-Hill, 2003.

Reisner, Marc. *Cadillac Desert: The American West and Its Disappearing Water*. New York: Penguin Books, 1993.

Rice, Sascha, director. *California State of Mind: The Legacy of Pat Brown* (documentary), 2012.

Rolle, Andrew F. *California: A History*. New York: Thomas Y. Crowell, 1963.

Schiesl, Martin, ed. *Responsible Liberalism: Edmund G. "Pat" Brown and Reform Government in California, 1958–1969*. Los Angeles: Edmund G. Pat Brown Institute of Public Affairs, 2003.

Schrag, Peter. *Paradise Lost: California's Experience, America's Future*. Berkeley: UC Press, 1998.

Schuparra, Kurt. *Triumph of the Right: The Rise of the California Conservative Movement, 1945–1966*. Armonk, NY: M.E. Sharpe, 1998.

Umbach, Kenneth W. "Pat Brown's Building Boom: Water, Highways and Higher Education." California Research Bureau, California State Library, Sacramento, 2006.

CHAPTER 8
1966: Voters Give Greater Power to a Full-Time Legislature

Behind-the-scene glimpses of Jesse Unruh's rise to power, his speakership, and his drive to professionalize the state assembly can be found in the Jesse M. Unruh Papers at the California State Archives, and in the following oral histories from the State Government Oral History Program, also at the California State Archives in Sacramento:

Broaders, Halden. Conducted by Carole Hicke, 1990.

Margolis, Larry. Conducted by Carole Hicke, 1989.

Whitaker, Clement S., Jr. Conducted by Gabrielle Morris, 1988–89.

Winton, Gordon. Conducted by Enid Hart Douglass, 1987.

Narratives of Ronald Reagan's initial campaign for governor can be found in several oral histories conducted by the Regional Oral History Office, Bancroft Library, UC Berkeley, including:

Christopher, George. "San Francisco Republicans." Conducted by Sarah Sharp and Miriam Stein, 1977, 1978.

Reagan, Ronald. "On Becoming Governor." Conducted by Sarah Sharp, 1979.

Roberts, William E. "Professional Campaign Management and the Candidate." Conducted by Sarah Sharp, 1979.

Spencer, Stuart. "Issues and Innovations in the 1966 Republican Gubernatorial Campaign." Conducted by Gabrielle Morris, 1979.

Weinberger, Caspar. "San Francisco Republicans." Conducted by Gabrielle Morris, 1978, 1979.

And from the State Government Oral History Program, California State Archives, Sacramento:

Hill, Gladwin. Conducted by Carlos Vásquez, 1987.

The following interviews were conducted by the authors for use in this book: John Burton (Sacramento, January 7, 2014), Sherry Bebitch Jeffe (telephone interview, October 15, 2014), Steve Merksamer (Sacramento, November 5, 2014), Ethan Rarick (Berkeley, July 8, 2014), and Richard Ratcliffe (Sacramento, January 27, 2014). Newspaper, periodical, and online sources for this chapter include: the *California Journal,* the California's Capitol website (www.californiascapitol.com), the *Los Angeles Times,* the *Napa Register,* the Newsmax website (www.newsmax.com), the *New York Times,* the *Oakland Tribune, Reader's Digest,* the *Sacramento Bee,* the *San Francisco Chronicle,* and *Time.* Other key sources include:

Allen, Don A., Sr. *Legislative Sourcebook, 1849–1965.* Sacramento: Assembly of the State of California, 1965.

Assemblyman X, as told to Lester Velie. "This Is How Payola Works in Politics." *Reader's Digest,* August 1960.

Bagley, William T. *California's Golden Years: When Government Worked and Why.* Berkeley: Berkeley Public Policy Press, Institute of Governmental Studies, 2009.

Boyarsky, Bill. *Big Daddy: Jesse Unruh and the Art of Power Politics.* Berkeley: UC Press, 2008.

———. *The Rise of Ronald Reagan.* New York: Random House, 1968.

Cannon, Lou. *Governor Reagan: His Rise to Power.* New York: Public Affairs, 2003.

———. *Ronnie and Jesse: A Political Odyssey.* Garden City, NY: Doubleday, 1969.

Dalleck, Matthew. *The Right Moment: Ronald Reagan's First Victory and the Decisive Turning Point in American Politics.* New York: Oxford University Press, 2004.

Green, Mark, and Gail MacColl. *There He Goes Again: Ronald Reagan's Reign of Error.* New York: Pantheon Books, 1983.

Jacobs, John. *A Rage for Justice: The Passion and Politics of Phillip Burton.* Berkeley: UC Press, 1995.

Jeffe, Sherry Bebitch. "For Legislative Staff, Policy Takes a Back Seat to Politics." *California Journal,* January 1987.

Mills, James R. *A Disorderly House: The Brown-Unruh Years in Sacramento.* Berkeley: Heyday Books, 1987.

Monroe, J. P. *The Political Party Matrix.* New York: State University of New York Press, 2001.
Putnam, Jackson K. *Jess: The Political Career of Jesse Marvin Unruh.* Lanham, MA:
    University Press of America, 2005.
Rarick, Ethan. *California Rising: The Life and Times of Pat Brown.* Berkeley: UC Press, 2005.
Schuparra, Kurt. *Triumph of the Right: The Rise of the California Conservative Movement,*
    1945–1966. Armonk, NY: M. E. Sharpe, 1998.
Swatt, Steve. "Reagan for Governor." KCRA-TV, January 1981.
Time. "Big Daddy." May 5, 1961.
Unruh, Jesse. Interview for "Reagan: The Governor." KCRA-TV, January 1981.
Whitaker and Baxter Papers, California State Archives, Sacramento.

CHAPTER 9
1974: Californians Pull Back the Curtain on Politics as Usual

Daniel Lowenstein, the first chairman of the California Fair Political Practices Commission, and Robert Stern, the commission's chief counsel, were largely responsible for early implementation of the state's landmark Political Reform Act. Stern, in an interview for this book, and Lowenstein, in an oral history conducted by Carlos Vásquez in 1989 for the State Government Oral History Program, California State Archives, Sacramento, discuss Jerry Brown's involvement in the inception and enactment of the PRA. Other oral histories of value concerning the role of lobbyists and political reform efforts include:

Beverly, Robert. "Legislative-Governor Relations in the Reagan Years: Five Views."
    Conducted by Steven D. Edgington, 1983, for the Regional Oral History Office, Bancroft
    Library, UC Berkeley.

And from the State Government Oral History Program, California State Archives, Sacramento:
Broaders, Halden. Conducted Carole Hicke, 1990.
Meade, Kenneth A. Conducted by Timothy Fong, 1987, 1988.
Nannini, Rico. Conducted by Gabrielle Morris, 1987.
Nielsen, Vigo G., Jr. Conducted by Ann Lage, 1989.
Zelman, Walter A. Conducted by Carlos Vásquez, 1989.

The following interviews were conducted by the authors for use in this book: John Burton (Sacramento, January 7, 2014), George Deukmejian (Long Beach, December 17, 2013), Hedy Govenar (Sacramento, January 11, 2014), Ross Johnson (Sacramento, December 19, 2013), Richard Ratcliff (Sacramento, January 27, 2014), Robert Stern (Los Angeles, December 15, 2013), and Jerry Zanelli (Sacramento, March 11, 2014). Accounts of Brown's early political career and the effort to enact political reform were gleaned from the following publications and broadcast media: the *California Journal,* KCRA-TV, the *Los Angeles Times,* the *New York Times,* the Politico website (www.politic.com), *San Diego Magazine,* the *San Francisco Chronicle,* and *Time.* Other key sources include:

Alexander, Herbert E., and Brian A. Haggerty. "Political Reform in California: How Has It
    Worked?" Citizens' Research Foundation, University of Southern California, February 1, 1980.
Allswang, John M. *The Initiative and Referendum in California, 1898–1998.* Stanford, CA:
    Stanford University Press, 2000.
Bagley, William T. *California's Golden Years: When Government Worked and Why.*
    Berkeley: Berkeley Public Policy Press, Institute of Governmental Studies, 2009.
Bipartisan Commission on the Political Reform Act of 1974, "Overly Complex and Unduly
    Burdensome," 2000, http://www.fppc.ca.gov/pdf/McPherson.pdf.
Cannon, Lou. *Ronnie and Jesse: A Political Odyssey.* Garden City, NY: Doubleday, 1969.
Jacobs, John. *A Rage for Justice: The Passion and Politics of Phillip Burton.* Berkeley: UC
    Press, 1995.
McFadden, Chuck. *Trailblazer: A Biography of Jerry Brown.* Berkeley: UC Press, 2013.

Michael, Jay, and Dan Walters. *The Third House: Lobbyists, Money, and Power in Sacramento*. Berkeley: Berkeley Public Policy Press, 2002.

Monagan, Robert T. *The Disappearance of Representative Government*. Grass Valley, CA: Comstock Bonanza Press, 1990.

Rapoport, Roger. *California Dreaming: The Political Odyssey of Pat and Jerry Brown*. Berkeley: Nolo Press, 1982.

Rawls, James J., and Walton Bean. *California: An Interpretive History*. New York: McGraw-Hill, 2003.

Samish, Arthur, and Bob Thomas. *The Secret Boss of California*. New York: Crown, 1971.

Swatt, Steve. "Brown: The Governor." KCRA-TV, January 1983.

CHAPTER 10
1978: Proposition 13 Launches a National Tax Revolt

This chapter draws extensively from state and national news organizations that covered the Proposition 13 debate and analyzed its effects years later, including: the American Prospect website (www.prospect.org), the Associated Press, the Bloomberg News website (www.bloomberg.com), *California*, the *California Journal*, *California Northern Magazine*, *Investor's Business Daily*, the *Los Angeles Times*, the *Sacramento Bee*, the *San Bernardino Sun-Times*, the *San Diego Union*, the *San Diego Union-Tribune*, the *San Fernando Valley News*, the *San Francisco Chronicle*, the *San Francisco Examiner*, *Time*, and the Zócalo Public Square website (www.zocalopublicsquare.org).

Particularly helpful were the following oral histories from the State Government Oral History Program, California State Archives, Sacramento:

Behr, Peter. Conducted by Ann Lage, 1988, 1989.

Gann, Paul. Conducted by Gabrielle Morris, 1987.

McCarthy, Leo. Conducted by Carole Hicke, 1995, 1996.

Papan, Louis. Conducted by Carole Hicke, 1988.

Torres, Art. Conducted by Steven D. Edgington, 2003.

The following interviews were conducted by the authors for use in this book: Mark Baldassare (Sacramento, September 5, 2014), Willie Brown (San Francisco, August 31, 2014), Joel Fox (Sherman Oaks, December 16, 2013), John Lewis (telephone interview, September 2, 2014), Steve Merksamer (Sacramento, November 5, 2014), and Robert Stern (Los Angeles, December 15, 2013). Other key sources include:

Allswang, John M. *The Initiative and Referendum in California, 1898–1998*. Stanford, CA: Stanford University Press, 2000.

Bagley, William T. *California's Golden Years: When Government Worked and Why*. Berkeley: Berkeley Public Policy Press, Institute of Governmental Studies, 2009.

California Taxpayers Association. "Proposition 13 Revisited." June 6, 2013. www.caltax.org/Proposition13Revisited.pdf.

Center for Governmental Studies. "Democracy by Initiative: Shaping California's Fourth Branch of Government." 2008. www.policyarchive.org/collections/cgs/index?section=5&id=5800.

Citrin, Jack, and Isaac William Martin, eds. *After the Tax Revolt: California's Proposition 13 Turns 30*. Berkeley: Berkeley Public Policy Press, Institute of Governmental Studies, 2009.

Fairbanks, Robert, and Martin Smith. "There's Gold in Them Thar Campaigns." *California Journal*, December 1984.

Fischel, William. "Did Serrano Cause Proposition 13?" *National Tax Journal*, December 1989.

Fox, Joel. *The Legend of Proposition 13*. Bloomington, IN: Xlibris, 2003.

Jeffe, Sherry Bebitch. "California: The Not-So-Golden State Legislature." In *The Reform of State Legislatures,* by Eugene W. Hickok, Jr. Lanham, MA: University Press of America, 1992.

Lo, Clarence Y. H. *Small Property Versus Big Government: Social Origins of the Property Tax Revolt*. Berkeley: UC Press, 1995.

Mathews, Joe, and Mark Paul. *California Crackup: How Reform Broke the Golden State and How We Can Fix It*. Berkeley: UC Press, 2010.

McFadden, Chuck. *Trailblazer: A Biography of Jerry Brown*. Berkeley: UC Press, 2013.

McWilliams, Carey. *California: The Great Exception*. Santa Barbara: Peregrine Smith, 1976. First published in 1949 by Current Books.

Martin, Lisa. "Exploring the Gann Limit: Then and Now." Cal-Tax Digest. July 2000.

Moore, Stephen. "Proposition 13 Then, Now and Forever." Cato Institute. July 30, 1998. www.cato.org/publications/commentary/proposition-13-then-now-forever.

Rapoport, Roger. *California Dreaming: The Political Odyssey of Pat and Jerry Brown*. Berkeley: Nolo Press, 1982.

Salzman, Ed. "Life after Jarvis." *California Journal*, August 1980.

Schrag, Peter. *Paradise Lost: California's Experience, America's Future*. Berkeley: UC Press, 1998.

Schwadron, Terry, ed. *California and the American Tax Revolt: Proposition 13 Five Years Later*. Berkeley: UC Press, 1984.

Time. "Nation: Maniac or Messiah?" June 19, 1978.

——. "Sound and Fury over Taxes." June 19, 1978.

Tipps, Dean, ed., and Robert Kuttner, contrib. *State and Local Tax Revolt: New Directions for the 80's*. Piscataway, NJ: Transaction Publishers, 1980.

Valentine, Phil. *Tax Revolt: The Rebellion against an Overbearing, Bloated, Arrogant and Abusive Government*. Nashville, TN: Nelson Current, 2005.

CHAPTER 11
1980: Technology and Money Forever Change Political Campaigning

The Institute of Governmental Studies at UC Berkeley houses a 232-box collection of campaign materials from 1968 to 2003 as well as redistricting data from Berman and D'Agostino (BAD) Campaigns and its principals, Michael Berman and Carl D'Agostino—two important players in Democratic politics and reapportionment campaigns. Sources on government campaign spending include the California Secretary of State and the Fair Political Practices Commission. Perspectives from major participants in the state assembly's unprecedented speakership fight can be found in oral histories in the State Government Oral History Program, California State Archives, Sacramento, including:

Bane, Tom. Conducted by Steven Isoardi, 1995.

McCarthy, Leo. Conducted by Carole Hicke, 1995, 1996.

Papan, Louis. Conducted by Carole Hicke, 1988.

Vicencia, Frank. Conducted by Raphael Sonenshein, 1987.

The following interviews were conducted by the authors for use in this book: Howard Berman (Berkeley, April 8, 2014), Barry Brokaw (Sacramento, August 23, 2014), Willie Brown (San Francisco, August 31, 2014), John Burton (Sacramento, January 7, 2014), Hedy Govenar (Sacramento, January 12, 2014), Ross Johnson (Sacramento, December 19, 2014), Sam Paredes (Placerville, August 22, 2014), H. L. Richardson (Placerville, August 22, 2014), and Jerry Zanelli (Sacramento, March 11, 2014). Key newspaper, periodical, broadcast, and online sources include: the *California Journal*, the Fox and Hounds website (www.foxandhounds-daily.com), the *Glendale-News Press*, KCRA-TV, the *Los Angeles Times*, the *Monterey Park Progress*, the *National Journal*, *New West*, the *Sacramento Bee*, the *Sacramento Union*, and the *San Francisco Chronicle*. Other key sources include:

Brinkley, Douglas. *The Unfinished Presidency: Jimmy Carter's Journey beyond the White House*. New York: Viking, 1998.

Brown, Willie. *Basic Brown*. New York: Simon and Schuster, 2008.

Follow the Money website. National Institute on Money in State Politics. http://beta.

followthemoney.org/election-overview?s=CA&y=2014.

Goldmacher, Shane. "The Waxman-Berman Machine Finally Shuts Down." *National Journal*, January 14, 2013.

McGee, Marcus. *Willie: The Man, the Myth and the Era*; *The Speakership Battles*. San Jose: Pegasus Books, 2011.

Meyerson, Harold. "The Liberal Lion Winter." *Los Angeles Times Magazine*, December 4, 1994.

———. "Liberalism's Legislative Genius Calls It Quits." *American Prospect*, January 31, 2014. www.prospect.org/article/liberalism's-legislative-genius-calls-it-quits.

Miller, Alan. "Mr. Inside and Mr. Outside: The Audacious Berman Brothers Built a Powerful Progressive Machine in California. But Can They Survive a New Political Order?" *Los Angeles Times*, March 29, 1992.

Richardson, James. *Willie Brown*. Berkeley: UC Press, 1996.

Walters, Dan. "Money and the Legislature: Lobbyists Charge 'Shakedown.'" *Sacramento Union*, January 2, 1984.

———. "Money and the Legislature: Special-Interest Money Plays a Critical Role." *Sacramento Union*, January 3, 1984.

Wolf, Jamie. "Howard & Leo & Willie & Carol & Art & Michael & Vasco & Janis & Jacqui & Jack: A Speakership Fight in California." *Los Angeles Review of Books*, October 13, 2012.

CHAPTER 12
1990: Californians Punish Lawmakers with Term Limits

Major newspaper and periodical sources used in this chapter dealt with the political environment that led to the creation of Proposition 140, the campaign for its passage, and analyses of its effect on California's legislature. Those sources included: the Associated Press, the *California Journal*, CBS News, *Capitol Weekly*, KCRA-TV, the *Los Angeles Daily News*, the *Los Angeles Times*, the *New York Times*, the *Sacramento Bee*, the *Sacramento Union*, the *San Francisco Chronicle*, the *San Jose Mercury News*, the *Santa Cruz Sentinel*, and *Time*.

The following interviews were conducted by the authors for use in this book: Mark Baldassare (Sacramento, September 5, 2014), Barry Brokaw (Sacramento, August 23, 2014), Willie Brown (San Francisco, August 31, 2014), John Caldwell (Sacramento, September 10, 2014), Cathy Gardella (Sacramento, September 20, 2014), Hedy Govenar (Sacramento, January 12, 2014), Ross Johnson (Sacramento, December 19, 2014), Jerry Lewis (telephone interview, September 29, 2014), John Lewis (telephone interview, September 2, 2014), Gregory Schmidt (Sacramento, September 10, 2014), and Lewis Uhler (Roseville, October 1, 2014). Other key sources include:

Allswang, John M. *The Initiative and Referendum in California, 1898–1998*. Stanford, CA: Stanford University Press, 2000.

Bagley, William T. *California's Golden Years: When Government Worked and Why*. Berkeley: Berkeley Public Policy Press, Institute of Governmental Studies, 2009.

Cain, Bruce E., and Thad Kousser. "Adapting to Term Limits in California: Recent Experiences and New Directions." Joint Project on Term Limits, National Conference of State Legislatures, Washington, DC, 2004.

Citrin, Jack, and Benjamin Highton. *How Race, Ethnicity, and Immigration Shape the California Electorate*. San Francisco: Public Policy Institute of California, 2002.

Jacobs, John. *A Rage for Justice: The Passion and Politics of Phillip Burton*. Berkeley: UC Press, 1995.

Lustig, Jeffrey, ed. *Remaking California: Reclaiming the Public Good*. Berkeley: Heyday Books, 2010.

Nalder, Kimberly. "The Effect of Legislative Term Limits on Voter Turnout." *State Politics and Policy Quarterly*, CSU Sacramento, Summer 2007. http://spa.sagepub.com/content/7/2/187.full.pdf+html.

Public Policy Institute of California. "How Have Term Limits Affected the California
Legislature?" November 2004.

Putnam, Jackson K. "The Pattern of Modern California Politics." *Pacific Historical Review*
61 (February 1992).

Schrag, Peter. "The Populist Road to Hell: Term Limits in California." *American Prospect*,
December 19, 2001.

Schabarum, Pete F. *Enough Is Enough: Term Limits in California*. Self-published, 1992.

CHAPTER 13
Still in the Game

Significant sources for this chapter are interviews with decision-makers and political analysts,
and news articles concerning four elections whose impact will need more time to fully
assess. The following interviews were conducted by the authors for use in this book: Mark
Baldassare (Sacramento, September 5, 2014), Ted Costa (Sacramento, October 15, 2014), Dave
Gilliard (telephone interview, October 10, 2014), Gary K. Hart (Sacramento, November 9,
2014), Steve Merksamer (Sacramento, November 5, 2014), Barbara O'Connor (Sacramento,
October 21, 2014), Dan Schnur (telephone interviews, October 17 and 18, 2014), George
Skelton (Sacramento, October 28, 2014), Richard Temple (Sacramento, September 29, 2014),
Dan Walters (Sacramento, October 9, 2014), and Carroll Wills (Sacramento, October 15,
2014).

The major newspaper, periodical, and online sources for this chapter include: ABC News,
American Conservative, the Associated Press, the Calbuzz website (www.calbuzz.com),
the *California Journal*, *Capitol Weekly*, the *Contra Costa Times*, Fivethirtyeight.com, the
Fox and Hounds website (www.foxandhoundsdaily.com), KCBS-TV, KQED Radio, *Latino
Magazine*, the *Los Angeles Times*, *Mother Jones*, the *New York Times*, the *Orange County
Register*, the *Palm Springs Desert-Sun*, the *Sacramento Bee*, the *San Diego Union-Tribune*,
the *San Francisco Chronicle*, the *San Jose Mercury News*, and the *Washington Post*. Other
key sources include:

1994: Public Benefits Are Denied to Illegal Immigrants

HoSang, Daniel Martinez. *Racial Propositions: Ballot Initiatives and the Making of Postwar
California*. Berkeley: UC Press, 2010.

Garcia, Ruben J. "Critical Race Theory and Proposition 187: The Racial Politics
of Immigration Law." *Chicano-Latino Law Review* 17 (Fall 1995). http://hei-
nonline.org/HOL/LandingPage?collection=journals&handle=hein.journals/
chiclat17&div=11&id=&page=.

Iyengar, Shanto, and Richard Reeves, eds. *Do the Media Govern?: Politicians, Voters and
Reporters in America*. Thousand Oaks, CA: SAGE Publications, 1997.

Olmsted, Kathy. "California's Crisis and the Collapse of the Republican Party."
Edge of the American West website. May 29, 2009. chronicle.com/blognetwork/
edgeofthewest/?s=Proposition+187.

Pachon, Harry. "A Flirtation with the GOP Turns Cold Politics: Wilson's Embrace of Prop.
187 Will Have Repercussions as New Latino Voters Enter the Electorate." *Los Angeles
Times*, November 6, 1994.

Wroe, Andrew. *The Republican Party and Immigration Politics*. London: Palgrave
MacMillan, 2008.

1998: Two Elections Shatter National Spending Records

Alexander, Robert M. *Rolling the Dice with State Initiatives*. Westport, CT: Praeger
Publishers, 2002.

California Common Cause. "Stacking the Deck: Gambling Industry Emerges as Top

Campaign Contributor in California." Report. June 2000 (updated July 2001). www.stand-upca.org/Local%20Government/fppc-and-fec/Stacking%20the%20Deck.pdf.

Dunstan, Roger. "Gambling in California." California Research Bureau, California State Library. January 1977. www.library.ca.gov/CRB/97/03/Chapt5.html.

Lombardi, Michael. "Long Road Traveled II." California Nations Indian Gaming Association (CNIGA). Undated. www.cniga.com/facts/History_of_CA_Gaming_Part_2.pdf.

Lubenow, Gerald C., ed. *California Votes: The 1998 Governor's Race*. Berkeley: Institute of Governmental Studies Press, 1999.

Matheny, Keith. "Once-Poor Tribes Parlay Casino Revenues into Political Power." *Palm Springs Desert Sun,* January 27, 2013. archive.desertsun.com/article/20130126/NEWS06/301260014/Once-poor-tribes-parlay-casino-revenues-into-political-power.

Michael, Jay, and Dan Walters. *The Third House: Lobbyists, Money, and Power in Sacramento*. Berkeley: Berkeley Public Policy Press, 2002.

2003: Gray Davis Is Recalled from Office

Baldassare, Mark, and Cheryl Katz. *The Coming Age of Direct Democracy: California's Recall and Beyond*. Lanham, MD: Rowman and Littlefield Publishers, 2008.

Gerston, Larry N., and Terry Christensen. *Recall!: California's Political Earthquake*. Armonk, NY: M.E. Sharpe, 2004.

LaVally, Rebecca. *California's Laws of the Century*. Sacramento: Senate Office of Research, December 1999.

Lubenow, Gerald C., ed. *California Votes: The 2002 Governor's Race and the Recall that Made History*. Berkeley: Berkeley Public Policy Press, 2003.

Mathews, Joe. *The People's Machine: Arnold Schwarzenegger and the Rise of Blockbuster Democracy*. New York: PublicAffairs, 2006.

Mathews, Joe, and Mark Paul. *California Crackup: How Reform Broke the Golden State and How We Can Fix It*. Berkeley: UC Press, 2010.

Public Policy Institute of California. "Just the Facts: Recall Election—One Year Later." October 2004.

Public Policy Institute of California, "Reforming California's Initiative Process." Panel discussion. October 24, 2013. www.ppic.org/main/event.asp?i=1392.

Schecter, David L. "California's Right of Removal: Recall Politics in the Modern Era." *California Politics and Policy* 12, no. 1 (December 2008).

Weare, Christopher. "The California Electricity Crisis: Causes and Policy Options." Public Policy Institute of California, 2003.

2010: Californians Experiment with Electoral Reform

Citrin, Jack, Gabriel Lenz, and Doug Ahler. "Can California's New Primary Reduce Polarization? Maybe Not." The Monkey Cage website. March 27, 2013. www.themonkey-cage.org/2013/03/27/can-californias-new-primary-reduce-polarization-maybe-not/.

Grose, Christian. "The Adoption of Electoral Reforms and Ideological Changes in the California State Legislature." USC Schwarzenegger Institute. February 25, 2014. http://www.schwarzeneggerinstitute.com/images/SI-Adoption%20of%20Electoral%20Reforms%20Report.pdf.

INDEX

A

abortion, 162, 164

African Americans, 21, 100–101, 108–109, 111–112, 218, 259; see also discrimination

Agnos, Art, 221, 231

Alien Land Law (1913 and 1920), 100

Antonovich, Mike, 234

aqueduct, see Los Angeles Aqueduct; Aqueduct, California Edmund G. Brown, 139

Article XIX (1879; anti-Chinese provisions), 33

Assemblyman X, 147

assessor corruption, 195–196

Associates, the, 6, 7, 14; see also the Big Four

Austin, Mary, 48–49

Australian (secret) ballot, 64, 168

B

Bader, Tom, 277, 279

Bagley, William, 173, 189–190, 207, 234

Baker, William, 241, 243

Baldassare, Mark, 211, 260, 281

Ball, George, 95

Ball, Hunt, Hart, Brown, and Baerwitz, 186

Bane, Tom, 224, 235

Baxter, Leone, 82–83, 87, 88, 94, 108; see also Whitaker and Baxter

Bear Flag Revolt, 22–23

Beery, Wallace, 90

Behr, Peter, 193–194, 199

Bell, Theodore, 69–70

Bellows, Jim, 201

Berman, Howard, 216–226, 229, 231

Berman, Michael, viii, 215–218, 220, 222, 223, 224–228

Beverly, Bob, 173

Bierce, Ambrose, 17, 64–65

"Big Daddy," see Unruh, Jesse

Big Four, the, 3, 7, 10, 12–13, 14–15, 16–17, 18, 61–62, 64; see also the Associates

Bird, Rose, 237

Bradley, Clark, 181

Braude, Marvin, 208

Brewers Institute, 169, 170–171

Broaders, Halden, 185

Brody, Ralph, 138–139

Brokaw, Barry, 214

Brown v. Board of Education, 21, 108–109, 117

Brown, Bernice, 121

Brown, Dennis, 206–207

Brown, Jerry (Edmund G. Jr.), ix, xi, 115, 123, 139, 141, *141*, 168, 175–191, 198, 200, 204–206, *205*, 207–208, 212, 218, 219, 221, 227, 237, 250–251, 259, 263, 266, 288

Brown, Kathleen, 256, 257

Brown, Pat (Edmund G.), 99, 115, 118, 121–124, 128–142, 149, 150–152, 153, 154–156, 158–159, 162, 175–176, 186, 197, 202

Brown, Ralph M., 148, 149

Brown, Willie, x, 160, 173, 218–219, 222, 225–226, 228–231, 233–236, 238, 239, 240–241, 242–244, 249, 250, 258

Brulte, Jim, 247, 260, 278

Budd, James "Buckboard Jim," 64, 65, 169

Burns, Hugh, 138, 144–145, 154, 155, 167, 176

Burton, John, 175, 189, 229, 274

Burton, Phil, 235

Bustamante, Cruz, 279, 280

Butcher, Bill, 194–195, 200, 204

C

Caldwell, John, 249

Calhoun, John C., 25

California Aqueduct, 139

California Derby Club, 173, 190

California Independent Voter Project, 285

California League Against Sinclairism (CLAS), 86, 90

California Medical Association, 93

California State Water Project, 137–139, 176

campaign management, 78, 83–84, 86–95, 108

campaign spending, 83–84, 161, 168–169, 175, 176–177, 179, 182, 185–192, 215, 224, 226, 229–232, 240, 253, 261–267, *265*, 268–270, 271, 272, 286–288; see also special interests

ABOUT THE AUTHORS

STEVE SWATT is a veteran political analyst and public affairs executive. He is a former award-winning political reporter with twenty-five years of journalism experience with the *San Francisco Examiner, United Press International* in Los Angeles, and KCRA-TV (NBC) in Sacramento. He received a BS in business administration and a master's degree in journalism, both from the University of California, Berkeley.

SUSIE SWATT is a member of the National Advisory Council of the Institute of Governmental Studies at UC Berkeley. She spent nearly forty years as a key staff member in the California Legislature. As a special assistant for the Fair Political Practices Commission, she researched and authored a study that won a national award for "investigative work in the public interest."

JEFF RAIMUNDO recently completed twenty-five years as a political and public-relations consultant based in Sacramento. Previously, he enjoyed a twenty-year career as a newspaper reporter and editor with the *Sacramento Bee* and McClatchy Newspapers in Sacramento and Washington, DC.

REBECCA LaVALLY, PhD, teaches rhetorical criticism and persuasion at California State University, Sacramento. She is a former editor of the California Senate's public-policy research office and a former Sacramento bureau chief for United Press International and Gannett News Service.

BRUCE E. CAIN is the Charles Louis Ducommon Professor of Humanities and Sciences, and the Spence and Cleone Eccles Family Director of the Bill Lane Center for the American West at Stanford University.

ABOUT THE CALIFORNIA
HISTORICAL SOCIETY BOOK AWARD

In 2013, after a twenty-year collaboration and with a shared commitment to finding new and inclusive ways to explore California's history, the California Historical Society and Heyday established the California Historical Society Book Award as a way of inviting new voices and viewpoints into the conversation. Each year, we bring together a jury of noted historians, scholars, and publishing experts to honor a book-length manuscript that makes an important contribution both to scholarship and to the greater community by deepening public understanding of some aspect of California history. For more information, please visit www.heydaybooks.com/chsbookaward or www.californiahistoricalsociety.org/publications/book_award.html.

ABOUT THE CALIFORNIA HISTORICAL SOCIETY

Established in 1871, the California Historical Society inspires and empowers people to make California's richly diverse past a meaningful part of their contemporary lives. We hold one of the top research collections on California history, which includes over 35,000 volumes of books and pamphlets, more than 4,000 manuscripts, and some 500,000 photographs documenting California's social, cultural, economic, and political history and development, including some of the most cherished and valuable documents and images of California's past.

ABOUT HEYDAY

Heyday is an independent, nonprofit publisher and unique cultural institution that promotes widespread awareness and celebration of California's many cultures, landscapes, and boundary-breaking ideas. Through its well-crafted books, public events, and innovative outreach programs, Heyday is building a vibrant community of readers, writers, and thinkers.

HEYDAY
into California

It takes the collective effort of many to create a thriving literary culture. We are thankful to all the thoughtful people we have the privilege to engage with. Cheers to our writers, artists, editors, storytellers, designers, printers, bookstores, critics, cultural organizations, readers, and book lovers everywhere!

THANK YOU

We are especially grateful for the generous funding we've received for our publications and programs during the past year from foundations and hundreds of individual donors. Major supporters include:

Advocates for Indigenous California Language Survival; Anonymous (3); Arkay Foundation; Judith and Phillip Auth; Judy Avery; Carol Baird and Alan Harper; Paul Bancroft III; The Bancroft Library; Richard and Rickie Ann Baum; BayTree Fund; S. D. Bechtel, Jr. Foundation; Jean and Fred Berensmeier; Joan Berman; Barbara Boucke; Beatrice Bowles, in memory of Susan S. Lake; John Briscoe; David Brower Center; Helen Cagampang; California Historical Society; California Rice Commission; California State Parks Foundation; California Wildlife Foundation/California Oak Foundation; Joanne Campbell; The Campbell Foundation; Candelaria Fund; James and Margaret Chapin; Graham Chisholm; The Christensen Fund; Jon Christensen; Cynthia Clarke; Community Futures Collective; Lawrence Crooks; Lauren and Alan Dachs; Nik Dehejia; Topher Delaney; Chris Desser and Kirk Marckwald; Lokelani Devone; Frances Dinkelspiel and Gary Wayne; Doune Trust; The Durfee Foundation; Megan Fletcher and J.K. Dineen; Michael Eaton and Charity Kenyon; Richard and Gretchen Evans; Friends of the Roseville Library; Furthur Foundation; The Wallace Alexander Gerbode Foundation; Patrick Golden; Erica and Barry Goode; Wanda Lee Graves and Stephen Duscha; The Walter and Elise Haas Fund; Coke and James Hallowell; Theresa Harlan and Ken Tiger; Cindy Heitzman;

GETTING INVOLVED

To learn more about our publications, events and other ways you can participate, please visit www.heydaybooks.com.